HOW TO WORK IN STAINED GLASS

How to Work in Stained Glass

ANITA and SEYMOUR ISENBERG

Second Edition

Copyright © 1983, 1972 by Anita and Seymour Isenberg
Second Edition   All Rights Reserved
Published in Radnor, Pennsylvania 19089, by Chilton Book Company
Designed by Arlene Putterman
Manufactured in the United States of America

Library of Congress Cataloging in Publication Data
Isenberg, Anita.
    How to work in stained glass.
    Bibliography: p. 321
    Includes index.
    1. Glass painting and staining—Technique. 2. Glass
craft. I. Isenberg, Seymour. II. Title.
TT298.I83 1983   748.5′028   82-73537
ISBN 0-8019-7354-6
ISBN 0-8019-7355-4 (pbk.)

    11 12 13   1 0 9 8 7 6 5

For John Marion

Contents

Part I
Materials and
Equipment

Part II
Procedures

Part III
Projects

Part IV
Artists
and Their Work

Part V
The Commercial
Glassworker

Appendix

Preface

Today, stained glass is an enthusiastic pastime for tens of thousands of people. It is also, either wholly or partly, the livelihood of a host of suppliers, manufacturers, designers, teachers, photographers, inventors, and retailers. Many of these businesses began as hobbies. It is not immodest to state that at least a portion of the popularity and growth of stained glass is due to this book.

When *How To Work in Stained Glass* first appeared over a decade ago, there was no text suitable for someone who wanted to learn about the craft. The few books available were calculated against the prerequisites of commercial studios.

Our desire was to provide a book with which beginners could have a relationship, a book that would be not only a factual source but also a companion. A book that would encourage, teach and enlarge horizons. A book that would keep back no secrets, that would give procedures all the way to completion. A book that would be precise yet inclusive in the quality and quantity of its information— from scoring glass to scoring with clients if its readers wanted to progress that far.

The fact that we succeeded in this far better than we ever dreamed is evidenced by the volume you are presently reading. No other book dealing with stained glass specifically for the hobbyist-craftsperson has maintained a viability necessitating a second edition. To be sure, imitations have

flourished. If this were the sincerest form of flattery, our heads would have been turned long ago. But these come and go. *How To Work* endures.

Many of our old students—those we taught personally, as well as those who learned from our book (the latter are far more numerous)—are now respected personages in the glass world. We meet them from time to time at conferences and hear them say, "It was your first book that got me started in glass. As far as I'm concerned, it's the Bible of the glass craft."

We are, to be sure, grateful to hear this. Bibles, however, do not need revision. Books dealing with less certain truths and consequences do. Such is the case with *How To Work in Stained Glass*. In a field that has become an industry in less than seven years, and one that continues to move ahead with lively spurts of technology, there must be allowances for new techniques and materials, and revised procedures. An example of such reorientation is in the use of copper foil. When the first edition was written, there was no adhesive copper foil made specifically for working with glass. The available adhesive foil was produced for electronic work and the glue backing, when raised to glass-foiling temperature, ran faster than Idi Amin. Foiling was thus done from sheet copper cut to size by the worker, applied by hand instead of by a foiling machine, and if any adhesive agent was used, it was Vaseline. That procedure is outmoded today.

In such a vivacious field as glass crafting, there will always be new procedures and promotions literally knocking at the door before one has welcomed the last. Most of the devices that are now appearing, however, seem to be modifications of previous developments. We believe that by incorporating these latest releases from the manufacturers we can assume a pretty complete survey. That, at least, is our intent.

But this edition of *How To Work in Stained Glass* is more than a compendium of tools and devices. Glassworking remains a handcraft constantly generating ideas and methods. In this regard we have substantially increased the size of the original book, providing a new and enlarged color section. Many of the old black and white photos have been replaced. A number of informative drawings and pictures have been added. Old chapters have, in the main, been expanded or reduced as their importance was reconsidered. Several subjects have been added, including hazards of crafts, an issue much discussed these days. We have also incorporated many of the processes and projects of well-known stained glass artisans around the country who thus share with you their creative juices. In response to many requests, we have provided more information on the history of the subject so far as it relates to the practicality of working with it.

In short, this is more than just a revised *How To Work in Stained Glass*. It is, for all practical purposes, a new one.

In bringing the work thus far, we cannot claim total responsibility. There were many people who helped along the way. Our appreciation is extended to the many artists, retailers, manufacturers, students and collectors who offered information and photographs, as well as to the people at Chilton Book Company who have nurtured *How To Work in Stained Glass* from the beginning. Two of these deserve specific mention: Alan Turner and Kathy Conover, who gave this manuscript, more than personal attention and consideration.

ANITA ISENBERG
SEYMOUR ISENBERG
Norwood, N.J.
May, 1983

HOW TO WORK IN STAINED GLASS

Introduction

GLASS IN THE ANCIENT WORLD

The transformation of a handful of sand, practically while it slips through your fingers, into a solid sheet of air is a potent alchemy. We take this process for granted, of course. Our capacity for surprise has been blunted by a host of scientific wonders that shrugs off so prosaic an activity as glass manufacture. Still, one wonders who first thought of it? Perhaps it was the same unlikely individual who first considered eating an oyster. No doubt the discovery was accidental. There is the story of Pliny's Phoenician sailors, who, going ashore to cook their meal, found nothing to rest their pots on and, returning to their ship, brought back blocks of niter. This substance, sodium bisulphate, when heated united with the sand on the beach to form a crude sort of glass.

However the discovery occurred, the *whenever* is ancient. Glass and glaze, for instance, have an almost identical chemical content. If we consider glazed tile as a forerunner to glass, we can trace the material to prehistoric Egypt. Among early glazed objects of this civilization is a vase bearing the cartouche of a ruler of the First Dynasty.

From the glaze in which clay objects were dipped, beads were probably a subsequent development. Beads were made by taking a fine rod of hammered bronze and dipping it into the molten glaze and twirling it around rapidly until it cooled. The ball that formed could be slipped off the rod, which contracted when it cooled. Cylindrical beads known as bugles were made of a tube of glass cut into lengths. Such a technique is still used today for certain types of tube glass.

Beads are the most widespread and hence the most frequently found of all glass objects since they were used as coins. Glass beads were usually opaque and made in many colors, and they represent varying degrees of skill in manufacture. Most of these early beads give no clues to date or place or origin, but they were in common use by the fourth millennium B.C. Beads were prized for their color, and stringing beads was both child's play and a business endeavor. Strands of beads were made into necklaces, collars, and fringe for clothing and headdresses. Some of the mummies are covered with a fine network of beads over the linen wrappings.

The Egyptians did not aim to make colorless glass. They sought primarily to use glass to imitate the hues of precious stones. Pliny calls such early attempts at cheating customers "a far more lucrative deceit than any devised by the ingenuity of man." The coloring of these forgeries possessed a rare brilliancy, the workers copying with astonishing perfection the characteristics of the natural stones.

As with today's colored glass, metal was used extensively as a coloring agent. Copper was a favorite. Turquoise blue is a dominant color in glass and glazes of all periods. Genuine stones in blues and greens were rare, and perhaps these colors were used in glass to make up for this deficiency. The characteristic glaze was made of a silicate of soda, lime, and copper. Intensity of color was governed by firing temperature, the lighter tints being produced from hotter exposure. Cobalt is used in semitransparent blue glass even today. Transparent ruby tints were not perfected until the Middle Ages. An opaque red glass seems to have been used almost exclusively for inlay work, probably because this color had a strong tendency to oxidize. Purple was derived from manganese and used in glazes of the First Dynasty. Manganese was used for brown, but it was not a color extensively employed. Yellow, a popular color, probably came from iron or antimony.

This imitation of precious stones seems to have been of more consequence to the glass workers than the making of vessels. Expert resemblances to amethyst, emerald, sapphire, lapis lazuli, jasper, carnelian, and diamond were produced by the Egyptians. Probably the next step beyond the manufacture of beads and gems was the making of small vessels of glass used to contain perfumes and other liquids. Before the blowing iron was devised, vases were probably made over an iron tube to which a bag of sand was firmly tied in the shape desired. Molten glass was poured on the metal and sandbag and colors introduced in a zigzag or crescent effect upon each layer of the hardening glass. The object was kept in motion until the shape became defined. As it cooled, the metal contracted and could be removed. The sandbag was then punctured and allowed to empty. In this process the metal served to shape the neck. It is assumed that as the workmen developed a familiarity with the process they saw that the sandbag was unnecessary. The vitreous substance was finally discovered to be able to be blown through a tube by hand or with bellows.

This discovery of the blowing iron is to glass manufacture what the potter's wheel is to pottery. With this device the glass objects could be made much more easily and use of this instrument became second nature. The blowing iron, even today, is a long hollow tube, nothing more. A mass of molten glass is fixed on the end and is shaped by the amount of air that is blown into the glass. The general appearance of the object, as well as the thickness of the walls, is determined by the force of air applied, the rhythm of the reheating, and the shaping tools and processes—to say nothing of the skill of the worker. Early glassware shows many lines of contrasting color. Forms were kept simple. Once the blowing iron came into use, more variety of shapes was possible, many of these having very long necks and elliptical bodies.

The Egyptians also understood the processes of glass cutting, engraving, and grinding. What they did not seem to be interested in, however, was making sheet glass. Nor were the Greeks much interested in this process—or in glass at all to any great extent. Instead, they were preoccupied with ceramics. The Greeks, who had a word for everything, had none for glass, calling the material, awkwardly, "melted stone."

The Romans, however, were fascinated by glass. They built furnaces, made vases, and used glass for much of their intricate mosaic work. They employed gold leaf to back transparent pieces of glass to provide a glittering effect—again, a very modern approach. While the Romans used glass in sheets for windows, these were essentially small surfaces; they also used mica, alabaster, and shells. It would appear that they cast their flat glass on a stone, with consequent unevenness and defects. Although such glass was capable of transmitting light, it must have given a unique view of the outside world.

THE MEDIEVAL WINDOW

A medieval stained-glass window, ablaze with the sun behind it, gives an effect of

Fig. 1 *The Massacre of the Innocents. A 15th-century panel that for all its busyness is coherent rather than chaotic.*

Fig. 2 *Fragments of glass, probably from the 9th or 10th Century. This reconstruction suggests a head of Christ, and it may be the earliest extant pictorial stained-glass piece.*

splendor so intense that the air itself appears to be burnished. The transmuted light is splintered into a shower of colors that waver before it, replenished and muted as the light brightens and fades. To come upon such an incandescence unexpectedly, in turning down the aisle of some quiet church during the course of a solitary ramble, is an unforgettable experience.

There are a number of reasons to substantiate the claims made for the supremacy of the early medieval stained glass. Every writer on glass points to the twelfth- and early thirteenth-century windows as incomparable. The early Chartres windows are referred to as perfect and irreproachable. Not only were the choices of colors and their placement aesthetically masterful, but there was the superiority of the glass itself. Its color has never been surpassed.

Fig. 3 *The Wissembourg Disk, an 11th-century Carolingian head of Christ. Such classic simplicity lasted to the beginning of the 15th century, when "painted glass" overloaded the medium and stained glass became a canvas for painters to show their prowess.*

Rough and uneven in texture, its very crudeness brought about prismatic effects and added enormously to the brilliancy of color. The phrase "imprisoned sunlight" sums it up. Designs relied upon action and rhythm. Naive, quaint, often piquant and always sincere in his direct and unstudied manner, the glass artist of the day was unique. His designs grew out of the glass itself. His technique belonged to his medium in a manner that is rare today.

The subjects of medieval windows—indeed, the windows themselves—were religious celebrations. The earliest known representation of a stained-glass window, the Wissembourg Disk with the head of Christ, goes back only as far as the late eleventh century. Stained glass likely has some of its antecedents in the miniature paintings of Charlemagne's era. These illuminated manuscripts do bear a certain resemblance to stained-glass windows.

For the medieval churchman, stained glass had a mystical significance. He saw in this substance that modified, shaped, and colored the light passing through it a parallel to the divine word, enhancing the body of man by passing through his spirit. The religious prejudice eventually served to imprison the medium and left stained glass for a time more or less in the background as a secular art form. For worldly endeavors artists preferred material less sacrosanct.

THE VICTORIAN PERIOD

Much of the stained-glass work done in this country toward the end of the nineteenth century, and quite a lot done right up through the 1920s, might be lumped together as "Victorian." The name does not so much represent a style of work as a convenience. There was a pragmatic aesthetic involved, combining the architectural and the decorative. In Victorian homes practicality was an essence: Windows were meant to fit a specific opening and to let in light. There are only a limited number of positions for this in most homes. Staircase landings offered a particularly good opportunity for stained glass. Hall door panels were also considered appropriate, for the obscuring effect of the colored glass would offer privacy. Glass was not only useful but decorative, intending to harmonize with other decorative features of the surroundings without overpowering them. The purpose was not to call attention, but to be subordinate to other decor. Many people today see the word *Victorian* as pejorative. They equate the term with a decorative aspect that is old-fashioned. What they are probably judging are the mass-produced imitation pieces. The Victorian ideal—nature and natural forms—still presents an ever-fresh aesthetic.

A great number of Victorian windows provide lovely scope and form. The medallion window was an especially popular shape. It had a squared background, in the center of which was a round area of glass containing some type of central focus, either a detailed leaded design or a painting. Ultimately these windows were so du-

Fig. 4 *Illuminated manuscripts may have been the antecedents of stained-glass windows.*

Fig. 5 *Examples of early painted glass canopies.*

Fig. 6 Most stained-glass windows are narrative or allegorical.

Fig. 7 Some stained-glass windows merely point a moral.

plicated and imitated that their vitality was diluted. But it was from this style that the great works of John La Farge and Louis Comfort Tiffany came into being.

THE TIFFANY ERA

For the new glass aesthetic that emerged from the Victorian period, Louis Comfort Tiffany's name is recognizably the standard-bearer. The Victorian motif, trapped in imitative artificiality, caught between building component and art form, constantly measured against the twelfth-century heritage of stained glass as modified by dollars and cents, was unable to evolve further. Sheer commercialism ended its pretensions to any validity as an art form. Studio after studio turned out, by the yard, basically the same window.

Tiffany was more an aesthete than a practical glass worker. He was, however, a practical man of affairs and his interests covered many decorative media. While not setting himself up as a representative of American glassworking, he did visualize himself as the man of the moment to enhance American tastes in art. This new art, or *art nouveau,* was his trademark. To extend the boundaries of expression through plastic forms, he began to investigate the possibilities of widening the range of his materials. For his experiments with glass he used not the European transparent glass, but the American opal or "milk glass," which had come into being as a substitute for china. By the 1870s there was a great deal of opal glass being used in decorative windows as well as in cups and saucers. It was available in a wide assortment of colors, textures, and densities. Eventually it become so popular that it threatened to outsell the imported variety.

Fig. 9 Using glass without regard for its particular character results in an imitation canvas. The lead lines disrupt the linear quality of the subject.

Fig. 8 Detail from a design by Edward Burne-Jones for a window, Rottingdean Parish Church, England. Note the calm, almost dreamy expression of these ethereal creatures and the lovely flow of line, both painted and leaded, the one complementing the other.

Whether it was Tiffany or La Farge who invented the process of applying the iridescence to glass, as well as extending the hues and tones, is debatable. Christopher Durand, another famous artist of the period, was also experimenting in this area. But Tiffany got the credit, and the glass goes by his name more than *his* name for it, which was favrile, from the Latin *faber* for *smith* or *hand-worked.*

The strength of color and variety of form finally achieved in favrile glass is still unequaled, although some of the newer glass companies have come close in their own output. Tiffany used his glass in vases and lamps as well as in windows. Many of his windows incorporate painted details in enamels. He also used rocks, seashells, pebbles, and other material that would enhance a specific effect. But these details never overwhelmed the glass. His employment of filigree overlays and even his ornate lamp bases are enhancements, never diminutions or compromises, of the medium.

Graceful designs characterize his work, and because of the nature of the small-pieced undulating break lines, he used—and possibly devised—a method of joining his glass pieces together with copper foil. The more supple foil could take the multiple tiers of his fenestrations without giving the bulky, staggered appearance that lead would present. Foil provided an equally natural adaptation to the three-dimensional form, for each piece of glass wrapped in its thin edging could be made to conform to the molded surface and then be soldered to its neighbor. Making such designs of small pieces of glass held together with copper foil and involving extreme technical skill has become known as the "Tiffany foil method."

Fig. 10 *The six panels in this Swiss work are crowded, the leading is awkward, and the figures are poorly drawn and inconspicuous. From Maurice Drake, A History of English Glass Painting (1912).*

Fig. 11 *Heraldic panels. From Maurice Drake, A History of English Glass Painting (1912).*

Fig. 12 *A modern design by Susan Dodds Stinsmuehlen. "Thor Medallion," laminated, etched and painted. The sources of subject matter for stained glass are inexhaustible.*

Fig. 13 *Corrosion holes. The large medallion, c. 1317, has a green center with four yellow lobes arranged round it. Lead lines are contemporary, except for the straight, flat lead that bissects the medallion. In front are an oblong scrap of Perpendicular white and two triangular Decorated fragments where decay has attacked the smooth surfaces and spared the outline color. The surface of the piece in the lower right-hand corner has deteriorated completely, except for a narrow rim protected by the lead line. Behind is a Perpendicular scrap, c. 1440, showing coarse grozzed edges and many small corrosion holes. The terms Perpendicular and Decorated are period styles. Not even stained glass lasts forever. From Maurice Drake,* A History of English Glass Painting *(1912).*

Fig. 14 *A modern copy of a medieval roundel. Note how the leaded lines are used as outlining elements for discrete portions of the figures and yet how they communicate a linear flow on their own. Collection of the authors.*

Fig. 15 The design format of one of Marc Chagall's Jerusalem Windows, Hadassah-Hebrew Medical Center, Jerusalem. The linear flow here is even more emphatic than in Figure 14.

Fig. 16 Linear flow of course is not reserved for lead lines. This wallpaper pattern has a forceable flow of line, one, in fact, similar to the linear qualities of the Chagall window in Figure 15.

STAINED GLASS AND THE HOBBYIST

After this history, where do you come in? You enter the exciting world of stained glass through the pages of this book. If you have never worked in stained glass, or if you tried it and found you did not have enough proper guidance to keep you going, you can start from scratch right here.

No other craft offers such inherent means of dramatic projection. The material proclaims itself even before you start to shape it. In fact, it has been said that even terrible stained-glass work still looks good because the glass itself makes such a powerful statement. That doesn't mean that terrible work should be your norm. It does mean that you can effect a working compromise with your material. You do the best you can; it will take up the slack. As you get better, your personality rather than that of the glass will glisten forth. But unless you try hard to make it happen, your final result will never be a disaster. This means that you will never waste time, material, or effort. Time is always a learning process. Material can always be reused in another project as you advance in technique. Effort builds on effort, and no step in this craft is ever taken in vain.

While the technique involved in working in stained glass is exacting, it is not difficult. It requires only the willingness to learn, the desire to explore your own creativity, the need to impress your personality on an inanimate if not lifeless modality. Since there are many good techniques, we cannot assume that our way of working with or teaching stained glass is the only way. We can say that it is the best way we have found. In this regard we would caution that stained glass is both art and craft. Thus it becomes a discipline. You should follow instructions in sequence. To attempt any stained-glass project and invest the progress with shortcuts, skimping on procedures, will usually lead to confusion and loss of morale. Despite this warning we have found that some students just have to

Fig. 17 This "fish window" by Anita Isenberg demonstrates linear flow. Note how the lines have been arranged to avoid a congruence at the same spot. Too many leads joining at the same place lead to a heavy blob of solder at that point. Generally, three lines crossing or meeting at the same spot is plenty.

Fig. 18 A "mushroom" window design by Anita Isenberg. The geometric style is pleasing to the eye because of the linear flow of background and foreground.

Fig. 19 Two completed windows showing a pleasing flow of line in a pictorial design.

learn by trial and error. You shouldn't have to. We made all the errors for you before we wrote the book.

Often we have heard the two excuses for shying away from glass. "I can't cut glass," and, "I'm not artistic." Actually anyone can learn to cut glass in half an hour. But even if you feel all thumbs when it comes to glass cutting, some of the newer cutters practically do the job for you anyway. And once you have felt the power of having a piece of glass score and break precisely where you wished it to, you will have trouble letting the cutter out of your hand.

As for not being "artistic," that's no problem at all. In fact, it can be a positive advantage. Many artists coming to glass attempt to apply principles from their prior discipline that are out of order where glass is concerned. And to assume that because you can't draw you are excluded is equally a misjudgment. Anyone can, with the help of a ruler, draw a straight line, follow a curve with a guided edge, make a circle with a compass. You then can produce a square, put a diamond in it and a circle around it; you have a design that, transposed into stained glass, will delight you with its sophisticated appearance. Once you have acquired the confidence this initial attempt provides, you can take it to any lengths.

It's that simple—and that intriguing.

MATERIALS AND EQUIPMENT

I

1
What Is
Stained Glass?

Before getting started in working with stained glass, every craftsperson should understand certain concepts about glass itself. The propensities of this material establish and guide the techniques that are able to be employed with stained glass. Many beginners tend to forget that. Imparting color to the glass modifies its physical capabilities to some extent, so stained glass has certain requirements of its own. In order to design with glass, the craftsperson must keep the characteristics of the medium very much in focus. Most people know instinctively that (1) glass cuts you, and (2) you can see through it. But in working with stained glass this is not always the case. The principles here are (1) you cut *it*, and (2) you *cannot* always see through it.

Glass is a *vitreous* substance. When liquid glass right from the furnace cools, it does not crystallize. Most other liquids—water, metals, fats—do crystallize. The word *crystal* itself can be confusing too. Most people visualize crystal as being transparent (quartz being a familiar example), and they assume that glass is similar. In fact, the word *crystal* is often applied to glass, but it is used only in a comparative sense to distinguish exceptionally clear glass from muddy or colored varieties. In a true crystal state, the atoms composing the substance have a regular arrangement rather like a military lineup. When they break, crystalline objects are likely to do so along specific planes of cleavage. Such objects constitute true solids.

When a vitreous substance cools, it does not crystallize, so it cannot be considered a true solid. Except to the touch, it does not have the properties of a true solid. That is as far as it goes, however. The atoms composing this "frozen liquid" are randomly arranged and allow microscopic fractures that do not follow the clean cleavage planes of true solids. If it is maintained for a long period at a temperature somewhat above its softening temperature, any vitreous substance will devitrify—that is, crystallize. In this state it will have a frosted and muddy appearance.

The American Society for Testing Materials, through its Committee on Glass and Glass Products, has adopted the following as standard definition of glass: "An organic product of fusion which has cooled to a rigid condition without cyrstallizing. It is typically hard and brittle. It may be colorless or colored, and transparent to opaque." But no definition of glass is satisfactory in terms of describing all the permutations of this remarkable material. Physically it is a paradox, chemically it is idiosyncratic, artistically it is challenging, pragmatically it is ubiquitous, prismatically it is spectacular, ocularly it is both near- and far-seeing. As an enamel, it becomes a thin glassy coat that can be applied to metals, other glasses, or ceramics, either clear or colored. As a glaze, it is used more specifically in pottery. Whatever your particular definition of glass may be, it must go beyond something that cuts you and can be seen through.

THE STAINING PROCESS

One common misconception about stained glass is that it is window glass that has in some way been "stained" or colored with dye. Nothing could be further from the truth, even though the name "stained glass" is misleading.

For some reason there has developed a misnomer in the form of a shortcut: "stain glass," which is being used more and more by people who should know better. Using this term among glass people will immediately single you out as a novice, and a careless one at that. In a field that is already beginning to suffer from imprecise nomenclature, this is a habit that should be nipped in the bud. If the term *stain glass* must be used, it should be for plastic sheets stained with colored dyes to resemble true stained glass, or for plastic imitation "Tiffany" lamps. Here at least the pejorative overtones of the term would be precise.

Stained glass is actually impregnated with color in the factory while still in raw chemical form. In medieval times the "colors" or metallic oxides were added to the "batch" while it was molten, but most factories today mix the elements before putting them into the furnace. Adding color is an integral part of the entire process.

Stained glass is composed of silica sand with approximately one percent iron, soda ash, limestone, and some borax. The percentage of iron in the sand is important. Sand can contain up to ten percent iron. The iron content has to be checked, for too much of it will give a greenish cast to the glass, rather like the color of a Coca-Cola bottle. Such an overlay could be disastrous to the product the factory is trying to produce. To put the color into the glass,

the factory mixes in various metallic oxides at the very beginning of the operation. Each color has its own formula and may be mixed by a special worker, who is an expert in the particular mixture. Some of the chemicals used for coloring glass are: sugar and sulphur for amber; dichromate for green; copper oxides for blues; and the addition of cobalt for still stronger blues. Red colors, which include rubies, oranges, and yellows—in short, the entire royal family—come from selenium or in some instances from gold salts, which explains the higher cost of this glass. Cadmium is another element whose oxides give the glass a yellow color. Other common elements used in an oxide state are nickel and iron.

Coloring the glass is not so simple as mixing pigments into sand and limestone and applying heat. Humidity and temperature play a great part in the end result, as does the thickness of the furnace and the coefficient of expansion of the different oxides within the molten glass. It is because of this last factor especially that the finished stained-glass sheet may behave more peculiarly than regular window glass when you cut it. The internal stresses and strains can be immense, especially in sheets with more than one color, such as "streakies." Keep in mind that glass is a homogeneous liquid—not a solid—and thus is susceptible to the laws of hydraulics just like other liquids. That means if you put pressure on one particular part of it with a glass cutter, you may set up a strain pattern through the sheet so that a fracture appears some distance away. The force that is transmitted is similar to that of the hydraulic brake in a car. The larger the sheet you use, the greater the possibility of this happening. Regular window glass will almost always transmit the pressure equally in a radius surrounding the moving cutter and generally behaves itself much better than the stained glass with its nervous oxides. Some highly neurotic stained-glass sheets fly apart at the merest touch of a cutter. Fortunately they are in the minority, but even for those of us who have worked in the medium for years, there come times when we find our skill challenged by a sheet of glass that insists on running its own way no matter how effective the score.

TYPES OF STAINED GLASS

Stained glass may be broken down into two main categories: antique and cathedral. Within these are found individual characteristics involving the transparency and texture of the finished sheet. Although the mixing of pigments basically follows the same process in all stained-glass manufacture, from then on, the process varies depending on what the end result is going to be.

Antique Glass

Antique glass is not so named because of its own specific antiquity but because it is hand-blown, as was the glass in medieval times. Once the glass has become molten in the furnace, a glass blower picks up a certain amount of it on the end of his pontil and blows it into a long cylinder (Fig. 1–1). Sometimes the cylinder is blown into a mold. Such a mold can be made of apple wood and may have designs carved into it to give the finished glass a pattern. However, most of the "seeds," "bubbles," and other "movement" within the glass itself that are so characteristic of antique hand-blown glass come from the art of the glass blower. "Trapped sunlight" is the way one admirer of antique glass expressed his pleasure at these small air pockets, which give the effect of miniature reflectors when tbe light flashes among them.

Once the antique glass cylinder has been blown, the ends are cut off and it is sliced down the center with a hot knife. It is then placed on its side in an oven, cut side up, and allowed to fall flat with the heat, thus making it into a sheet of glass. Such a blown cylinder may be done free form—that is, without a mold—and it will

Fig. 1–1 *A cylinder of stained glass with top and bottom "bottle bottoms" cut off. This cylinder is cut in half when hot, placed in an oven, and flattened into a sheet of stained glass.*

be extremely uneven in thickness. Even the ones blown in a mold may vary in thickness from ¼" to almost ¾" in the same sheet.

In the past, hand-blown glass was made mostly in factories in France, Germany, and England, and its purchase entailed the additional expense of any imported item. With today's increased demand for these transparent hues and tones of all possible varieties, factories in this country have set up a determined challenge to what was for years mostly a European enterprise. The Blenko Glass Company has long promoted antique glasses in the traditional sense. In an effort to enhance an aesthetic that seems unbounded, comparatively new companies such as Uroboros and Bullseye are producing sheets of "designed" cathedral glasses. These may be mixed with antique glasses for specific effects that go beyond the art of the medieval and Tiffany craftsman, or they may be used on their own, with results as overpowering as the hand-blown glasses. It is not exaggerating to say that a revolution in thinking about glass has lead to a revolution in its manufacture.

Glass has become more than "decor" for its own sake. Even when a stained-glass piece is commissioned primarily for ornament, the range of material now available can transform it into an aesthetic statement. The eye of the beholder may be the final judge, but the choices of glass, now so plentiful, exercise a range of subtleties that influence such judgment. And antique glass is no longer the only glass category in which these subtleties are found.

Cathedral Glass

All glass that is not mouth-blown is by definition cathedral. Cathedral glass encompasses a wide variety of machine-made vitreous sheets. Its manufacture is either by a single- or double-rolling process in which the glass is forced between rollers or impressed in its molten state against a flat surface by a top roller alone. These rollers may be embossed with a texture to be impressed on the glass sheet. The glass is of a constant thickness—usually ⅛"—and in general is easier to score and cut than antique glass, although this is by no means always the case. Since cathedral glass is made in the United States, it is cheaper than the imported antique glass, and is both beautiful and striking in its own right. The worker in glass today will find that this glass will be a never-ending delight.

Opalescent Glass

A large proportion of cathedral glass is "opalescent glass," which, as its name implies, is opaque. However, the opacities vary. Rather than allowing the light rays to pass directly through, it spreads them within its surface, giving the effect of being lighted from within. Opalescent glass is seldom of one color, except when it is pure white or pure black. Even when it is pure white, it is usually a white-on-white design. Dramatic mixtures of colors

are spread throughout the sheet in whorls and darting lines, and these give movement and life when light illuminates the glass from behind (Fig. 1–2). Opalescent, alone among stained glasses, also reflects light. Because of its dense makeup, it does not lose its hues and tones with the disappearance of backlighting as do most stained-glass windows when the sun goes down. This quality makes it a natural choice for objects with a consistent color tone, such as lamps and room dividers, which are not always provided with backlighting. In lamps it is a particularly happy choice, for the opalescent glass hides the bulb, which through transparent glass would be seen as a "hot spot."

Because of the linear flow of color across an opalescent sheet, beginners can be misled into thinking that the glass has a "grain" somewhat like wood. The question then arises whether to cut with or across the "grain." In fact, glass has no grain whatsoever, and the appearance is misleading. Opalescent glass is somewhat more difficult to cut than other types of stained glass; it is harder and requires a special cutter and generally more pressure than antique or other cathedral glass.

Fig. 1–2 *A sheet of opalescent glass held up to the light. Note the whorls of color and "grain."*

Machine-Streaky Glass

Machine streaky glass is similar to opalescent glass. However, instead of using an opal base, it begins with a flint (clear) glass base. Both opalescent and machine-streaky are available in a wide variety of color combinations. Opalescent glass can be either machine-rolled or hand-rolled and is formed by mixing an opal glass (white as opposed to clear) with one or more colors.

Manufacturing techniques differentiate one glass type from another. In addition to some of the standard glass types we will discuss, there are ranges of specialty glasses, some of which are considered more sophisticated than others in both manufacture and aesthetics. There is also a practical basis to specialty glasses, some being more appropriate to certain uses than others. It is profitable labor to experiment with the different glass varieties, although it is not always necessary to purchase entire sheets of each particular type just for experimental use. Small pieces will do for a start. It is wise not to overburden yourself at the beginning with an extensive stock of different glasses that you may not get to use for some time.

Flashed Glass

Flashed glass is a form of antique glass that is usually made with one color layer on top of another. Various combinations are available—for example, blue flashed on yellow, red on white, red on yellow, and blue on orange. You can tell a piece of flashed glass by scratching a corner with a glass cutter and chipping a small bit away. The underlying color will show through. Any color flashed on white or clear glass is particularly easy to tell by holding an edge of the glass up to the light. You should make out the clear underlying portion with the thin layer of top color.

Flashed glass has two main purposes. The first is to combine two colors so as to get a melding of both that will add yet another hue to the color range; the second is for etching purposes. By using the proper

Fig. 1–3 *Detail from the "Pirate" window. The pocket buttons, and sleeve stripes were all etched from flashed glass.*

materials, it is possible to dispense with portions of the flashed upper layer according to a predetermined design and thus allow the bottom layer to show through. The procedure can be as complex or as simple as you care to make it—from simply etching out the eye of an animal on a small figurine to the lacy effects of stained-glass windows by Chagall.

Streakies

Streakies follow their name: Sheets of colors are streaked across the surface. They are similar in this to opalescent glass, but being transparent they have an airy delicacy that can be breathtaking when the light streams through. Some of the best streakies—many of them English—could be put in a frame as they are. In fact, unless you are cutting fairly large pieces of such glass, you can mar more than you make since you may lose much of the color flow. Many of the English streakies, in addition to combining a coloful palette, also add a rippling of the glass itself—a textural component that lets the colors dance across the sheet, though providing uncertain cutting. We have in our studio several German streakies that we have never been able to bring ourselves to cut. There seems to be no way to improve on the beauty of the glass as it is.

Streakies are particularly effective as sunsets, cloud-filled skies, ocean waves, landscapes, rainbows—or even the Manhattan skyline. They also serve well as mountains or abstract colorations in non-specific works. They may be employed in free-form objects and for animals—butterfly wings made from them are especially alluring.

Textured Glass

Granite-Backed Glass: This is a low-relief "granite"-type texture, and the rough back disperses the light more effectively. A common question is, which is the "right" side, the side to face outward? The "right side" of any glass is the side you think is best for your purpose; there are no hard and fast rules. Don't try cutting on the granite side at first. Just one look at it may make your glass cutter's wheel fall off. If you cut on the smooth side, remembering to reverse your pattern if you want the granite side up, you should find granite-backed glass no more difficult to work with than any of the other cathedral glasses. It does scare some beginners though.

Granite Ripple: This is a heavier granite-type backing to which is added a rippling of the glass surface itself. This traps the light at the same time that it is diffused and so conveys a sense of spread to the illumination as well as added texture to the glass.

Drapery: This is the heaviest of the ripple glasses and is used, as the name implies, mainly for clothing, room furnishings, and waves—any object that requires a three-dimensional projection. Tiffany windows make use of drapery glass. Its use can point up a dramatic situation or pro-

Fig. 1–4 *Two examples of heavy ripple or "drapery" glass.*

vide necessary relief from a noncontrasting backdrop. Used to best effect, it emphasizes the work over all, rather than standing out itself as a novel element.

Pebbled Glass: The surface of pebbled glass displays a smooth facing rather than a granulated one with deep, irregular indentations.

Pebble-Ripple: A combination of pebbled glass and granite ripple. This unusual, indented glass gives a peculiar diffusion of an irregular light that can be highly dramatic.

Cutting Textured Glass

Although textured surfaces tend to look awesome to those not used to working with them, they can be cut with relative ease by employing a few simple procedures. Try these hints, from the folks at Uroboros Glass the next time you are face-to-face with a textured surface:

1. Make sure your cutter is clean and sharp. Carbide cutters work best, and we recommend the MacInnes with a Number 4 wheel.

2. Lubricate the cutter by dipping it in ker-

osene before each score. A dry cutter produces an uneven score and causes extra wear on the wheel.

3. Place the sheet of glass on a thin, dense foam pad, such as the ⅜-inch Ensolite pads used by backpackers. This evenly distributes the pressure of the cutter over the entire sheet.

4. Score on the smooth side of the sheet and avoid applying too much pressure.

5. With the ball end of the cutter, tap the textured side along the length of the score. For particularly difficult cuts, develop the crack visibly by tapping along the entire length of the score. (Experts can tell by the sound of the tapping if the crack is adequately developed.)

6. With fingers or grozzing pliers, gently separate the glass in the usual manner for smooth glasses.

7. Extremely acute angles with thick textures can be easily cut with a small diamond bandsaw.

8. Remember to be patient. Every glass manufacturer makes glass of different hardness and cutting qualities. It sometimes takes a while to develop a feel for each of the different glasses.

Hammered Glass
Another type of cathedral glass, hammered glass looks as though it had been textured by a small, persistent hammer. The indentations are uniform and when the light hits them they act like facets. There is a rough and a smooth side to this glass, and the choice is yours as to which side you put forward.

Crackle Glass
Crackle glass is an antique glass that is dipped quickly in water immediately after being formed. The shock of this contact forms definite fracture lines throughout the sheet. The glass is removed from the water before the sheet can self-destruct. As the glass slowly cools, these fracture lines become embedded in the subsurface.

Crackle glass comes in almost all colors, although ranges within a specific

Fig. 1–5 *Crackle glass, showing the lines running through the surface.*

color may not be available. This is a type of "figured" glass with the figurations—the crackling—running throughout the sheet. There is usually no problem cutting this glass, but be careful since you are dealing with a rather fragile type.

Flemish Glass
Flemish glass has deep channels running helter-skelter throughout the sheet. These channels are caused by the rollers of the

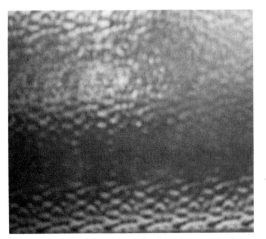

Fig. 1–6 *A sheet of Flemish glass showing highlights of the characteristic pock-marked effect as the light comes through.*

machine, and while the color may change, the indentations are all alike. This gives a lack of individuality to Flemish glass that is not noticed as much perhaps with either hammered or granite-backed glass perhaps because the indentations are so uninteresting and so readily apparent.

This should not be used in great quantity because it cheapens other types of glass used with it. Used alone it is monotonous and unimaginative. With Flemish glass more than with any other type discussed so far, a little bit goes a long way.

Fracture Glass

Historically, fracture glass was created by fusing thin glass flakes or "fractures" to a glass sheet during the rolling process. The best fracture glass was an artfully designed color collage, utilizing fractures of a variety of sizes and in a range of hues. The result was surprisingly organic and three-dimensional.

Uroboros Glass is one of the companies that has redeveloped true fracture-streamer glass. The technique fuses an artfully designed palette of fractures onto a carefully selected range of sheet-glass colors. Streamers are thin glass strings that in the past have been used in conjunction with fractures to suggest vines, twigs, or even pine needles. Today's artists also find use for them in conceptual designs.

The advantage to using this type of glass lies in the nonlinear color you have to work with. Standard sheet glasses are limited to streaks and swirls, even though nature's colors are often spotty or blotchy. Fracture glass visually suggests nature's nonlinear aspects. That is one reason why it works so well for foliage backgrounds and for abstracts.

When used on the front surface of the work, fracture glass provides a distinct and bold aspect, since the shiny edges of the flakes are evident. By placing the fractures on the back surface, you can soften the effect and cause the colors to fade into the background. Another common technique is to "plate" the fracture glass behind the front surface of the work. This is done in

Fig. 1–7 Uroboros fractures and streamers, in a typical collage on clear glass, is superb for viny, leafy backgrounds. Uroboros uses hot "trickles" of glass to form the streamers; as they cool the molten clear glass is poured over them and the mass is then rolled together. Fractures are produced by blowing out a bubble of glass to extreme thinness and then shattering it. These pieces are then impressed into the molten glass "bed."

as many as four layers, and it creates a superb three-dimensional effect.

Fracture glass is only one of the recently developed "design glasses" that the imagination of the manufacturer and advances in technology have made available to the hobbyist and professional alike.

Ring-Mottled Opalescent Glass

Like fracture glass, ring-mottled glass was reconstituted by Uroboros Glass Studios. The mottled opalescent effect was a glass-making secret thought to be lost with Louis Comfort Tiffany. Research by Uroboros into the use of gold as a colorant has opened up a range of hues that includes fuschias, purples, and hot pinks. These exhuberant colors can be used as a base for the creation of wildly exotic special effects, many of which are employed to the full by contemporary artists in the "new wave" of glass design. This glass also adds flair and know-how to the works of beginners with

Fig. 1–8 Ring-mottled opalescent glass in different colors by Uroboros Glass.

very little effort. The difficulties you as a beginner may run into with these glasses is by their overuse. It's tempting to take advantage of so presumptive a material.

Slab Glass

Slab glasses or *dalles de verre,* often just called *dalles,* are thick chunks of glass approximately 1″ thick by about 6″ to 8″ wide and 12″ long. To produce them requires a precise annealing system that relieves such masses of the innate stresses of cooling. This of course allows for easier cutting of the dalle and less chance of it fragmenting. In turn, this means less waste, more usable glass, and a lot less frustration.

Dalles requires special materials, mainly epoxy or cement, and special occasions to suit their characteristic design potential. They may be employed just as they come from the factory or, more likely, in broken or cut pieces acquired either by using a glass cutter or a slab-glass wedge. *Chunk glass* is the term often used for the broken pieces of dalles. These chunks, made to varying thicknesses by the worker, break up light along their various cleavage planes or facets and so provide yet another stained-glass luminescence, especially formidable when seen within a large cement or epoxy object. Light filtering through these chunks makes them look like so many precious stones.

Iridized Glass

Iridized glass is a specially formulated surface that reflects light in a manner similar to Tiffany's glass. It is effective when it is incorporated as part of the overall design, but, like Flemish glass, it can be used to excess. Certainly it is one of the more dramatic of the opalescents. It offers no special cutting problems and is fun to work with.

Glue-Chip Glass

You can make your own glue-chip glass in small quantities or you can buy it in sheets.

Fig. 1–9 *Pieces of slab glass* (dalles de verre) *and some blown cylinders that are in a preparatory stage in making sheet "antique" stained glass. Courtesy of Blacko Co.*

This glass is patterned on one or both sides, but the pattern is not impressed by a roller. Today, it is used for office doors, partitions, glass tabletops, room dividers, as parts of stained-glass windows, and sometimes as bordering pieces.

To chip glass you first need a special animal-product glue. Other glues will not work. You will also need a dessicant, such as silica gel. If the surface of the glass is smooth, you must roughen it either by sandblasting or by grinding it to allow the glue to adhere. The glue is then heated in a double boiler and spread on the glass with an ordinary paint brush. The glue now must be encouraged to dry. To do this as efficiently as possible, you must fashion some sort of drying or chipping chamber—anything from a plastic bag to a kiln. The dessicant is placed in the drying chamber to remove the moisture from the glue. During this process the glue literally tears itself away from the glass surface, taking with it some of the surface flakes. Indeed, the force of this tearing away can send chips of glue-laden glass flying if the chamber is not enclosed. It is the curling of the glue away from the glass that forms the distinctive pattern on the glass surface, like a whisper over it, or, more characteristically, like snowflakes or feathers. The consistency of the glue and the thickness with which it is applied determine the depth of the chipping.

Most hobbyists do the chipping over small, specific areas. Sheets of glue-chipped glass are available at most stained-glass distributors. If you want to work with this surface pattern, it might be worth buying several sheets. (For a more complete description of glue-chipping, see Chapter 17.

Waterglass

Waterglass is a trade name rather than a specific type of glass. Made by the Spectrum Glass Company, this nonmechanical rippled glass has gained enthusiastic acceptance by artists and craftspeople in the stained-glass field. Its high luster as well as the feeling of liquidity it projects makes its name almost automatic. Its resemblance to water is given greater depth in Paul Marioni's famous window (see color section). Spectrum also produces Wispies, its name for translucent mixes.

It is interesting to note that Spectrum

Glass is the only glass factory to use large electric furnaces to feed molten glass in a continuous ribbon through a 200-foot digitally controlled annealing lehr. This unique process attempts to assure uniformity of composition and minimal internal stress within the glass. All glass factories do their best to make their glass readily workable. Workable glass scores easily and breaks along the score line precisely. It does not shatter in one portion of the sheet when another part is being worked on. It also grozzes smoothly and does not tend to chip and flake. In short, it works *with* rather than against the craftsperson.

Glass workers establish individual preferences based on experience, but they also pay attention to manufacturers' claims. And glass manufacturers are very much attuned to their response. This provides a give and take to the industry that is not present in most others. Where a particular glass does not live up to expectations, it is generally taken off the market and reconsidered. As you make your initial acquaintance with the material, you do not have to assume that it is always right and you are always wrong. You may have purchased a sheet of glass that is poorly annealed. If this happens, always discuss it with your retailer. He is there not only to sell you glass. It is to his advantage that you be happy with it. Then you will be back for more.

The boundary between what makes a generic type of glass made by all companies and an individual trade-name item is not well defined. In a nomenclature that is growing rapidly and that many workers individualize according to their own rules, it is easy to get confused. When ordering glass of any particular manufacturer, it is well to study its catalogue and terminology. Such information is readily available from retailers who sell these brand names and who are knowledgeable to point out differences between the glasses of specific manufacturers. Some of the varied differentiations of glasses from different companies are listed in the Appendix.

STAINED-GLASS DESIGN EFFECTS

To achieve its true measure of power, stained glass must be backlighted. But this is not a limiting factor, as many prospective clients suppose. In fact, it is dramatically advantageous. During the day stained-glass windows are infused with light. As the daylight changes, so does the character of the stained glass and the nature of the design. A diminishing of the daylight does not have to diminish the effect of the stained glass. Instead, as the waning light strikes the glass from a different aspect, certain features and colors that were muted before now become highlighted. Many people have favorite hours for viewing a particular panel or window; for some it is not the noon of bright sun, but the meditative light of afternoon or even the solemn perspectives induced by gathering twilight.

Once night comes, the window or panel is extinguished from within. But outside the window glows, providing a different aura courtesy of the electric company. This is all a lot of activity for a single art form, and the designer of stained glass must be prepared to deal with it. But you don't have to make an entire window to get your effects. A small panel or small, free-form objects will also light up your chosen spaces. Stylized animals, flowers, and insignias will do the trick. Placing objects in the window is simple enough. They can be suspended from the wooden molding or hung from plastic suction hooks attached to the clear glass of the pane. Make sure the window surface you are going to use for a suction hook is clean, or the hook may shortly gasp and fall, taking your pride and joy with it. It is best to use a clear fish line to attach your pieces, since metal wire is noticeable and looks awkward.

Stained-glass mobiles also give an intriguing effect to a space. It is not necessary for these to be constructed entirely of glass pieces; stained-glass hangings interspersed with many other materials, from pieces of forged metal to lengths of bam-

Fig. 1–10 Detail from the "Pirate" window—leaded-glass windows within a leaded-glass window. Close to a hundred small pieces of glass were foiled together to form these background windows.

boo, provide an interesting arrangement. The spatial propinquity is what gives charm and wit to the material, although no amount of arrangement can enliven an essentially dull piece.

MAKING A LIGHTBOX

If you want to make stained-glass panels but cannot take up window space, display your work in a lightbox. Oils and watercolors are often lighted individually to emphasize their personas. So why not stained

Fig. 1–11 A more ornate shutter that employs lead lines in a diamond pattern.

Fig. 1–12 Door panel in the home of Mr. and Mrs. William Lee, New York.

Fig. 1–13 *Free-form duck in our studio window. The ducks in the background are real.*

Fig. 1–15 *Stained-glass clock face. The piece is illuminated during the night and reflects the daylight at other times. (Courtesy: Elliot Weiner)*

glass too? A lightbox need not be expensive. It is easy to make one yourself for about the cost of a reasonably priced frame. The lightbox should be made of a type of wood that will set off the panel. It should stand away from the wall as unobtrusively as possible, leaving only enough space to accommodate the fluorescent lights in their crafted recesses. The back of the box is usually covered with silver foil. A 1/4" wood molding will serve to hold the stained glass.

It is important to screw the back panel of your lightbox into place rather than nailing it. Sometimes it's easy to forget

Fig. 1–14 *Stained-glass room divider. The metal frame is hinged together. (Courtesy: Hope Pepe)*

that the light bulb will eventually have to be changed, and of course it's easier to remove screws than nails.

The lightbox should weigh only slightly more than a framed picture of approximately the same size. If it is much heavier than that, you have either used too dense a wood or provided more space within than necessary. You can make the lightbox lighter by using frosted plastic for the diffusing screen rather than frosted glass. The diffusing screen supports the stained-glass piece and allows the fluorescent light to diffuse from within. Although it's best to make the screen light, if it is somewhat heavy, you can allow for the extra weight by providing a stronger hook for suspending the box. To turn the lightbox off and on, a line switch will do, or you can set a small toggle switch into the box itself.

The most ornate type of lightbox is the stained-glass lampshade. The glass used in lampshades is generally of an opalescent or granite-backed cathedral variety—both to diffuse the light and to hide the bulb. Shades come in all shapes and sizes, although basically they are of four types: the straight panel, usually with a skirt of some sort; the bent panel, which generally has a crown; the small, pieced lamp, which may be fabricated over its entire surface or only in its lower portion, having bent panels for the top; and the lantern, basically a straight panel lamp with a small inside dimension.

Room dividers and fireplace screens—a type of modified room divider—have been produced by stained-glass workers, as well as clock faces, three dimensional panels, double-glazed hangings to give the effect of glass on glass, self-supporting abstracts, figurines (in one case a full orchestra), tryptichs, and entire ceilings. The interaction of light and color produces a vivacity that seems to enhance the imaginative powers of those working with the material, so almost anything becomes a possibility.

Before you undertake a large window, keep in mind certain practicalities relative to the medium. They are most important

in window fabrication because they are amplified considerably in these necessarily larger dimensions.

Without exception, always remember that you are designing for glass—not for wood, plastic, or metal—and that certain designs cannot be cut in glass. Also remember that leaded glass work is essentially linear; too many or too few lines can either overwhelm the glass or overstress it. Add to this the various characteristics of the type of glass, such as granularity, transparency, opacity, streakiness, rippled or hammered, antique or cathedral, fractured or crackled, mottled or frosted, and realize how its appearance, much less the color, can work either for or against you. Keep all of this in mind before you even begin to draw your first pattern line.

Certain generalizations can be made for starters about the various glasses:

1. Textured surfaces can be used to suggest the lifelike dimensions of leaves, flowers, or tree bark in representational windows and lampshades. Textured surfaces can also be used to add depth and optical brilliance in nonrepresentational work.
2. Fracture-backed, streamer-backed, or mottled glasses are generally used for foliage or backgrounds.
3. Flemish or hammered glass is used where a specific texture is necessary to convey the nature of an object. Rarely are these glasses used in backgrounds. Both may be used in lampshades, but they are more decorative as skirt strips than as panels.
4. Iridized glass surfaces give an added dimension of reflected color. Beginners do not often start working with iridized glass, although you may want to experiment with small pieces of it. It is usually expensive and used most often to provide emphasis to a particular area.
5. Opalescent glass may be used in windows, but it is usually used for lampshades. Combining opalescent and transparent glass in a window takes skill and experience.

2
Lead
and Other Came:
The Ubiquitous
Skeleton

Lead, that stoic, ponderous, and occasionally murderous element is paradoxically the main ally of flights of fancy in stained glass. And it has been from the start. Like a bony skeleton, it is rigid where necessary, yielding where required, innevitably compliant. Lead *came*, is available in 6-foot lengths of various dimensions and in coiled spools of 25-foot lengths. The spools are convenient because they cut down on waste and they store easily.

The word *came* is Old English for *string* or *length*. It is also spelled *calme* in older books. The lead cames used in working with stained glass are made by an extrusion process whereby the molten metal is shaped, channeled and pressed through a steel die. Usually, lead came is pure. Some companies add alloys to toughen it or to make it bright or encase it in a brass "skin" to provide a measure of inflexibility. Certain cames are more difficult to cut and bend than others. Round came, for instance, is generally more stubborn than flat came. Other metals have become popular, such as zinc cames, copper foil, and brass rods, but lead is still the major material, still the old, reliable companion, still the classic partner in this long-standing ballet of line and light.

shaped pieces of glass. However, this practical medievalism has its aesthetic investment in that the flow of the design is emphasized and often derived from the linear quality of the lead. Thus knowledge of the idiosyncracies of came is essential to anyone who wants to work with stained-glass. The lead is as crucial to the overall statement as the glass itself.

How Came Is Measured

Lead came is always measured across the top surface, not across the channeled side. Nor is the depth of the channel necessarily a factor in measuring lead. Since the channel may be artificially pinched or widened, such a measurement would be inconstant. The top surface, however, does not change to any degree, and it's here that we measure whether the lead is $1/16''$, $1/8''$, $3/16''$, or $1/2''$. Hobbyists generally stay in the range of $1/16$ to $1/4$ inch lead came, but if you undertake an extensive project of wide dimensions, especially if large pieces of glass are being used, you might want to use the large leads both for strength and design (Fig. 2–2).

Whether came is round or flat applies also to a description of the top surface. Most leads come either way.

LEAD CAME

Lead came has two principal purposes. The came is made to hold together the different

H or U Cames

H cames have two channels, one on either side with a wall or "heart" in the middle,

Fig. 2–1 This extrusion press produces lead pipe. The only difference between this and came is the die. Courtesy National Lead Company.

Fig. 2–2 A length of lead came showing the "heart" and the top, or measuring, surface.

Specialized Cames

In addition to the regular H and U cames, there are a number of other, specialized cames. Among these are cames to hold glass in a three-dimensional position and for right turns and other angles. Many of these cames are used primarily for lamp manufacture; others are used in free-form sculpture and in self-sustaining glass wall pieces. Today, there is a came for practically any use. If you do not find the came you are looking for in one of the many catalogues, no doubt one of the large lead companies, such as Gardiner, is either working on it or only waiting for enough requests to do so.

The amazing number of shapes of lead cames does not mean that the old standbys have fallen by the wayside. These standard leads still do most of the work; their more exotic brothers only point up certain shortcuts for specific effects. In general, the more involved the design of the lead, the more expensive it becomes. Inevitably there comes the point where you may find it cheaper to take more time and combine the standard leads you have, especially if you are not producing that many items. Don't invest in leads just because they are exotic. If you are mass producing items, however, the specialized cames are great timesavers.

shaped like an H on its side. This lead heart is usually ¹⁄₁₆". H cames are "inside" leads, accommodating themselves to pieces of glass in each channel. U cames, or "high heart" cames, are "outside" leads used for finishing a single surface that will show, such as unframed panels or the skirts of lamps. Their single channel is considerably deeper than an H channel, and they give a completed look to the edges of a piece. Rarely do you use H came on the outside of a work. For if you do, you will then have to slice away the remaining open channel. This makes the whole piece look sloppy.

The Degrees of Lead Came

1. The two consistencies of lead came are pure and mixed. Pure lead came is exactly that—the lead content is 99 percent. No alloys have been added to toughen it or to give it a bright sheen. Mixed lead may contain quantities of tin or other alloys to provide a particular advantage, usually to make the lead more hardy or to prevent or slow down oxidation.

2. The two silhouettes of lead came are flat and round. Looking at the came in cross-section, flatness or roundness is determined by the shape of the top and bottom lips. Although rounded came is ac-

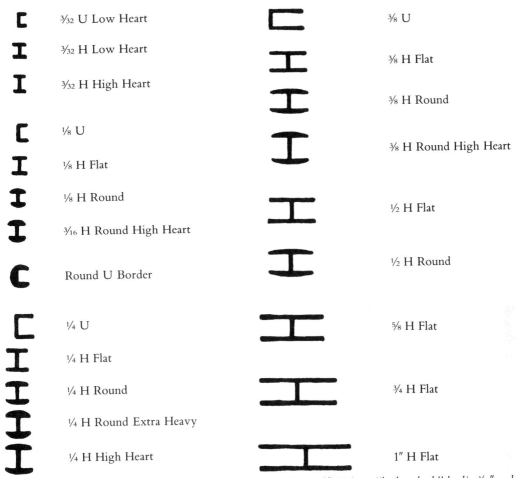

⅜ U	
⅜ H Flat	
⅜ H Round	
⅜ H Round High Heart	
½ H Flat	
½ H Round	
⅝ H Flat	
¾ H Flat	
1″ H Flat	

3/32 U Low Heart

3/32 H Low Heart

3/32 H High Heart

⅛ U

⅛ H Flat

⅛ H Round

3/16 H Round High Heart

Round U Border

¼ U

¼ H Flat

¼ H Round

¼ H Round Extra Heavy

¼ H High Heart

Fig. 2–3 *Some common lead came silhouettes. Most hobbyists use ⅛″ U (as a "back-to-back" lead), 3/16″ and ¼″ H, either round or flat, and ¼″ U as an outside finishing lead. Rarely will it be necessary to use a lead size larger than ⅜″.*

Heart Thickness

Channel Width

Face Width

Fig. 2–4 *The basic anatomy of came, here H or two-sided came shown on its side. Heart thickness and channel width may vary in the same came from different manufacturers.*

tually stiffer than flat came of the same dimension, since more metal is used to round the surfaces, the choice of one over the other is generally a function of the design, not a matter of stability.

3. The two cross-section dimensions of lead came are height and width. The cross-section height depends on the came "heart" or central support (or, in U came, the border). A "high heart" lead is one with a wider channel (or channels) than a comparative "low heart" came because of this taller support. This type of came is

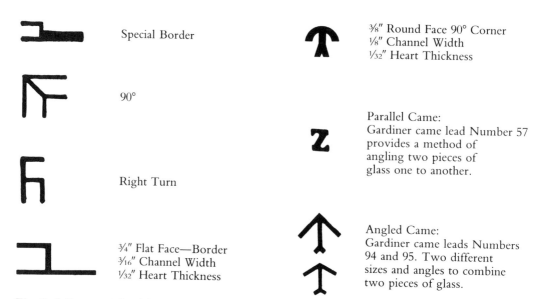

Special Border

90°

Right Turn

¾" Flat Face—Border
³⁄₁₆" Channel Width
¹⁄₃₂" Heart Thickness

⅜" Round Face 90° Corner
⅛" Channel Width
¹⁄₃₂" Heart Thickness

Parallel Came:
Gardiner came lead Number 57
provides a method of
angling two pieces of
glass one to another.

Angled Came:
Gardiner came leads Numbers
94 and 95. Two different
sizes and angles to combine
two pieces of glass.

Fig. 2–5 *Some specialized lead came silhouettes. Chances are you will order these rarely and in small quantities unless you are mass producing a piece.*

Dimensions of Standard Lead Cames

No.	Approx-imate Strands Per Box	Face Width	Channel Width	Heart Thickness	Wt.Per Lin. Ft. In Ozs.
1	195	.313"	.125"	.031"	1½
2	118	.375"	.156"	.031"	2½
3	195	.156"	.156"	.031"	1½
4	131	.219"	.375"	.031"	2¼
5	148	.188"	.188"	.031"	2
6	107	.438"	.156"	.047"	2¾
7	131	.250"	.188"	.031"	2¼
8	195	.156"	.156"	.031"	1½
9	118	.438"	.188"	.031"	2½
10	131	.188"	.172"	.031"	2¼
11	195	.125"	.188"	.016"	1½
12	74	.750"	.156"	.047"	4
13	118	.250"	.172"	.031"	2½
14	169	.406" (Overall)	.156"	.031"	1¾
15	79	.625"	.156"	.031"	3¾
16	169	.219"	.125"	.031"	1¾
17	40	.734"	.422"	.094"	7¼
18	84	.344"	.188"	.047"	3½
19	19	.969"	.250"	.125"	15½
20	91	.500"	.141"	.047"	3¼
21	53	.750"	.234"	.047"	5½
22	74	.625"	.219"	.047"	4
23	84	.516"	.250"	.047"	3½
24	65	.438"	.188"	.047"	4½
25	91	.313"	.188"	.047"	3¼
26	107	.500"	.156"	.047"	2¾

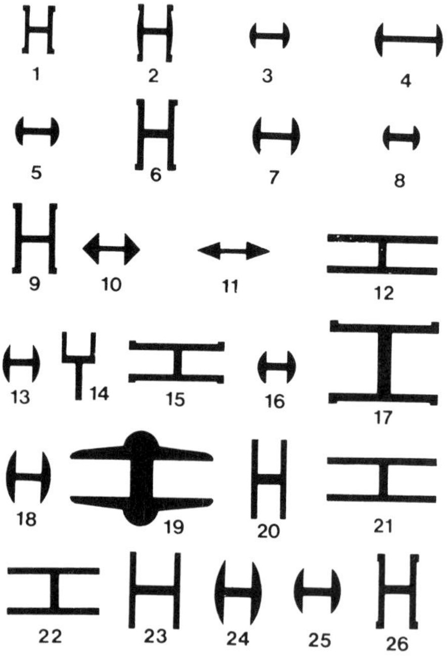

Dimensions of Standard Lead Cames (cont'd)

No.	Approx-imate Strands Per Box	Face Width	Channel Width	Heart Thickness	Wt.Per Lin. Ft. In Ozs.
27	98	.375″	.297″	.047″	3
28	148	.250″	.188″	.031″	2
29	84	.469″	.172″	.031″	3½
30	84	.500″	.188″	.031″	3½
31	53	.625″	.172″	.031″	5½
32	42	.750″	.188″	.031″	7
33	24	1.000″	.234″	.125″	12
34	118	.328″	.172″	.031″	2½
35	195	.156″	.188″	.031″	1½
36	169	.313″	.188″	.031″	1¾
37	84	.500″	.172″	.109″	3½
38	65	.484″	.234″	.125″	4½
39	98	.563″	.188″	.047″	3
40	29	1.000″	.188″	.047″	10
41	43	1.250″	.219″	.031″	6¾
42	19	(.250″)(.500″)	.125″	.125″	15¼
43	290	.125″	.125″	.016″	1
44	98	.313″	—	.156″	3
45	37	1.500″	.219″	.047″	8
46	118	.375″	.156″	.031″	2½
47	118	.188″	.172″	.063″	2½
48	148	.281″	.156″	.031″	2
49	84	.625″	.172″	.031″	3½
50	230	.125″	.203″	.031″	1¼
51	107	.313″	.219″	.047″	2¾
52	56	.625″	.250″	.031″	5¼
53	195	.188″	.125″	.031″	1½
54	45	.875″	.234″	.047″	6½
55	169	.234″	.156″	.031″	1¾
56	84	.281″	.250″	.031″	3½
57	65	.344″	.266″	.063″	4½
58	79	.750″	.188″	.031″	3¾
59	98	.328″	.234″	.047″	3
60	230	.188″	.156″	.031″	1¼
61	195	.188″	.203″	.031″	1½
62	65	.500″	.188″	.047″	4½
64	118	.234″	.234″	.047″	2½
65	53	1.000″	.156″	.047″	5½
66	118	.375″	.203″	.031″	2½
67	148	.281″	.203″	.031″	2
68	107	.375″	.156″	.047″	2¾
69	70	.500″	.203″	.047″	4¼
70	84	.344″	.125″	.047″	3½
90	295	.104″	.172″	.041″	1
91	165	.172″	.188″	.078″	1.8
94	110	.266″	.203″	.078″	2.6
95	98	.313″DIA.	.188″	—	3
707	195	.188″	.156″	.047″	1½
727	84	.500″@90°	.188″	.035″	3½

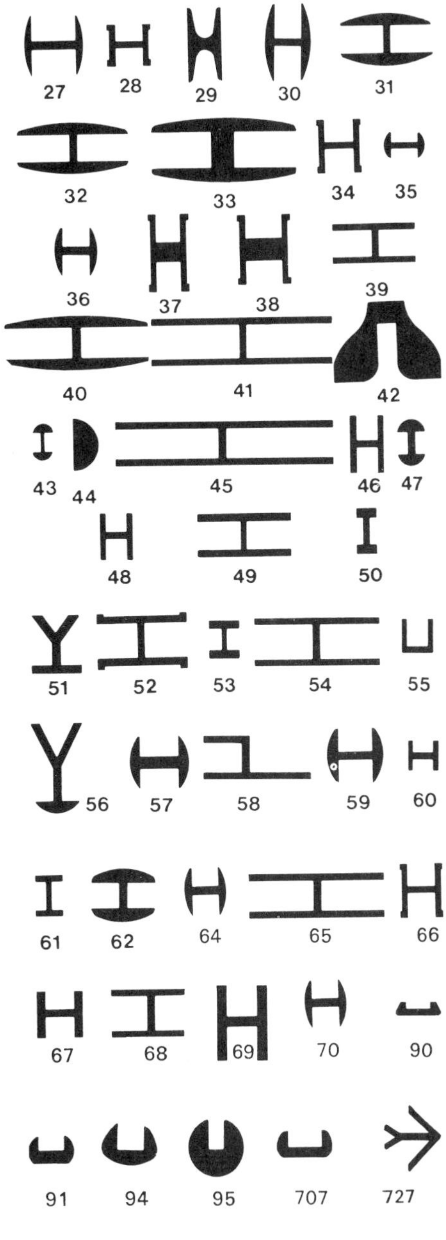

Fig. 2–6 *RSR Corporation's standard lead cames. RSR manufacturers two alloys—a 99.9% pure lead came and a special alloy of ¾ antimony and ¼ tin, which gives a shiny finish to the came and slows down oxidation.*

Table 2–1 Decimal Equivalents

.016	1/64	.313	5/16
.031	1/32	.328	21/64
.047	3/64	.344	11/32
.063	1/16	.375	3/8
.094	3/32	.406	13/32
.109	7/64	.422	27/64
.125	1/8	.438	7/16
.141	9/64	.469	15/32
.156	5/32	.484	31/64
.172	11/64	.500	1/2
.188	3/16	.516	33/64
.203	13/64	.563	9/16
.219	7/32	.625	5/8
.234	15/64	.734	47/64
.250	1/4	.750	3/4
.266	17/64	.875	7/8
.281	9/32	.969	31/32
.297	19/64	1,000	1

stead, although the empty channel, hanging as it were in midair, tends to provide an anticlimactic look.

6. Lead came comes in many styles. Cames of convenience is the name of the game. In addition to all the extra rounds, extra high hearts, and extra thins, there are special bordering styles such as 90-degree turned came with a 45-degree heart and a right-angle came with a 90-degree heart—actually a combination of two U leads. Many of these bordering leads are especially useful in lamp making, but they also serve well in stained-glass sculpturing, since they offer more support than copper foil.

used for extra thick pieces of glass, such as English streaky. The cross-section width is the dimension that gives the came its essential identification, and it is the same as the linear width.

4. The two linear dimensions of lead came are length and width. The standard came length is six feet. If you buy the lead in three-foot lengths for the sake of convenience, you are buying half a strand. Linear width is the same as cross-section width and generally is measured in multiples of sixteenths—1/16″, 1/8″, 3/16″, and 1/4″. To determine the "size" of a came, all you need do is measure the side-to-side diameter. After you have worked with came for a while, you will quickly be able to size it by eye. Came widths extend up to one inch. Such leads may be used in large windows with large, individual pieces of glass. Although this may be an architectural necessity, a good stained-glass designer will make the lead complement the design.

5. The two structures of lead came are U and H. U leads, or bordering leads. These have a single channel and may be rounded or flat. The one channel allows the lead heart to supply a finished, smooth surface around the object. This does not mean that you cannot use an H lead in-

Widening and Narrowing Channels

The channel width of lead came measures about 1/4″ and accommodates the majority of different colored glasses. For hand-blown antique glass, the lead channel may prove either too wide or, more often than not, too narrow. English streaky glass, with its variable thicknesses throughout the sheet, is especially difficult to get into the lead channel.

To narrow the channel, pinch it against the glass by pressing with the broad blade of a lead or putty knife. To widen the channel, a special instrument called a lathkin is used. If a particularly thick piece of glass is to be accommodated, a portion of the lead channel must be opened so wide that it may gape. This is acceptable if enough of the channel margin grasps the edge of the glass without threatening its stability. However, if the opening of the channel does not allow a sufficient grasp of the piece of glass, use a larger lead or a thinner piece of glass, even if you slightly compromise the color scheme. Nothing looks more unprofessional than pieces of tortured came, the edges of which seem to be all but nonexistent around the glass. These areas stand out accusingly no matter how hard you try to convince yourself that no one will notice.

Fig. 2–7 Lead came arranged for top and side (channel) viewing. The widest (top) is ¾". Some of the channels, in two of the cames on the right, are grooved. The treatment of the channels depends on the manufacturer. That grooving adds flexibility is debatable.

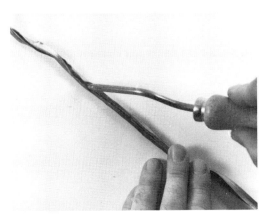

Fig. 2–8 Widening the lead channel. The lathkin's metal point opens the came from roughly the middle of the picture toward the left. The pinched portion of came is grasped with the other hand.

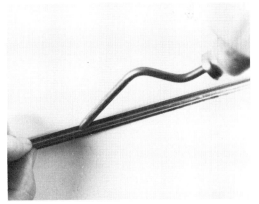

Fig. 2–9 Opening the came from the top. The channel is upward, and the lathkin presses downward. Your other hand stabilizes the came and keeps it from rolling over.

Lead and Other Came: the Ubiquitous Skeleton **35**

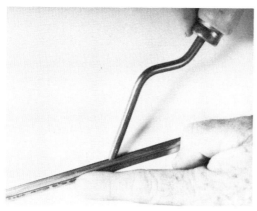

Fig. 2–10 *Opening the came from the side. The lathkin presses sideways, and your other hand presses the came against it to keep it from slipping.*

Fig. 2–12 *Place the blade of the lead knife under a piece of glass you want to seat in a channel. This will raise the edge of the glass just enough to clear the lower flange of the lead.*

Fig. 2–11 *Slipping the glass edge into an open channel of the lead. The glass should fit snugly but easily in its entire length. You should be able to accomplish this without pressing, pushing, shoving, or hammering.*

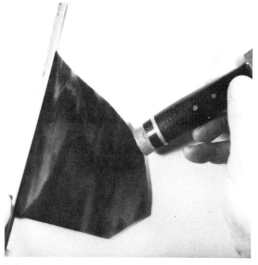

Fig. 2–13 *Tapping glass into the came. Use the back end (weighted for the purpose) of your leading knife. Tap gently. Try to tap against a stable surface of the glass. Avoid tapping against corners, since these may break off easily and leave you with a piece of glass that no longer fits the pattern.*

Fitting the Glass to the Came

While fitting the glass to the came during the leading process should be a simple process, it can turn into a contest if you have not used the materials effectively. Force should not enter the picture, although beginners inevitably attempt to use it to im- pose their will on the stubbornness of the came. The idea is to slip the edge of the glass into an open channel of the lead, which you may or may not have widened beforehand (*Fig. 2–11*). The other channel may already be affixed to a piece of glass

(Fig. 2–12). The piece of came is flat against the table as is the glass being applied. In your attempts to push the glass edge into the lead channel, you may continue to find that edge seating improperly. Patience gives way to tapping the glass with the handle of the lead knife. After a few minutes of frustration, you will discover that the glass was pushing against the bottom lip of the piece of came. Now you can see the results: one piece of came to be replaced because of a mashed channel and possibly one piece of glass with a chipped edge because of all that unnecessary tapping.

The point is that glass usually goes into the lead channels readily enough if it is lined up properly. A slight amount of tapping is all that may be needed to finish seating it. If the came doesn't comply, you can try sliding the blade of your leading knife under the glass, thus raising it slightly above the table. This will allow it to slip right over that lower channel lip. It will take little, if any, tapping to lock it securely into the lead or leads. Where more than one lead is involved, as in Figure 2–12, the same rule applies. It would probably be best to seat the glass into the lower came first, then slide it into the front channel. Once the glass is grasped by the first came, it is automatically raised to the proper height to slide into the adjoining came.

Tapping Glass into the Came

Tapping is not always necessary or wise. Most cames will accept their glass borders without any extraneous urging. Tapping can become a habit, and it's not a good one. A slight push of the finger against the glass will correctly seat it within the came; if it rocks, it usually means that the glass has been incorrectly cut to fit the space and no amount of tapping will make it fit. In fact, tapping in this instance may rearrange all the pieces that have been set so far.

Whenever you tap, for whatever reason, do it with caution. *Never*, as we have seen students do, tap glass into came with

a hammer. You will apply far too much force and possibly shatter the glass or chip it badly. Instead, use the back of the lead knife, which is weighted for the purpose. But even with the knife tap gently. Remember, if you have taken the pains to see that your glass fits correctly, you will need little, if any, tapping to make it seat properly. If the glass does not fit correctly, all the tapping in the world will not seat the came, and most likely you will turn a misfit into a disaster.

Stretching the Came

All lead came below ½", and sometimes even that, must be stretched. Came should be stretched only prior to use. This process not only straightens the came of all kinks and twists, but it makes it much easier to work with because it firms up and tones

Fig. 2–14 *Two styles of lead stretchers. Both have serrated jaws that grip the lead, both are attached firmly to the work table. You can use a bench vise rather than a lead stretcher, but it is more work to close the jaws and more likely the vise will tear the lead through excessive crimping. The jaws open and close quickly with little effort.*

Fig. 2–15 A lead stretcher on a long metal tongue that fastens to a swivel. The swivel can be fastened to the work table with a vice grip. This means that you can stretch the lead while standing at any angle, since the swivel will always face you. It also allows you to move the stretcher around the studio, since it need not be permanently affixed to a table. (Courtesy of Anderson Stained Glass Studios)

the lead. The process of stretching is easily done by placing one end of the came in a lead stretcher or vise and pulling, gently at first, with pliers at the other end. You will actually feel the lead give and elongate. A sharp jerk will probably snap the lead and send you flying across the room. Keep one foot behind you during the stretching process: Lead came has a definite sense of humor. Another method of stretching the came is to step on one end and pull upwards on the other. This procedure works only for the thinner leads from $1/16''$ through $3/16''$. It is not a good idea to work with unstretched lead. It will not follow the vagaries of the design but will tend to stand away from the glass.

Storing Lead Came

Lead came resembles long strands of spaghetti combined with the sinuousness of snakes. All sorts of methods have been devised to store them so that the various styles may be readily identified and the individual lengths easily separated. A number of these methods are ingenious and serve the purpose well, especially where only a dozen or so came lengths are involved.

The cames can be doubled over and hung from padded hooks to avoid kinking, laid out in individual bundles, placed in long boxes with dividers for the different types, or placed in heavy, color-coded cardboard tubes to avoid mix-ups. Many workers store lead came in the long wooden boxes they are shipped in, and, indeed, if you buy large amounts, this is obviously the best way to store it. The way *not* to store cames is to throw them together in a bin—unless you want to spend all of your creative glass-working time untangling them.

If you store came in a box or boxes, you must decide how and where to store the boxes. One obvious place is under the work table. Lead cases can be stored on shelves, with each shelf holding a separate type came. Since the cases will be stacked one on top of the other, it's a good idea to remove the end of the case so that you can pull the came out easily. One disadvantage of this system is that once you pull the came out and decide not to use it, you can't very well put it back unless the box is partially empty. Instead, you could set up a row of hooks. Pulling the came out of a full box is not quite so easy as it sounds. The strands seem determined to mate during the process, and all too often you will have to flap the came about to get it to slide free.

If you are selling came, you will almost certainly end up with more of it out of the box than in by the end of the day, since customers seem unable to imagine what an entire length looks like from a sample and inevitably request several strands more than they buy. The best way to avoid this problem is to arrange the cases so that the came can be lifted from the top. You can buy or build a case rack to suit the number of cases you intend to store (Fig. 2–16 A, B). Lead came, of all stained-glass materials, is the most difficult to find a proper home for in the studio or store; your choice of location should be anything but slapdash. It can make working with the stuff a chore or a pleasure right from the start.

Fig. 2–16A Lead came storage rack made of sturdy metal posts. This design takes up little room, but it will hold 14 boxes of 100-pound lead came. Dimensions are 51" × 72" × 57" high. (Courtesy: CAC Company)

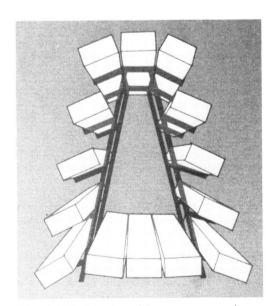

Fig. 2–16B Side view of the came storage rack.

Physical Characteristics of Lead Came

Lead has a tendency to form an oxidative coating on its surface when it is exposed to air. The process is gradual, but even the thinnest coating will diminish the ability of the surface to accept solder, and a heavy coat of oxidation will stop the process altogether. This thickening barrier cannot be removed even by the strongest flux. If your lead isn't absolutely shiny, it has oxidized to some degree. If it has a dull finish, the oxidation is extensive. There is no problem removing this coating once you understand what has occurred. It is best removed by scrubbing the surface with a stiff wire brush, either brass or copper bristled. Steel bristles are likely to scratch the surface rather than buff it. Brass- or copper-bristled brushes can be purchased in most hardware stores.

The oxidative coating does not have to be removed until you are ready to solder. The coating has no effect on the malleability or the firmness of the came. When you are ready to solder, scrub each joint with the wire brush. You will see the shiny, newly minted surface of the lead appear fairly rapidly. Some workers make it a habit to scrub each joint even if the surface still looks shiny, claiming that the solder spreads more evenly over the joint.

While there is no way to prevent the oxidative process, it can be slowed down. Since exposure to air accelerates oxidation, store the lead came in a dry area. Dampness and humidity will quickly dull the shiniest lead. You can further protect the came by storing it in plastic wrap. Keep all storage boxes tightly covered. Separate layers of came in a single box by paper to avoid dampness seeping through from one layer to the next. This will also help keep the came from tangling. Most factories ship came this way. You should keep the lead away from any chemicals you are working with. The fumes from inorganic acids such as hydrochloride, sulphuric, and nitric can affect the surface of the lead even if they don't come into direct contact with it. And one final note: Don't stretch the lead came until just before you are ready to use it.

Cutting and Mitering

Came can be cut straight across or mitered at an angle to fit against its neighboring leads as snugly as possible. The close butting of the cames allows for smooth soldered joints, which will enhance the linear quality you are trying to achieve. This provides a neat, professional-looking final result.

Several items on the market can be used for cutting lead. Mitering, however, is not always so easily accomplished. But first, a couple of tools that should *not* be used. Chief among these are ordinary scissors or tinsnips. The blades of these tools tend to crush the channels or deform the cut end, and it must be restructured before it can be used. Cutting came with scissors will also dull and ruin the scissors eventually. Mitering with these items is awkward and time-wasting.

One dangerous lead-cutting tool is the hand-held razor blade. For all its multipurpose uses, cutting came is not one of them.

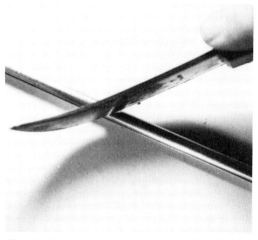

Fig. 2–18 Cutting lead came at an angle (mitering.) The degree of angle is scratched on the top surface of the came and the knife blade is matched to it. The force applied is the same as with a straight cut.

Even thin cames are tougher than they look, and razor blades cannot withstand the stress of cutting through them. Also, a corner can chip off and hit you in the eye. Or the brittle blade may twist and shatter, mitering your fingers instead.

A utility knife can be used to cut came because it has a more rugged blade than a razor blade. It is awkward, but it's safe. A heavy-duty linoleum knife can be used as a lead knife if one edge is ground onto the back (convex) surface. Treated thus, it resembles a professional leading knife and is at least a step in the right direction. You need a bench grinder to put the edge on the blade, as well as a good quality steel to maintain the edge. But in the long run, it is less work to buy a leading knife.

Using a Leading Knife

Make the cut across the top surface of the came regardless of the size came being used. Never make the cut across the channeled surface because you can damage the delicate channel edges. Mitering is most effective when done from the top surface of one came to that of another. With the blade of the leading knife resting on top of

Fig. 2–17 Cutting lead came straight across. The knife blade forms a right angle to the lead, and the force is downward with a side-to-side jiggle.

Fig. 2–19 *Some substitutes for the leading knife. Above is a standard utility knife and below a linoleum knife. Sharpening the convex curve of the linoleum knife will provide an edge with a shape similar to a leading knife, if not the proper weight and balance. Beware of the pointed blade on the utility knife, which is too fragile for came. If you use a utility knife, always use the blade, never the point.*

Fig. 2–20 *Two versions of the essential leading knife. Top: a smaller, nonweighted knife with a steeply rounded cutting edge. Bottom: a weighted-handle variety with a more gradual blade curve.*

the came, gradually increase the pressure and work with a side-to-side rocking motion. The combination of these forces sends the blade cleanly through the came. A rocking motion front to back is not as effective. Excessive pressure will crush or otherwise distort the came. Without the rocking movement the knife will push

rather than slice, and this will crush the came.

A new item on the market, a came cutter, does a similar job to the lead knife. This is a specific tool for the purpose, not one adapted for the procedure. A good came cutter can also be used for cutting items other than lead, such as copper foil, zinc came, and wire. The sharp nose and the keen edges of this tool enable you to cut came without distorting the channels and also to miter. Although we find the lead knife an indispensable item, in many ways an extension of the hand, many stained-glass workers prefer a came cutter (Fig 2–21). Our recommendation is to learn to use a lead knife regardless of any subsidiary items you add later on. We can all use all the help we can get. The leading knife, however, remains the basic precision instrument for the leading operation.

In addition to the leading knife and came cutter are lead-came choppers and lead saws. Hand-held and electric choppers are available (Figs. 2–22 and 2–23). The

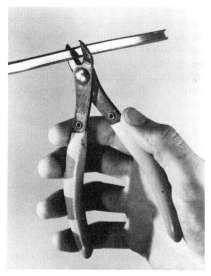

Fig. 2–21 *The Big Shear 1755 came cutter from Plato Products cuts lead and zinc came, foil, and wires. Its sharp nose and keen edges enable you to cut came without distortion. It is a comfortable instrument to use.*

electric model is useful primarily when a quantity of came of similar length and miter has to be prepared. The tool cuts this rapidly and precisely. The hand chopper is used more for individual leads. The angle of the miter is scratched upon the surface as a guide and the blade hammered home. Providing a sharp blade is used, the cut is clean, and the came does not have to be restraightened. As with came cutters, lead choppers are ancillary to the essential leading knife.

Widening the Lead Came Channel

A number of tools can be used to widen the came channel. Usually widening is necessary to fit an especially thick piece of glass or to reexpand a channel that has somehow gotten pinched in the rough and

Fig. 2–23 The electric lead chopper for cutting lead in quantity. (Courtesy of Anderson Studios)

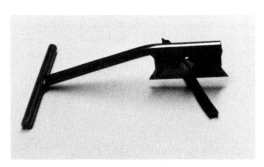

Fig. 2–22A Lead chopper poised in position over a piece of lead; it is self-sustaining.

Fig. 2–22B One quick tap with a hammer and the lead is cut neatly.

Fig. 2–24 The came saw makes straight cuts and miters. A handy little device, especially for cutting zinc, brass, and brass-crowned lead came. (Courtesy of The Window Works)

tumble of the storage area. Special instruments called "lathkins" present various streamlining, come in various shapes, and are made of various materials, from Mylar to wood to metal (Fig. 2–25). Sometimes a lead pencil, the simplest kind of lathkin, can be run into the narrowed portion of the channel side to open it.

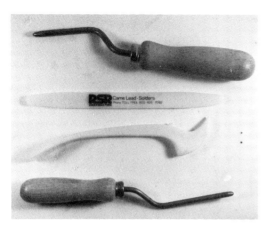

Fig. 2–25 *Lathkins. Top and bottom are two sizes of the angled wood/metal variety that are very useful. In the center are two Mylar shapes. You can also use bone, pencils, or dowels, but you should get used to the feel of one regular tool to gain efficiency.*

When using a lathkin to widen a channel, it is important not to snag the came. A good lathkin will slide easily along the length of came. The shape of the lathkin you buy or make yourself is up to you. We prefer the wood-handled model with an angled metal tube that can be used in a pushing fashion. The point of the metal plows through the channel while we hold the came firmly on the work table with our other hand. These lathkins can also be used point downward, scraping against the channel wall or heart. An lathkin can also be pulled toward you.

If the came is positioned channel up, the pressure from the lathkin is down (*See Figs. 2–9 and 2–10*). If the channel is positioned sideways, the balancing pressure of your other hand comes from the other side The best position usually depends on the length of the came. So long as you are comfortable and the job is being done efficiently, the positioning of the came is immaterial.

Cornering

Whenever you work on corners, such as the outside edges of a window or panel, you will encounter some special leading

problems. Most workers prefer to use U leads on these outside borders because they provide a neat, finished appearance. Simply butting the corner leads one against another is one technique. However, for purposes of strength, as well as to provide a trim look, it is advisable to interlock these cames at the corners. Just running one came over the other makes the corners bulge; this is emphasized by the subsequent soldering. We splice these corners, one into anoher, in a sort of lock-and-key process (*Figs. 2–26 and 2-27*). This is not a procedure universally adhered to by any means, and we do not always follow it ourselves, but it does allow for good, tight corners that hold up well.

Lead Poisoning

The danger of lead poisoning is one of the first questions asked by cautious beginners in stained glass. And it is interesting to note that many professional workers in the craft know little about this subject. The fact of the matter is that the body can absorb lead. Anyone who handles lead for periods of time will find a residue on the fingers of lead oxides. If you practice good hygiene and wash your hands with soap,

Fig. 2–26 *The locking-corner technique with lead came. The came on the left has been cut out to allow the one on the right to fit in the alotted space.*

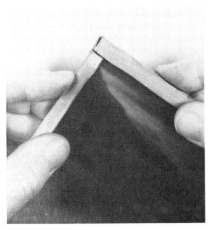

Fig. 2–27 The two corners are brought together and locked into position. They will then be soldered. This maneuver gives added strength to the joint and makes for neat soldering joints. If you prefer just to butt the leads, you will have an open channel in one of the two butting Us

water, and a brush when leaving the studio, these deposits will come right off and there should be no problem. However, if you are in a rush and decide to eat a sandwich, or if you unconsciously lick your fingers to turn pages while reading instructions, a certain amount of lead will be absorbed. The worker who is clean and thoughtful in his work habits need have no fear of lead poisoning. As for the danger of lead fumes liberated during the soldering process, see Appendix.

Lead particles and lead oxides become lodged in the pores of the skin. They are not absorbed into the body unless ingested. Naturally, if you have any cuts on your fingers, they should be well bandaged before working with lead cames. We don't advise wearing gloves, but you should wash your hands throughly before leaving the workshop. Needless to say, all lead should be kept out of the reach of children.

DESIGNING WITH LEAD

Artists in other mediums who begin to work in stained glass often continue to think in terms of their previous craft, be it oils, watercolors, or sculpture, and attempt to adapt that knowledge to stained glass. They soon find that the stained-glass medium has rules of its own in terms of design. One must always keep in mind not only what can and what cannot be cut in glass, but what the leading procedure will do to these cut lines. Points, especially, tend to disappear, swallowed up by the lead. If you have a number of points coming together at any one place, you will end up with a mass of lead and solder that bears no resemblance to your original design. Let the lead work with you in the design. If you need a long, thin line, don't try to cut it out of glass; use a wide piece of lead instead. If you want the eye to follow along a certain path, let the lead lines carry the flow to that area. Remember, lead came is an integral part of the design; it is not there simply to "glue" the glass pieces together. Lead lines that wander erratically over the surface of a work to no ostensible purpose detract from what otherwise might be a very pleasing prospect. The type of lead you use depends on the effect you want to produce and the amount of strength you need. Don't fall into the trap of designing with small pieces of glass, then allowing them to be swallowed up with large pieces of lead.

In this regard, consider mixing various sizes of lead within the same panel, as a painter would mix different brush strokes depending on what he wanted to emphasize and what he wanted to tone down. It is not essential or artistic to stick to one type of lead throughout a window or a panel. All of this must be noted in the original design or blueprint, and only when this is completed to the worker's satisfaction should the actual glass cutting and leading begin.

H Cames

H cames, as previously noted, are inside leads used within a panel or lamp to accommodate a piece of glass to either side. While there are almost infinite styles and

Fig. 2–28 A bold pattern showing sweeping lead lines radiating from an off-center focus. Leads used here were mostly ¼" and ⅜".

Fig. 2–31 Another detail shows an ornate and nimble flow of lead line in the bouquet of flowers. This was difficult leading but worth it in terms of the end result.

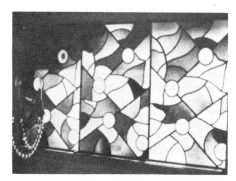

Fig. 2–29 A more delicate pattern of lead lines giving a spidery effect, the curves complement the roundels scattered through these panels. Lead sizes are ¼" to ³⁄₁₆".

Fig. 2–32 Rose pattern design on a stained-glass lamp in copper foil. Note the intricate glass cutting. (Courtesy: Uroboros Glass)

Fig. 2–30 Detail of a garden scene. It shows a stark, emphatic use of line with fairly wide leads— ¼" to ½".

variations, six major H leads are in common use. Keep in mind that lead cames may be made for special purposes if you want to invest in the special dies. But dies are expensive. If you have a milling machine, you can make your own style came lead, and indeed, there are also cames that are sold specifically for milling. You could then turn out an almost endless supply of unusual leads. But if you are like the rest of us, you will settle for some of the tried and proven ones, such as those described in Figure 2–10.

1. *⅛" Came—No Room for Error*. The smallest H came, ⅛" H came is very thin lead indeed. In rounded form, it appears even thinner than it does in flat, since the edges are foreshortened. There is no room for error in using this lead. Your glass cutting must be precise because there is very little channel to cover mistakes. In fact, this lead is not advised for beginners unless the glass edges are sanded, and even then, if the sanding is not done correctly, the sanded edge will show beyond the limit of the came. This lead is used mainly for small pieces of glass, or for large pieces where the lead line is so secondary to the overall design that just a hint of it is required. Of course it furnishes little strength, so a design using a long, unbroken length of this came must be carefully thought out in advance. It is used extensively in hanging objects, such as mobiles or small animals, since it goes around only small pieces of glass.

2. *³⁄₁₆" Came—A Beginner's Lead*. Here is the novice's friend—wider than the ⅛" but not as bulky to inexperienced fingers as the ¼". As is true of all these leads, ³⁄₁₆" comes in both round and flat shapes, with the flat being somewhat easier to manipulate. Glass cutting need not be as specifically precise as with ⅛" came, though, of course, it is a good habit always to cut your glass as precisely as possible. Because of the small overhang in this lead, it will not accept thick pieces of antique glass, and if you use such glass in your design, don't use the ³⁄₁₆" lead in those areas. Witb this one exception, you will find that this basic lead is good for intermediate panels, mobiles, and windows, since it furnishes a feeling of delicacy without fragility and adapts well to inner and outer curves.

3. *¼" Came—Lamp Makers Pride*. This is the most popular lead for paneled lamps, especially in rounded form, but it is also useful for other objects as well. In its flat shape it is used more in windows. The ¼" rounded lead gives enough room for lamp panels to angle within it, without showing the edge of the glass. Yet it does not appear too bulky or make the lamp too heavy. This lead also contributes enough strength to hold the lamp firm. The rounded edge serves to intensify the three-dimensional effect of the lamp and gives the surface a finished appearance. In windows or panels, ¼" flat lead provides a more definite line to the work than either ⅛" or ³⁄₁₆", and it also adds more rigidity.

4. *⅜" Came—For Professional Windows*. With this size we leave the hobbyist leads and go into leads used mainly by professional studios. A stiff, heavy lead, ⅜" came firmly clutches the glass on either side and gives a definitive linear quality to the window. It will not conform well to sharp curves, though with care it can be used at

Fig. 2–33 Some H leads. From left to right: thin ⅛", heavy ⅛", ³⁄₁₆" round, ¼" round, ½" flat, ¾" and 1" flat.

such points in the design. In its rounded form it can be used in the larger lampshades, but it will be more bulky than the ¼". With the ⅜" we get into heavier and therefore more expensive leads. Lead is priced according to weight.

5. *½", ¾", and 1" Lead Cames—Strength and Flexibility.* These professional leads are rarely used by the hobbyist, if at all. Providing more strength than flexibility, these leads are rugged and difficult to work around curves and are mainly used in large windows. They provide a definitive linear flow to the design and complement large pieces of glass. Although these leads are more massive than the hobbyist leads, they are worked in the same way. They need not be stretched; indeed, above ½", they *cannot* be. Occasionally a section of one of these wide leads is used in a small work with a thinner and more delicate line. Here the lead forms a stark break in the pattern, so it calls for the utmost discretion on the part of the designer, since there is the possibility of unbalancing the entire work for this one novel effect.

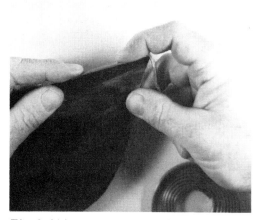

Fig. 2–34A *Wrapping a piece of glass with ⅛" U lead (back-to-back.) The lead is placed along the glass edge and pressed to it with the fingers. It is especially important to do this with straight edges, as shown, and to make sure that the lead has been stretched adequately. Otherwise it may come away from the glass.*

U or End Cames

U or end cames are used on borders or on glass surfaces where no other piece of glass abuts. These are finishing cames, giving the work a finished appearance, enclosing it rather than leaving an empty H channel dangling. Popular with hobbyists, these leads are seldom used by professional studios. This is because studios mainly create large windows designed for an existing framework. Instead, studios use H leads as bordering leads both to furnish more strength to the borders and allow leeway in fitting the window into its space. That extra, empty channel can always be shaved to allow more room for a proper fit, keeping in mind that it will eventually be covered by molding.

1. *1/16" Styles—Back-to-Back Leads.* These leads are mobile and accommodating. They are available in at least two

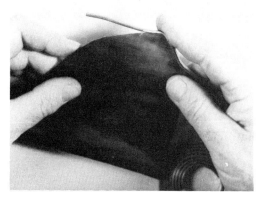

Fig. 2–34B *Where curved surfaces are being wrapped, the flexibility of this lead follows the curve precisely. The lead must be tight against the glass.*

widths of channel—¼" and ⅛"—for different thicknesses of glass.

The ⅛" U width is popular with hobbyists because it has a flexibility that approaches foil yet the sturdiness of a leaded line. Actually, it is used like foil; each piece of glass is leaded in a wraparound technique, and these leaded borders are then soldered together. The line of solder is "beaded," meaning that it is laid down to an extent that the leaded line becomes convex. This lead is dear to the heart of free-form designers, since it can take angles up to 60 degrees and more and still cling to the glass, provided it is pressed firmly around a smoothed edge. Its flat, outer surface is perfectly suited to the application of a sister lead against it. This is the "back-to-back" technique.

In using this lead, each piece of glass after being cut is wrapped with the came. The ends are soldered together and the wrapped pieces are placed back on the pattern and solder flowed along the surfaces where they meet. This is a rapid technique for putting together free-form objects such as hanging mobiles, small animals, shade pulls, and pendants. It is one of the more popular techniques among beginners.

2. *³⁄₁₆″—Finish for Small Panels*. This is the first of the truly "high heart" cames. It is used along flat surfaces as a finishing lead for a panel that is to be hung in a window. No framing need be involved. This lead will take curves if they are not too abrupt.

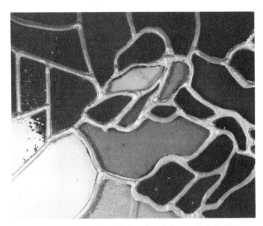

Fig. 2–35 *Example of the flexibility of ³⁄₁₆″ H leads used throughout and then "tinned." The solder joints as well as the tinning—the flow of solder over the leads themselves—is neat and orderly.*

If the curve is not a gentle one, this lead will tend to kink. To prevent this, you must smooth it gently as you go, or you must cut small triangles out of the sides to take the bend and solder the lead at these areas after pulling them together, like taking a dart in the material for a dress. There is no rounded version of this lead. A popular lead for the bottom of the skirt of paneled lamp shades, it is also used where three-dimensional objects must be soldered together at angles, where use of an H lead would involve too much bending of the channels. This lead is amenable to a number of shapes and designs if it is worked carefully and with patience. It can prove balky if it is tugged or pushed into awkward curves. Because of its flat surface, it will fit against a sister lead with little trouble, providing the glass has been cut accurately.

A secondary use of this lead is as a "belt" to close the seams of lamps. When ³⁄₁₆″ U is flattened out completely, it has just the proper shape and width to form a smooth bridge over the seam between body and skirt.

3. *¼″ Round—A Lamp Lead*. This lead is especially designed for curves of three-dimensional objects, the most common of which are the skirts of straight-panel lamps or the bottom curved portion of lamps with bent panels. It may also be used to wrap roundelles—spun glass circles—within a flat panel, providing you press the lead firmly enough against the roundelle's surface to make sure it grips. This lead does its job superbly where it is called for, although it is not called for too often. It is also used in stained-glass jewelry and stained-glass free-form items such as belt buckles, where peculiar curves must accommodate all sorts of angular offshoots. It is a heavy lead and comes only in rounded form, looking more like a C than a U shape. It complements ³⁄₁₆″ L and ¼″ H leads. Since ¼″ H round is used extensively in paneled lamps, the ¼″ U round may be a good choice for the skirt if the curve is too abrupt for the ³⁄₁₆″ U.

Portfolio / Kathy Bradford

Kathy Bradford discusses her work
in Chapter 18.

Not a Rack Behind. *William Shakespeare
broods over two versions of the Globe Theatre,
while in the foreground lies a fallen rose in this
multi-layered, sandblasted, stained glass roundel.*

Zingers. *Bicycle race, in three panels.*

Detail, Zingers.

Running Woman in X Fence. *40" x 42" wall panel; etched and painted glass, laminated fabrics, jewels, brass, zinc.*

Barren World. *32" x 32" wall panel; laminated, etched and painted glass, brass, wood, zinc.*

Chan Kite. *30" x 50" wall panel; etched and painted glass, fusing, brass, zinc.*

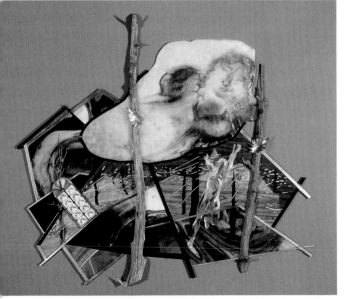

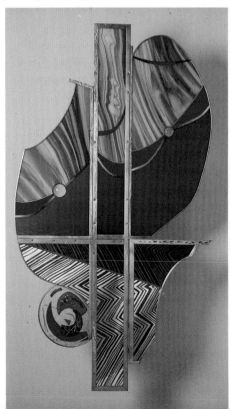

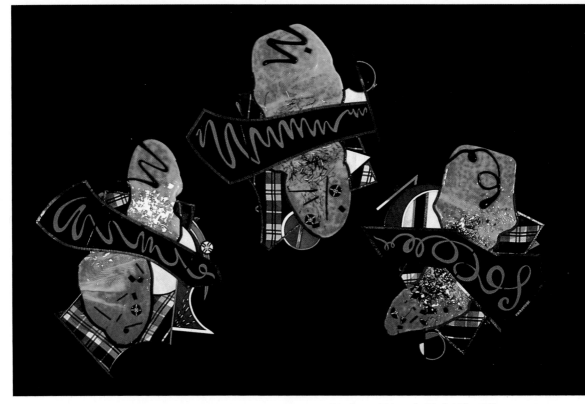

Uroboros Triptych. *Each 32" x 32";
hand-rolled glass, etched, painted, laminated;
brass, copper, lead.*

Alchemical Resolution, *detail. Etched
and painted glass, with painted lead and
polished copper.*

Portfolio / Garth Edwards

Fallen Man. *Panel, Fisher and Uroboros glass.*

Strap on Features. *3' diameter. Combination of leaded glass, lead overlay holes and sheet lead. The holes in the round panel were blasted, then cleaned with a router. The eyes and mouth are sheet lead, cut to the pattern and glazed like glass, then scored and drilled. The eyes are copper foiled; the overlays are copper and lead.*

Commuter. *Window, copper-foiled glass.*

My Aunt. *19½" x 18" leaded glass panel.*

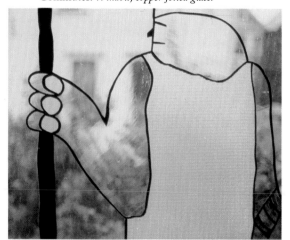

4. *³⁄₈″—For Large Panels and Windows.*
This is the largest size U lead in general
use. It complements ¼″ H leads. Keep in
mind the deep channel, a space almost ³⁄₈″
deep, when you plan your design. Otherwise you will discover too late that any
part of the design that encroaches on the
borders of the panel will be swallowed up
by this rather hungry channel. Another
problem arises when beginners cut their inside H leads too long. Here, the ³⁄₈″ U will
overlap these inside lengths, causing bumps
in the bordering lead. The inside leads
must be pulled out and trimmed. This lead
will not take curves well, and as a wrap-
around lead, it is unwieldy and bulky.

Some Specialized Cames

Specialized cames have some particularly
distinctive feature that marks them for specific use. They are not general all-purpose
leads and they are more expensive than the
leads so far described.

1. *Reinforced Cames.* These are leads
with a hollow heart (see *Fig. 2–38* and accompanying table on page 52). Through
this portion runs a flat steel rod that provides a stiff support for the came. Although these leads may conform to gentle
curves of glass without too much trouble
and to moderate curves with some effort,
their main purpose is to add strength to the
object. Because they run side to side within
a window, an outside reinforcing bar is unnecessary. They may be worked into a design and still furnish needed support. They
may also be used as border leads, although
here of course they are much less difficult
to use, since they would run straight from
side to side. Because of the inner bar, reinforced cames cannot be cut with a leading
knife or hand came cutter effectively. Instead, you must use a hacksaw. If you intend to use this lead in a design, you must
allow for its wider heart and calculate your
pattern accordingly.
Reinforced cames are usually reserved

for large windows or glass sculpture involving heavy pieces that require firm support. Using these cames within a window,
whether in one area or several, does not
mean that you can discount the outside
reinforcing bars automatically. This lead
does limit their use, but depending on the
design and dimensions of the window, you
may need outside support bars anyway.
However, you will need fewer of them
than you otherwise might without the
reinforced came, and you can probably
place them away from the part of the design that the reinforced came supports.

2. *Colonial and High-Heart Cames.*
These rather ornate leads are applicable to
special types of windows, usually in
"leaded windows"—that is, where clear
glass is cut into shapes of recurring patterns, such as diamonds, squares, and rectangles, rather than in windows of colored
glass in a pictorial or free-form pattern.
Use of these cames is an adventure in discretion, since they can be overpowering.

3. *Off-Center Cames.* In these H leads,
the heart is placed away from the center,
infringing on one channel. Thus one channel is shallow and the other channel is
deep. This lead can be used where two
pieces of glass abut, one of which is thin,
the other extremely thick. The thick piece
can be given a wider flap of lead to fit into,
whereas the thin piece will be satisfied with
a narrower channel. In this manner, for example, you can get away with using ³⁄₈″
lead rather than going into a heavier ½″ or
¾″ or even 1″ lead, which will overbalance
the window with its wider lead line.

4. *Extra Wide Cames.* These widths
may be purchased with a channel that is almost double the width of the usual sized
channels. This is to allow the placing of
either very thick pieces of antique glass or
the process of "double glazing," where one
piece of glass is placed on top of another of
a similar or different color, the two then
embedded into this wide channel of lead.
Interesting and novel effects can be obtained in this fashion, and two and even
three tiers of glass can be placed together,

depending upon the effect you want to achieve.

Outside Lead

Sometimes it is necessary to use H came as an outside lead. Since professional studios are involved in making large windows, the edges of which will be covered with molding, whatever lead they use around these edges will not show. The use of an H lead leaves an empty channel, which gives a certain margin for error should the dimensions of the window prove too tight. In this case, the extra channel may be shaved off to make the window fit. Hobbyists may follow this idea in making a panel to fit into a wooden frame, such as a door panel. However, where the outside border is going to show, a U lead is recommended.

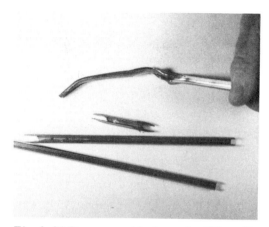

Fig. 2–36 Brass-crowned lead came is stiff but still flexible, as the top piece demonstrates. Advantages of this came lie in its color and in its support qualities for specific items. One disadvantage is that solder joints must be touched up since the joints will appear silvery-gray. We electroplate our brass-came joints. (Courtesy of Nervo International)

Buying Lead Came

Lead is sold in six-foot lengths and, in some cases, rolls or spools. It varies greatly in price, so shop for the best deal. The prices of reinforced or other specialized came may be quite high. The beginner will initially work with the thinner and lower priced leads.

Brass-Crowned Lead Came

One of the newer types of lead came is a sandwich of lead and brass. The coating, or crowning, of brass that covers the top and bottom surfaces of the lead (the channeled areas remain uncoated) serves several purposes. Although the came is extremely stiff, it can be used to encompass stained-glass pieces of reasonably curved borders. It is true that more effort is required, but the end result is fascinating. The use of this material makes the piece very firm—an advantage in lamps and boxes—and the lead lines, now brass lines, provide an entirely new effect.

Brass-crowned lead came is of special value for its strength in beveled windows, where the weight of the plate-glass pieces

is generally taken up by zinc came. Zinc came is as valuable as ever for this use, but the brass/lead combination provides another alternative. The brassiness of a panel, free-form objects, or lamps completed with this came is not only as novel, but another kind of creative statement. You can express your ingenuity by mixing brass-coated cames with regular ones in the same piece of work. While you should proceed cautiously here, there is certainly a lot to be said for this kind of experimenting, which, if nothing else, is a lot of fun. It goes along with some of the newer techniques using lead came, such as painting the surfaces with various colors to match or offset the glass (see color section). Brass-coated came comes in a number of different styles and widths, and is more expensive than regular lead came.

Zinc Came

Zinc came strands are formed into shapes similar to lead came. The advantage of zinc over lead lies in the increased strength along with the decreased weight. Zinc cames are generally cut with a hacksaw.

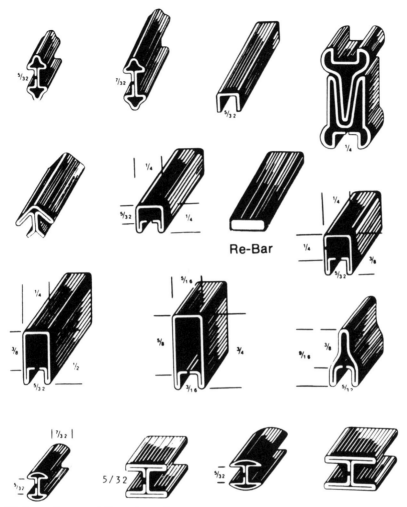

Fig. 2–37 *Some shapes and dimensions of zinc came.*

These cames are far more rigid than lead cames, although they become more mobile when heated, for example in making beveled panels of ¾″ plate glass. Here strength of the holding metal is a prime consideration, as is the overall weight of the finished panel. As a structural material, zinc came is used in borders and at selective areas within a stained-glass panel. It can also be used between sectional windows.

Zinc requires little solder to make a smooth, tight bond. If the zinc is clean, the solder flows evenly over the surface. There is no reason to have large, unsightly joints merely because zinc is being used, although some workers not used to the material are of this opinion. Oleic acid is a good flux for zinc soldering. We use 60/40 solder with zinc as well as with lead came. Zinc strands come in 6 and 8-foot lengths.

Fig. 2–38 *Dimensions of Reinforcement Lead Cames*

Came No.	Approximate Strands Per Box	Face Width	Channel Width (Inside)	Heart Thickness (Overall)	Steel Bar Size	Wt.Per Lin. Ft.In Ozs.
100	84	.500″	.172″	.125″	$^3/_{16}″ \times ^1/_{16}″$	3½
101	84	.438″	.188″	.188″	$^1/_4″ \times ^3/_{32}″$	3½
102	74	.500″	(.219″)(.250″)	.203″	$^1/_4″ \times ^1/_8″$	4
103	91	.500″	.234″	.203″	$^1/_4″ \times ^1/_8″$	3¼
104	74	.625″	.250″	.203″	$^1/_4″ \times ^1/_8″$	4
105	65	.750″	.250″	.219″	$^1/_4″ \times ^1/_8″$	4½
106	49	.500″	.250″	.219″	$^1/_4″ \times ^1/_8″$	6
107	53	.625″	.234″	.219″	$^1/_4″ \times ^1/_8″$	5½
108	37	1.000″	.250″	.219″	$^1/_4″ \times ^1/_8″$	8
109	42	.750″	.234″	.219″	$^1/_4″ \times ^1/_8″$	7
110	26	.750″	.313″	.250″	$^1/_4″ \times ^1/_8″$	11¼
111	98	.438″	.156″	.125″	$^3/_{16}″ \times ^1/_{16}″$	3
112	74	.625″	.156″	.141″	$^3/_{16}″ \times ^1/_{16}″$	4
113	53	.625″	.250″	.219″	$^1/_4″ \times ^1/_8″$	5½
114	74	.500″	.188″	.188″	$^1/_4″ \times ^1/_8″$	4

(Courtesy of RSR Corporation)

The Reinforcing Bar

The Re-Bar or Brace Bar is used to back up a large window to prevent bowing. In days of old, a steel rod was used for this purpose. No attempt was made to work the rod into the design of the piece it was to brace, and the eye tended to overlook it. The steel rods spanned the window usually at specified intervals and were attached to the framework. They were also attached to the window lead joints. Since steel does not solder, copper wire was wrapped around portions of this rod and these areas were soldered to the underlying leaded joints. Today, rods have given way to steel bars. These bars, although providing as much support, can be bent to conform in some measure to the design, thus becoming comparatively obscure. The steel bars used today are about ⅛″ thick and are immersed in a bath of molten solder or electroplated or galvanized to permit them to accept solder directly to their surface. They are then soldered directly to the lead joints of the window where they will provide maximum support.

3
The Soldering Process

Soldering is a process for joining metal to metal. Metals do not adhere directly; instead, an alloy, a mixture of metals, is used to bind them through the application of heat. Solder is the alloy that "wets" the metals and enables them to adhere.

SOLDERING PREREQUISITES

In order for the soldering process to take place certain things are necessary:

Solderability. Solder is a tin-lead alloy. Most of the metals used in stained glass, including lead, tin, sheet metal, bronze, copper, and white metal are solderable.

Heat. The soldering process occurs when the metal pieces to be soldered are heated above the melting point of the solder itself. The heat source used must rapidly reach a temperature of about 100 degrees over the melting point of the solder. Since lead has a fairly low melting point, care must be taken to heat it without melting it. This is a common mistake among beginners.

Flux: Flux is a chemical that loosens the oxides from the metal to be soldered and allows the molten solder to flow onto the surfaces of the metals to be joined. A good flux must fulfill a number of requirements:

1. Be easily applied, preferably with a brush in liquid form for maximum penetration.
2. Readily deoxidize the metals to be joined. It should begin this activity directly upon application and complete the job in a few seconds, depending on the thickness of the oxide coat.
3. Reduce the surface tension of the molten solder, permitting it to flow freely over the deoxidized surfaces of the metals to be joined. In this way, a smooth, wide bond of solder is laid down.
4. Not emit harsh or toxic odors. This means that it should not smoke, fume, bubble, hiss, steam, or spit.
5. Not be so strong as to pit the soldering iron.
6. Clean up easily. This means it should not leave a cloudy layer on the glass or a sticky scum on the lead joints. It should leave as little residue as possible.
7. Leave no dangerous elements behind as byproducts of the soldering process.
8. Not be caustic to the skin.

Solder: The correct solder alloy or tin-to-lead ratio allows the metals to bond when the proper soldering temperature is reached. The solder flows over the

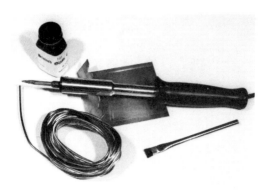

Fig. 3–1 *Flux, flux brush, solder (60/40 solid core ⅛"), soldering iron, and stand.*

surfaces of the opposing metals by capillary action to produce neat, smooth joints. A proper solder should flow easily over the heated surfaces. It should not be necessary to keep going over a joint to even it out. If you have to fuss with it, something is wrong with the solder, the flux, the metals to be joined, or the soldering equipment.

Welding is another process for joining metals, but it is not used in stained-glass work. Braising is closely associated with welding because of the high temperatures required to do the job. Both braising and welding involve joining metals of higher melting points than lead. The only way lead strips can be joined together in a metal-to-metal bond is by soldering.

CHARACTERISTICS OF SOLDER

When we use the term "solder" or "soldering," we are not speaking of so-called liquid solder or cold solder. Both of these are really glues. Plastic bonds formed by the liquid solders break down and disintegrate at temperatures that are well below the melting point of the tin-lead combination that forms the metal-to-metal bond. In fact, such cold solders should not be used where a strong metal-to-metal joining is required.

The most extensively used solders are

composed of lead and tin in specific percentages. In naming any alloy, the more expensive metal is always given first place. Thus, a 60/40 solder is one containing 60% tin and 40% lead. This solder is the only one that is extensively used in stained-glass work. This process occurs very quickly; this precise timing is what provides a good solder joint.

Lead has a melting temperature of 621°F. Tin has a melting temperature of 450°F. However, combined in solder form, they melt at 361°F. To get a completely molten state of combinations of the two is to run a gamut of temperatures between the solid to partly solid, partly liquid, to the fully liquid state. For example, a solder of, say, 20/80, which would be 20% tin and 80% lead, would have to be heated to 531°F. to be completely liquid. This is a very high temperature for use in stained glass, indeed almost as high as the melting temperature of lead. This particular percentage of 20/80 liquifies slowly and sluggishly and has a temperature range of 361 to 531 degrees before it is entirely liquid. This percentage of solder is more of a paste, and it is used mostly for plumbing work, although it is really too sluggish even for that. Certainly it is too unwieldy for the pin-point soldering of lead joints, which requires a fast melt and a fast freeze with as little heat as possible. On the other hand, a 60/40 solder need be heated only to approximately 370° before it achieves a completely liquid state. It becomes solid again at 361°, leaving a working zone of temperature of only 9 degrees. This is exactly right for stained-glass work.

One combination of tin and lead goes immediately to a liquid from a solid with no working zone at all. It is practically instantaneous. This is a combination of 63% tin and 37% lead. The instant shift from solid to liquid is called the *eutectic* point of the solder.

A Summary

The more tin you add to lead, the lower the melting point of the lead-tin combina-

Table 3–1 Melting Points of Tin–Lead Alloys

Composition % Tin % Lead	Complete Liquidation Points Degrees F.	Solidification Points Degrees F.	Composition % Tin % Lead	Complete Liquidation Points Degrees F.	Solidification Points Degrees F.
0–100.0	620	620	52.5– 47.5	403	358
2.5– 97.5	608	570	55.0– 45.0	392	358
5.0– 95.0	597	522	57.5– 42.5	381	358
7.5– 92.5	586	475	60.0– 40.0	370	358
10.0– 90.0	576	435	62.5– 37.5	361	358
12.5– 87.5	565	397	63.0– 37.0	358	358
15.0– 85.0	554	358	65.0– 35.0	360	358
17.5– 82.5	545	358	67.5– 32.5	363	358
20.0– 80.0	536	358	70.0– 30.0	367	358
22.5– 77.5	525	358	72.5– 27.5	372	358
25.0– 75.0	514	358	75.0– 25.0	378	358
27.5– 72.5	504	358	77.5– 22.5	383	358
30.0– 70.0	496	358	80.0– 20.0	390	358
32.5– 67.5	486	358	82.5– 17.5	396	358
35.0– 65.0	477	358	85.0– 15.0	403	358
37.5– 62.5	468	358	87.5– 12.5	410	358
40.0– 60.0	460	358	90.0– 10.0	415	358
42.5– 57.5	448	358	92.5– 7.5	424	358
45.0– 55.0	437	358	95.0– 5.0	432	358
47.5– 52.5	424	358	97.5– 2.5	441	358
50.0– 50.0	414	358	100.0– .0	450	450

COMPLETE LIQUIDATION POINT: Point at which all is liquid.
SOLIDIFICATION POINT: Point at which the alloy begins to change from the solid to the liquid.

Fig. 3–2 Melting Point Chart

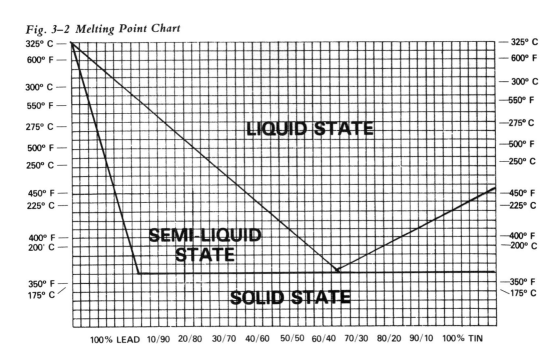

tion and the smaller the workable zone of the solder; that is, the zone where it goes from completely solid to completely liquid. A solder of 63/37 would have no workable zone at all, since it would go solid-liquid, liquid-solid instantaneously. The closest solder to that point which still has a workable zone—that is, a 9-degree zone in which soldering is possible—is 60/40. The addition of tin beyond this point will raise the working zone gradually between 361° and 450°, the melting point of tin.

"SHAPES" OF SOLDER

Solder is generally sold as bar solder and wire solder. Wire solder comes in different dimensions. The best shape of solder for stained glass is ⅛″ solid-core wire solder. This width allows the maximum amount of solder to flow onto the iron and then to the lead to give the neatest joint. Using a solder with a diameter less than ⅛″ is inefficient. Bar solder is totally inadequate for stained-glass work, and we mention it only to decry its use.

CORE SOLDER

Some solders on the market contain a core of material, usually a resinous flux. These should be avoided since the resin will eventually gum the soldering tips and even the glass. In fact, it continues to ooze from the soldered joints long after the piece has been finished. It is best to use solid-core solder in percentages of 60/40 (occasionally perhaps 50/50) and to avoid these problems.

PROCEDURE FOR A GOOD SOLDER JOINT

While it is the soldered joints that hold the stained-glass work together, they should stay modestly in the background. Nothing is more ungainly than bulges of solder arthritically sitting in great humped masses over the joints of a panel or lamp. Leads

that have been pitted and burned in an attempt to solder them will add to this crippled bravado.

The procedure for making a neat, substantial solder joint involves five steps:

1. Clean all joint surfaces with a wire brush
2. Make sure that your lead cames are properly mitered, that they abut one another as closely as possible with minimum space between
3. Make sure that you use the correct soldering flux for the particular work
4. Keep your iron at the proper temperature and use the proper solder
5. Make sure each joint is clean and smooth after you have soldered it

Let's discuss these steps point by point:

Cleaning the Joint Surfaces

A clean surface is most of the battle. Any particles of dirt or grease or any oxides covering the lead will interfere with the soldering process. Do not use a cleaning solution on lead came. Instead, clean it with a copper wire brush (Fig. 3–3). This will not scratch the glass but will have enough abrasive quality to strip the oxide coat from the lead. In cases where the lead

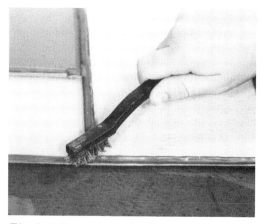

Fig. 3–3 A copper-wire brush can be used to clean the joints to allow the solder to flow evenly.

is so old and oxidized that even a wire brush will not remove the coating, scrape it off with the blade of your leading knife to the shiny underportion. Only this surface is solderable. Of course the soldering tip should also be clean or it will not only refuse to pick up solder, but its application against an otherwise clean joint will dirty it and make it unsolderable. Do not use strong, inorganic acids such as hydrochloric or sulphuric acid as cleansing agents. These acids release highly toxic fumes, and the acids themselves are extremely dangerous.

Fitting the Lead Cames

The lead cames should be measured in such a way that the solder can be easily drawn over the ends with one touch. This means that the cames should be mitered or cut to correspond closely with each other without gaps between the ends *(Fig. 3–4)*. Leads should be sliced with a sharp instrument, preferably a leading knife, which provides a clean and true end-to-end meeting. Attempting to bridge a gap between the leads will not only result in a hunchbacked solder joint, but will waste solder, time, and temper. It is better to do a leading job correctly step by step than to try to make up

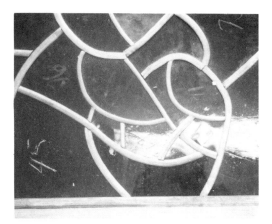

Fig. 3–5 Note how the leads are mitered to fit snugly.

in Step 3 for what should have been done in Step 1.

Using the Right Flux

Be sure that the flux is the correct one for the work. If the joint surface is not clean, no amount of flux will help. The flux may be applied to the parts to be soldered by brushing. We rarely dip joints into flux in

Fig. 3–4 The lead came should butt together as shown, allowing for a smooth soldered joint.

Fig. 3–6 Different width acid-resist flux brushes.

stained-glass work. In brushing flux onto a joint, it is important to use an "acid" brush. This is a stiff bristle brush that is itself impervious to the flux. Its stiffness is essential to work the flux into the lead surface and through any remaining oxide coat. The better you work the flux into the surface of the lead came, the more easily the solder will flow. It is not necessary to flood the area with flux. That will only make a mess on the glass. A small amount properly applied will work better than an ocean of it merely poured on. Don't be afraid to scrub the flux into the joint with the flux brush. Simply wiping it on gently is not sufficient.

Keeping the Soldering Iron at Proper Temperature

The soldering iron is the best tool for heat application. It is important to select an iron large enough to have sufficient heat capacity to perform its function at a reasonable rate of speed. But don't let it get too hot. An overheated iron will refuse to pick up solder and will melt the joint surfaces. This cratering effect of the lead cames is unsightly; they then must be replaced. Do not try patching the burned surfaces with solder. Watch your iron. Don't let it get so hot that it takes over the job. On the other hand, if your iron is not hot enough, you will end up "dragging" the solder, with an end result showing waves of frozen metal in peaks and valleys over the joint. No amount of resmoothing with a sufficiently hot iron will remedy this.

No matter how much soldering you may have done in wiring circuits or plumbing or other work around the house, you will find that soldering lead is a unique situation. Practice on scrap lead for fifteen or twenty minutes until you get the feel of the material. You will be amazed how rapidly the lead will melt away from your overheated soldering iron. Better to have this happen on scrap rather than on the lead you will use in a piece of finished work. Of course, if you are not using the proper solder, you will be hindered all along the line, even if your iron is hot enough.

Cleaning the Joints After Soldering

Flux residues make the glass tacky and smudgy. Organic solvents may be used as cleaning agents, such as carbon tetrachloride, but we mention this specific agent only to condemn it. While it is an excellent solvent, it is so dangerous that it should be ruled out completely, no matter how well your studio is ventilated. Unfortunately, simple soap and water will not clean away the flux residues and oxide coatings from the glass, nor will any of the standard glass cleansers like Windex. The best material is a cleaning and polishing powder we make ourselves, a 75:25 mixture of calcium carbonate and diatomaceous earth. It can be used either wet or dry over the entire surface. The powder probably works best when used dry, although it does tend to fly around the room. So close the doors when you are working with it. Used wet, it forms a paste, and while more elbow grease must be applied to get it to work properly, it doesn't produce as much dust. Plain whiting is also good. The cleaning agent should be sprinkled over the entire finished work on one surface and then the glass and lead alike scrubbed with a heavy bristled floor brush. The cleaner should not only pick up and break down all flux residues and dirt that have collected on the glass and lead, but it also should dry the putty with which many finished stained-glass panels are impregnated.

THE FLUXES

Without flux the solder will roll off the lead surface. Flux removes oxides from the metal surface during its heating and soldering and prevents any oxidation of the molten solder. A flux must be readily displaced by the solder so as not to interfere with the wetting and bonding of the solder to the

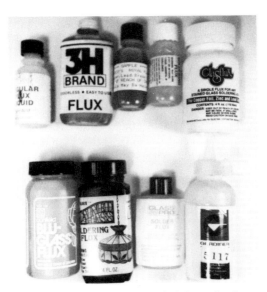

Fig. 3–7 Different fluxes. To find the perfect flux for you, sample as many as possible.

Fig. 3–8 A flux that we use often is Glastar's Glasflux.

underlying metal. The flux must remain stable over the soldering range. A good soldering technique calls for the selection of the mildest flux that will do the job. Fluxes fall into three main classes: corrosive, intermediate, and noncorrosive. Noncorrosive fluxes are too weak, and corrosive fluxes are generally too strong for stained-glass work. A noncorrosive flux, such as is used in resin "core" solder, will ooze from the lead joints. A corrosive flux—for instance, one containing an inorganic acid—eventually attacks the lead, leading to pitting of the surfaces.

Most fluxes used in stained-glass work are in liquid form, since they are easier to work with that way. A paste flux can be used, but for ease of operation, a liquid is preferred. It is easier to scrub a liquid into the lead with the soldering brush than a paste, and it's much easier to get out of the jar. One basic disadvantage of liquid flux is the readiness with which the jar tips over, fluxing the tabletop in the process. In order to frustrate this particular tendency, keep only a small amount of flux in the bottle while working, so when the soldering iron cord tangles with it, or the piece you are working on bumps against it and it overturns, you will not lose the entire amount of flux.

Today, there are innumerable fluxes for specific stained-glass requirements. The aim has been to develop a flux that promotes rapid activity on the work surface and not on the worker. It's nice to have one that also can do several jobs—on lead and foil, for instance. A good one is Royal Flux, made by Kierco, which works well on lead, copper, brass, and zinc. This company also makes Golden Flux, a real friend when it comes to taking off thick oxide coats from leaded windows that need to be repaired. Only a minimum of wire brushing is needed. Golden Flux requires Kierco's flux neutralizer to inactivate it. This renders harmless the residues that are left on the work, and will also clean the glass to some extent. This neutralizer will work on almost all brands of flux to clean up the remains of soldering activity.

Glasflux, made by the Glastar Company, can be used with copper foil, zinc, or lead soldering. You may prefer to use specific fluxes for individual metals. Traditionally this has been the case, with one flux for lead, one for copper, and one for everything else. However, Glasflux will not corrode copper foil or discolor lead, the basic problems leading to the two-flux situation. Glasflux, a gel, permits a smooth brush-on application without unpleasant fumes or the use of a strong cleaner such as alcohol to clean up the soldering residues afterward. And it can be added to tip-cleaning sponges. It cleans the soldering-iron tip from all the dross that accumulates during soldering.

Fluxes, like most of the tools and supplies in stained-glass work, are individualistic. Workers develop their own preferences bases on experimentation. A host of fluxes are shown in Figure 3–7, although these are by no means meant to represent the entire field. Your local distributor or mail-order supplier will carry a number of fluxes based on the wants of craftspeople in the area.

One of the best ways to test a wide variety of fluxes is to attend a trade show such as the Stained Glass Expo. Manufacturers offer samples of their products both old and new for you and your retailer to test. The Canfield Company, for instance, has developed what it calls Instant Solder, a solder and flux formulation that allows preplacement of the exact amount of solder necessary for a particular joint. Other chemicals in its armamentarium are Action Tin, a tinning paint for applying a coat of solder on metals before joining; Sil-Can White Creme Brazing Flux for use with their brazing alloys; Copper-Mate, a soldering paste flux; and Solder-Mate liquid soldering fluxes. The Plato Company produces its own brand of flux, which rounds off a complete list of soldering products for this company, including soldering irons. Some workers feel secure with a product from a manufacturer that hits all the bases this way. Other workers prefer a company that deals in a particular product. Lake Chemical Company concentrates on flux products. Its La-Co liquid flux is recommended for general soldering of lead and zinc. It is water-soluble and has an easy cleanup. La-Co also works well for cleaning and tinning soldering irons and is readily brushed onto the joint. Lake Chemical also produces a high-heat resistant flux paste, used mainly for copper-foil work. The La-Co Flux Stik is a unique item. Re-sembling a crayon, it can be applied in pin-point areas, and it's good for overhead soldering, which is always a frustrating endeavor. La-Co Flux, according to the manufacturer, requires no hazardous warning.

The Kester Solder Company makes several good fluxes, among other soldering items. Its oleic acid flux is an old standby. Try as many of the varieties as you can. Soon you will settle down with a few favorites. Perhaps "settling down" is not the phrase to use for a field that in itself is in a state of flux.

THE HEAT SOURCE

The best heat source for soldering is one that will assure a strong bond between the metals in a fast, efficient manner. A torch is certainly fast, but since the lead would turn to rivulets, it's hardly efficient. A small heat source that takes many minutes to heat the solder is obviously too slow. For the type of soldering done in stained glass, there is only one real option—the electric soldering iron. But first, here are several soldering irons that you do not want to use in stained glass.

The Featherweight: This particular "find" costs somewhere between $1 and $3 and is available on the bargain counter of your hardware store. The tip is not replaceable. Wattage varies between 25 and 50 watts. Such an iron is strained beyond its capacity when it comes to melting solder over a wide unit area, such as a lead joint. The pin-point soldering of electrical connections is more in its line. The result of using it on lead joints is an impatient dragging rather than an even flow of solder over the joints. The beginner compensates for this by pressing barder with the iron against the joints in an attempt to flatten them. Novel, haphazard effects can be achieved in this manner, although none of them will be what you want.

The Heavyweight: Here is the other extreme: an iron endowed with such overabundant electrical vivacity as to cleave through solder, lead, and fingers and crack the glass in the bargain. Usually it has a tip large enough to fry an egg. For some reason, workers who use this iron invariably are attempting the most delicate joint soldering.

This iron gobbles solder at an alarming rate and generally spews it in absentminded dribbles over tabletop, floor, and shoes, and only seldom on the work in progress. One can barely touch a joint with it lest it evaporate. Great clouds of steam and a residual hacking cough mark its operator's position in the studio.

The Antique: Occasionally a beginning student appears in class proudly displaying a soldering device that has been "in the family" for generations but that still "has a lot of life in it." Sometimes the handle is in several pieces held loosely together with tape. The tip, on the other hand, is tight, frozen to the barrel, pitted and rusty. This medieval memento when plugged in may cause the electric company to go into shock. Nevertheless, the owner is insistent on saving money and may indeed finally turn out some work despite the handicap—although far less than the rest of the class, and with much more effort. He may even insist that he is having fun. Certainly he has a lot of space in which to work, with his neighbors to either side shying away for fear of electrocution. Such devices often end up showing more sense then their operators. They know when to quit, and often they do so right in the middle of an extensive project. Technology being what it is, and common sense being what it is, owners of such antiques spend more money to get them fixed than it would ever cost to buy a new one.

The Blow Torch: No one who has done even the slightest work with stained glass would consider using a blow torch on a lead joint. It is mentioned here only because the question of its use is constantly raised. Using such a flame thrower would burn the leads right off the panel, as well as shattering the glass. For creative endeav-

ors, the blow torch is better left in the hands of the plumber.

Soldering Guns

In the past we have been emphatic about classifying soldering guns as negative items. We were convinced that if you must pack a weapon in stained-glass work, a leading knife would be more practicable. Then we received a number of letters, some irate, from people who insisted that they used soldering guns with no compromise to the quality of their work. To be fair, we tried to find at least one type of soldering gun that could be reasonably used in the craft. We found it in the Lenk Company soldering gun *(Fig. 3–9),* which is similar to an iron with a pistol grip but with no trigger. The tip is copper, pyramidal, and not interchangeable. It tends to corrode rather rapidly and must be re-tinned. Heating capacity is 75 watts, which is reasonable for soldering moderate joints. The balance of this tool is comfortable, and its use, keeping the above considerations in mind, is not unreasonable if you must use

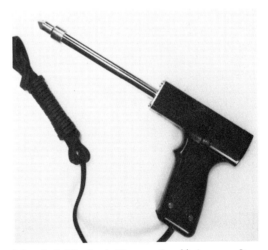

Fig. 3–9 The Lenk Company's soldering gun. It works, but it is not meant for stained-glass work. Even if you are used to a soldering gun for circuitry soldering, you will find it easy to change over to an iron.

a gun. But the question remains, why must you? Irons are where the action is so far as the latest developments and efficiency of production are concerned. Our original prejudice against guns still stands, although we direct it at those products made for circuitry soldering and that have a trigger on/off switch and a thin tip. They have achieved amateur status only because some workers have one lying around the house and see no reason not to use it. Unfortunately, there can be no changing of tips in such an instrument, no mobility in the soldering of different joints, angles, or objects, no wide overlay of solder because of insufficient surface heating. As for "tinning," that is, drawing a line of molten solder over a joint, it is ineffectual. There's no fast draw with a soldering gun. It is interesting that in our survey we have seen fewer and fewer workers attempting to use them.

Soldering Irons

The first thing to look for when choosing a soldering iron is the Underwriters Laboratory listing. Many people forget this little item. All the irons that are produced for the stained-glass field are so listed, so you don't have to worry there. But if you have an iron at home that is a strange brand, make sure it has a UL listing before you use it.

Other than that, the choice of a soldering iron depends on how up to date you want to be. It is a good idea to check that all the parts of your iron-to-be are easily interchangeable. We like to have maximum flexibility for selecting the exact combination of handles, temperatures, and tips for any stained-glass soldering application. The Unger iron, with its thread-together design, is strong in this regard and makes changing heaters, tips, or handles an easy, fast operation. Of course, you want to keep the cost down, and the most logical way to do this is not to have to throw away your iron when an irreplaceable part goes bad. You should be able to replace any worn-out component, not the entire iron.

Since you will be using the soldering iron over long periods, a fatigue factor comes into play. The heavier the iron, the greater the fatigue. So you want a device as light as possible and one that is easy to use, not one that fights you and throws you off balance every time you pick it up. *Comfort* is the key word here. In this regard, the handle and shape of the iron are modifying factors. Handles are as diverse as the Unger cork or plastic finger grip to the streamlined Esico handle that serves both their bent and straight irons so well. Speaking of which, it is the tip of the iron, not the handle, that is supposed to heat up, and companies have spent a lot of time on

Fig. 3–10 Anatomy of Esico's soldering iron with its Vitacote tip. Among its features are the stainless-steel case, nickel wire leads, ceramic insulator, and grounding screw. The handle conforms to the hand and remains cool.

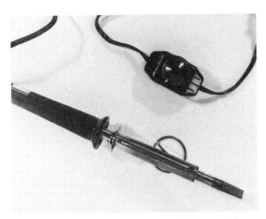

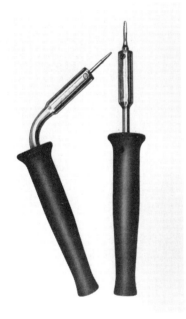

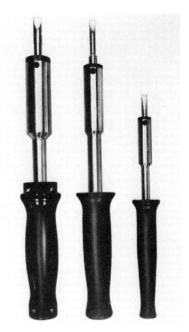

Fig. 3–11 The Lenk Company's 100-watt soldering iron. Note the rheostat control on the line.

Fig. 3–13 Esico irons, from medium to heavy. Any of these are used for work in stained glass from 85 watts to 125 watts, depending on the project. Even the heavy-duty iron is easy to handle, and the handle stays cool. So do you.

Fig. 3–12 Two soldering guns by Esico, the "hatchet" or "bent" on the left and the straight iron on the right. These are made specifically for stained glass.

which ensures cooler handles. Handle streamlining varies from "pen grip" to "fist grip," depending on the delicacy or rugged character of the soldering.

Irons come in "bent" or "hatchet" styles as well as straight. Even here, the design can make or break your relationship with the iron. Esico offset or hatchet irons are offset 70 degress to form an included angle of 110 degrees. You may find that this shape is the most comfortable to work with over a period of time. Hexagon provides a hatchet style of 90 degress, a more acute angle than Esico, and you may prefer this kind.

The wattage is an important consideration, as is the length of time it takes for the iron to heat up. What you want is an iron that is engineered for quick heat production, transfer, and recovery. Wattage

design and material to provide this discrimination.

The Hexagon deflector is designed to keep the heat where it should be—in the tip—as is Esico's stainless-steel stem, confines lie between the 75-watt iron and the 125-watt iron. Fewer than 75 watts provides sluggish heat and slows down the work. More than 125 watts slows down the work because you must be so cautious about not burning the work. As we will see, this explanation is an oversimplification because most soldering irons, once plugged into a wall outlet, just get hotter and hotter; what you really want is a tempered heat that peaks rapidly and stays put. Standard irons operate on 120 AC and DC. Most of the plugs can go only into the socket one way for proper grounding.

The tip of an iron can be held in the barrel by a set screw or it can be threaded. We have never had good luck with a threaded tip. Invariably it freezes in place and the flexibility of the iron, which depends on the ability to change to different shaped tips for different projects, is lost. Even a set screw may freeze. However, at least you can drill it out if all else fails. But you cannot drill the frozen tip out of a threaded barrel.

Finally, there are some things to look for in a soldering iron, or at least to know about, that most people never consider. Figure 3–10 shows the anatomy of a typical iron. When you go comparative shopping, look for these features.

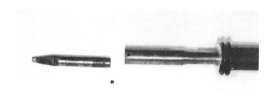

Fig. 3–14 Soldering iron with tip removed shows the ease of changing tips. The tip slides into the barrel and is held by a set screw.

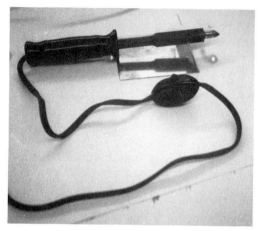

Fig. 3–15 The line-cord switch is located at the proper working distance from the iron.

Our Preference

The best soldering iron we have found is a 100-watt, ³⁄₈″ bore iron with a set screw to allow for changing the tip. It comes straight or hatchet shaped. The iron is designed and constructed to give constant production performance. Its handle does not get hot, and it has the latest in heating elements, the elements being easily replaceable should one burn out. It is light enough to be held easily, heats up readily to a workable temperature, and maintains that temperature for long periods (*Fig. 3–11*). The tendency for any "uncontrolled" iron is to get too hot for the lead cames, so a certain amount of plugging in and unplugging of the iron into the electrical out-

let becomes necessary to maintain a constant temperature. A "controlled" iron will save you excess wear and tear by maintaining the ideal heat and allowing work to proceed unhindered by continual stooping and searching for the outlet. Such an iron employs a rheostat.

The set screw on the iron is particularly important. Screw-in tips tend to freeze into place with the continued expansion and contraction as the iron heats and cools. The hammering, oiling, squeezing, twisting, and sweating that result when you discover that a tip cannot be removed from the iron provides a colorful break in routine, but generally it results in the purchase of another iron. The set screw in a new iron should be loosened after the first few uses. Once the iron has been broken in, you may rely on it to open and close readily.

The Switch

One way to avoid plugging and unplugging the iron to maintain constant temperature is to put a line switch on the cord *(Fig. 3–15)*. This is easily accomplished, and, providing you remember to use it, you won't wonder why your lead is melting or your solder isn't. Caution should be exercised in placing the switch. If you place it too close to the iron, it will clatter against your work. If you place it too far away, you will have to stoop and bend to find it. Putting it in the middle of the cord will probably have it catching the edge of the table and pulling the iron out of your hand. A fairly safe rule of thumb is to put the switch approximately 12 inches from the end of the iron and check it before cutting the cord to make sure that is where you want it.

The Stand

Irons generally come equipped with a little stand to rest the iron on when it gets hot. It's a good habit to use your stand, even for a cold iron. Some workers plug in their iron and leave it on the table top just for a moment to warm up while they arrange their equipment. Somehow the stand is the last thing they locate, and charred wood is the result.

The stand is one of the easiest items to lose. If you misplace it, get another one. Trying to rest your iron on a hammer or wrench or pair of pliers as a temporary stand only results in the iron rolling off and burning either the table or yourself. There is no room for improvisation here.

The Rheostat Control Unit

For the serious worker in stained glass, the rheostat control unit is a must. It effectively controls the amount of heat going through the iron and does away with the plugging in and unplugging, switching-on and switching-off ritual that is the plague of beginners in the field. Such a unit pro-

Fig. 3–16 *Soldering-iron stands.*

Fig. 3–17 *Rheostat control unit with iron attached. (Courtesy: Esico)*

Fig. 3–18 *Glastar's rheostat control unit. Competitively priced and, like Esico's, built to last.*

The Soldering Process **65**

vides manual control of soldering iron tip temperatures with automatic corrections for voltage fluctuations up to 80% of the full wattage of the heating element. It also allows operation without control at 100% of full wattage. A pilot light on the instrument indicates cycling of the current. Rheostat control units are not inexpensive, but they last indefinitely. The only part that may need to be replaced is the small fuse.

A number of companies make rheostat controls, among them Glastar, Kindig, and Esico. On its Model 222, Esico has incorporated a self-contained electronic solder station for the rheostat, soldering iron stand, and tip cleaner. It is a compact combination.

Fig. 3–19 *Esico's combination soldering-iron holder, tip cleaner, and rheostat control. Who could ask for anything more?*

The Tip Cleaner

The tip cleaner is designed to clean a Vitacote or copper soldering tip quickly and efficiently. A stroke across the wet vertical sponge removes undesirable residues, which fall into the tray at the base. Solder on the tip's working surface is not destroyed. The top cover lifts off to refill the water reservoir that keeps the sponge wet at all times. It is certainly a friendlier way of cleaning the tip than shaking the iron across the floor and across your neighbor's foot.

A number of other styles of tip cleaners are available from Esico as well as other manufacturers. Ingenuity is catching, and we have the Esico Model HC–4 Iron Holder and Tip Cleaner combined as the round cleaner or with a flat tip cleaner *(Figs. 3–21 and 3–22)*. Esico also makes an under-the-bench iron holder–tip cleaner combination that is easily installed with only two screws. This quality unit is convenient, safe, and, especially for workers with limited space, compact. Low sulphur content, heavy-duty sponges are used in all Esico tip cleaners.

The Plato Company makes rotating tip wipers, claiming (we cannot say otherwise) that soldering tips last longer when they are wiped on clean, damp, sulphurfree cellulose sponges. You can't overwipe

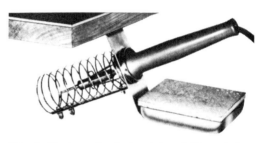

Fig. 3–20 *An under-the-bench iron holder and tip cleaner combination.*

Fig. 3–21 *Esico's soldering-iron holder and tip cleaner.*

Fig. 3–22 *Esico also makes a flat tip cleaner.*

Fig. 3–23 *Plato's rotating tip cleaners and soldering-iron holders.*

a tip when you use a rotating wiper because the design causes the sponges to rotate through the water reservoir when pressure is applied. This is a nice touch. Sponges sear when they are dry. Plato also makes a tip-wiper iron-holder stand. This convenient holder stand for pencil-type soldering irons is a heavily plated double-steel coil-cage construction that protects the worker against burns from accidental contact with the hot iron. A stable base of four rubber-capped legs keeps the holder where you place it.

Soldering Tips

Tips for soldering irons come in all thicknesses and shapes; if you cannot find a shape that suits what you have in mind, you can have a company that deals in these items make one up for you. However, the chances are that you cannot conceive of a shape that has not already been made.

Widespread as may be the choice of dimensions and shapes of tips, the material they are composed of is limited to copper—either pure copper or plated copper. Some workers rarely use plain copper tips anymore, unless a specific necessity calls for them, such as not having a plated one of requisite shape. Although the copper tip is cheaper than the plated one, it is difficult to maintain in even moderately pristine condition, and the number of styles available are limited compared to the plated variety. Time was when the plated tip was a novelty, but no longer. At the same time, this doesn't mean that the pure copper tip is on the way out. Many beginners start

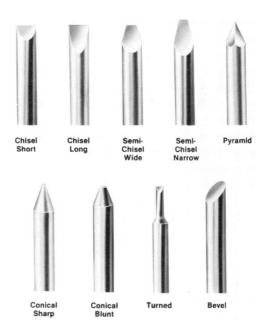

Fig. 3–24 *Esico's plated soldering-iron tips.*

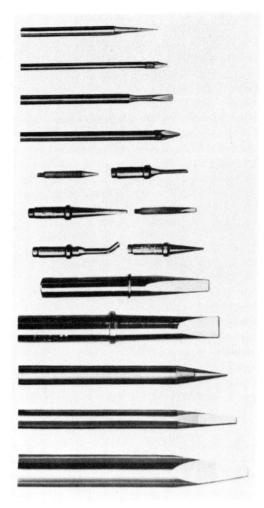

Fig. 3–25 *Plato's plated soldering-iron tips.*

covering this bare, clean copper surface with an even layer of solder. This layer should remain in place until the next tinning is required. There are several steps to the operation.

1. Allow the tip to cool if you have been using the iron. To clean the tip well, you must remove it from the iron.
2. Remove scaly oxides from the working surface. Use a file, an 80-grit abrasive polyurethane foam stick available from the Plato Company *(Fig. 3–26),* or 100-grit emery cloth. While sanding or scraping, be careful to maintain the tip's original shape. You don't want to change a pyramid to a chisel shape, for instance. Once you have filed the copper tip down to a shiny surface, it must be fluxed and retinned.
3. Put the tip back in the iron, and coat the working surface of the tip with flux, either liquid or paste. Do this before turning on the iron.
4. Turn on the iron, and, when the tip is at working temperature, run solder over the surface. If the tip does not accept solder, it is probably too hot. Cool it to a point where it will accept the solder.
5. If the tip is not completely tinned, apply more flux and solder while the tip is hot.

As you now continue working with this newly tinned tip, you will see it gather up more and more oxides until once again

off with several of these rather than investing in the more expensive plated tips, and some experienced workers insist that they get a better joint with a copper tip than a plated tip. One of the inconveniences of the copper tip is the frequency of retinning.

Tinning the Copper Tip

Tinning involves scraping off the dirt and oxides that have gathered on the tip surface from previous soldering operations, then

Fig. 3–26 *Plato's tip-restoring bar restores detinned tips if they are not pitted or worn. Use only on cold tips.*

you will have to go through the tinning process.

Plated Soldering Tips

Plated soldering tips last longer than plain copper ones. They need only moderate care—wiping with a sponge—and give maximum performance uninterrupted by a cycle of retinning. The core of plated tips is made of copper, which is highly conductive. The working surface and shank are iron-plated. The tips are pretinned and the entire shank is alloy-plated and ready for immediate use. These tips are considerably more expensive than the plain copper ones, but they are far more convenient. They do not require rough filing even when retinning becomes necessary, since filing can remove the iron coating and ruin the tip. These handy devices reduce soldering time and add neatness and a great sense of satisfaction to the activity.

You should have a number of different shapes of soldering tips in your working area so that you can choose one that best fits the needs of the moment. If you have two different size bore irons, you may want to stock two sets of tips to accommodate them. Most workers stay with a single bore, usually a ⅜″, even if they have more than one iron, and avoid having to stock a double supply of tips. Both copper tips and plated ones are available for all size bores. We keep several bores of irons on hand, including a ⅝″ for extra heavy joint soldering, and one for pretinning sheet foil for special projects. This iron uses copper tips.

Tips to Keep Your Tips in Shape

Even plated tips are subject to wear. To keep yours in tip-top condition:

1. Inspect all tips periodically to make sure they are clean and that the tinning has not worn away. Plated tips occasionally require tinning, and the procedure is the same as for copper tips, except that with plated tips you never use a file and never

Fig. 3–27 *Using a spool of Plato's desoldering braid.*

grind them unduly against any gritty surface.
2. Flood the tinned working surfaces of a plated tip with solder before using it. This will provide a fresh protective surface on the tip.
3. Clean the tip on a wet cellulose sponge as necessary as you continue to work with it.
4. Excessive pressure of tip to joint surface or rubbing a tip over a joint does not improve heat transfer or make the solder flow better. Beginners seem to believe that it does. The best solder joint all but creates itself. All you furnish are the materials for it to do so.
5. In the process of making a solder joint, apply fresh solder to the metals being joined, *not* to the hot tip.
6. Apply fresh solder on the tip before placing the iron back in the holder after soldering.

THE DESOLDERING PROCESS

Sooner or later, you will make a mistake. We all do. Moreover, you will not only make it, you will solder it. But don't despair. A soldered area can be unsoldered without burning away the leads, cutting away the joint, or breaking out the glass. Several companies make solder removers. Plato makes one of the best, called Soder Wick, and with a spelling like that you might wonder about its effectiveness. It works very well. All you need do is place a small portion of the wick (it comes on a spool) directly on the solder to be removed and put the hot iron tip on top of that. As the solder melts, it is drawn up the wick and off the joint. You just keep cutting away the used wick and replacing it until all the solder is gone. It beats the old method of melting unwanted solder and then shaking the piece to get it off. Hexagon Company makes a solder remover with the same type of tinned braid, and it also uses the same type of capillary action to pick up the solder. In addition, Hexagon makes a Solder Sucker, which is a Teflon tiplet attached to a rubber ball, similar to a plastic eyedropper. The idea is to melt the solder and, when it is molten, dip the tip of the tiplet into it and release pressure on the rubber ball. The suction then absorbs and gathers the molten solder into the ball. This technique also works, although the wick method is more effective.

A SUMMARY

The soldering process, including the use of an efficient soldering iron, is an integral part of working in stained glass. Your finished product reflects the tools that you have used. While we do not recommend that beginners go out and immediately purchase professional soldering irons and a complete set of iron-coated tips, we do feel they owe it to themselves to use equipment that will give the best performance for the time spent.

Approach the entire matter of soldering cautiously at first. Initial attempts may look delightful, only to look second rate under critical appraisal. This in itself will lead to the urge to acquire the proper tools for the job. To sum up:

1. In most instances use 60/40 solid core solder. It makes a difference whether you call it 60/40 or 40/60, since the solder is composed of tin and lead, and the percentage of tin is placed first in the equation. Any percentage other than this can make the soldering process difficult. If you use a "resin core" solder, you will have sloppy joints; the resin will ooze over the glass and be almost impossible to remove. It will also eventually gum up your soldering tip.

2. Use an iron that is hot enough. Irons below 80 watts are not recommended because they take too long to heat up and don't last. Also, the tips available for such irons are too small for use on large joints. There is no question that a small iron will eventually do the job, but you will spend too much time on this one procedure. And by the time you have gone through several small irons, you will have paid for a large one. So, if you intend to do any extensive work in glass, why not get the right iron to begin with?

3. Make sure your soldering tip is clean. If you are using an ironclad tip, wipe it every so often on its sponge to remove excess flux and solder. You will notice a considerable difference in solder flow if you do. If you prefer a copper tip, check to see that it is properly tinned and fluxed. The tinning and retinning that are necessary with a copper tip are a nuisance, but more of a nuisance is solder that keeps rolling off the soldering tip because of the barrier of dirt on its surface. Refile the copper tip, flux it, and tin it with solder.

4. If your tip is clean and still won't pick up solder, the solder rolling off and away from the tip, your iron is too hot. Allow it to cool somewhat. Ideal heat is when the solder, touched by the soldering tip, instantly melts and clings or is "picked up" by the tip to be transported to the work in progress.

5. If your soldering leaves sharp pointed ends on your joints, you are "dragging" the solder and your iron is not hot enough. Solder properly applied should flow smoothly.

6. Use the right flux. A liquid or gel works best.

4
Tools
of the Trade

Stained glass is a hand craft and the hand has always had a soft spot for a good tool. A good hand tool is an investment that repays itself many times over. It is loyal and capable and soon becomes an extension of yourself. No tool, of course, regardless of how ingenious or sophisticated it is, creates by itself. At least, not yet. Only you can do that. But the efficiency and comfort of the tools you acquire will allow you to create more effectively and productively. The stained-glass field has recently seen a revolution in new tools and equipment. It is impossible to review them all, but some of the more provocative ones will be illustrated and explained. Which fulfill the most necessary functions of the craft will depend on you. Some of the devices make the technique of stained glass possible; others simply make it comfortable. There is a thin line between the two.

GLASS CUTTERS

What is a glass cutter? It's a device consisting of a handle attached to a hard steel or carbide wheel rotating on a bronze axle. As the cutter is pushed or pulled along the surface of the glass, the wheel turns and plows a groove through it. This causes a fracture over the surface and a weak area along the length of the score. Pressure applied properly along this weakened area will serve to break the glass into two

pieces. Pressure applied improperly, or if the score line is imperfectly made, will result in a large number of glass pieces. The type of cutter you use is the first element toward the successful or unsuccessful score.

Probably no tool in the stained-glass armamentarium is as personal or as individual to the worker as the glass cutter. This was not always the case. When this book was first published, choice was pretty well limited to the so-called classic model. This is still the choice of a great number of workers today. Many people who first got to know glass through their fingertips guiding one of these cutters see no reason to change from a device that has become so much a part of themselves. But the classic design can take some getting used to. For the elderly person, for the arthritic, or simply for one whose fingers just can't manage to grip this style of cutter, where once there was nothing to do but struggle with it, now there are styles of cutters to fit just about any hand and any inclination.

The term *cutting* is not an accurate one in stained-glass work. Glass can only be *scored*, scratched, or grooved. The word *cut* is legitimized by the name *glass cutter*, but this instrument should more accurately be called a glass *scorer*. Scoring means to fracture the glass along one of its surfaces. To "run" the score is to deepen this fracture through to the other surface. To break the glass means to separate the two pieces along the line of the score.

Glass cutters can be divided according to which portion of the hand is emphasized in their use. Accordingly, we separate them into "finger" cutters and "palm" cutters. Some of the other kinds of cutters can be found in the Appendix.

Don't skimp on stained-glass tools, least of all on your glass cutter. If you buy a cheap cutter, you will be sorry. Good glass cutters, especially carbide cutters, are not cheap. At the start, decide what you can affort to outlay for tools and supplies. If you must cut costs, at least initially, the glass cutter is not the tool to do this with. Purchase less glass or lead or foil, or do without one of the pliers, but don't hamper your efforts by not getting a good cutter or two.

The Classic Cutter

The classic glass cutter design is a product of the Fletcher-Terry Company, which first manufactured it in 1869 as Bristol Diamond steel-wheel glass cutter. The design, with some modifications, is still used today in its line of Gold Tip glass cutters. Most of us who have been involved with stained glass for many years still use and cherish our Fletcher Gold Tips. We use other style cutters as well, but it would be impossible for any new cutter design, even Fletcher's own Scoremaster to replace these tried and true friends completely.

With the classic cutter the finger tips grasp the cutter and guide it; the upper portions of the fingers, toward the web of the hand, supply stability. The Fletcher-Terry Company provides the accompanying table as a guide to its Gold Tip line of steel-wheel glass cutters.

Table 4–1. Steel-Wheel Glass Cutters

Number	Wheel Angle (degrees)	Wheel Size	Suitability of Cutter
01	124	7/32	General purpose, boxed
02	124	7/32	Same ball end
01CP	124	7/32	Same-card packed
02CP	124	7/32	Same-card packed
06	114	7/32	Cathedral opal glass
07	114	7/32	Same ball end
08	124	5/32	Pattern cutting
09	124	5/32	Same ball end
01F	134	7/32	Heavy glass, 1/4"
02F	134	7/32	Same ball end
08F	134	5/32	Soft stained glass
09F	134	5/32	Same ball end
086	114	5/32	Pattern cutting, extra hard glass
096	114	5/32	Same ball end

(Courtesy of Fletcher Terry Co.)

Fletcher-Terry also makes a line of carbide wheel cutters, coded CA1, CA2, and so on, which follows the chart, and a special carbide cutter (CA-F) with a high angled wheel for softer glass. There is no flaking of the score line with this particular cutter.

All of these cutters, as well as the carbides, have the "classic" cutter design as shown in Figure 4–2.

The two major categories of these cutters fall into steel wheel and carbide wheel. There is a great difference in price between

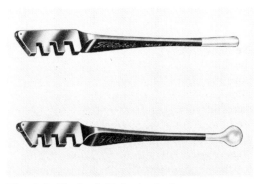

Fig. 4–2 Fletcher bold tip classic glass cutters.

Fig. 4–1 The original 1869 patented "Bristol diamond" steel-wheel glass cuter. Courtesy: Fletcher Company

the two, and for good reason. Carbide cutters, if treated properly, will last about five times as long as steel cutters. Beginners in stained glass should have at least two steel-wheel cutters: an 08 pattern-cutting small-wheel cutter and an 06 hard cutter. One of them should be ball-ended. To make things easy for yourself, add a general purpose carbide cutter to these two.

The ball on the end of a cutter allows you to tap a "score line" into a "run line." (See the actual technique of cutting glass in Chapter 6.) Only one of your cutters need be ball-ended. This will leave you a hard, straight end on the second cutter to use as a fulcrum for breaking a straight score.

A word about turret and wood-handle cutters. Some individuals complain about the thinness of the metal handles on those shown in Figure 4–2, and you may decide wood-handle cutters are more to your liking. The handles are stouter and fill the fingers more securely. These cutters are somewhat lighter than the metal-handle ones. Be careful how you hold the wood-handle cutter or you may chafe your fingers. Experiment with these lighter, thicker-handled cutters to see which work best for you.

Turret, or multiple-wheel glass cutters have no place in stained glass. The extra wheels in the turret get in the way of fine pattern cutting, and by the time one of the wheels gets dull and needs to be changed, you probably will have misplaced the cutter anyway. They are fairly expensive, but if you can afford it, get a carbide.

The Wheel Size

The smaller the glass cutter wheel, the more readily the cutter will steer. When following pattern borders, a small wheel makes life easier. A $5/32''$ wheel is a good size here. Larger wheels are useful for scoring straight lines. A large wheel might last longer than a small one, but when cutting to pattern, a small wheel tends to provide your hand with more dexterity.

Fig. 4–3 A Fletcher "refill"-style glass-cutter wheel on U-shaped axle.

Fig. 4–4 A Fletcher glass-cutter wheel many times magnified.

The Bevel Angle

The angle at which the wheel was ground is important as far as the kind of glass it is meant to score. In general, broad beveled cutter wheels are designed to score soft glass, while the steeper beveled ones are meant for hard glass. Plate glass, despite its thickness, is really a soft glass. The best cutter to use on it is an old one; one where the wheel has been dulled by use and consequently has a broader angle. Thus it plows a wider scoreline.

Handles

The Fletcher-Terry cutters have metal handles. These may be too thin for some individuals. You can try to broaden this stem in order to grip it better by wrapping it in a piece of surgical tubing. Some workers wrap their cutter handles with tape which tends to get sticky during use and is hardly comfortable. Actually these handles are made to their dimension because the instruments balance best that way. Get used to the cutter as it is; don't try to redesign it. A good tool often demands a learning process, during which time it may also be learning about you. Our experience has been that most people want to impose their will on tools, glass and teacher all at once. The tools and glass may not stand for it.

Ball-Ended Cutters

The ball is used to tap a score and cause it to run, thus deepening the fracture of the glass and making it easy to separate into pieces. It is possible to tap the score with the tooth side, the underside of the cutter, but this does not work as well and requires more skill in tapping. If the ball on the cutter is not smooth, sand or file it smooth for good tapping results. Some cutters have a small ridge around the ball that interferes with accurate tapping. This should be sanded down. *Never* tap with the cutter wheel.

Grozzing Teeth

If the glass didn't follow the score line, or if the piece was a little too large, grozzing

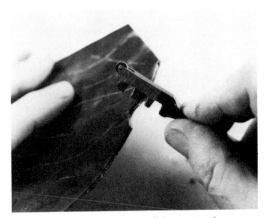

Fig. 4–5 Grozzing a piece of glass using the grozzing teeth on a glass cutter.

will chip off small pieces of glass to let you get exactly the shape you want. It also smoothes the edging *(Fig. 4–5)*. The three slots found on the underside of most cutters were once used for grozzing. These teeth, originally cut into brass or soft iron, are not of much use in stained-glass work. The soft metal would allow you to break off small pieces of glass without cracking the rest of the piece. Today, grozzing slats are made of hard metal, and they can break more glass than they save. Instead of using grozzing teeth, get a good pair of glass or grozzing pliers, which are made of special soft iron.

Carbide Glass Cutters

Some carbide cutters have the word *carbide* engraved on the cutter handle. Others may be color coded. Since a Fletcher carbide cutter looks like any other cutter, mark yours so that you will be able to distinguish it from your regular cutters. Carbide cutter wheels are made of silicon carbide and can be resharpened by the manufacturer for a nominal charge. Good carbide glass cutters are a pleasure to use.

Sharpening Glass Cutters

A glass cutter can be resharpened, but it takes patience and the right type of stone—a white Arkansas stone. The cutter is held at a slant to match the original angle of bevel of the wheel and run back and forth over the stone. Use a lubricant. Usually it is not a good idea to resharpen cutters, especially steel-wheel cutters. Once you resharpen one, it seems to dull quickly. Buy a new one when the time comes. A poorly resharpened cutter may ruin the glass instead of saving you money.

Cutter-Wheel Lubrication

Keep your cutter wheel lubricated. This will make it score better and last longer. Otherwise you can ruin it in one stroke.

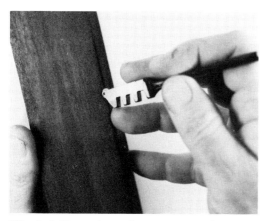

Fig. 4–6 Sharpening a glass cutter on a whetstone. If you don't keep the identical angle to the original, you will ruin the wheel.

Store the cutter in a heavy jar or glass, and place a pad of steel wool at the bottom so that the cutter wheel doesn't rest against the glass. This padding will also turn the wheel as the cutter is moved, causing the lubricant to circulate over the axle. About ¼″ of kerosene in the bottom of the jar or glass will work well as a lubricant. Do not use oil or turpentine; turpentine especially will gum up from the friction of use and immobilize the wheel. If the wheel is stuck when the cutter is used, a flat spot may burn into the wheel and take it permanently out of round. There are special cutter lubricants that are less volatile than kerosene and will last longer, but kerosene is probably the handiest.

Testing for Sharpness

Test a glass cutter for sharpness by comparing the way it scores to a new cutter. As you learn the feel of your cutter, and as you cut more and more glass, you will be able to tell easily when a cutter is going dull. When your old cutter seems sluggish and you don't get that "singing" from the glass when you move it across the surface, try a new one. A dull cutter may make a

score, but that doesn't mean the glass will separate cleanly. When the glass is difficult to separate, and when your break line looks ragged, the cutter is probably getting dull. Always keep a few new cutters on hand. It's no fun trying to cut glass with a dull cutter, and it's also expensive in terms of broken glass. A cutter can also get flat spots and dents in the wheel from cutting on dirty glass or from rough handling. Such a cutter will go "tic, tic, tic, tic" as you make a score. No matter how good the cutter is otherwise, it is useless with this defect. Such problems are generally caused by dropping the cutter on the wheel end or from inadequate lubrication. If you take care of your glass cutter, it will serve you well for a reasonable length of time depending on the type wheel and amount of use.

Advanced-Design Cutters

The Palm Rest and the Scoremaster

The Fletcher-Terry Company manufactures two new types of cutters. Both are calculated to make glass cutting easier, especially for individuals who have trouble gripping the classic cutter. One is actually a modification of the classic cutter. This Palm Rest handle attachment *(Fig. 4–7)* improves the conventional holding technique by putting the entire palm to work instead of three fingers. Made of spring steel, it fits snugly in the palm of the hand, maintaining a constant and firm contact throughout the scoring procedure. For beginners, it offers a secure guide to the process, as well as a steadier grip and better cutter stability and control with less hand fatigue.

The Palm Rest is easy to attach to the regular Fletcher cutter by sliding the clasp on or off the handle. You can adjust the support to the size and shape of your hand. The device works equally well for straight-line or pattern cutting *(see Figs. 4–7 through 4–10)*.

Fig. 4–7 The Fletcher-Terry Palm Rest is designed to be used with Fletcher's regular or "classic" Gold Tip cutter design.

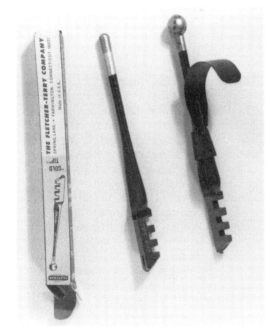

Fig. 4–8 Left: The Fletcher Gold Tip cutter; right: a similar cutter with the Palm Rest attached.

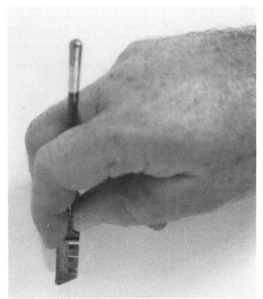

Fig. 4–9 Standard three-finger glass-cutting grip.

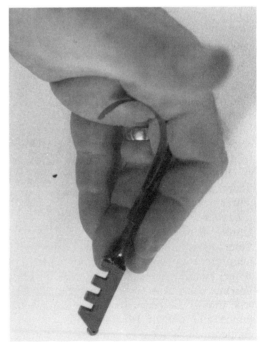

Fig. 4–10 The Palm Rest allows a more secure grasp, and more security as well in facing the glass, than the three-finger grip.

Fletcher's second new design, the Scoremaster glass cutter, differs in a number of ways from the Gold Tip classic design. Instead of the thin-stem handle, which tends to wobble between inexperienced fingers, then flattening as it approaches the

Fig. 4–11 Fletcher-Terry's Scoremaster.

Fig. 4–12 The Scoremaster and proper grip.

grozzing teeth, this cutter has a contoured handle. The finger grips allow for comfortable placement of the fingertips. Unlike many thick-handled cutters, this one thins out as it goes past the knuckles and then widens again immediately thereafter so as to preserve the balance. There is no danger of chafing at the web of the hand. The Scoremaster is an anatomically pleasing cutter; it is hand-sure. Gone are the useless grozzing teeth, a feature that is absent in almost all of the newer cutters. Instead, there is a precision-made head assembly to keep the wheel firmly in place, allow full wheel visibility for accurate pull or push scoring, a replaceable carbide wheel and axle that gives the cutter a sense of permanence, and a lubricating wick that can be dipped into light oil, so no oil reservoir is needed. Altogether, the Scoremaster seems to know the score in more ways than one. A ball end tops off the handle, providing

both a tapping mechanism and a balancing function. At the other end, serrated indentations provide nonskid fingertip control just above the head. The cutter can be used for flat clear glass and all types of stained glass for pattern or straight cutting.

Hold the Scoremaster however it is the most comfortable. Make sure that the wheel is straight up and down and the handle perpendicular to the glass. The amount of force applied depends on the type of glass you will be cutting. The basic rule for cutting is to apply as much force as you can without crushing the surface of the glass. If you find a white, gritty scoreline developing, you may be pushing too hard. Try to maintain uniform speed and force until the wheel runs gently off the edge of the glass. Never retrace the line of cut.

The Ultima 9000

The Ultima 9000, made by Ultima Industries Inc., is a palm-grip cutter with an extension for the index finger along the shaft. It allows maximum flexibility of the wrist with full wheel visibility at all times. The cutter is designed to be used in either sitting or standing positions, and it can be pushed or pulled. Both right- and left-handed workers can use it easily. And beginners usually adapt to it quickly. The cutter is comfortable and takes only fifteen minutes for the most inexperienced glass cutter to get used to.

Ultima claims that this cutter requires about half the scoring pressure of traditional glass cutters. Just the right amount of pressure will make a small groove with only one fracture running down, and the break will follow the score line. Our feeling is that the pressure is more or less divided between wrist, shoulder, and index finger. The index finger provides a great measure of control, especially for inexperienced glass cutters. A tapping ball is provided at the front of the cutter, just above the index finger position. Changing a dull wheel is simple; you place the axle pushpin on a flat surface point up and push the axle

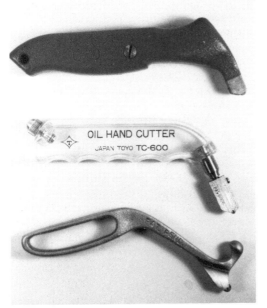

out, replace the new wheel, line up the axle holes, and push the axle back in place again with the back of the axle pushpin. This well-designed cutter could easily become a standby.

The Oil Hand Cutter

Glass Accessories International revolutionized the glass-cutting market with its series of Supercutters (see *Crafting in Glass*). Its new design, the TC 600, unlike the pengrip Supercutters, is a palm-grip cutter with an oil reservoir located in the plastic handle. The serrated lower surface of this lightweight, see-through tool provides comfortable finger grips. The cutting head itself is magnificent. The cutter may be held either in a fist grip with the thumb

Fig. 4–13 *Palm Rest glass cutters.* Top: *Fletcher's heavy-duty cutter, which produces 40 percent more pressure power than regular models, is designed to supplement, not replace, conventional handled cutters.* Center: *Glass Accessories' oil hand cutter.* Bottom: *the Ultima 9000.*

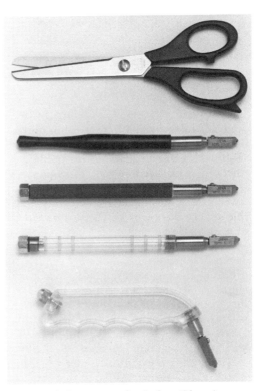

Fig. 4–15 *Assortment of tools from Glass Accessories International.* Top: *pattern scissors;* Middle: *Supercutter glass cutters;* Bottom: *the palm oil cutter.*

Fig. 4–14 *The grip for the Ultima 9000.*

resting as a guide or in a palm grip with the index finger acting as the guide. Don't hold this or any other palm-grip cutter with all fingers completely wrapped around it. Such a grip limits wrist mobility.

The Raven Glass Cutter

The Raven glass cutter, made by the Raven Tool Company, is one of the more original designs. It is a fingertip cutter with a stabilizing, screw-out support for the knuckles. The manufacturer calls this a palm rest, but the support is provided more from the base of the fingers than from the underside of the hand. The cutter is the heaviest we have tested, being made of brass. However, its design enables the weight to work for, not against, the operator. It is directed through the cutting wheel and onto the glass, so less shoulder pressure is required. The cutter has four parts: the wheel, the cutting turret, which has a lock-nut arrangement to permit various wheel angles, the body, and the shaft. The body looks ungainly until you position the cutter in your grasp. Then the two wide upper and the single lower grooves make sense. Index and third finger tips fit above, thumb below. The shaft screws outward until its T-bar design meets the under surfaces of the knuckles. The horizontal bar slips below the knuckles; the vertical bar slips between them. This sets up an extremely stable support, but it does take getting used

Fig. 4–17 *The Raven glass cutter from the side.*

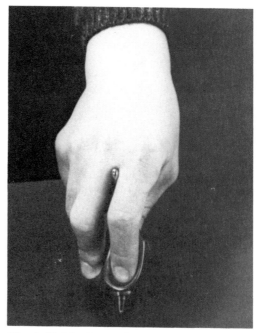

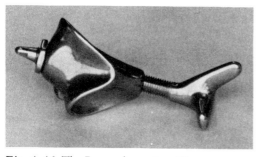

Fig. 4–16 *The Raven glass cutter. (Courtesy: Raven Tool Company)*

Fig. 4–18 *The Raven glass cutter from the front. A great deal of wrist mobility is permitted.*

to. One advantage is the wrist mobility that is permitted, especially when cutting curves.

The cutter comes in right- or left-handed models and is self-adjusting from the shaft screw-out provision. In addition, you can push or pull the score. Individual tips are available, and all cutting wheels are tungsten-carbide.

The Diamond Cutter

The diamond cutter usually is not used in stained-glass work because following a paper pattern is impractical. It works well for straight lines, but is expensive and used mostly for mass-production work. Using a diamond cutter requires more skill than a wheel cutter, but of course it cuts more easily. There are different kinds of diamond cutters for different kinds of glass. The handle may be made of wood or plastic, without a ball, and prices range from $3 for a questionable one to $24 and more for a commercial, high-grade one.

Circle Cutters

Circles can be cut freehand with a regular glass cutter or with a machine that can cut circles to almost any dimension. Circle cutters come in several styles, and cutting a circle in glass is simple with any of them. For small circles, from ⅜″ to 5″ in diameter, Fletcher-Terry's compact rotating-handle instrument can be used. Once the circle is inscribed, it is broken out of the glass by scoring lines at right angles to it and pulling off the pieces with glass pliers. For larger circles, from 2″ on up, a suction-cup circle cutter may be used. This has three pieces: a cup stand, a movable turret with a screw gauge, and a rod on which the turret travels. The further the turret is placed from the cup stand, the wider the diameter of the circle will be. The cup does not have to be braced by hand if it has a good suction base. The cutting wheel is similar to that on a regular cutter, and it should be lubricated and kept clean. When the wheel

Fig. 4–19 *Fletcher-Terry's small "lens" or circle cutter mounted on a wooden stand. The diameter of the circle is limited by the length of the cutting bar, which is limited by the size of the machine. A larger model is made by Stanford Engineering.*

becomes dull, attach a replacement wheel. Usually all you have to do is loosen and tighten a single screw.

The Odd-Shape Cutter

A logical next step from a machine that cuts circles is a machine that cuts curved shapes. The hobbyist making one-of-a-kind items may have little use for this, but the hobbyist-businessperson who is producing multiple items may find this machine to be a real help. With this machine each piece will be exact, and each will be scored in a minimum amount of time.

The Fassglass cutting machines *(Fig. 4–21)* are efficient, rugged, and accurate. Fassglass I will cut virtually any shape you can cut by hand, even squares and triangles. The cutting head raises out of the way in an instant to make changing templates easy. The machine comes with a template layout tool and easy instructions. The Fassglass II does the same work but has five times more cutting area. It measures only 24″ by 24″. Templates are easy to make.

Strip-Cutting Devices

Cutting glass into long, narrow strips using a ruler and glass cutter alone does not appeal to many workers' sense of humor.

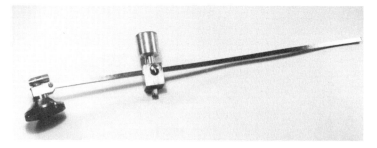

Fig. 4–20 *Glass Accessories'
circle cutter has a suction-cup
base and a bar placed on a
swivel. The unit is well balanced and never moves once
the suction is applied. It can
cut large circles.*

Fig. 4–21 *The Fassglass I odd-shape cutter. Courtesy: de Groot Fabricating.*

Fig. 4–22 *The Fassglass II odd-shape cutter.*

The ruler invariably slips, no matter how
securely you hold it, and it is hard to keep
the cutter moving with the same force
along the entire length of the cut. So when
the time comes to break out the glass
strips, the uneven pressure may provoke a
break line that is not quite even with the
score line. This, in turn, gives you uneven
strips that have to be grozzed—and that
means extra work even if you do manage
to straighten out the borders. Strip cutters
make such a project a lot easier.

Figure 4–24 shows a strip- and circle-
cutter combination made by Glastar that
can cut squares, rectangles, and diamonds
from ½″ to 12″ wide. The circle-cutter attachment cuts circles from 3″ to 24″ in diameter with accuracy to a fraction of an
inch. This timesaver is especially useful in
cutting repetitive and often tedious border
pieces. It is lightweight, constructed of extra hard, glass-filled Acetel and contains
three pieces: a 12″ T-bar with a 6-cutter-
wheel turret, a circle-cutter base, and a
stripper base. The T-bar attaches to either
base. To provide durability, the six cutting
wheels are on the T-bar turret. By turning
a screw, a fresh cutting blade rotates into
place, replacing the worn blade. The circle
cutter is held by three small rubber points
that anchor securely to the glass.

For stripping, nail a standard 1 × 2″
board to the worktable, and place the glass
against the board. The stripper rides on the
edge of the board as you draw the cutter
over the glass. Thus all glass pieces are cut
to exactly the same size.

If you want to cut strips, Diegel Engineering's tool allows you to do it quickly

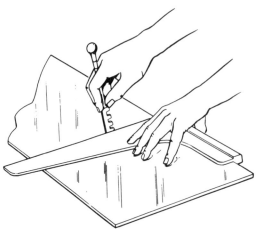

Fig. 4–23 *The highly accurate 12¼" glass square, designed by Glastar specifically for squaring off and cutting the edges of stained glass, is made of structural foam. The square is thick, sturdy, lightweight, and moves easily on glass. It is accurate to ⁵⁄₁₀₀₀th of an inch. The square will make up to a 12½" cut. By using a straightedge as an extension, it can cut glass as wide as three feet.*

Fig. 4–24 *Glastar's combination strip and circle cutter.*

and easily *(Fig. 4–25)*. Its multiple-strip cutter is designed with the same precision as its other products, notably its foiler and crimper. This machine, usually only for large shops, cuts strips, squares, and rectangles from 1" to 20" wide and uses twelve cutting heads, with more to be added if needed. One push on the handle bar oils all cutters simultaneously.

If you want to cut only single strips, Diegel makes a less imposing device with a less imposing price *(Figs. 4–26 and 4–27)*.

GLASS PLIERS

Glass pliers have a number of specialized applications, although one pair of pliers may be used for various operations without too much trouble. This means that you can probably buy a single pair of pliers initially, so long as you avoid household "electrician's" pliers. Glass pliers go by various names, such as grozzers, breaking pliers, running pliers, and lead-cutting pliers, and there are various categories within each of these according to manufacturing characteristics.

Glass or Breaking Pliers

These all-purpose pliers can be used for breaking and grozzing—that is, trimming away pieces of glass that extend beyond the bordering edge of a cut portion and that are too small or too awkward to remove by hand. Some breaking pliers are made with underslung jaws to grip the glass below the score line and nowhere else. Others are made with parallel jaws so as not to pinch the glass, but rather to apply even pressure above and below.

They are made both with and without grooves in the jaws; grooved pliers have an advantage in that they also can be used for rough grozzing. To be used in this fashion, the jaw of a grooved glass plier is worked over a glass edge more or less like a file. Be careful—if too much pressure is applied, the glass will splinter, and the edge will be in worse shape than before. Grozzing takes practice, and fine grozzing should only be attempted with special grozzing pliers. Only the more obvious points and imbalances can be aligned with a breaker, but this it will do well.

Glass pliers can also be used to break a piece of glass after it has been scored. Once the score is made, providing it is a straight

Fig. 4–25 *Diegel Engineering's multiple-strip cutter has a 36" by 36" base and cuts glass from .030" to ¼" thick. Maximum sheet size is 30" by 30". Score length is 30".*

Fig. 4–26 *Diegel Engineering's single-strip cutter for cutting long strips of glass.*

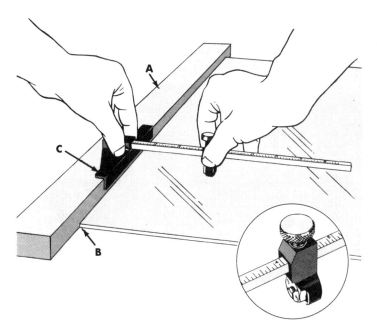

Fig. 4–27 *Using Diegel Engineering's strip cutter. Fasten a 1 by 2" board to the work-table, and place the edge of the glass against the board. The strip cutter goes against the protruding edge of the board and slides as you draw the cutter over the glass. Insert: the turret and the multiple cutting wheels.*

Fig. 4–28 Glass Accessories' straight-line cutter is 57½" and made of sturdy aluminum. On the bottom, in grooves, are two rubber strips to prevent the cutter from moving on the glass. At the end is a metal plate providing a straightedge guide to line the cutter up with the edge of the glass.

Fig. 4–31 The cutter itself consists of a spring-loaded plastic handle with an oil reservoir for the cutter wheel at the bottom. The spring-loading keeps the wheel out of the way when the cutter is not in use. Finger pressure releases it. This whole arrangement slides readily in a groove the length of the cutter, so all that is required to cut long glass strips of precise dimension is a quick arm-and-finger motion. Multiple strips can be cut with ease.

Fig. 4–29 On top of the cutter, in brackets of its own, is a marking pen that can be used . . .

Fig. 4–30 . . . to run alongside the straightedge guide to calculate glassy strips before the cutter itself is used. Note the groove in which the cutter mechanism rides.

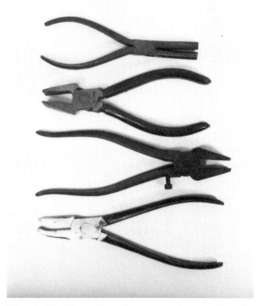

Fig. 4–32 Glass pliers; from top to bottom: Round-barrel grozzers; breaking pliers; running pliers; and heavy-duty grozzers.

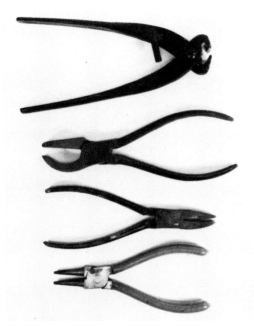

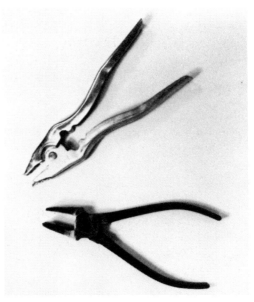

Fig. 4–35 Bottom: *glass breakers;* Top: *chain pliers.*

Fig. 4–33 Glass pliers; from top to bottom: Heavy-duty glass nippers; underslung-jaw breaking pliers; small grozzers; and round-jaw grozzers.

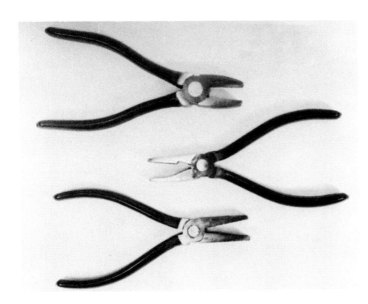

Fig. 4–34 Diamond Tool pliers: Top: Glass-breaking pliers; Center: rounded-jaw grozzer; Bottom: flat-jaw grozzer.

cut, the glass is laid flat on the table surface with the score uppermost. The glass should be extended over the edge of the table until the score is directly above the table edge. Now, with the glass pliers, firmly grasp the glass piece directly at the score line so that the pliers' lower jaw is almost against the table's edge. With the left hand, press the furthermost section of glass against the table to keep the piece from moving. The pull on the pliers should be out and slightly down, and the two pieces will separate with a musical "ting." Keep your feet out of the way; occasionally the glass will break into more than two pieces. Glass pliers should not be used to break sharp curves unless you are skilled in their use. Because the width of their jaws makes the procedure somewhat chancey, it is better to use grozzing pliers. An excellent beginner's pliers is one with either a 6" or 8" handle with a ¾" or 1" grooved jaw.

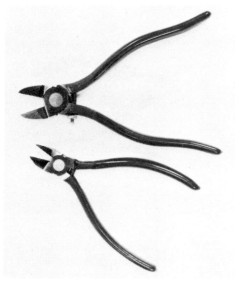

Fig. 4–36 *Came-cutting pliers.*

Fig. 4–37 *Using grozzing pliers. Narrow trims can be removed and sharp corners rounded by nibbling the edges as shown, using the serrated surfaces of the jaws in a filelike fashion. (Courtesy: Fletcher-Terry Company.)*

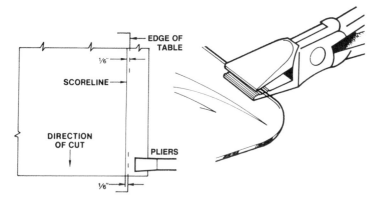

Fig. 4–38 *Breaking pliers can either break glass or nip projecting shards. For breaking, calculate their accuracy for trims up to 2" wide. The point of application of the pliers is important. The ends of the jaws must be as parallel to the score line as possible and no more than ¼" away. Locate the glass so that the score is parallel to the table's edge and about ¹⁄₁₆" in from it or right above it. To break out the glass trim, grip the sheet with the pliers and pull out and down, stabilizing the sheet with the other hand. (Courtesy: Fletcher-Terry Company.)*

86 *Materials and Equipment*

Grozzing Pliers

Grozzing pliers have narrow jaws with fine teeth and are used strictly for grozzing or for carving difficult shapes out of glass. They are made of soft metal, and any use other than glass grozzing or occasional breaking may damage them. They are also good for nibbling away the fine points and inconsistencies left on the glass from less than perfect cuts. Using these pliers requires more practice than other pliers, but they're worth the effort.

Make sure the pliers are well oiled, so they will open and close with minimal work of the hand. It's best if they open with the weight of their bottom handle alone. If you hold the grozzing pliers with one handle up, the joint should be so free that the lower handle will drop. Keep all your pliers this spry. It eliminates the tiring motion of constantly having to open them by pushing in with your fingers.

When the teeth wear down, recut them with a fine file. With care, grozzing pliers will last for a long time.

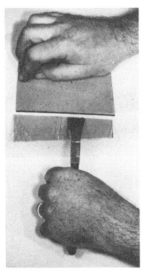

Fig. 4–39 Breaking pliers in action. The two pieces of glass are separated, and the trim breaks clean. Grip the center of the glass with the pliers; the force of the pull should extend equally to both ends of the score. You can use flat-jawed breaking pliers or underslung jaws.

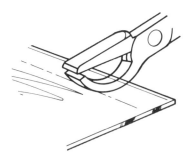

Fig. 4–41 Underslung-jaw breaking pliers gripping at the score line. The top jaw holds, while the bottom exerts pressure from below.

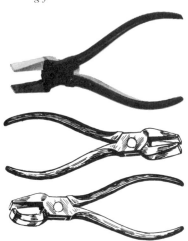

Fig. 4–40 Top and Center: Flat or straight-jaw breaking pliers; Bottom: underslung-jaw breaking pliers.

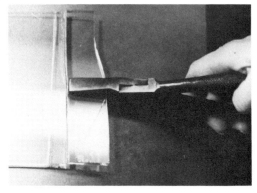

Fig. 4–42 Grozzing pliers can also be used to break glass along a score line.

Running Pliers

Probably the most difficult cut to score and break out of a piece of glass is a thin, long strip. This break tends to run off the score line somewhere along its length. Running pliers help such breaks run true. Unfortunately, they are expensive.

Fig. 4–43A *Using running pliers. The pliers are lined up with the score line directly in line with the guideline on the pliers. The set screw is tightened so that the pliers jaws just grip the glass.*

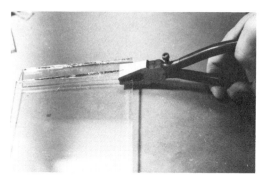

Fig. 4–43B *As pressure is increased, the score "runs" and the glass breaks clean.*

The jaws of running pliers curve into one another. The top jaw is concave and the lower convex. The lower jaw thus becomes a fulcrum for the two pressure points of the upper jaw. Such an arrangement allows even pressure above and below the score line. To ensure even pressure, a screw gauge is provided on top of the pliers. This screw is turned so that the pliers are permitted to grasp only the surfaces of the glass with the smallest amount of pressure—just enough to fracture the score, but not enough to crush the glass. You must spend a minute or two arranging the pliers at the score line, since the central mark on the pliers must be matched to the score line. The procedure:

1. Score the glass in a straight cut.
2. Bring the glass over to the table edge so that the table edge is at right angles to the cut. Take the running pliers and line up the score on the glass with the guide line shown on the upper jaw of the pliers.
3. Turn the screw gauge so that the jaws of the pliers grasp the glass as lightly as possible without slipping. Then loosen the screw perhaps half a turn more. Press firmly on the handles and the cut will travel along the score line.

A new style of running pliers, called the Glassnapper, is specially designed with narrow jaws. The handles are spring-loaded for easier handling. This lightweight tool, manufactured by Glastar, is molded of a strong, durable, glass-reinforced Acetel. With the narrower jaws,

8" Models   6" Models

Fig. 4–44 *Fletcher-Terry's running pliers. Special jaw inserts permit firm but gentle gripping of delicate surfaces up to ¼" thick without danger of scratching the glass. The jaw inserts have special plastic anvils designd for perfect alignment under the score for a perfect edge. All can be quickly and easily replaced.*

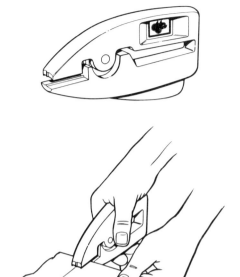

Fig. 4–45 Top: *Glastar's Glassnapper running pliers.* Bottom: *"Snapping" or running the score line.*

compared to other running pliers, the tool can break much smaller pieces of glass. It works equally well with large pieces.

The spring-loaded handles are a special advantage since they are always open to ³⁄₁₆″—the perfect spacing for the insertion of an ⅛″ piece of glass. Some workers tend to have trouble opening pliers with one hand. Since the bottom jaw of the Glassnapper extends beyond the upper jaw, it is easier to insert the glass in the jaws.

SPECIAL PURPOSE PLIERS

Round-Barrel Grozzers

Round-barrel grozzers will grozz a small half-moon out of glass rather than a straight line like square-jawed pliers will. They are handy when grozzing inside curves and will work well when small concavities must be taken piecemeal out of a

pattern. They should not be used as breaking pliers; their grip on the glass, because of the barrel shape, is applicable only to a small surface area. In effect, these are more of a crushing pliers than other types, and their use is more specific. Still, when they are necessary, they are very welcome.

Heavy-Duty Grozzers

Heavy-duty grozzers essentially do the same work as small grozzers, but they rest more firmly in a large hand and provide more leverage against the glass edge. It is a matter of individual preference whether to use these or the smaller version. Some workers use the small grozzers exclusively because they do not like the wider grozzing jaws, perhaps feeling that grozzing more surface at a time leads to rougher results. Others feel just the opposite. Preference to an extent depends on the strength and the size of the hand. The large grozzer is 7¾″ long with a jaw width of ⁷⁄₁₆″. The small grozzer measures 6″ in length with a jaw width of ⁵⁄₁₆″. Although these differences seem small, they make a considerable difference in the amount of leverage obtained, the area encompassed, and the grip and consequent stamina of the hand muscles. The width across the widest point of the large grozzers with the jaws closed is 2¼″; that of the small pair is 1¾″.

Glass Nippers

Glass nippers are not grozzers. Their function is to chew into the glass edge rather than file it. The jaws are two sharp-edged pincers that catch the glass between them and literally bite it away. Some workers use them mainly for rough "grozzing" of areas that will not sustain a cutting and breaking technique, particularly inside curves. These nippers work well if you avoid taking larger and larger bites. Using this tool unskillfully will inevitably lead to breaking the glass.

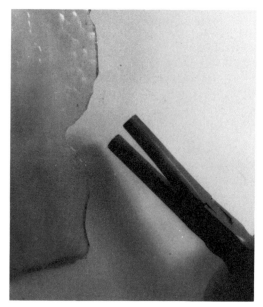

Fig. 4–46A *Barrel-jaw grozzing pliers, and their effect.*

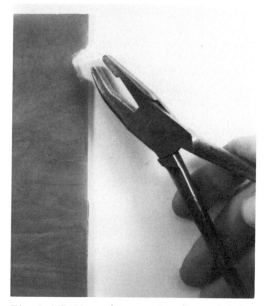

Fig. 4–46B *Heavy-duty grozzing pliers and their effect. A very controllable tool.*

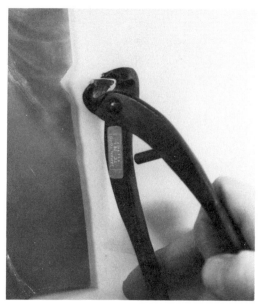

Fig. 4–46C *Glass nippers and their effect. Control of this tool is difficult. The glass can break if too large a bite is taken. Small nibbles are best, from one side of the grozz to the other.*

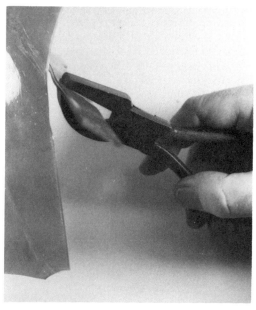

Fig. 4–46D *The underslung-jaw pliers breaking away a mild inside curve. The glass is held only by the front of the jaws, which apply "line" pressure.*

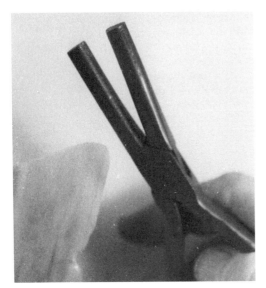

Fig. 4–47 *Barrel-jaw grozzing pliers also can be used to round a sharp corner.*

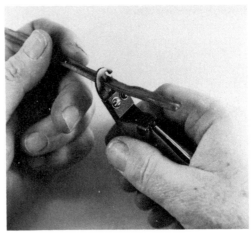

Fig. 4–49A *A lead came nipper in position to slice a piece of came.*

Fig. 4–49B *The configuration of this lead nipper is designed to support the came while cutting it; therefore no distortion of the came occurs. The front section supports the came, and the blade comes up behind and cuts it. A neat device.*

Fig. 4–48 *Round-jaw pointed pliers and their effect. Take small nips.*

Underslung-Jaw Breakers

A variation of regular glass pliers, underslung jaw breakers provide a more direct line of pressure under the score line during the breaking process than do regular glass breakers. They also allow you to see more precisely where that lower jaw is. Some workers swear by them. However, our security feels threatened by the missing grasp of the lower jaw on that area of glass in front of the score line. Once the glass breaks, the fragments tend to fall out of the pliers unless a substantial piece is being broken.

Round-Jaw Grozzers

The smaller version of the round-barrel grozzers can be used where tiny curved areas are to be gnawed out of pieces of glass. However, this process is time-consuming. Unless you have the time and patience, forget them and use regular grozzers. The pointed jaws are roughened rather than grooved. Such roughing is essential, given the tiny grasp of these jaws.

Flat-Jaw Grozzers

Flat-jaw pliers have angled rather than parallel jaws and thus do not provide optimum grozzing force. Instead of a flat-surfaced edge to the glass, you will find a slanted one following their use. This sloping edge throws off precise borders of the piece, and attempts to fix it by grozzing off the jutting shelf only compound the problem. Foiling a slanted edge is difficult because the foil will not sit properly, nor will such edges abut the way they should. Flat-jawed pliers, or any angled-jaw pliers, are not therefore recommended for stained-glass work.

Chain Pliers

If you make and wire stained-glass lampshades, chain pliers are a must (see Chapter 14).

Came-Cutting Pliers

Some workers use came-cutting pliers in addition to their lead knife (see Chapter 2).

PATTERN CUTTERS

Pattern Scissors

Pattern scissors come in at least two sizes, $\frac{1}{16}''$ and $\frac{1}{8}''$, the measurement referring to the amount of paper cut away between pattern pieces to make room for the lead came. If you're using lead up to $\frac{3}{8}''$, you are probably better off with a $\frac{1}{16}''$ scissors. For anything over that, you might want

the larger size. Ideally you should have both sizes, since you probably will be varying lead sizes within the framework of certain designs.

Pattern scissors consist of three blades, two below and one on top. The bottom two blades are joined to allow a slight

Fig. 4–50 *Two styles of pattern scissors.*

Fig. 4–51 *Pattern scissors cutting in a single-blade-up position. The cutting should be done closer to the juncture of the blades than shown here.*

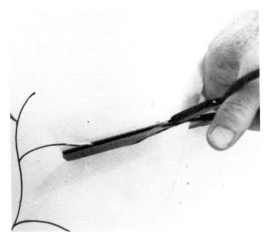

Fig. 4–52 Pattern scissors cutting in a double-blade-up position. This is about where the scissors should be cutting.

space, which is commensurate with the size of the paper cut out. It is into this space that the top blade falls. Thus the paper is cut precisely and with guillotine sharpness. This sharp edge on the paper pattern is important. A pattern with a poor memory for its horizons is a cloudy guide.

Using the scissors for the first time is an experience. Rather than cutting as with ordinary scissors—by taking a bite the length of the blade—the best way to use pattern scissors is to take small bites with the back of the blades, inching up on the pattern with a crafty maneuverability. Turns and angles can be cut readily after some practice.

Pattern scissors can be used either top blade up or double blade up. If you use the top single blade up, you can sight along the blade against the line being cut. If you want to use the scissors with the double blades on top, sight between the two blades and make sure the line being cut falls between them. Once the pattern is cut, you cannot trim uncertain edges with regular scissors because the space between patterns will be awry. Cut your pattern correctly the first time. Practice using the scissors on scrap paper before going on to your project.

Pattern Knife

The simplest way to allow space for lead lines in a pattern is to go over the pattern lines with a medium-size magic marker, then cut these lines away with a razor blade. This is tedious and imprecise, but some workers become good at this technique and would work in no other way. A pattern knife utilizes this technique, but more comfortably and precisely than a razor blade, though not as comfortably as pattern scissors.

A pattern knife, consists of double blades in an angled handle. The width between the blades is adjustable. The blades are kept razor sharp. This tool takes some adjustment initially to get the blades even. There are some disadvantages. When you pull the knife toward you, you will be working in your own shadow. You can, although it's awkward, reverse the direction and push the knife from you, reversing the handle as well. But now you find you are still in the dark, since the line you are cutting away is hidden by the blades. Most workers who use pattern knives develop specific techniques, such as viewing from the side of the blades or looking over

Fig. 4–53 The Artmob Inc. pattern knife is comfortable, efficient, and precise. The dual left and right bevel blades are polished and tempered Blue Spring steel and have a double bevel to add strength and life to the sharpened edge.

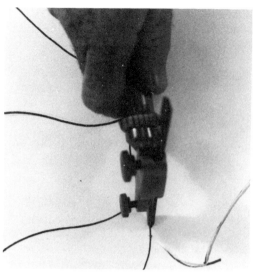

Fig. 4–54 *Cutting a pattern with the pattern knife. Put a piece of cardboard under the pattern paper to allow the knife to cut more cleanly. It also prevents the blades from digging into the table surface. Here the knife is pulled toward the operator.*

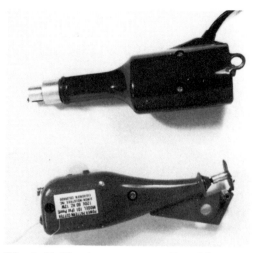

Fig. 4–55 *Electric pattern cutters. Top: The Carrousel electric pattern shears (Courtesy: Carrousel Development Company). Bottom: The Power Pattern Cutter (Courtesy: Simon Industries, Inc.).*

them, which allow moderate dexterity with the tool. In skilled hands, patterns can be cut fast and accurately. It depends what you get used to. One big advantage to the pattern knife is its price—much cheaper than scissors.

Electric Pattern Cutters

Relatively new devices, two electric pattern cutters are available, and both make for sophisticated pattern cutting. The Carrousel pattern cutter cuts a single-size channel, has a rheostat on the side to speed up or slow down the cutting. There are five speeds to give fast or intricate cutting on papers up to a 10-point stock.

The cutter made by Simon Industries, the Power Pattern Cutter Model 101, has a laminated blade that makes the accurate cutting of complex patterns easy. It does not have a rheostat. However, disregarding these slight differences between the two, it's impossible to decide which does the better job. Each is a tremendous advantage to a hobbyist turning out a reasonable

amount of work; for an active studio situation, the time saved with one of these devices is incalculable. The heads on both cutters are reversible. And using them is a lot of fun.

NECESSARIES

Lead Knife

One of the most essential tools in stained-glass work is the all-purpose lead knife, which is at once a cutter, fitter, hammer, flange, straight-edge, bender, and straightener of lead came. In effect, it provides the worker with another set of fingers. Leading knives without weighted handles are cheaper than weighted ones, but we do not recommend them. You can put your own weighted end on a knife by carving down the wood and melting lead into the space. This is what many oldtime glass workers did before weighted knives were made commercially. But it's easier to let the factory do the work. The blade of the leading knife comes either straight or curved, and here individual preference takes over. The

Fig. 4–57 Lead knife with weighted handle. One of the most useful of all tools.

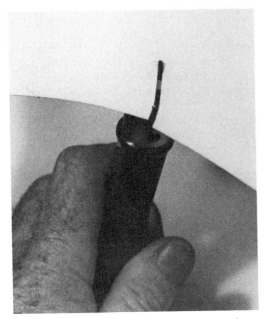

Fig. 4–56A The Carrousel power cutter seen from above cutting a piece of pattern paper, the cutting head at the end of the slit. Note the clean edges of the cut.

Fig. 4–56B The Carrousel pattern cutter seen from below. Note the curl of paper from the cutting process in front of the cutting head.

curved blade can be put to more uses than the straight one.

The point can be used to hook and position leads within a panel prior to soldering. Cutting the leads with the sharp surface is a technique in itself. With the soft leads, such as ⅛", ¹⁄₁₆", ³⁄₁₆", either "U" or "H", the danger is that by applying too much force your knife will crush the channel. You then have the additional job of opening the crevice and restraightening the lead. A professional leading knife is made of the best steel and will keep its temper far longer than the operator who is inefficiently wielding it. It's not necessary to come down with it like a guillotine against the lead, nor should you apply straight pressure hoping to push it through the came. Let the knife do its job.

The best way to cut lead came with it is to lay the blade straight on top of the came with a small amount of pressure and wiggle it from side to side. It will cut through the channel with surprising dispatch, and the lead will hardly be bent at all. For cutting leads such as ¼" and up, the same principle is used—except that it is safer here to use more pressure on the knife. With heavy leads, you may have to use both hands, but wiggling it from left to right will enable the blade to gain purchase on each level of the came it is slicing through, and you will find you are making neat, able cuts.

A word of caution: A professional leading knife is a precision tool and occasionally needs to be sharpened. Do not use a kitchen knife sharpener, since it will chip the blade. An Arkansas whetstone will put an edge on your knife with ease, and it will then be ready for another year or so of use. Such a sharpening process involves strapping the knife across the stone, which is oiled with light machine oil. Don't be impatient with this process, and try to keep the angle at which you are strapping the knife the same with each stroke.

The leading knife is a basic tool that ranks next to the glass cutter and soldering iron in importance.

Lathkins

Lathkins widen and straighten the lead channels so that the glass will "seat." No advanced worker in stained glass would

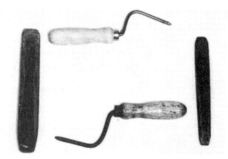

Fig. 4–58 Lathkins: two different sizes of metal ones—a thick and a thin; two different shaped wooden ones. The left wooden lathkin was originally a pool cue.

Fig. 4–59 Opening a piece of came with a plastic lathkin.

consider beginning a project without this convenient item at hand to avoid frustration.

Metal lathkins come in two sizes, thick and thin, and they can either be pushed or pulled through the came channel. If you want to push the lathkin through the came, hold the instrument with the rounded end within the channel and wiggle it slowly through the came, using the force of your arm to push it along. You must keep the lead straight and braced behind the instrument as you go. If you would rather pull the lathkin through to straighten the channel, dip the point into the channel and pull it toward you. Don't pull it too hard, especially if the piece of came is twisted, or you will tear the lead.

You can make your own lathkin out of wood. Many workers do this, making personalized tools to fit their hand. Start with a hard wood such as oak, walnut, or maple, and sand it with a bench sander to the appropriate dimensions. Dipping it in a hot oil will lubricate it and seal the wood. Let the wood stand in oil overnight. An old pool cue cut down to size is an excellent base for a wooden lathkin. It is already almost entirely shaped for your grip. Wooden lathkins, however, no matter how hard the wood, will wear out in time, and will begin to chip and fault irregularly along the working surface.

Many lathkins today are made from plastic. This material wears well and is so smooth that it slides readily through the lead channel. Various sizes and shapes are on the market, since no lathkin design has yet achieved general approval. In an emergency almost anything that will widen or open a lead channel will serve the purpose, even the point of a pencil.

Lead Stretcher

The lead stretcher is a device, actually a specialised vise, to hold lead came. It is composed of a fixed lower and a movable upper jaw. It can be screwed firmly to a shelf or table, which itself must be strong enough to withstand the pull of the worker at the other end of the came.

With the top jaw laid back, one end of the came is placed against the lower "teeth" and the top jaw closed firmly. The lead is not yet snuggled into the vise; this happens as the came is pulled. The teeth, or ridges, are so angled that when the came is pulled they automatically lock against it. To remove the came, simply open the vise. You can use a regular vise to accomplish the same purpose, but more work is involved in opening and closing it. Also, a regular vise will hold the came by crushing the end, thereby weakening it and allowing it possibly to tear loose during stretching. Most stained-glass workers buy a lead stretcher sooner or later; it is too convenient an item to do without.

Leading Nails

Leading nails are an excellent means of stabilizing lead came. With their flat sides, they minimize gouges in the lead came and help prevent chips in the glass. A good leading nail should have certain characteristics:

1. Not be so fat so that it will split or chip the glass edges it is meant to hold.
2. Not be so thin that it will fail to maintain a proper purchase into the wood of the workboard.

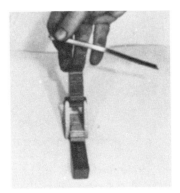

Fig. 4–60 *The lead stretcher, open to receive a came.*

3. The taper should be gradual so as to allow removal by the fingers.
4. There should be a strong point, but not one so sharp that it will blunt or turn after the first few times' use.
5. The nail should be high enough to stand reasonably above the working area, but not be so high as to interfere by catch-

Fig. 4–61 *Imported leading nail, exact size*

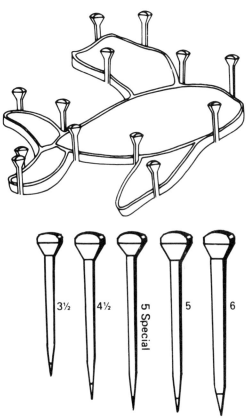

Fig. 4–62 *Five diamond horseshoe nails shown actual size. Sizes 3½ and 4½ are packed in 1-pound boxes; sizes 5 and 6 are packed in 5-pound boxes. The nails hold a piece of leaded stained glass prior to soldering the lead joints. Note that the widest flat side of the nail is against the leaded surface of the glass.*

ing the sleeve of the worker—or worse, the hand—during the course of the leading procedure.

Remember that any movement of the glass pieces while you are leading them up can mean redoing a section of the work in progress. This is frustrating. You are dependent on leading nails to hold the completed pieces where you have set them. After all, once you take the time and effort to draw a design, cut a pattern, and cut glass to match the pieces, you should know that the pieces will at least stay put.

Neither "common" nails nor "finishing" nails will do the job. The ideal nail is shown in Figure 4–61, and even here the point is a trifle thin. These imported German leading nails are hard to obtain, but you can get them from some glassworking supply outfits. If you can obtain them, you will find they are practically indestructible. The second choice is the horseshoe nail. These are sold by many stained-glass distributors. Get top-quality horseshoe nails of Swedish steel. These are boxed approximately 150 to 160 a pound for use in stained glass.

You can also use pushpins, depending on the material you intend to push them into. It is tiring to push them into plywood. They are usually used with Homosote boards. These pins come with aluminum or glass heads, measuring about ⅝".

Glass Drills

Drilling a hole in a piece of glass is not quite as simple as doing it in a piece of wood or metal. A special drill bit must be used. Glass drill bits fit into standard hand drills, and can be used with water lubricant. However, if too much heat is generated by the procedure, the glass will crack. This usually occurs right when the job is almost done. The tendency to avoid cracking leads to overuse of the lubricant. This, if it puddles over the surface, will prevent the drill bit from acquiring purchase on the glass.

The best way is to go by sound. If you hear no sound at all from the grinding process, and the bit keeps turning in the hole with no perceptible progress, chances are you are using too much water. (Some workers prefer to use light oil as lubricant.) If, on the other hand, you begin to hear the "cry" of the glass as you drill—a grinding sound that increases in intensity and manifests itself as well in an increased frictional resistance to the drilling—you need more lubricant. You will also see quite a bit of glass "dust" coming up from the hole. Diminish the sound with lubricating material so that it is faint but still audible. If you can maintain it at this volume, you should be able to drill safely through the glass. The average hole should take no longer than a minute or two.

Carbide glass bits are available in different shapes, from spear-headed to triangular. Price varies according to size and shape, and they are expensive. Dimensions are from ⅛" to ¼". The most frequently used size is ³⁄₁₆". This size serves the purpose for most people of drilling a hole to hang small objects.

Fig. 4–63 *Three types of glass drill bits.* Top to bottom: *reamer; spear point; and three-corner types.*

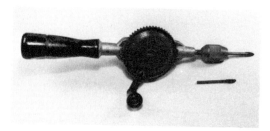

Fig. 4–64 *A spear-pointed Carborundum drill bit held in a hand drill. Glass drilling must be done carefully so that too much heat from the drilling doesn't fracture the glass.*

Glastar makes a new type of glass drill bit (Fig. 4–65) with a specially designed diamond-coated surface for round glass holes. It will cut a ¾″ diameter hole in ⅛″ glass in less than fifteen seconds. Also available is a ¼″ drill bit.

Diamond-coated bits are far superior to the traditional carbide-tipped spear-point bits. They are far easier to use, more convenient, and their life is many times that of the carbide-tipped drill bits.

If you want to use a carbide-tipped bit in an electric drill, as opposed to a hand drill, you have to build a dam of putty on the glass and fill it with kerosene. Then a slow speed of about 400 RPM would be used to drill through the glass. This is a time-consuming, tedious process, and cracking the glass is likely. With diamond-coated drills you merely sponge out a teaspoonful of plain water on the glass. Then you quickly and easily make a hole at any speed, depending on your drill. Breakage is minimal. Such a bit can make several hundred holes before it has to be replaced. This is many times more than the spear-point drill bit can do. The diamond bits will fit any standard portable drill.

Another use for holes in glass, incidentally, other than for hanging small objects, is for installing jewels to simulate eyes in animal suncatchers. Inlaying is more professional looking than mere surface gluing.

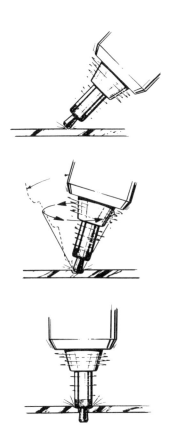

Fig. 4–65 Cutting a hole in glass using Glastar's new diamond-coated drill bit in a standard drill. Top: The hole is started by placing the tip at an angle to the glass. Center: The drill is gradually straightened as it gains purchase on the surface. Bottom: The hole is completed with the drill vertical to the glass.

Glass Grinders

No recent piece of technology has so changed the aspect of stained glass as a hobby and art form as has the introduction of the glass grinder. The notion of using a rotating wheel, lubricated and diamond-coated, to grind pieces of glass into shapes that could be cut only with great difficulty by a glass cutter, was taken from the lapidary industry.

Basic to the function of the glass grinder, or glass router as it is also called, is the head. Many shapes are offered for grinding various types of surfaces. The heads are divided into two groups depending on whether their main purpose is grinding or cutting holes (see Fig. 4–66). Such heads provide grinding sleeves of a metal/diamond process, allowing for a controlled and consistent grinding surface for the life of the sleeve. Brass and stainless steel have been used for grinding bodies to prevent corrosion and freezing in the motor shaft. Silica powder, generated by grinding glass, tends to creep between the grinding body and the motor shaft. There it solidifies and freezes the body in the same manner as rust and corrosion will do. Using

Router Grozzing Heads		*Hole Cutters/Engravers*	

Mini-Router Head
⅝″ Dia. Sleeve

Engraver/Hole Cutter
⅛″ Dia. Pointed

Single (Economy) Head
¾″ Dia. Sleeve

Hole Cutter
¼″ Dia.

Standard Combination
½″ & ¾″ Dia. Sleeves

Hole Cutter
⅜″ Dia.

Pro Combination
(Industrial Grade)
½″ & ¾″ Dia. Sleeves

Hole Cutter
½″ Dia.

Industrial Head
¾″ & ¾″ Dia. Sleeves

Hole Cutter
⅝″ Dia.

Precision Head
⅜″ Dia.

Hole Cutter
¾″ Dia.

Micro Head
¼″ Dia.

Tiffany Head
¾″ Angled

Fig. 4–66 Some different router-grozzing heads from the Glasscrafter Company. (Courtesy: Kindig Enterprises)

Fig. 4–67 Glastar's diamond heads include standard 100 grit and extra smooth 220 grit.

Delrin, a tough industrial plastic, solves this problem.

Wire Brushes

Wire brushes are not to be confused with flux brushes. They have a stiff copper-bristled, fairly wide scrubbing area and are used to scrub the oxidized surface off lead prior to soldering a joint. Their use is especially advised where joints have been allowed to sit for some weeks prior to soldering. The more oxidation formed on the

Fig. 4–68 *A newer model grinder from Glastar. On top is a grooved Delrin plate that supports the glass during grinding and prevents scratching. The plate snaps into place, which makes cleaning easy. A waterproof plastic on-off switch prevents electric shocks.*

Fig. 4–70 *An attachment that enables accurate grinding.*

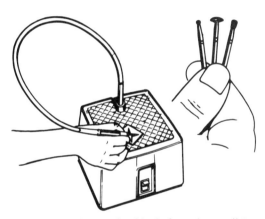

Fig. 4–71 *Glastar's flexible shaft attaches to all its glass grinders. This ancillary tool is especially useful for engraving on glass. Three diamond-plated tools for grinding and engraving come in a kit: an inverted cone, a ball, and a disc.*

Fig. 4–69 *Glastar's "Starlet" performs as well as the larger, more costly glass grinders, even Glastar's G-4 model with the 1" head. It has two diamond heads—⅝" and ¼". Supporting the glass is a grooved Delrin top plate.*

The 3,400-rpm motor is not so powerful as that of the larger model, but it grinds glass swiftly and efficiently.

Fig. 4–72 *Wire brushes. Make sure the bristles aren't too rough for the lead.*

surface of the lead, the more difficult a time you will have getting the solder to "take." Employing this sort of brush with a little elbow grease cuts the frustration factor considerably. Don't get a brush with tough steel bristles. This will scratch the glass and probably tear the lead away from it. An instrument more in the nature of a heavy suede brush will do. A few sweeping back-and-forth motions should give a nice shiny surface to the lead, which will then take the solder well.

If you have a large window to do, and a number of oxidized lead joints, you could use a round brush with a central axle that fits into an electric hand drill.

These brushes should be used with reasonable control, and if you get a soft enough one, it will not mar the glass. A little cleaning and polishing powder placed over the glass before brushing will clean off oxidation even more speedily. Be sure when using an electric drill that the machine doesn't go out of control.

Marking Pencils

Crayons for marking on glass come in various colors, but white, red, and black are the most popular. Marking pencil can be

Fig. 4–73 *Two types of marking pencils. Those on the left have a string that unravels the crayon; those on the right have a twist-top that projects the crayon from the end.*

used to calculate the cuts when laying out a pattern on a piece of glass. They are also useful in marking an edge for trimming. Never use them in place of a paper pattern, however, and always clean the pencil marks off any glass pieces to be fired in the kiln; such marks will bake right into the glass. If you are making a large piece such as a window with many pieces, mark each piece of glass by number with your pencil to correspond to its paper pattern.

Pattern, Abrasive, and Kraft Papers

Pattern paper is a heavy-duty paper not as thick as moderate cardboard. This dimension is critical. The paper must allow for a certain amount of wear and tear when used as a pattern, yet be thin enough so that the glass-cutter wheel can ride along its side without being raised from the glass surface. Use white or a light color paper to contrast with the glass. The shirt-backing cardboard from laundries is usually too thick and may not allow you to follow its outline with the glass cutter, since it prevents the wheel from scoring effectively. Pattern paper, when cut with a pattern knife or pattern scissors, should leave a sharp border. Ordinary cardboard tends to fray. Be as accurate as possible in pattern cutting; any inaccuracy here will lead to disproportionate pieces.

Kraft paper is a rugged brown wrapping paper that artists use for making an original drawing, or cartoon. This cartoon will be with you throughout the course of your project and will be subject to nail holes, spilled flux, and hot solder. Kraft paper holds up well through it all, whereas a lesser strength paper may disintegrate, guidelines and all.

Abrasive paper is a special type of wet-dry sanding cloth that will take rough edges off glass pieces if you do not have a grinder. It is best used wet. Dip it in water, and place the glass on the worktable, allowing the surface to be sanded to extend over the tabletop. Abrasive paper works surprisingly rapidly, and it will last indefinitely if you let it dry after use and shake out the glass dust. Or rinse it out in running water to get rid of the glass dust. Using abrasive paper dry considerably shortens its lifespan.

Putty

Stained-glass windows or panels that will be exposed to the weather, or that are larger than one square foot, should be puttied. This weatherproofs the work and adds strength by supporting the glass within the lead cames. Linseed oil putty is preferred because it is freely workable, and tends to harden as the linseed oil evaporates. It is either white or black.

The Slab-Glass Wedge and Hammer

Slab glass, also called *dalles*, usually measures 8″ × 12″ with a thickness of 1″. Dalles are too thick to be leaded or foiled as made. They can be used as small pieces or "chunks" of unequal sizes and shapes, which then furnish enough surface to be foiled into a stained glass object for a three-dimensional or other unusual effect.

Dalles may be embedded in cement or epoxy in heavy walls or large embrasures. They are rarely used full size, and are shaped with a slab-glass wedge. The wedge is placed underneath the piece of glass below the cut line. The glass is tapped directly above the wedge with a slab glass hammer, and the force of the tap carries through the glass to the sharp edge of the wedge beneath and fractures cleanly. The hammer comes in small and large and is shaped like a mason's hammer. It comes to a sharp angle at either side of the head; thus the force of the blow is concentrated

Fig. 4–75 *Some glass "chunks" broken with the hammer-and-wedge technique along straight lines and one showing facets along a curved line. "Dalles" can also be sawed with a glass bandsaw.*

Fig. 4–74 *Slab glass wedge embedded by its handle in a lead form and a wood block for support*

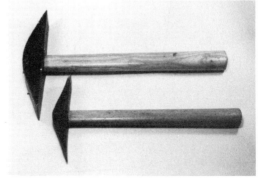

Fig. 4–76 *Two sizes of slab-glass hammers.*

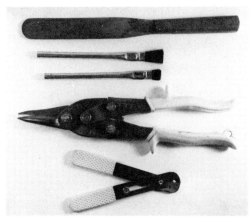

Fig. 4–77 Miscellaneous tools. Top: *spatula for mixing paint and a pair of "acid" brushes for flux. The top brush shows the length of bristle as it comes; the bottom shows a trimmed brush, ready to use. Trimming the bristles makes them stiffer and facilitates scrubbing the flux into the lead or copper surface to be soldered.* Center: *all-purpose metal cutting pliers.* Bottom: *wire strippers, good for wiring stained-glass lamps.*

into a narrow line, allowing for a fairly gentle tap to be highly effective at the point of impact.

Antiquing Patina

Antiquing patina is a copper sulphate solution that changes soldered joints from a bright, shiny surface to a coppery, aged look. It will not work directly on the lead came; the chemical reaction occurs only in the presence of tin. Therefore, if you want to antique an entire length of came, you must "tin" the entire length of lead. Antiquing solution works best when it is warm, or if the joint is warm, such as a freshly soldered one. It will work cold, but in a slower fashion. Either way, it should be rubbed on with a flux brush, wiped off, and then reapplied until the desired color is achieved. Don't use the same brush both for flux and antiquing; the antiquing solution will contaminate the flux and interfere with its activity.

Miscellaneous Tools

"Acid" brushes are cheap and are the best way of spreading flux onto a joint. These look like library "paste" brushes. You may

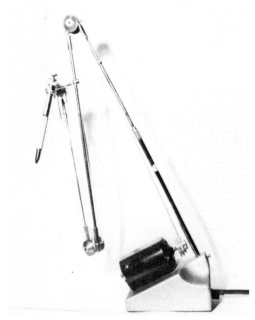

Fig. 4–78 A dental drill complete with handpiece is a delight for grinding and polishing. Often these can be purchased used. A foot switch is handy to control the rpm's.

Fig. 4–79 The ubiquitous foot switch for use with various machines. It allows control of the machine without taking a hand away from the working surface. With variable-speed machines, foot pressure may slow down or speed up the drive.

also need all-purpose metal cutting shears. A spatula for mixing paint and a pair of wire strippers for wiring stained-glass lampshades are items that may seem at different ends of the creative pole, but they are both tools that will make your creative life a lot easier. Another, less expected item is a dental drill. You may do work with metals and plastics ancillary to glass, and these materials require grinding, poking, and scoring. A dental drill is the tool to accomplish this. These units are available from dental supply houses. You do not need the entire unit with the seat and the sink; just the table-based drill is sufficient.

5
Baubles, Bangles, and Beads

GLASS JEWELS

Glass jewels can be used to add character to objects, point up a whimsical creation, or brighten a window. As such, they serve as punctuation marks in the grammar of stained-glass design. Jewels are made from molten glass that has been pressed into three-dimensional form. Many glass jewels were made by the Heidt Company of Brooklyn and were known as "Heidt jewels." The end of a solid colored glass rod was heated to molten state in a beehive oven, then quickly placed into a Swedish steel mold press. The glass jewel was pressed out, placed in a lehr, and allowed to cool slowly. Most of these old molds have been lost to us, but if you can find these jewels, they will add a charming, antique look to your design.

Using old as well as new jewels in abstract and Victorian windows can dramatically emphasize and heighten the effect of the piece. Jewels also may be used in free-form hanging objects as the central portion of a glass arrangement and as intriguing mobiles.

Jewels are much in demand, particularly reds, golds, and yellows. We have found old stained-glass windows in antique shops that, even though mistreated over the years, still yielded up a handful of old jewels. New jewels, often clearer in color than the older ones and of more modern design, are inexpensive and provide lovely ornamental fillips to a creation.

ROUNDELS AND "BOTTLE BOTTOMS"

Roundels are circles of glass that have been hand-spun or pressed by machine. They come in most colors and in sizes from 2″ up to 12″ or even larger. It is not always easy to tell the difference between a spun and a pressed roundel. Both types are beautiful, and both are equally effective used within panels or free-form mobiles, or even just leaded up as is and hung. A spun roundel usually contains more whirls of color within it than one that is pressed by machine. These whirls give a soft, beguiling appearance that, added to its geometric shape, makes the roundel one of the more popular stained-glass jewels. Since roundels come with a rounded edge, they are not difficult to lead. But too narrow a lead will prevent the rounded flange from going into it. Designing a window or panel with roundels is a tricky task because it's easy to get carried away and overdo it. These colorful circles may then take over the figuration of the window, overwhelming rather than intriguing the eye.

Roundels are fairly expensive, but you can make your own. Glass circles that resemble roundels are available, and they also may have swirls of color within them. These are "bottle bottoms"—bottoms of cylinders that are cut away after the manufacture of stained glass sheets. These can be used as decorative pieces. They are usually irregular in shape with rough edges. You may have to trim them before incorporat-

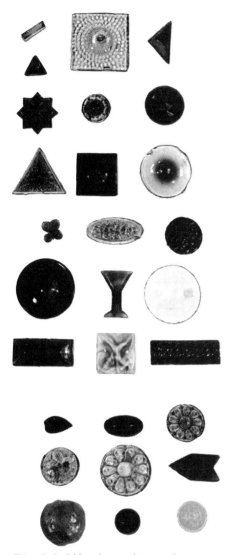

Fig. 5-1 Old and new glass jewels.

Fig. 5-2 Corner jewels and apples.

Fig. 5-3 To make jewels, molten glass is pressed into a mold. The jewels are then cut apart, usually with a glass bandsaw, after they have cooled. Shown are some fragments of jewel complexes, which may consist of a dozen or so similar jewels.

ing them into a design. Even so, the work is worth the effort, for they are impressive, and their effects often equal those of roundels. Added to this is their comparative cheapness.

Bottle bottoms can be opalescent or clear, just as roundels and are about 8″ in diameter. They can be cut across the center fairly easily, broken into two halves, and then leaded into abstract free forms.

MILLEFIORE

Millefiore are short multicolored cylinders, also known as Venetian beads or tube beads. Peeking down at a random few seen on end is like looking at a cluster of dimin-

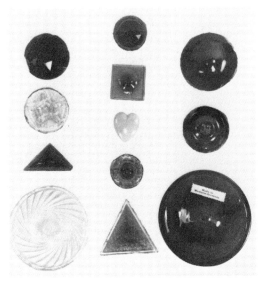

Fig. 5–4 Glass jewels and roundels.

Fig. 5–6 An effective use of roundels and odd jewels within a new window. Courtesy: Edward Martin.

Fig. 5–5 Larger roundels of different colors.

Fig. 5–7 A decorative roundel focal piece made from a circle of opalescent white glass decorated with a flower design. This glass, striking in itself, picks up additional vivacity in the light. Such designs can be handpointed or silk-screened and then fired in. (Courtesy: D and D Glassworks, Lake Geneva, Wisconsin)

utive pizza pies. Designs vary from stars to fleur de lis, to concentric rings of color. When these beads are heated in a kiln, each flattens into a circle of multicolor whirls. When a bead is placed on top of a piece of glass and heat is applied, it melts into the glass base and forms a technicolor ink blot. Millefiore do not have to be heated to be effective. Used as eyes for small glass animals or grouped in patterns and glued in abstract designs, they form unusual three-dimensional effects with two-dimensional free-form glass mobiles. While millefiore are fairly expensive, a few will go a long way.

GLASS GLOBS
Glass globs are transparent or opaque marblelike humps of solid glass in various

Fig. 5–8 *Glass circles fired into roses in the kiln. A leaf is attached to the one in upper left. You could use different colors of glass here, from dark red to clear.*

Fig. 5–10 *These flower-bud roundels started as small circles that were then draped over or sunk into molds. They have been glued together to form an abstract bouquet.*

Fig. 5–9 *Two rose molds on the left, and on the right are two roses of opalescent white glass that have been taken out of the molds.*

colors and shapes. Unlike some baubles, they are not individually molded but produced in free-form fashion. While they are not as instantly captivating as millefiore, they have a character of their own, and they can be foiled, leaded, or glued to enhance a creation.

Glass globs usually have one fairly flat

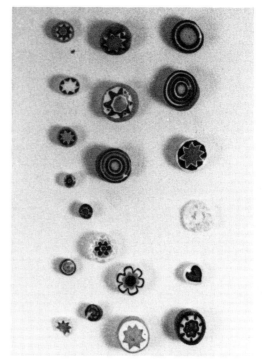

Fig. 5–11 *Millefiore or Venetian tube glass viewed on end.*

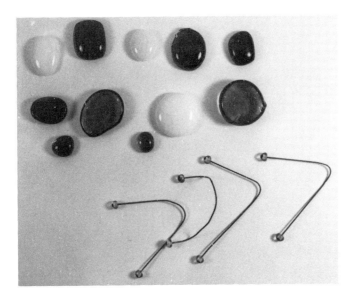

Fig. 5–12 *Glass globs, some showing the flat undersurface. At the bottom are some glass eyes on wire stalks.*

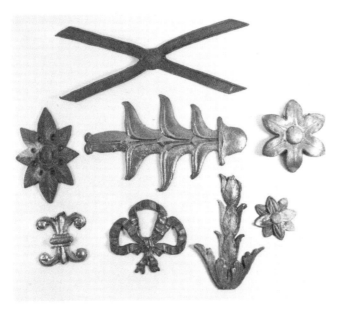

Fig. 5–13 *Lead casts that can be used for decorations within windows or panels. These are mostly old castings, but with the amount of scrap lead you will be accumulating you will be able to melt your own castings using a plaster-of-paris mold. It's fun.*

surface for applying glue. This surface is where the glob itself rested while it was being formed in the kiln. Occasionally you will find twinned globs or globs of interesting deformities among a particular batch. Such unusual configurations may themselves be put to imaginative use.

Globs can be used as eyes, the petals of flowers, decoration for glassware, bottles, or jars, to make candleholders, or as lamp ornaments. If you have enough different sizes and colors, you can create a mosaic effect. Spaces between may be grouted or filled with liquid lead or glued with special glues that dry to a transparent, rapid finish and will not shrink. Beware of

Fig. 5–14 *Hanging owl, 10″ × 6″. The eyes are bottle bottoms cut with a carborundum blade.*

the general all-purpose hardware store glue which will lose its holding power as it dries.

Glass globs are extensively used in stained-glass jewelry (see Chapter 16).

METALLIC EMBROIDERY

Copper sheeting can be used to cut leaves, wings, or other filigree items. This material is so malleable that designs may be embossed on it with ease, and it solders beautifully. The proper thickness also cuts easily with an ordinary pair of scissors. Brass is another interesting entity. While somewhat more difficult to work with than copper, it will impart more rigidity, and as an axial skeleton for a glass sculpture, it's second only to galvanized steel.

Some workers use parts of wire hangers for skeletal structures, such as flower stems or backbones of animals, which must stand to a certain height. Using metal or wire hangers for this purpose involves a certain amount of fuss, since the metal must first be sanded clean of paint and then fluxed vigorously with an inorganic acid

flux (such as hydrochloric acid in glycerin) and then tinned. Tinning is impossible unless a strong flux is used because the solder will roll off the metal. After tinning and soldering, the hanger becomes a convenient stem, wand, spike, handle, or body in its new incarnation.

Galvanized steel bars are used for bracing windows that need more strength than lead and putty can provide. Older windows were braced with ungalvanized steel. Since steel cannot be soldered, copper loops were wound around these bars at juncture areas and these loops were then soldered to the leads. Coating the bracing rods with zinc did more than make the bar itself solderable. In the process, the rod became a metal strap, averaging ½″ wide by ⅛″ thick. It is flexible and, unlike the rod, can be made to conform to the design. Larger spans involving heavier areas take a heavier size.

Pieces of galvanized steel scraps cut to size make excellent crossbars for the tops of lanterns to support the underlying socket and the hanging ring above. If you want to try this, be sure to get a wide enough piece of metal to allow for the hole you must drill through it for the socket. If you don't want to go to the trouble of drilling through one of these metal straps, cut two of them to size, leaving room between them for the socket nipple, and rely on the pressure of the hanging ring to maintain stability.

Zinc cames are also used in stained-glass work, but although they have flexibility, they cannot follow a curve readily. For outside edges, where rigidity is a must, they do a good job. They're also used in long windows or panels for straight side-to-side supports, instead of bracing rods. The design of the window must allow for them. They are generally H cames with wide channels and will nicely accommodate English streaky or thick French glass. The width of the channels enables even foiled glass to be tipped forward or backward and then fixed against the zinc came with solder for an off-center effect.

GLASS RODS

Glass rods are available in odd sizes and thicknesses. They can be cut with a glass cutter by nicking the rod and breaking it or by sawing through a thick rod with a carborundum blade fitted in any hacksaw handle. Glass rods can be melted in the kiln to interesting shapes and designs (the heat must go to 1800°F, since you are dealing with a solid glass core), and they may also be used for support, especially for mobiles. Fishline, which is all but invisible, can be purchased in any sporting-goods store to bear the mobile, and it can be attached to the proper balancing point on the glass rod by making a deep score around the rod at that area and wrapping the fishline into the groove. To smooth the ends of cut rods, polish with wet abrasive paper.

BOTTLES

Bottles do not have to be molded in a kiln to be used in stained-glass work. The bottoms of many wine and beer bottles, for instance, can gain a life of their own as decorative items. Not only the bottoms but also the sides of bottles because of their ready curvature, are natural for a boat's sails or any object requiring a bend. Even the tops of bottles can be strung together as wind chimes. Bottles can be cut with little difficulty using a hot wire or a carborundum blade in a hacksaw handle.

Electric bottle cutters are still available from the bottle-cutting craze of a few years ago. Here an electrically heated wire is wrapped around the bottle and the bottle put into cold water. It breaks apart neatly. The carborundum blade takes longer to do the job, with more work on your part, but it is equally effective.

One caution: Cutting bottles with a hacksaw blade can be tricky at first because of the round shape. Hold the bottle securely. Wear a glove, at least at first. Once you get used to handling the curved surface, you will find that bottle cutting, like glass cutting, requires nothing more than common sense to avoid injury.

Pirate Window.

Portfolio / Anita Isenberg

Roundel design.

Porthole.

Victorian transom.

Greek Baring Gifts.

Bird of Prey.

Overlaid Window; owl overlay courtesy Ed Hoy Co.

Lamp, completely restored from existing frame.

Detail of geometric-pattern shutters; opalescent glass with center break.

Diamond window.

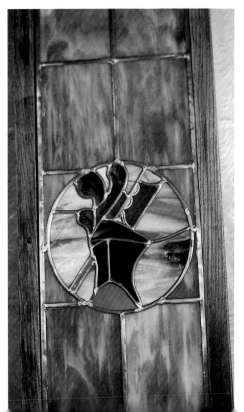

Detail of a room divider: rectangular plays on hot colors.

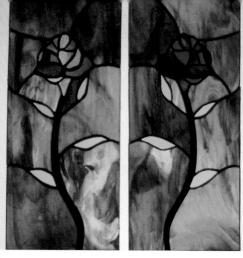  

Shutter panels.

Flower panel, demonstrating etching, painting, and use of glass color for effect.

Victorian panel.

Dutch Boy: *a scene in two panels.*

When one speaks of artistry, more than likely what one is really describing is a highly advanced degree of technical achievement. True artistry—that of a Shakespeare, a da Vinci, a Beethoven—is a modality beyond reasonable expectation either in ourselves or in others. On the other hand, technique has its own purity— and it has the additional advantage of being in reach, given adequate instructions and reasonable attention.

R. H. NEITERLUZ,
Qualifying the Fine Arts

PROCEDURES

II

6
The Art of Scoring and Breaking Glass

Cutting glass is different from anything you may have attempted in the crafts field. Yet anyone can cut glass—and there is really no right way or wrong way to do it. There is a more efficient and a less efficient way, but individual preference often develops individual efficiency, especially since so many different types of glass cutters are now available. We emphasize our own method because we have found that it allows the most hand flexibility, as well as being a good starting point so that you can go on to use any other cutter and any other method.

Glass cutting requires technique, just as playing the piano requires technique. The hand positions in cutting may seem awkward at first, but you will be surprised at how rapidly they will become second nature. The technique for cutting glass with a hand cutter is simple. You will need only minimal practice to develop a feel for scoring and breaking out the glass.

Paradoxically, the primary objective in glass cutting is to keep from breaking the glass. You must make a deep enough score to produce the run, or fissure, but not so deep that the cut edges are nicked and chipped. A nicked or chipped edge is a weak edge, and it may crumble.

SCORING THE GLASS

Choosing a Glass Cutter
The basic principles of cutting glass apply to all glass cutters. For illustration, we will use Fletcher cutters in this chapter. The choice of a cutter is an all-important first step, although initially almost any cutter will feel awkward in your hand. Even with cutters made by the same company, the choice remains, since some companies make a number of different cutters for different purposes (see Chapter 4.)

If you attempt to cut opalescent glass with a soft-glass cutter, you will have to use more pressure and more labor than if you chose the cutter meant for such a glass. And even at that you may get a poor cut. Cutters are labeled according to their type of wheel. For general, all-purpose cutting, a carbide cutter is best. This cutter will do equally well on opalescent as on cathedral, on plate glass as on window glass, and you need not worry about picking up the wrong cutter for the wrong piece of glass. Carbide cutters are expensive, and you may not wish to invest in one immediately. On the other hand, stay away from dime-store glass cutters. Tbey are extremely frustrating for stained glass. Get a reputable cutter, and make sure your choice is guided by the type of glass you are going to cut.

The Fissure
A glass cutter does not cut glass in the sense of shearing or sawing. Rather, it is a *force* generator. By rolling over the glass surface, the cutting wheel provides a minute fracture, called the fissure. A good cut

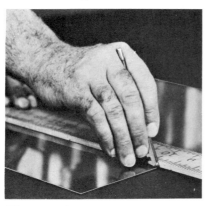

Fig. 6–1 The recommended way to hold the cutter. (Courtesy: Fletcher Company)

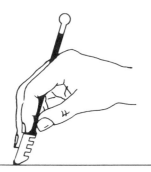

Fig. 6–2 Side view of the correct way to hold the cutter.

Fig. 6–3 An example of poor positioning for cutting. The elbow resting on the table limits wrist mobility. The glass cutter is slanted so the wheel will not meet the glass at the proper angle.

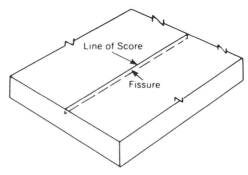

Fig. 6–4 The fissure runs from edge to edge of the glass.

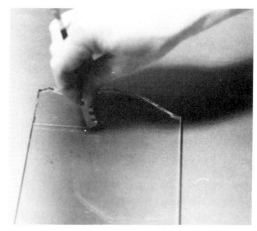

Fig. 6–5 Scoring the glass. Note that the fissure begins directly at the upper edge of the glass.

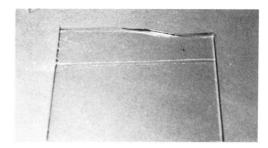

Fig. 6–6 The fissure ends directly at the lower edge.

edge can be attained at break out only if the wheel made a proper fissure.

Interestingly enough, the fissure that yields a clean, strong edge is practically invisible on the glass surface. It can be seen only by looking *into* the glass. The good fissure will reflect light and appear as a continuous narrow band of light. No glass chips or glass dust should appear on the surface if a proper fissure is made. If the surface is not clean and if the score is a white gritty line, you have made a gouge or scratch, not a true fissure. A sheet of glass can be broken out along a gouge or scratch, but the edge will be chipped and weak. Such an edge should be ground or belted to remove the nicks and avoid the almost certain fracturing of the glass.

The Table Surface

An important consideration in cutting glass is your work surface. It should be hard, flat, and clean and covered with an easily cleaned resilient material such as a sheet of wrapping paper. A permanent cover could be made of felt, but the felt should be not more than 1/16" thick. A thicker resilient cover or a deflecting surface hampers good cutting. A clean surface is vital. The height of the table is also important from the standpoint of comfort. You must be able to make the score comfortably without having to strain or change position.

Holding the Cutter

The cutter can be held in any number of ways—grip it in the fist, poise it like a pen, grasp it with grozzing teeth uppermost, squeeze it just above the wheel like a tube of toothpaste, or even grab it with both hands. All these methods will allow you to score glass. The idea, however, is to score glass that follows a pattern.

The first rule in learning to cut glass is hand position. Unless you learn to hold the cutter efficiently, you will have an awkward time cutting to pattern. To make up for a lack of wrist mobility, you will have

to contort your body. The proper hand position will let you get from one section of glass to another without having to take the cutter away from the surface or twisting your body. The recommended way to hold the cutter is shown in Figure 6–2. Place the handle between the first and second fingers as shown. The thumb supports the cutter on the underside. Use a free wrist motion. To prevent a blister, make sure the handle is not leaning backwards against the web of your fingers. In fact, the cutter should not be leaning backwards at all. It should be straight up and down or even tipped slightly forward. The wrist should be able to move up and down or side to side with ease. Pressure should be exerted primarily from the shoulder. Pressure from the wrist is a gradually tiring process and may give you a stiff joint. Let

Fig. 6–7 *Cutting with the diamond. The grasp is similar to that used with a regular cutter.*

Fig. 6–8 *Guiding the cutter with both hands is not recommended.*

The Art of Scoring and Breaking Glass **117**

the weight of your body apply pressure to the cutter through your shoulder, almost as though you were leaning on the cutting wheel. The grozzing teeth should be pointed down toward the glass surface. It is possible to cut with the grozzing teeth up, but this makes the cutter top heavy and throws it off balance, making it just one more thing for your fingers to fight.

Cutting Stance

If you're right-handed, stand with your left foot slightly forward and your right foot turned not quite at right angles to it. This will shift your balance toward your right arm, which is where you want your cutting strength. It also angles your body so that you are not pulling the cutter toward your stomach. The free space allows your wrist to move smoothly from the initial point of the cut to the end of the cut line. If you are left-handed, reverse this stance.

If you cut glass sitting down, you can't apply your body weight in the same way. You will have to use more wrist pressure, which can be tiring, and it's awkward to follow a pattern as accurately as when standing. If possible stand up to cut glass. If you must sit, you will have to experiment to find the most effective way to coordinate your weight and balance.

The Glass Surface

We score glass by pulling the cutter toward us. But it is not critical how the cutter is held, or whether it is pushed or pulled. The most convenient and comfortable grip and direction is always the best, providing that (1) the glass surface along the cut line is clean before the score is made, and (2) that the wheel rolls freely and is in direct contact with the glass to develop the proper fissure.

If the glass is dusty or dirty, much of the energy required to make the fissure will be lost. An irregular fissure or a skipped fissure will then be made, resulting in chipped and weak edges at the break out. So any lint, dust, or other debris that

accumulates so readily in a working area should be cleaned off the glass. Use a cleaner that will not leave a residue on the surface and make it slippery; we use soap and water, rinse, then wipe the glass dry with crumpled newspaper.

Manufacturers often coat glass with a special powder to protect it during shipment. This must be removed from the line of cut to prevent the cutting wheel from picking it up. Routine cleaning of the glass surface also removes the powder.

Before scoring the glass, be sure that the glasscutter wheel slot is clean and that the wheel rolls freely without drag. The wheel axle must be lubricated.

Which Side to Cut?

Before scoring the glass, examine it carefully to make sure that you are cutting on the right side. Unlike window glass, some stained glass has a right and a wrong cutting side. Obviously it's easy to tell the right side of granite-backed or pebbled stained-glass. With all glass, the rule is that the smoother side is usually best for cutting, but it is sometimes difficult to decide *which* side is the smoother. To determine this, make a small score on each side of the glass before making any major cut. On sheets of flashed stained glass, where one color is laid on top of another, cut on the white or under-color, side. Hold the glass on end up to the light so that you can see the distribution of the layers of color. If you still cannot tell, chip away a small corner to see which side contains the color and which one is uncoated. Cut on the un-coated side.

We use the terms *coated* and *uncoated* because flashed glass is not invariably a color placed on a white or clear surface. Red could be flashed on yellow, for instance. In this case, the yellow side might be the best cutting side.

Cutting Force and Speed

The force applied to the cutter is dependent on the wheel angle and the condition of the wheel. Regardless of the wheel angle, the maximum force that can be applied is easily defined: It is the greatest force that can be used without crushing the glass surface. When the score becomes a white gritty line, or if chips and glass dust are created, you have exceeded the maximum force. The resulting score line is a gouge, not a fissure. A good rule is that the best score is clean of glass chips and barely visible when looking at the glass surface.

Some practice is required to get the feel of applying the maximum cutting force without crushing. It is essential to maintain this force uniformly throughout the full length of the score. If the force varies, the depth of the fissure will vary and affect the quality of the break. When scoring and applying this maximum noncrushing force, make sure that the score is made continuously until the wheel runs off the edge of the glass. Forget the edge of the glass. If you think about the edge of the glass as you approach it, you will unconsciously vary the force and speed of the scoring stroke.

The depth of fissure is directly affected by the speed of the cut. The faster the wheel rolls, the deeper the fissure will be. But there is an inverse relation between force and speed. As the speed is increased, the force must be decreased to avoid crushing and gouging. Generally, the faster the score (below maximum noncrushing force), the better the cut. In hand-cutting, speed is not as critical as in machine cutting. What is important is that the speed be maintained uniformly throughout the cut until the wheel drops off the edge of the glass. If a good breakout is not achieved, you must make a new score with some increase in force. *Never* retrace the line of cut. A score can be made only once. Retracing creates a gouge and damages the wheel of the cutter.

Cutting Wheels

Cutting wheels are honed to various angles *(see Fig. 6–9)*. The recommendations are reliable if the described techniques are ap-

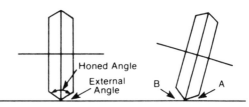

Fig. 6–9 *Proper contact of the wheel against the glass. Wheels are honed to various angles to score various types of glass. A and B show the tilt of the wheel.*

plied. Standard cutters offered in most hardware stores have wheels honed to 120 or 124 degrees. This is a good angle for glass ranging in thickness from .063 to .093 inches.

While flaking of the glass during a score can occur with any wheel, sharp-angled wheels (under 120 degrees) are more likely to cause this. Flaking can be delayed by wiping the area of the score line with a cloth dampened with kerosene or light oil. It is important to try to avoid the incidence of flaking during scoring because flaking will affect the quality of the fissure. Flaking can lead to chips when the breakout is made.

To determine the best wheel angle to use for a specific glass, start with any cutter, say with a standard 120-degree wheel. Then score the glass, using the maximum noncrushing force. If you are cutting thin glass and the wheel punctures it, switch to a sharper-angled wheel. The maximum noncrushing force will be less. If the score seems right but a good breakout does not result, use a higher-angled wheel. Here the maximum noncrushing force will be greater, but a deeper fissure will be made.

Whenever scoring, maintain the verticality of the cutting wheel. The cutter should be held straight up and down. Any tilt of the cutting wheel will affect the quality of the score. In Figure 6–9, the wheel tilt with a high-angled wheel is external angle A. The wheel tilt of a sharper wheel is external angle B. The applied force is insufficient for one side (A) and excessive for the other side (B). This results in gouging and a weak edge.

Cutting Oil

A special cutting oil is available that helps give more effective score lines. Brushed over the projected line of cut with a soft brush, it cleans the glass and helps to lubricate the surface as the wheel travels over it, thus minimizing the variables of the scoring process. The residue from the cutting oil will have to be removed before foiling or leading the glass. A thin water line over glass that has been thoroughly cleaned will give much the same effect as cutting oil. But essentially, if the glass surface is clean, you should be able to make precise score lines with the glass cutter alone, so long as you are using the correct wheel for the type of glass.

Summary on Scoring Glass

1. Use a good cutter that you feel comfortable with. Don't worry about initial awkwardness.

2. Have a flat, firm support for the glass. This is particularly necessary for some antique sheets, which may not lie flat. You will have to allow for the rock of the glass as you score, so your scoring will of necessity be slower than usual. Try to keep your speed constant; even after getting over the rocky area, do not speed up.

3. Make sure the glass is clean and that no glass crumbs from prior cuttings are on the table surface or embedded in the felt mat. If you use a mat, shake it vigorously before each scoring. Leftover tiny pieces of glass will act as levers to shatter the glass you are working on. Worse, they can also cut you.

4. To make a straight cut, draw the cutter along a straightedge once and only once. Never go over a score line. If the score line wavers or is otherwise unsatisfactory, do not try to correct it. Make another one some distance away.

5. Start a cut at the top edge of glass and allow the cut to run off the bottom edge—or vice versa. Do not let the cutter run off the glass edge with such force that it breaks the glass or penetrates the table-

top. The cutter should roll, not bounce, off the glass edge.

6. You may start a cut from slightly below the top glass edge, run it off the bottom edge, then go back, place your cutter wheel at the point where the score begins, and push backwards and off the top edge.

7. Use only enough pressure to make the score. This takes practice. If small slivers of glass begin to shower from your score line, you are exerting excess force. If the cutter is making no mark, you are not fissuring the glass.

8. The cutter should move along the glass evenly and not waver from side to side. If your handle wobbles, it means the cutting wheel is not plowing a precise groove. This will give a ragged break.

9. It is not the pressure of your wrist that counts, but the pressure of your shoulder and body. The pressure will also be guided by your cutting speed.

10. Thickness or thinness of the glass does not have a relationship to the amount of pressure needed to make a score but rather to the angle of the glass-cutter wheel. With the proper wheel angle for the proper glass, pressure can be mostly constant. If you are not using the proper wheel angle, certain glasses, particularly opalescents, will require more scoring pressure than other types of stained glass. Cutting a thin antique tint ($\frac{1}{16}''$ or less) or a thick English streaky, some portions of which can go over $\frac{1}{4}''$, is more a matter of the proper cutter than the proper force. Using the right cutter with the right wheel angle is the secret to good cutting.

11. You can lubricate the score line if you are having difficulty scoring.

12. For safety's sake, break each score line as you make it and before making another. Scoring a piece of glass weakens it. Don't allow it to break on its own.

BREAKING THE SCORE

The score can be broken in a number of ways, and each has its virtues, depending on the size and type of glass as well as the type of score—whether it be a straight line, outside curve, or inside curve.

The Tapping Method

Tapping the glass is usually done (and taught) incorrectly. There is only *one* right way to do it, and that is to hold the glass securely, both sides of the score between the fingers, and with score line uppermost, tap along its length from the bottom *(Figs. 6–11 and 6–12)*.

Glass is usually broken from the bottom opposite to the score line, rarely from the top. Tap with the ball of a ball-ended glass cutter. But don't swing it at the glass as though it were a wrecking ball or you may risk a splinter in the eye. It isn't nec-essary to tap *that* hard. The ball will give an inordinate force to a moderate tap. Furthermore, the ball should not be swung wildly. Balance the glass cutter in your hand and guide the ball with your finger against the handle. The object is not to smash the score, but to "run it"—to fracture the initial score line further through the surface of the glass.

As you tap along, hold the glass up to the light to see if the score is "running." You should see a deepening line appear and progress along the length of the score line. Once this line reaches the end of the score line, you can snap the glass by hand. Many beginners think that tapping alone will run

Fig. 6–12 Tapping a large piece of glass. The sheet is supported on the tabletop and one hand holds the scored pieces from separating too abruptly. This procedure takes practice.

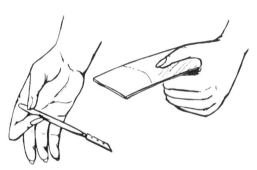

Fig. 6–10 Wrong way to tap a score. The glass cutter is being swung wildly, and the piece of glass is supported on only one side of the score line.

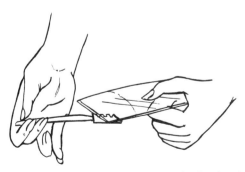

Fig. 6–11 The wrong way to tap. As the glass is struck, it will move upwards with the blow and most of the sharp force will be lost.

Fig. 6–13 The tapping method. A ball-ended cutter is tapped against the underside of the score line. Support is furnished by the fingers as well as the tapping hand to the glass on both sides of the score line. The ball is guided by the third finger from below in short, sharp taps.

the score, and often they tap recklessly, holding the glass by one edge until the pieces separate, one or both perhaps dropping to the floor. If you hold both pieces securely, neither will fall, and you will save yourself a lot of glass and a lot of grief.

Tapping need not always be done with the ball-ended cutter. Some workers tap with the grozzing teeth of the glass cutter. This furnishes less force and may be used where fragile tapping is required, such as on thin, delicate glass with tricky cuts. If you are scoring on a large area tapping is not recommended at all. It's dangerous to try to support large pieces of glass with one hand while tapping with the other.

Fig. 6–14 *The pieces of glass have separated, but are still firmly supported above and below.*

Fig. 6–15 *A score "running" and properly held across both sides of the line. As a safety measure, never tap and run a score line on a piece of glass you have used to practice scoring. The glass can shatter along any of these scores from the force of previous tapping.*

Their weight may cause them to separate abruptly, taking you by surprise. The tapping causes the surfaces to vibrate, like ripples in a pond, and the run line will wander erratically on and off the score line, giving a less than satisfactory break.

Tapping is overemphasized in beginning classes and taught badly in the bargain. One short, sharp tap against a well-supported score line is worth hours of timid pecks or exasperated whacks.

The Fulcrum Method

The fulcrum method is useful on moderate to large pieces of glass where a straight line or a gentle curve is scored. Once the score is made, the piece of glass is lifted on one end, and about ¼″ of the fulcrum, such as the straight end of a glass cutter, is placed directly beneath the score line. The glass is then pressed down by hand on either side of the score. The score should run true across the length of the glass.

Do not use a ball-ended cutter as a fulcrum. It is too thick and will transmit too

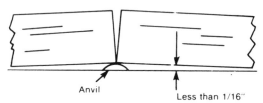

Fig. 6–16 *The fulcrum method: Breakout at a minimum angle using a thin fulcrum, or anvil, beneath the score line. The break is clean.*

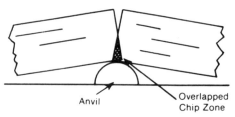

Fig. 6–17 *The fulcrum method: Breakout at an excessive angle using too thick a fulcrum or anvil beneath the score line. The back edges of glass crumple against one another, and the break line is chipped.*

much pressure. For long scores, a thinner fulcrum may be necessary to minimize the force. A leading nail or straightened paper clip can do the trick. Occasionally with this method you may hear a satisfactory crack only to discover that the score has not run all the way across. Turn the glass carefully or reposition your fulcrum and follow the same procedure on the opposite end of the score line. This should complete the job.

No method is foolproof. You may find after placing the fulcrum and pressing with care that the glass self-destructs. Now you have many small pieces for suncatchers. What happened? You may have pressed too hard, providing too much tension. The fulcrum may have been inserted too far under the score. The scoring could have been insufficient for the particular glass, or the glass may have contained an invisible crack. In addition, the fulcrum could be too thick, or it may have been the glass itself. Stained glass sometimes has a mind of its own, and it can work against you. When this happens, it's time to take a break rather than trying to make one.

Breaking by Hand

To break out a piece of glass by hand, hold it with your thumbs on either side of the score line. Keep your other fingers folded into your palms, away from sharp edges. The pressure during the breaking process is out and down, almost a rolling of the knuckles of one hand against those of the other. If the glass just won't break, don't try to force it. You still have other options.

The Tabletop Method

Place the glass over the edge of the table until the score line is parallel to the table

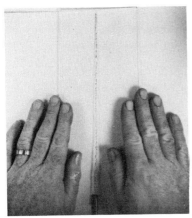

Fig. 6–18 The fulcrum method: The fulcrum, the back of a glass cutter, appears at the bottom. Pressure is applied by the hands equidistant from the score line.

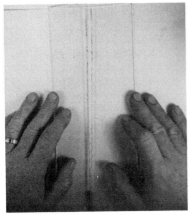

Fig. 6–19 The glass breaks evenly.

Fig. 6–20 The two pieces of glass perfectly broken down the center of a penciled score line.

The Art of Scoring and Breaking Glass **123**

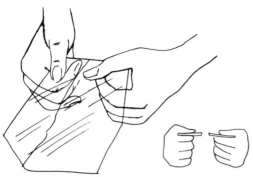

Fig. 6–21 *The incorrect way to break by hand. With the force of the snap, the two back edges of glass could dig into your palms.*

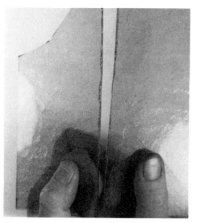

Fig. 6–23 *The breakout, the two pieces still firmly supported.*

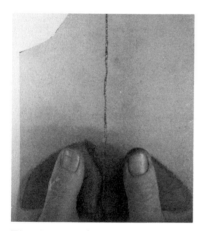

Fig. 6–22 *Breaking glass by hand. The safest way to hold the glass. This position allows maximum force to be exerted against the score line. The pull is to either side and down—circular—with the knuckles of either hand guiding the motion and preventing any sudden slippage.*

Fig. 6–24 *The tabletop method: Snapping the glass along the table edge. Both pieces are supported.*

breaking any size sheet of glass. Naturally, the procedure can be used only for straight-line cuts.

Breaking with Running Pliers
Running pliers are used for specialized cuts where long, thin pieces are required. Place the tool so that it lines up with the score, and apply pressure on the handles. The score will run automatically. These pliers are used mainly for straight cuts.

Breaking with Glass Pliers
Glass pliers are used to break score lines where the pieces to be broken are too small

edge. Then raise the glass and snap it smartly downward. The piece you are holding in your hand will come free as the leverage of the table snaps the score line (*Fig. 6–24*). Keep your feet out of the way when using this method. Large sheets of glass may be broken in this fashion with very little pressure. It takes practice—and courage—to apply this technique the first time, but it will not be long before you find yourself in control of the material. Then you will have no qualms about

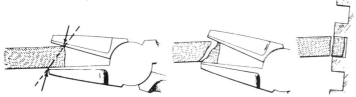

Fig. 6–25 Why not to use household pliers for grozzing glass? Ordinary pliers have angled jaws. The thicker the glass you attempt to grozz with them, the wider this angle becomes. Contact is made at only two points on the glass, and the resultant force is not at right angles to the surface. When the wrenching force of grozzing is applied, the end result is surface unevenness. The arrows show where contact is made; the dotted line is the resulting force. When the glass edge is left angled, as here, it cannot be leaded or foiled properly (See page 92). Even a glass cutter's grozzing teeth (right) do a better job than household pliers. Glass pliers are made with parallel jaws to avoid this, and they grip the glass securely.

or awkward to be broken by hand. They may also be applied to break off small irregular edges, whether the score is straight or curved. Hold the glass in one hand and the pliers with the other and carefully grip and pull out and down. You could also use the tabletop as a stabilizing surface instead of holding the piece in the air. Do not snap downward too abruptly with the pliers or the sudden force may break the glass. When using the tabletop, keep one hand firmly on the glass to immobilize it. You can use glass pliers also to some degree as grozzing pliers. Since both jaws are grooved with fine teeth, they may be used to nip away small outcroppings of glass from the score line.

Breaking Plate Glass

Plate glass can be broken by placing it on the table surface, score line down, and tapping from the unscored surface. This is the only type of glass so treated, mainly because of its thickness. A more accurate way to break plate glass is to use Fletcher's Plate Glass Breaker *(Figs. 6–26—6–29)*.

1. Run the score on thick glass—anywhere from ⅜″ to 1″. Fletcher recommends the carbide cutter (CA-B) that is enclosed with each breaker as the ideal choice for ½″ and thicker glass. The thicker the glass, the more essential it is to have a good score. The glass must be clean and

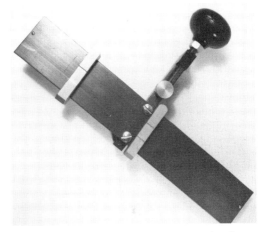

Fig. 6–26 The Fletcher Plate Glass Breaker furnishes two supports—the moving bars, which slide along a main brace and may be placed equidistant from the score line, and a screw fulcrum, just above the lower bar. Turning the knob raises and lowers the fulcrum.

tbe score continuous and uniform. When running a score on a large sheet of plate, the weight of the glass opposes the required bending motion. Place a small object like a pencil under the glass at each end of the score.

2. After scoring, pull the sheet of glass a few inches over the edge of the cutting table in the direction the score was made. Place the breaker tool on the glass with the screw knob down. Spread the

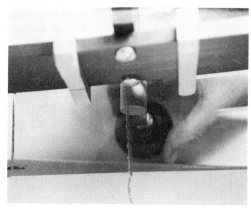

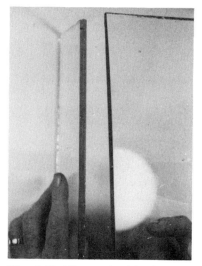

Fig. 6–27 The Fletcher Plate Glass Breaker in action. The breaker is placed in position so that the holding bars are above the glass, to either side of the score line. The fulcrum is positioned just below the score line. The knob is turned just tightly enough for the fulcrum to press firmly against the glass.

Fig. 6–29 The completed break showing the thickness of the plate and the precise running of the score. Fletcher's breakers are well worth the investment.

5. To break small pieces of thick glass, set the breaker tool on the table with the knob up. After scoring the glass, turn it over so that the score is on the underside. Insert the glass in the breaker, align the score, spread the sliding anvils as far apart as possible, and turn the knob.

Caution: Always wear protective gloves and arm covering when running a break.

Fig. 6–28 Turning the knob tightens the fulcrum against the glass, and the score line begins to run.

two upper anvils as far apart as the glass permits, but keep them equidistant from the score.

3. Locate the center fulcrum directly under the score. Turn the lead screw with the knob so that the fulcrum presses upward on the glass from below.

4. When splitting long, narrow pieces (lengths six or more times the width) place a second breaker tool at the terminal end of the run and tighten the fulcrum screw slightly.

Cutting Circles

Circles can be cut out of stained glass by using a freehand method with a paper pattern or by using a circle cutter. Circle cutters are of two basic types: those that use a central pivot with a variable arm, and those that use a stand with a limited arm but provide compactness and extra stability. Either will cut accurate circles.

Scoring the circle is not difficult with circle cutters, but it is only half the battle. The major·procedure is breaking the circle out of the glass *(Figs 6–30—6–35)*. Here glass pliers come in handy. (1) Cut the circle, using either a circle cutter or a pattern and standard glass cutter. (2) Cut tangential

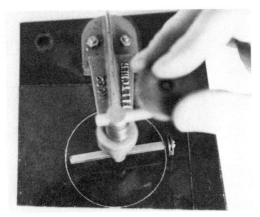

Fig. 6–30 *Scoring and breaking out a circle that has been inscribed with a circle cutter.*

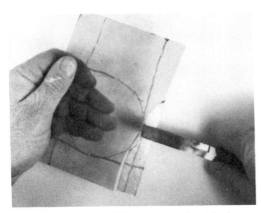

Fig. 6–31 *Tangential lines are scored and broken out.*

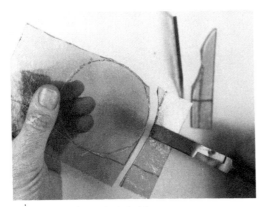

Fig. 6–32 *The circle is half out.*

Fig. 6–33 *The final section of the circle is ready to be broken out.*

Fig. 6–34 *Now only small pieces of glass remain to be grozzed around the circle.*

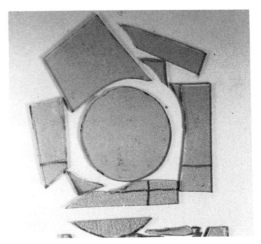

Fig. 6–35 *The final circle, grozzed but not sanded.*

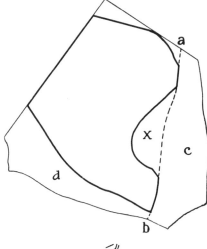

Fig. 6–36 Grozzing a deep inside curve. The piece is placed on the glass (left) and waste piece **C** is cut away by scoring line **ab.** Waste piece **d** is also cut away. On the right are the minicurves that will be cut slowly into the glass. If these curves are not cut carefully, a fracture at **fg** is likely. Note how each minicurve runs into the one behind it. This is to equalize the pressure of breaking so that the entire piece will not shatter.

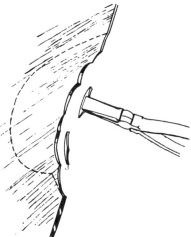

Fig. 6–37 Small areas of grozzing into a deep inside curve. This method, as opposed to the minicurve method, practically carves the projected cut out of the glass, but it requires patience.

Fig. 6–38 Breaking out the inside curve. A series of minicurves is scored within the boundary of the main curvature.

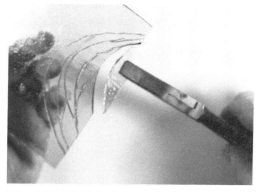

Fig. 6–39 The first minicurve is broken out with a large grozzing pliers. The glass is hand-held, although it can be rested over a table edge if it is too large to be held comfortably.

lines to reach from the circle to the edge of the glass. You can make as many of these lines as you wish. (3) Break these lines away, using the glass pliers.

Pliers will allow you enough strength to break the glass without breaking into the circle itself. Use caution here, and don't nip off too much at one time. Better to score a few extra lines than to try to get too much in one bit and break the glass. In this regard, keep in mind that in cutting

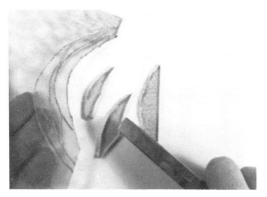

Fig. 6–40 About half the minicurves are broken out of the major curve.

Fig. 6–42 The final curve, all in one piece, and large grozzing pliers, a favorite tool.

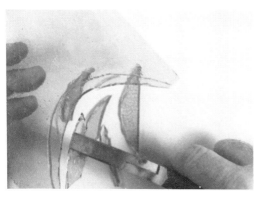

Fig. 6–41 Only the last minicurve remains to be broken out.

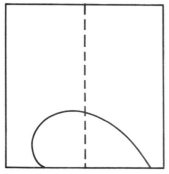

Fig. 6–43 Another way to make this cut is to follow the suggested score along the dotted line and then cut the two remaining, less extreme inside curves.

glass you cannot entirely save both pieces—the piece you want to use and the piece you are breaking away. Be frugal and get as much as possible out of your glass, but be willing to sacrifice your waste piece to save the pattern piece.

Cutting Inner Curves

Probably the most difficult cuts to break out are inner curves. Whereas outer curves such as circles allow the pressures of the break to run freely to the right and left, inner curves will not allow this and must be broken out in small pieces. Gradual curves may be broken out in a single piece. Sometimes an entire section of such a curve may be broken out by tapping, but in a sharp

curve the tap line may run off the score and ruin the piece.

The best procedure for breaking out inner curves is to cut duplicates of the inner curve within the hollow of the curve itself (Fig. 6–36). Run these curves into one another so that your pattern looks like that in Figure 6–38. Then, with glass pliers, break out each of the minicurves (Fig. 6–39). When breaking out the curve, grasp it at the narrowest portion and allow the tension to flow into the wider part, which can handle it better. This will give a controlled break. Don't grasp the minicurve in the center and pull or the scores may fly apart. Break out each little curve separately, using more and more care as

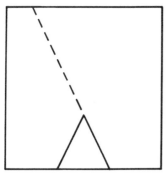 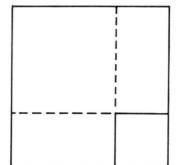 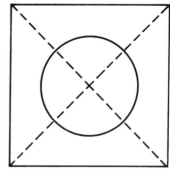

Fig. 6–44 *The V cut. The dotted line shows the recommended score. This cut cannot be done by hand otherwise.*

Fig. 6–45 *Incomplete scoring of the surface. You cannot cut the rectangle out of the piece of glass as such. You must continue your score along either of the dotted lines before making the second cut.*

Fig. 6–46 *Cutting an inside circle. The glass is cut along the diagonal lines. Then the comparatively mild inside curves are cut away from the remaining triangles. The four truncated triangles are then leaded back together, and the circle is established as a negative space.*

you get farther into the hollow of the major curve. When you get to a point where you are close to the original score line, proceed even more cautiously. You may want to grozz out the final minicurve, almost as though you were carving it. This technique should break out even the most severely shaped inner curves.

For less extreme inner curves, the same procedure is applied, but it is not necessary to make quite so many inside cuts. The cuts can be larger, and you can break them out right up to the actual score line without grozzing. As usual, successful scoring and breaking depends on the glass. Greens, reds, and yellows tend to follow a score line poorly, especially on inner curves. On the other hand, certain French antique glasses will break perfectly at a touch along the inner curve line. At first, don't try to put too many inner curves in your designs. As you gain experience, you can incorporate more.

Breaking Long Strips

Use running pliers, strip cutters, or a small fulcrum under the edge of the glass sur-

face. Trying to tap out a long strip of glass leads to jagged edges or disaster, since the run line usually leaves the score line to travel on its own.

INCOMPLETE SCORING AND OTHER PROBLEMS

Each score must run two edges. You cannot make a score and stop in the middle of the glass. And you cannot make a score and return to the same edge. In the beginning, avoid difficult score lines such as extreme inside curves involving C cuts or V cuts. There are ways to break these cuts, but while you are still getting familiar with glass, it is best not to throw yourself this kind of curve.

Points and Thin Cuts

Probably the most common designing error beginners run into is clustering points. If you design seven or eight crossing lines, don't expect to have this area remain a point after the glass is leaded and soldered. What you will get is a blob of solder. If

Fig. 6–47 *Points converging but not meeting in a veritable explosion of lead lines—all discrete and radiating from a central focus.*

Fig. 6–48 *The three-ring sign—the glass cutter's ultimate challenge.*

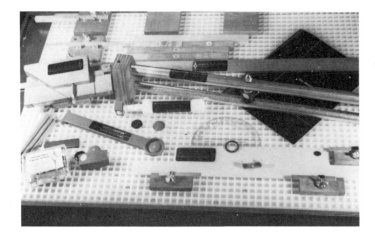

Fig. 6–49 *A sampling of the Morton tools and accessories available for use by hobbyists and professional workers alike. These are all described fully in the brochure accompanying the Morton System.*

you must have lines crossing, keep them to a maximum of three. If you want lines to cluster, leave enough room for each lead to remain clearly visible.

Remember that the lead takes up a certain amount of room. To cut and struggle over a piece of glass, perhaps ¼″ in breadth, and then see it disappear in the panel during leading can be discouraging. Avoid thin pieces, unless you have well calculated them for extremely thin lead or copper foil.

The Three-Ring Sign
Speaking of difficult cuts, the three–ring sign features what can only be described as impossible glass figurations. It has been in-

triguing glass cutters since the Middle Ages. Was it ever actually done? Can it be done? If you find it a challenge, make sure that you use inexpensive glass. You will be using a lot of it!

THE MORTON PORTABLE GLASS WORKSHOP
The entire glass scoring and breaking endeavor has in recent years been ingeniously reconditioned in the system designed by the Morton Company. The idea of creating portable working space especially for the cramped apartment dweller as well as the homeowner, has been the focus of this company's design concepts.

The Art of Scoring and Breaking Glass **131**

Fig. 6–50A The "Safety Break" system of Morton Glassworks. Here we see the pressure block to the right, and the running button to the left. The button is shown upside down to demonstrate the stem that holds it into one of the surface pockets.

Fig. 6–50B A long, thin strip showing the score line.

Fig. 6–50C The scored glass is positioned over the running button with the score in the center. The pressure block is then applied.

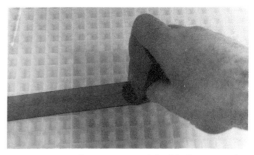

Fig. 6–50D The curvature of the block is over the score line. The glass is fed over the button and the block is pressed gently but firmly along the score. The score will soon start to run.

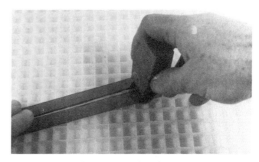

Fig. 6–50E The resulting break is neat and clean.

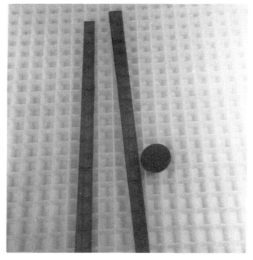

Fig. 6–50F The two pieces of glass alongside the running button.

Fig. 6–51 *The same strip and another above it broken out along the planned score lines. These were both done with the Morton Safety Break System.*

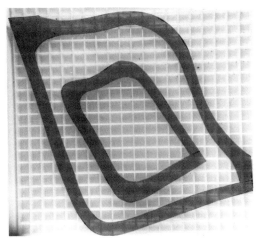

Fig. 6–52 *This was a solid piece of stained glass. The design was scored from it and broken out using Morton tools.*

Fig. 6–53 *Three planned scores and breaks done with the Morton Safety Break System.*

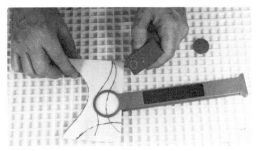

Fig. 6–54 *The Morton Quick Center device functions as a target to find the center of the breaking button in glass that is hard to see through. It makes working with translucent opals and mirrored glass easy.*

The Morton System begins with a special cutting surface that prevents the scattering of the many chips and shards that naturally occurs during the glass-cutting operation. This plastic "egg-crate" surface holds the glass dust, chips, and other debris, while the work piece moves smoothly over the top plastic rim. For free-hand cutting, the Morton surface is used much in the same way as a conventional wood or carpet surface. One exception might be when scoring a piece of glass smaller than a square inch. There it may be helpful to place a layer of cardboard between the surface and the glass to prevent the piece from tipping into one of the multiple plastic pockets.

To clean the cutting surface pockets of glass chips, you can use a vacuum cleaner or dump the chips on newspaper. If you use newspaper, be careful when you roll up the paper; the chips will be small and hard to see.

The Morton Safety Break System is a glass-breaking tool that enhances the glass-chip containment idea and allows a division along score lines that otherwise would be impossible. This is done by "slow breaking" from pressure over the surface at multiple contact points. The worker develops a "feel" for the glass. Conventional breaking methods are usually accomplished up and away from the scoring surface. These

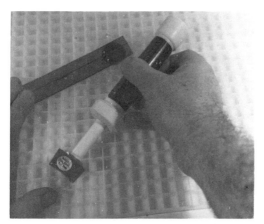

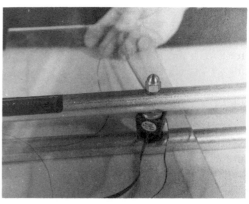

Fig. 6–57 *The Plate Breaker in action. The glass is fed under the system from behind; as the block is squeezed downward against the button, the score begins to run.*

Fig. 6–55A *Morton's "Maxi-Break" tool for thick glass comes in handy. It allows forceful topping of a calibrated degree along the score line.*

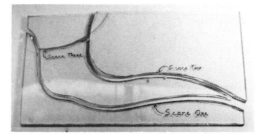

Fig. 6–58 *A piece of 3/8" plate glass scored and broken along lines that would be impossible to achieve without the Morton Plate Breaker.*

Fig. 6–55B *The glass is broken in the same manner as before.*

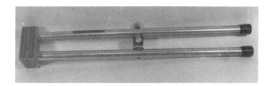

Fig. 6–56 *The Morton Plate Breaker.*

Fig. 6–59 *The Morton E-Z Angle (right). The cut angles in the foreground show the accuracy with which they go together to form geometric designs of any shape. This tool allows precise duplication of any angle.*

methods, however good, are less controllable for critical shapes than breaking on the surface. The control possible with Morton's tool means less scrap and less grinding or grozzing of the final work piece. It also reduces the need for run-out scores on inside and outside curves. More of the scrap glass is therefore intact and usable.

The basic components of the Morton System are the running button and the pressure block. These two items will enable the worker to break out almost any score. Patience is required, however. Many workers believe that breaking glass is an all or nothing procedure, and with standard tools that is true. However, with the Morton technique, the point-by-point guidance of the break is what permits it to follow critical turns and angles. Instead of an all or nothing break, it is a gradual one.

This philosophy is carried over to the newest Morton tool—the plate-glass breaker. It is best described as two pieces of pipe with a running button and pressure block between them. The squeeze permitted by this leverage allows you to guide "impossible" stained-glass scores on plate glass. When we experimented with this tool, we cut both ¼″ and ⅜″ plate curves and angles that could not have been accomplished any other way. Naturally, the thicker the glass, the more time involved in pressuring along the score over and over. When the glass finally does break, the resulting edges are flush, except for perhaps a slight fringe of glass on the back surface from surface tension. This is readily wiped away with the small abrasive stone that comes with the tool.

Morton's booklet gives a thorough schooling in its methods and tools, from the basic surface to the lightbox, layout blocks, and plate-glass cutter. Follow the directions before going off on your own with these tools. After that it is merely a matter of practice.

7
Cutting Patterns

Cutting the pattern for a stained-glass piece is an all-important first step in the process of transforming an idea into a work of art. The pattern is the guide from which all your further efforts will extend. If you make an error here, it will be compounded throughout the other steps. Use a medium oaktag for the pattern. This paper thickness will allow the wheel of the glass cutter to score but be sturdy enough to stand up well as a guide.

DESIGNING THE PATTERN

Every stained-glass piece begins as a drawing. When you make the first drawing, draw it as you see it in your mind's eye. Put everything on paper: perspective, shadowing, linear qualities, and even the colors if you want. Use pastels to match the colors you have in mind in order to see how they will blend.

Once you have a sketch on paper, it must be transformed into a cartoon, the blueprint for the work *(Fig. 7–1)*. The cartoon shows all cut lines and all the lead lines, both thick and thin, in their final dimension. The only aspect of the design that the cartoon does not have to show is color, but you may indicate that as well. Keep your lines easy and flowing.

CUTTING THE PATTERN

Once you have designed your pattern, the next step is to cut it, making sure that you leave room between the pieces for the lead. One tool to use for this purpose is a pair of pattern shears or scissors (see Chapter 4). Some beginners feel that if they make a mistake in cutting the pattern they can fix it later when it comes to cutting the glass. This ad lib method never works. If you make a mistake in cutting the pattern, you must substitute a new piece or everything will be thrown off. Using a pattern knife is one way to leave space for the came. However, it is somewhat more difficult to use than pattern scissors and does not give as satisfactory a cut. So, when you try a pattern knife, try a pair of pattern scissors as well.

Freehand cutting is the way beginners usually start with patterns. Trace over the lines of the cartoon with a heavy marking pencil. Then with either a razor blade or ordinary scissors, cut to either side of this black line. This will leave an empty space where the black line was, which is the space approximated for the leading. This is not a precise method of pattern cutting, and it is not recommended for any critical work, such as a design that must fit into existing dimensions—a window, panel for a door, or shutters, for example. As an introduction for cutting patterns for free-form objects, it works fairly well. Remember that not all magic markers are the same in width, and even those that are wear down as they are used. This will result in a variable line that may be thicker at the end

Fig. 7–1 *A paper pattern ready to be cut. Each line is a cutline drawn to scale. The next step is to number each piece to correspond with the working drawing.*

Fig. 7–2 *Cutting the pattern. The pattern piece is placed on top of the glass and the cutter will be run along its sides.*

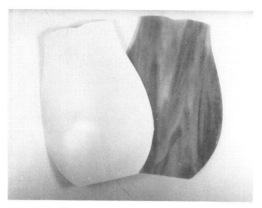

Fig. 7–3 *The piece of glass cut to pattern size.*

Fig. 7–4 *Pattern pieces cut to size and placed back on the cartoon.*

of the pattern than at the beginning, Also, the mechanics of cutting out the line furnish another area for error; since this cut must be done twice, it doubles the possibilities for carelessness.

USING THE PATTERN

Once you have the pattern cut to size, put each piece back on the cartoon. The cartoon piece should show its borders around its pattern piece. Occasionally the pattern will have shrunk away from the cartoon borders. If this happens, you have misjudged the lines and cut too closely within them, or the lines were not made dark enough for you to see properly while cutting. A piece of imperfectly cut pattern will lead to an imperfectly cut piece of glass. If the pattern pieces on the cartoon seem to fit correctly, the next step is to cut a piece of glass to match each of the pattern pieces. Place the pattern on top of the piece of glass and run the glass cutter around the edges of the paper to make the cut *(Fig. 7–2)*. Make each cut individually and break it out before going on to the next.

Never cut from a pattern *under* the glass. This is a very imprecise technique. Opalescent glasses as well as antiques may be too dark to see through but to cut accurately, the pattern must be placed on top of the glass surface. For precise pattern cutting, the glass cutter must be in direct contact with the paper edge.

A piece of pattern made from the proper paper should last for many cuts. However, if you are cutting a pattern over and over, such as a lamp panel, consider transferring your pattern to a thin piece of sheet metal instead of using pattern paper. Even pattern paper will tend to fray as the glass cutter rides against it time after time. Be sure in transferring your pattern to metal that the sheet metal is thin enough to allow the wheel of the glass cutter to contact the glass sufficiently to score it.

All pattern pieces should be numbered to correspond with numbers on the cartoon *(Fig. 7–4)*. In a small window or panel there is no major problem in finding the pieces of pattern, but numbering them is a good habit to get into so that when you make a larger piece of work, you will be able to tell exactly by number where the pattern fits. It can be frustrating to have nervous pieces of paper fluttering all over your worktable while you pick each one up by hand to try to find its place in the puzzle.

8
Designing for Stained Glass

The lead lines in stained glass hold the different pieces of glass together, just as melody and counterpoint hold the notes together in a musical composition. To the untutored eye, lead lines may not seem to make much difference to the work as a whole; just as to the untutored ear, all chamber music sounds alike. Stained-glass windows usually contain a foreground, which is the focal point, and a background, which fills in lesser detail and completes the composition. This is true whether the window is pictorial or abstract. In this regard, linear quality is most important. Be careful in designing so that the background does not become so overly complicated and busy that it detracts from the foreground. This is probably the most common mistake in stained-glass designing. Make the background simple and save your complexities in colors, cuts, and leading for the foreground. And always keep the question in the back of your mind no matter how ornate or how simple your cartoon: "Can these pieces be cut out of glass?"

BALANCING LEAD LINES

The lead lines act as guides for the eye. They move the eye either across the entire composition or to a certain focal point.

The design should not lead the eye into areas that are dead ends. Such breaks or snags in the overall pattern are disruptive. A good stained-glass design should be smooth and rhythmic, not a staccato jumble of lines. The eye tends to read a stained-glass window in much the same way that it reads the pages in a book, guided by the lines of type. The lines lead the eye to the other lines.

To strengthen the flow of line within a composition, follow these rules:

1. Avoid having too many lines meeting in one place. This acts much the same as a traffic snarl. The viewer will not be guided to get involved.
2. Try to mix leads. Don't use only one type throughout a panel unless it's a small panel. Try to keep the eye intrigued by a creative linear quality as well as a colorful one.
3. The lead lines should act as a creative force, either in terms of geometric balance or whatever imbalance you want to create.
4. Avoid passing lead lines through painted areas or through pieces of glass that have intricate line cuts. Both confuse the design by mixing a jumble of lead lines. It is always better to redesign your drawing if you see the concept is intolerable to the medium. In stained glass, technique and artistry go hand in hand.

Fig. 8–1A *Preliminary sketch for the "Pirate" window concentrating on background detail rather than the central figure.*

Fig. 8–1B *The color possibilities are added in pastels.*

Fig. 8–2 *An initial sketch of a cartoon.*

MIXING LEAD SIZES

In mixing leads there are no hard and fast rules. You can juxtapose a ⅛″ lead and a ¾″ if you have a good reason for doing so. Or you may want to go from ⅛″ to perhaps a ³⁄₁₆″ or at most a ¼″ lead and proceed to larger sizes in a stepwise fashion. It's also possible to get some magnificient

effects by leaping across lead sizes. Just be sure that the larger leads do not overpower the smaller ones.

You can use large leads on one small area of the window and tiny leads throughout the rest of the piece if you want that unbalanced effect. The line quality should be thought out and designed into the cartoon, not decided upon when the leading procedure is already in full swing.

One general rule is that small pieces of glass take small leads and larger pieces of glass take larger leads. This is not only a good design rule but it adds strength to the window. You may decide, however, that your large pieces of glass should take small leads as well as large. You cannot be so cavalier with the small pieces of glass; if you use large leads on them, they may sink into the channels and disappear entirely.

DESIGNING CORNERS

A number of lead lines meeting at one point will create an ugly soldering area. The

Fig. 8–3 The lead lines in this window panel flow out from the central focus and carry the eye along.

Fig. 8–5 Sketch of a design for a stained-glass border.

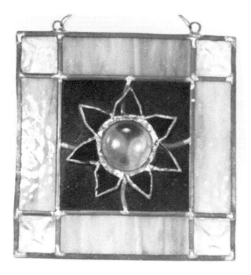

Fig. 8–4 This window panel shows how simple geometrical patterns may be employed to artistic advantage. The central flower has three-dimensional leaves jutting out from the ruby jewel. The severe border complements this rather ornate interior.

Fig. 8–6 A "porthole" giving an example of designing for a limited space. The rope effect is painted and baked onto the border glass, giving a tightly knit design concept.

more leads that meet this way, the more space you will take up with solder. In a pencil sketch it may look as if there is no problem. We emphasized this difficulty before, but since it is such a common design-ing mistake, here it is once again: If you want to have a number of lead lines meeting, arrange in the design stage that they won't meet at the same point. Let them converge toward several points in a similar area. Just keeping them an inch apart will make all the difference.

Fig. 8–8 *Designing for lead and foil. The design shows a crowding of the elements composing the horn of plenty without a crowding of the structural design.*

Fig. 8–7 *A "porthole" in a series of four designed to fit into shutters. Chunk glass is used for the sun with radiating rays of lead lines. A whale sports in the waves below. All lead lines are worked in as part of the design.*

One popular stained-glass design is a compass showing spikes radiating from a central hub. Such spikes may be cut to needle-point sharpness in glass, but when it comes to leading them up the ends have suddenly moved two or even three inches into the panel. All you have toward the border are two leads cramped close together with solder covering their surfaces. To avoid this, don't cut the glass to these needle-point edges. Leave enough thickness at the point so that the leads have room to grip the glass and still show glass between them. To make certain what the glass width should be, cut a piece of glass and measure two pieces of appropriate channeling against it.

DESIGNING FOR REINFORCED LEADS

Reinforced leads do not take sharp curves well. They have a much thicker heart than other leads to allow for the steel rod running through their center. The best way to determine the width of their space is to look at the lead in cross-section. You will be able to measure the lead heart with the rod inside. This will give you the exact amount of room that you must cut out of

your pattern. It's about the size cut by a large pair of pattern scissors—approximately ⅛".

USING REINFORCING RODS

If you are designing a stained-glass window of three feet by three feet or more, reinforcing rods should be placed at every two feet to brace the window. The rods must be cut with a hacksaw, and you should try to incorporate them into the overall design. If this is not feasible, modify your design so that the rods will not go through areas where their profiles will cast obstrusive shadows. Rather than using the old type of steel reinforcing rods, which cannot be bent, workers today use the galvanized reinforcing "strap." This solders well and has a certain amount of flexibility that will permit it to back up the line of a lead going across the width of the window. With the introduction of these flexible reinforcing straps, there is no reason to sacrifice strength for design.

DEVELOPING A COLOR SENSE

To use stained glass to its best advantage, you should have a thorough knowledge of the way colors blend. One way to achieve this is through the use of a color wheel. This is not a precise guide, since printed colors are notoriously disproportionate to glass colors, but it will help. The more

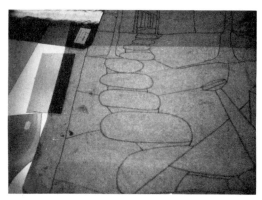

Fig. 8–9 *The work drawing on the light table with the colors placed alongside.*

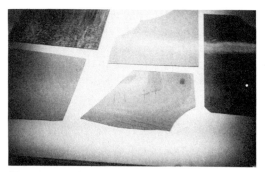

Fig. 8–10 *Balancing colors on the light table. The pieces are not cut to pattern, but placing the colors next to each other gives an idea of how they will relate.*

Fig. 8–11 *Rough-cut glass pieces on the light table to see how the colors blend.*

practical way is to get the boxes of samples that most glass manufacturers sell as a guide to their types of glass. The charge for these samples is usually minimal and always worth more than the price as far as training your eye. It is no exaggeration to say that hues and tones represented in glass are all but unending. But the interaction among them is not the same as with oils, watercolors, or pastels. Probably the closest parallel is stage lighting. The superimposition of colored lights provides a measure of what happens in glass with colors side by side: One impinges on or enhances the other. This dramatic effect is modified by the sizes of the glass pieces. Working with samples of similar size pieces on a

light table and then comparing them in daylight as well is excellent practice for training the eye to color subtleties.

Looking at a variety of works in stained glass can also educate the eye to a good color sense, as well as to a sense of design. Modern stained-glass works usually have a wider—and wilder—color spectrum than medieval ones, where the color range was more limited. But the matching of medieval colors is almost miraculous. So go to as many shows and museums and churches as possible. This is the best schooling in stained glass you can get.

Even after you have developed a good sense of color, it still will not be sharp enough. We don't mean the ability to pick and choose colors from the light table, but to know at the same time what these colors will be like in bright sunlight, cloudy daylight, and dusk. What color will blur out or be emphasized by the interplay of another tone elsewhere? What colors

Fig. 8–14.

Fig. 8–15.

Fig. 8–12.

Fig. 8–13.

will project best toward the street when the lights are on? Keeping your glass color sense sharp is a never-ending challenge.

COLOR AND THE LIGHT TABLE

Take your finished design and lay it over the light table. You will see that the light penetrates the paper fairly readily. Then take the colors of glass that you want to use and place them over those respective areas of the design without cutting the glass to size, simply to get a rough notion how the colors will mesh *(Fig. 8–10)*. Keep in mind that looking at colors on the light table is not the same as seeing them by true light. You should try to lay out as many colors of your choice as possible. Then stand over the design on a chair or small ladder, as far away as possible, and study the color pattern. You may find that what you thought was a good balance before laying it out now looks bland or even antagonistic. It is easier to change the color scheme now, before cutting the pieces. Don't be afraid to change all the pieces if you think the colors are not working well together. Hold a few of them up to the daylight if you're unsure of them and see what the quality is with this light. This will also give you some idea of the modification between daylight and the light table for all your colors.

A stained-glass composition is a relationship of design elements acting along and in conjunction with one another. The effect of the piece should be one of unity.

Subject matter has little to do with design and color. A blue horse, for instance, may be perfectly valid in the circumstance. But the type of blue might be critical. The shape of the horse may likewise be crucial to the overall design of the piece, whether it be realistic or surrealistic—if it can be cut or painted. The fun in working in glass is to explore the unique possibilities that the medium itself proposes. At this point, don't worry about what is good and bad. Be prepared to make mistakes—and enjoy them. You will make mistakes in your glass choices and designs. You will also break a lot of glass. It's all good practice.

9

The Copper Foil Method

Use of copper foil with stained glass came about in the Tiffany era, but whether Tiffany himself invented the technique is questionable. However, with it he produced along with La Farge and others intricate works that involved the juxtaposition of thousands of small, faceted glass pieces that were too delicate for the bulky lead came. These mosaiclike creations needed a supportive metal that was at once delicate, flexible, inexpensive, adhesive, readily solderable, and which could become rigid on demand. Copper foil met these requirements.

The edges of the glass pieces are wrapped with copper foil, the overlying foil pressed against the surface of the glass to either side, allowing a small lip of metal to show. The ends of the foil are soldered. The glass pieces are placed atop a pattern and soldered together. Because of the simplicity of the technique and the allowance it seems to provide for inexpert glass cutting, many beginners learn this method and no other. This is a mistake. It is also a mistake to consider copper foiling as "easy" or "easier" than leading and to prefer it for this reason. Neither is easier. They are two separate techniques, each with its own specifics.

FOIL SIZES AND THICKNESSES

Several thicknesses of foil are available for use in stained glass work. For convenience,

we may consider them as hard, medium, and soft. The degree of rigidity of the metal will depend on the thickness of the foil as well as on the amount of solder used in the final "tinning" process. "Hard" foil is .002″ thick, twice the dimension of the .001″ of the "soft" foil. "Medium" foil has a thickness of .015″. The weight of the foil determines the price.

Choice of thickness is dependent on the type of work being done. Small pieces of glass require only a thin foil to hold them together. However, you might want the bulky, rough effect of a heavier thickness even with small glass pieces. Not so much choice is possible when large foiled panels of glass are to go into a lampshade. Here heavy foil is essential for reasons of support.

Foil used to come in 6″ wide rolls from which strands of variable widths were cut depending on the needs of the worker. The introduction and perfection of individual rolls of from 5/32″ to 1/2″, with a pressure-sensitive glue backing that adheres the metal firmly to the glass, made foiling the comparatively simple process it is today.

Ideally, the thinner the foil size you choose for your work the better, since the effect produced will be more delicate with the least amount of metal visible. However, there is a point of no return. You don't want to use foil that is so thin it fails to fulfill its bracing function. The width

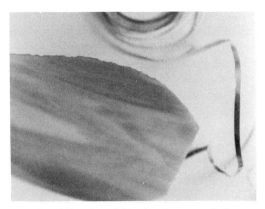

Fig. 9–1 *The edge of this glass is too rough for proper foiling; it must be sanded before foil is applied.*

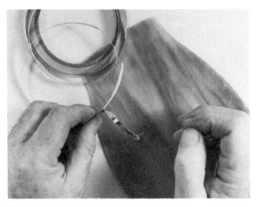

Fig. 9–2 *Beginning the copper foil process. The sticky tape is removed from its backing.*

size you choose should be roughly three times the thickness of your glass edge. This allows a delicate tracery of foil on the front and a substantive two-thirds unseen and contributing to stability.

The mistake so many beginners make in choosing too wide a foil size is to forget that while a single piece of glass may show only ¼″ of edging, when that piece is placed in the design it will juxtapose a similarly foiled piece. The two edges combine to show a wide line. The amount of visible foil—the amount overlapping the glass—will double by the time the piece is completed. Once solder is applied, your delicate line can become a rampart.

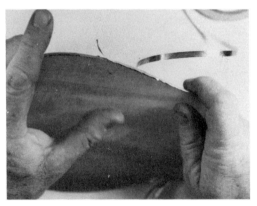

Fig. 9–3 *The overlapping end sticks up as the glass is edged with foil.*

COPPER FOILING: STEP BY STEP

1. Draw a design for a free-form hanging, such as a suncatcher.
2. Cut it out of glass and grozz the glass edges until they are reasonably smooth. Sand them with carborundum paper if you want. The smoother the glass edge, the better the foil will adhere to it.
3. Choose a width of foil that will accommodate the edge of your glass. As a beginner, you can arbitrarily select a ¼″ foil to allow for miscutting on the glass edges.

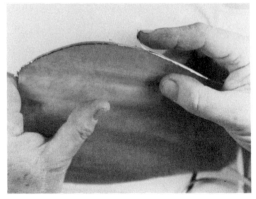

Fig. 9–4 *The overlapping edge is turned down as the wrapping proceeds.*

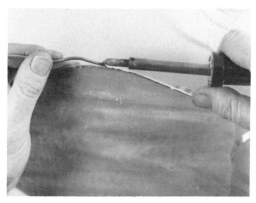

Fig. 9–5 *Soldering the rim of foil together. A touch of the iron is all that is needed.*

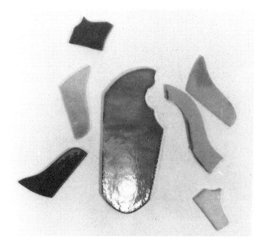

Fig. 9–6 *Even odd shapes can be foiled. The piece in the center has been neatly crimped.*

4. Anchor the end of the foil against the starting area of the glass with your fingertip. As you wrap the foil round the glass edge remove the paper backing. Press the foil firmly and evenly against the glass edge as you go. If you are foiling a square piece, check the corners for evenness of the foil; if the piece is circular, spot-check as you foil.

5. When you get back to your starting place, overlap the foil about ¼″ and cut away the excess.

6. Press down (or fold over) the foil that is standing around the circumference

of the glass onto the front and back surfaces of the glass. Expecially on the front, this lip of metal should be as even as possible. The pressing motion should be toward the center, not peripheral. Once the foil has been hand-pressed, you can iron out any wrinkles with a knife blade or similar tool. Corners especially may need this treatment. If you are working with a textured glass, you may need to spend more extra time ironing the foil against this rough surface.

7. Once you are satisfied that your foil is even and flat, solder the ends together with a small amount of solder.

If you have any trouble soldering, scrub the foil gently with a wire brush and reflux it. Soldering the overlapping joint allows the piece to be put down without the foil popping out of position. It is also easier to press each portion of the foil down firmly without it slipping. Go through this procedure with each piece of glass, and then place each piece in its proper position on the work drawing or cartoon. You should be able to see the ink line around each piece of glass on the drawing when the glass is put in place.

After all the pieces are properly foiled and placed in position, hold them with leading nails around the outside so that they are bound according to the lines of your design. Find out if they do not fit before soldering the individual pieces of glass together. Very often the pieces do not come together because the foil on one or more is not pressed tightly. This will take up room and extend a piece over its cartoon lines.

8. Treat each piece of glass in your pattern in this manner. Use your fingers to press the foil as tightly and as evenly as possible into every cranny. Be careful not to tear the foil against a sharp edge of glass or by pushing too forcefully into a deep curve. If the foil should tear, remove it from the piece and refoil. Do not attempt to overlap the foil, do not ignore the tear on the assumption that the solder will cover it, do not cut and patch. You will probably end up doing one or all of these

Fig. 9–7 *Foil can be used effectively around large pieces of glass as well as small. This real butterfly is encased between two large watch glasses held together by copper foil. The finished appearance is trim; the foil is less obstrusive than the thinnest lead would be. A problem with lead came here would be its tendency to separate from the glass. (Courtesy: Camur Design Products)*

Fig. 9–9 *Detail of foiled side door panel. The beading was purposely made heavy to give depth to the pieces and thus emphasize them.*

Fig. 9–8 *A foiled Christmas star. The ribs of the star angle out toward the viewer. Such 3-D techniques are more easily accomplished with foil than with lead. In the center is a small glass "glob" foiled in.*

things anyway, and you will find out they just waste time. It is easier to start the piece over.

9. Once all your pieces are foiled, place them on the cartoon and make sure they lie snugly against each other. The covering of foil should not have changed their relationship, so if they do not come together you have not cut them correctly. You should have noticed that before. You may have ignored it. In any event, you must now recut those pieces that are throwing off your pattern. Do not try to justify the new relationship among the pieces no matter how tempting it might be.

10. Once the pieces fit snugly, solder them together. Some workers add a step and, after they foil each piece, flux and solder the rim of copper—a process called "tinning." This not only makes the soldering of the pieces easier during assembly, since solder flows to solder very readily, but tinning makes the copper foil rigid, and preventing it from coming loose. It's up to you. Be careful in tinning each piece not to leave irregular areas of solder on the

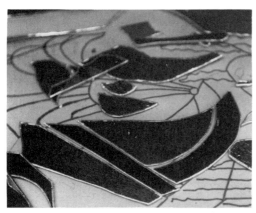

Fig. 9–10 *Copper-foiled glass pieces being fitted together on a cartoon for a window.*

Fig. 9–11 *Lead came and copper foil in combinations. The central portion of the flower is foiled, while the outside skein is all caming.*

edges of the pieces. This will prevent them from fitting properly.

11. Tinned or not, the assembled pieces are soldered in the same way. We may "tack solder" an assemblage, especially if there are many pieces in a sculptural arrangement. Tack-soldering means placing a small amount of solder in a few critical areas just to hold the pieces together to obtain a perspective. If the pieces are all in one plane, you may solder completely two pieces at a time. If one or two pieces are arranged in a three-dimensional fashion, we tack-solder those first, since all other pieces must relate to them. The ad-

vantage of tack soldering is the ease with which these few spots can be unsoldered if necessary. It is all but impossible to unsolder two foiled pieces that have been fully soldered. In that case, the foil must be stripped away, solder and all, and you are back to step one.

Once all the pieces are arranged, we like to tack solder them at the corners or any place that will hold them together. Once they are tacked, you can take out the nails and more easily solder up the entire panel. Do not let the iron get too hot during this procedure or the solder will flow through the joints to the other side. Flux all visible copper to make it solder readily. When your panel is finished, there should be no evidence of foil showing underneath the solder.

12. When you have soldered all the exposed foil on one side of your suncatcher, turn the piece over and solder the foil on the other. You must do this not only for looks, but for strength. It is sometimes more difficult to solder a back surface because it may have picked up dirt from the tabletop, and dirt and flux may have percolated from above. Clean this back surface before attempting to solder it. Once this back side is soldered, clean the piece and stand back to admire it.

SOLDERING FOIL

Any soldering tip can be used for foil. Many craftsmen prefer a thin tip, since it allows more control for the thin edge. The same iron used for leading is used for foiling. Although foil will not melt from the heat of the iron as lead came will, the solder will tend to flow between foiled pieces rather than over them if the iron is too hot. The effect most workers want to achieve in soldering foil is "beading."

BEADING

Beading is the final step in copper foiling after all the pieces have been firmly soldered together. It establishes a rounded

Fig. 9–12 *Ornate foiling in the "Tiffany" style. Such an intricate pattern could only be foiled and still have its delicacy preserved.*

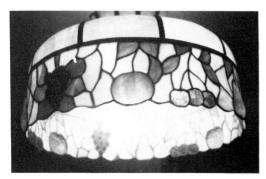

Fig. 9–13 *A "fruit" lamp showing less intricate foiling on the border than Figure 9–12. While the copper is malleable when it is being worked, once it is "tinned" with solder it becomes stiff and holds even large pieces of glass firmly.*

curve of solder over the foil line giving depth to the pieces of glass. They are aesthetically discrete rather than obviously joined. Beading is done with a moderately heated iron. Some sort of rheostat control is necessary to prevent constant switching of the iron on and off or, worse, plugging it in and unplugging it.

Beading can be frustrating for the inexperienced worker, who may find the "bead" of solder flattening out and running onto the table. If you are especially inept, you may loosen some of the pieces as well. Beading is not a simple, last-minute icing

on the cake. It is an integral part of the work. Keeping a cool head together with a cool iron is imperative. The idea is to have the rheostat control reading about one-half to three-fourths line voltage. If you have no rheostat, use a line switch and keep your iron as cool as possible, just able to melt the solder. Try to keep the solder plastic rather than liquid. This will allow it to build up on the previous layer.

We like a U-shaped lead came or a flat strip of metal around the outside edge of a foiled panel. We solder it into place, and tack it to each foiled line running into it. You may want to solder a loop for hanging the panel. A copper loop should be "tinned"—at least where it will be connected to the panel. For easy attachment of the loop, clean it in flux before soldering.

TROUBLESHOOTING

Here are some common reasons for problems with foil:

1. If tinning is not done smoothly, the surface will be irregular and the pieces of glass will not meet each other. Overtinning also gives an additional thickness to the copper.

2. Unclean foil. Copper will not take solder if it has an oxide coat or is dirty.

3. Not enough flux or the wrong type of flux, which may be too strong to bond the solder. This can also create a foul odor and dangerous fumes.

4. Watch your iron temperature. If you're having trouble flowing solder, your iron may be too cold. If the solder runs, the iron may be too hot.

5. If you're having trouble soldering into the glass concavities, you are probably using the wrong shape or size tip. Your best bet here is a flat, thin, chisel shape, such as a 3/16" or a flat 1/4".

6. Poorly cut glass presents problems. If the glass does not conform to the pattern to begin with, the foil will follow this ad libbing, and you will end up with a design that has no relationship to your pattern. If the glass is cut to the correct shape but has

splintery edges, your foil will not adhere smoothly and a chipped edge of glass may be visible alongside the edge of foil. This is unprofessional and sloppy. Glass cutting must be precise and the glass sanded so that it shows no discrepancies in the edges.

7. Make sure that your foil is pressed tightly around the glass. No matter how well the glass is cut, if the foil is not crimped to the edges, it will loosen.

COMBINING COPPER AND LEAD

The copper foiling and lead caming techniques are not mutually exclusive. Copper is usually used with small pieces of glass; in a lampshade, for instance, the curve is produced by foiling small pieces over a form. The smaller the pieces of glass, the greater the bend or curvature that may be achieved. To shape large pieces of glass, the glass must be fired over a form in a kiln.

While leading gives a bold, emphatic look to a piece, copper foil provides a delicate, lacy effect. Foil is not ordinarily used for the long spans of glass that lead can handle with ease; nevertheless, provided a panel is given proper support with brace bars and the design is well planned, foil can be used throughout an entire window.

Leading and copper foil may be combined in a window where small and large pieces of glass are used together, or where the design involves "foiling in" jewels, chunks, globs, stones or seashells.

Adhesive-backed copper foil, precut in rolls, allows even the most inexperienced worker to achieve a finished, professional look. The inclusion of the copper foil technique into "classic" stained glass opens up great new possibilities. Its use provides effects not possible with lead.

Fig 9–15 A copper foiling machine by Diegel Engineering. As the paper backing is stripped away, it is guided to a waste bin on the floor. Diegel has a special crimping device that can be attached to the machine or hand-held as a second process.

Fig. 9–14 A foiling machine originally manufactured by Sunshine Glass and now made by Glastar, holds three different sizes of copper foil—¼", ³/₁₆", and ¹/₃₂". It dispenses the foil, splitting off the paper liner in the process, centers it on the glass, and crimps it around the edge.

Fig. 9–16 Foiling with a manual copper foiling machine from Lamps Ltd. The glass is held against the front "forming" wheel which applies and crimps the foil in one operation.

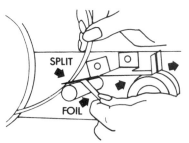

Fig. 9–17A *The Elite "1" foiling machine. (Courtesy: Stained Glass Design Hasbrouck Heights, New Jersey) As the foil comes off the feed wheel, it is split away from its paper backing. This leaves the sticky surface facing up.*

Fig. 9–17B *The foil travels toward the front of the machine.*

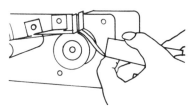

Fig. 9–17C *At this point the glass is brought to the foil and contact is made.*

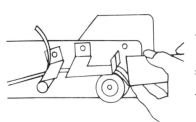

Fig. 9–17D *The glass is brought against the foiling wheel and pressed firmly against the foil.*

Fig. 9–17E *The glass is turned so that its edges meet the foiling wheel.*

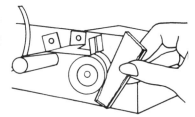

Fig. 9–17F *The foiling is now almost completed.*

Fig. 9–17G *Foiling the piece with simultaneous crimping along the sides of the glass. The foil is torn and a slight overlap is allowed where the two ends meet.*

FOILING MACHINES

Foilers run the gamut from the simplicity of a bare wheel attached by screws to the worktable as a mere holding unit for a roll of copper foil to electric ones that apply the foil, strip away the paper backing, and even crimp the edges around the glass. The more sophisticated units will hold several different sizes of foil for different glass thicknesses. Thus the multiplicity of hand operations is transformed into a single machine procedure. Since hand foiling could not be made easier, the object of the foiling machine is to make it more productive and the end result more professional looking. The carelessness of many workers in keeping their foiled overlap even is compensated for by the machine. This alone, for a worker who does only a minimum of foiling, would make the purchase of even a cheap foiler worthwhile. If you do a lot of foiling (and some workers do almost all of their stained glass this way), any of the sophisticated machines is a dream purchase.

Essentially all foilers work alike. The roll of copper foil is held by the unit and fed into a smaller wheel against which the glass edges are hand turned. The advantage of an electrically driven wheel against a hand one is the lessening of fatigue quotient. Electric foilers are run by foot pedals guided by the operator.

10
Finishing Techniques

Enthusiasm provides the design, and ambition the fabrication process. Both can wane when the nitty gritty of cleanup begins. Some workers skimp on the final touches that must be applied to any stained-glass work, partly because they feel these won't make much difference. But any stained glass that is not thoroughly cleaned and puttied remains forever unfinished and can come back to haunt you should you sell it. The finishing processes are just as important as the designing and the fabrication of your work.

CLEANING THE GLASS

Once all soldering has been done, clean the piece as soon as possible. The longer you allow the finished piece to sit before cleaning, the more difficult it will be to get it clean. The flux residues and the general grime that has accumulated during the fluxing and soldering operation will form a crust over the lead and the glass. No matter how tired you may be upon completion of the work, start cleaning!

Rinsing in soapy water is just a first step. The object may appear clean while it is wet, but when the water is wiped off it will be smudgy, tacky, and probably still weeping flux from the joints. Few things are more scruffy looking than an uncleaned

stained-glass object. And your chances of selling any item are certainly better if it is nice and shiny.

Cleaning the glass comes first. The panel should be laid flat on the table and cleaning and polishing powder sprinkled over it. Sift the cleaning and polishing powder over the glass with a small strainer so that you cover tbe surface. Lumps and other debris may get into the powder, and they can scratch the glass. With a floor scrubbing brush with bristles that are flexible enough to ride over the leads without tearing them loose, brush the powder all over the glass. You can use a great deal of force pressing straight down, providing the object is lying flat. If you work in an enclosed area, keep a handkerchief over your nose; the powder can fly about and you may find yourself sneezing it onto the work.

Once the surface is clean, turn the panel over and apply powder to the other side. Then with a vacuum cleaner or with a rag, remove the powder. This powder is not to be reused. Tap the panel against the table to remove the remaining powder from under the cames and hold it up to the light. You might still have a few pieces of glass that look smudgy or feel tacky. Repeat the process for their benefit. Once the panel is clean and leads are uniformly shiny, use soapy water or Windex to clean the surfaces further.

Fig. 10–1 *Cleaning the completed panel. The cleaning and polishing powder is rubbed dry against all surfaces of lead and glass. A fine steel wool pad or a floor scrubbing brush may be used.*

Fig. 10–2 *Puttying the panel. Putty is pushed under all lead flanges.*

PUTTYING

Putty is used to weatherproof windows and provide support. For stained glass, putty with a linseed oil base is best. Linseed oil putty hardens after a time and provides a stiff lining between the lead came and the glass in the channels.

When getting ready to putty, first get an old pair of kid gloves or coat your hands with a protective glove coating such as Pro-Tek. This DuPont product guards the skin against, oils, grease, and oxides, and it washes off with water. It prevents the putty from sticking to your fingers. Pro-Tek is greaseless and within a few moments after applying it to your skin, you will not even know it's there.

Take a handful of putty from the can and rub it into a ball between your palms. If it is too sticky and moist, add a little cleaning and polishing compound to it to stiffen it up. If it is too adherent, it will come out of the came as fast as you push it under, preferring to stick to your fingers.

After getting the putty to the right consistency, snip off a bit with your fingers and start pushing it under the cames with your thumb *(Fig. 10–2)*. Each piece of lead should have putty under it. This is not as painstaking a procedure as it may sound. In fact, many workers find it relaxing. Be careful that you don't crack any pieces of glass by getting too relaxed. The

border leads should also be puttied. Be careful when pushing the putter under them that you do not push them away from the glass.

When you are done, you will find a sloppy object in front of you covered with gobs of putty. Take a bent putty knife or even a lead knife and turn down the cames against the glass surface. Putty will ooze out from beneath them *(Fig. 10–3)*. With a nail or an ice pick, go around each border of lead *(Fig. 10–4)*. The putty will easily cut loose from the came. Scoop up any excess putty with your hand, roll it into a ball, and pop it back into the can. Seal the can tightly. If you leave the lid even slightly ajar, the putty will harden. After puttying, clean and polish the piece again.

Putty comes in black or white. Black putty will leave a black line under the lead; white putty will leave a white one. It is especially important if you are using black putty to protect your hands. The carbon that furnishes the color is difficult to remove from skin.

You should warn anyone buying your stained glass, if the puttying has been done only within the past several days, that the work will continue to ooze putty for at least another week. Ask them not to clean it. After several days the putty will set, and they can go around the leads with knife to clean away the excess, and then clean the panel with Windex.

Fig. 10–3 Turning down the leads in a panel after puttying. Be careful not to apply too much force.

Fig. 10–4 Removing excess putty using an ice pick. The point is passed around the surfaces of the lead.

BRUSHING THE LEADS

The leads must also be cleaned, even though they were cleaned with the glass. Brush the leads with fine steel wool that has been dipped in the cleaning and polishing powder, then scrub along the lead surfaces. The leads will become bright and shiny as you strip away grime, soldering residues, and the oxide coat. The shiny surfaces start to darken again after cleaning, but they should all darken evenly. The soldered joints will also darken in time.

"ANTIQUING" LEADS

If you don't want to wait for the leads to age naturally, applying antiquing patina will provide an "aged" look. Brushed on surfaces, the patina will change the lead

color from a bright silver to a dark copper. For this to occur, the lead came must be tinned; that is, solder must be run along whatever length you want to treat. This procedure is not only time consuming but also costly because of the amount of material used. If you are making a commissioned object and antiquing was requested, include the extra materials and labor in the price.

Clean the entire panel before antiquing the leads. If they are covered with oxides and flux residues, you will have a difficult time. Leads can be cleaned again after the antiquing patina is applied, but not with steel wool and cleaning and polishing powder. This would strip away the copper coat provided by the copper sulphate solution and once again make them shiny. When you tin the leads, use flux sparingly and if any should spill on the glass wipe it off immediately.

FILING SOLDERED JOINTS

After soldering, your joints should be smooth and look finished. Until you master soldering, they may be ragged and

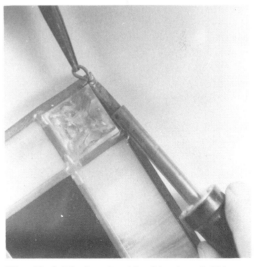

Fig. 10–5 The loop is soldered in place, held in position by needle-nose pliers.

rough. Instead of spreading solder wildly around with the iron and making things worse, you might be better off to file them smooth. Use a small flat, fine file, but be careful not to scratch the glass. Don't try to make a masterpiece of each joint; just file away the rough edges that you were unable to smooth out with the iron.

APPLYING THE HANGING LOOPS

Copper loops that are used for hanging stained-glass panels or objects should be tinned before being affixed. Use a pair of needle-nose pliers to hold them. Holding the loop in the pliers, dip it into a jar of muriatic acid. This will remove the oxide coat instantly. Muriatic is a strong, inorganic acid that should be treated with caution. Please keep it away from children.

Once the loop has been dipped in this acid bath, it should be dried, fluxed, and tinned immediately. Do not attempt to tin it without using flux (it won't accept solder) or without drying it off, since the acid will pit soldering tips and cause dangerous fumes.

A copper loop ready for tinning will allow solder to run full circle with one application. Keep holding the loop with needlenose pliers, since copper transmits heat readily to unwary fingers. Apply the loop at the balancing point of your piece, or use two or more loops at either corner for balance. One may have to be placed behind the panel in order to support it from the bottom or the middle. By pretinning the loops, you will find it simple to solder them to your piece, which you may find yourself one-handed, one-elbowed, or even with your chin during this activity. This is not the time to find solder rolling off an untinned loop.

11
All About Slab Glass

Slab glass, or dalles de verre, or simply dalles, is a fascinating medium that few glass hobbyists have worked with to any great extent. As it happens, the slab glass technique lends itself well to contemporary designs in architecture. As produced by the Blenko Glass Company, these slabs weigh about eight pounds and are about ⅞″ thick and are made in more than 200 shades.

SHAPING SLAB GLASS

There are several ways to cut and shape slab glass.

Breaking on the Anvil

The slab-glass anvil is a triangular steel saddle with a rounded edge. The slab is scored with a straight line using a standard glass cutter. With the score line uppermost, the slab is placed directly above the anvil and the slab rapped smartly against it. It will break precisely along the score. This process can be continued to fairly small pieces until it becomes unwieldy. Then the slab glass hammer is used.

Breaking by Wedge

This device comes to a much sharper presenting edge than the anvil. Glass is shaped by holding the bottom surface against the wedge and tapping from above with the hammer.

Scoring with Cutter and Chipping Hammer

Curves are broken out in this manner. Taking the smallest rectangle of glass you can break out, the curve is scored and a chipping hammer is used to follow it around, taking a little bit of glass off the surface at a time. The glass is propped against the anvil for support.

Faceting

This process involves chipping small pieces off the glass surface, allowing more light to pass through and reflect from the glass, like a diamond. The smooth side of the glass is usually the interior surface; the rough side is the outside. The unofficial rule is to place ⅛″ facets over about 30 percent of the glass in a window and leave 70 percent of it untouched for contrast. Faceting is generally done with hand-held pieces, the force of the chipping hammer being minimal.

Shaping with Hammer Alone

As the pieces get small enough, they can be shaped on the anvil by taps of the slab-glass hammer without the benefit of an underlying score line. The hammer must have carbide tips to be effective. Steel will not last.

Fig. 11-1 *The slab-glass wedge as we use it.*

Fig. 11-3 *Positioning a piece of chunk glass for breaking.*

Fig. 11-2 *The slab glass wedge inside its lead base, which is itself supported by wood. The hole drilled in the lead slab is just sufficient to allow the lower portion of the wedge to go through. A piece of the wood base was removed to show this. The wood base levels the lead and the wedge by allowing room for the stem to come through.*

Fig. 11-4 *Breaking a slab glass chunk with the wedge and hammer. A sharp tap will do the job.*

Using the Band Saw

Diamond band saws made for glass will shape slab glass easily and precisely. A saw is used both to break out difficult shapes and to save glass, since the amount of waste here is minimal. The results are smooth and finished. Glass band saws are now available at a reasonable price.

A general impression of slab-glass cutting by those who have never seen it done is that pieces of glass fly like bullets across the workshop as hammers slam against dalles. Actually, the force is more a tap than a slam. All the same, it is wise to

Fig. 11–5 *Note the even surface of the new break.*

Fig. 11–6 *The pattern placed in the bottom of the wooden frame.*

Fig. 11–7 *Rubber cement is used to hold the pieces of chunk glass to the work drawing so they will not move out of place when the epoxy is poured.*

wear goggles and best to use gloves when involved in this activity. Once the glass has been shaped, it is color coded to its place on the cartoon.

THE CARTOON

The cartoon, usually drawn on kraft paper, is worked up from a design similar to that used in a stained-glass window. Patterns may be taken from it and used as guides to shape the glass. These shapes should be simple, rough hewn, and fairly large. Don't try to produce a delicate effect, at first. The material does not respond well to this kind of statement. If you plan deeply cut facets, block them in the dalle with bits of clay so that the epoxy or cement does not flow into and abolish them. This clay is removed after the epoxy has set, leaving the original facet. If your cartoon calls for a long, narrow piece of dalle, say 1″ by 8″, cut four pieces to that dimension and place them in the design about ½″ apart so that the epoxy will flow between. After you pour the epoxy, even though they are interrupted you will see the individual pieces as a single line of color.

Curves are done as discussed above. Where dimension is required, it is not pos-

Fig. 11–8 *Detail of panel done in cement.*

sible to stand one piece of dalle atop another any more than you can stand a jewel atop an underlying bit of slab glass. The holding material will seep between them and provide opacity. For a three-dimensional surface stand some of the dalle pieces on end. This will raise them above their neighbors and give contrast without you having to get technically sidetracked.

CEMENT AND EPOXY

If you use a cement mix, place reinforcing wires on top of your cartoon before laying your chunks upon it. Then cut holes in this wire to allow the chunks of dalles to fit within. The epoxy technique needs no such reinforcing. Using cement with dalles has not proved satisfactory as an architectural holding material because of the stresses provoked by cold weather outside the building wall and heated air within. Between an outside temperature of zero degrees and an inside one of 80 degrees, the inch or so of cement separation soon develops hairline cracks that begin to leak air. This problem does not occur with epoxy.

The main consideration with epoxy is that it must be mixed well. It comes in two separate cans—one a monomer, the other a polymer; or one the epoxy itself, the other the hardener. Once the two are mixed, hardening begins. Premix the epoxy for about five minutes before adding the hardener. Without a good premix, the panel will not set up properly and soft spots will develop. After premixing the epoxy, pour in the hardener and mix for another five minutes. There is not a 50:50 ratio; the ratio is 1 gallon of epoxy resin to ½ pint can of hardener. If you use less than a full gallon unit at a time, use the ratio of 100 resin (the heavy, thick epoxy) to 2½ of the clear, yellow hardener. That is 100:2½ by weight. If you use the entire unit once, which is generally the case, then simply pour the entire contents of the hardener into the can of epoxy.

One gallon of the epoxy-hardener mix will cover four square feet, figuring half epoxy and half glass.

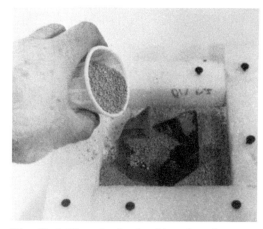

Fig. 11–9 *Glass chunks placed in a Styrofoam frame as the first step in making an epoxy panel. The upper-right piece has a clay dam in one deep facet. The sand is poured over the surface.*

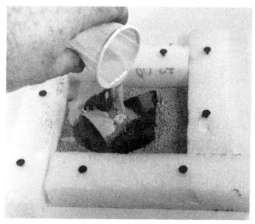

Fig. 11–10 *Pouring the epoxy over the even surface of sand.*

MAKING AN EPOXY PANEL

Framing

Frames for an epoxy panel can be made of wood pieces nailed together or, more simply, of Styrofoam sides attached by nails through prepunched holes to a flat piece of Styrofoam. The sides can be used over and over to form squares or rectangles. The edges of the frame correspond to the borders of your cartoon. You must leave a good inch outside perimeter between frame and glass for chunks. Otherwise, you will not have room to pour the epoxy; it will be crowded between frame and glass and will not be able to level out. If the frame is made of wood, treat the sides with a mold release to keep them from adhering to the

Fig. 11–11 *The completed pour. The glass on the lower right has been splashed. This will be chipped off when dry.*

the epoxy from running and smearing the surface. Each piece of glass should be clean or the epoxy will not adhere. Alcohol or acetone may be used as a cleaning agent. The chunks should be large enough to allow light to penetrate the panel. Too small pieces may get lost in the epoxy.

Another method—and the one we favor—is to pour roofing sand between the glass pieces to a level of ¼". Maintain this level throughout the framed area; if it becomes too deep, the epoxy poured on top of it will be overly thin. The sand is readily poured from a plastic cup. It prevents the epoxy from sticking to the paper. It also keeps the pieces of glass from moving during the pouring process, as well as giving an interesting texture to the surface.

epoxy. Wrapping them with waxed paper, as some workers do, is a nuisance. Nor do we use wax paper on the cartoon, since the rubber cement we use to hold our chunks in place sticks better to the kraft paper than to wax paper. We rip the paper away afterward.

The frame, whether of wood or Styrofoam, should be smooth. Every indentation or knob will appear in the border of the finished epoxy panel. These panels are heavy, so don't make them larger than roughly 2½ by 3 feet. For your beginning panel, even smaller dimensions would be advisable.

Place the frame over the cartoon, remembering to leave room at the perimeter and making sure that the kraft paper is flat and unwrinkled under the frame. Panels are usually cast approximately 1" in thickness, so judge the width of your frame accordingly. With the frame in place, you are ready to place your shaped chunks within it.

Placing the Glass

If you are going to pour directly on the kraft paper, use rubber cement to hold the glass chunks in place. This also prevents

Pouring the Epoxy

Epoxy poured from a cup will allow you more control than pouring it from the gallon container. It is best to pour the entire panel at one time. If you don't have enough epoxy and pour half today and half tomorrow, a demarcation line will appear between the two pourings. If you must pour on separate days, roughen the surface of the old area with a file or chisel before pouring fresh epoxy. This will make the bonding more effective.

Pouring is not really the word for this process. It is more a trickling of the epoxy between the glass pieces. If any epoxy gets on the glass don't wipe it off. Wiping leaves a smear, which is much harder to get off than just allowing the epoxy to harden and then chipping it off.

Epoxy sets up in about twenty to thirty minutes, so don't dawdle during the pouring; on the other hand, you needn't rush unduly and make a mess. Once you have the epoxy to the proper thickness, seed the top surface with coarse or fine sand or leave it smooth.

When pouring epoxy, the more ventilation in the room the better, and anything that will help get rid of the odor is good. Epoxy contains no solvents, but the smell can be quite strong. Epoxy can irritate the skin if you have a sensitivity to it, so when working with it, wash off any epoxy with soap and water. Avoid using solvents, since these remove fats from the skin and can themselves be a source of irritation.

Double Casting

Double casting permits the glass to protrude from the epoxy on both sides of the panel. Once you lay the glass in the frame, pour ½" of roofing sand (instead of ¼") around the pieces. Then pour ¼" of epoxy and let it sit overnight. Next day turn the panel over, frame and all, and let the sand fall out. If the panel comes out of the frame, replace it. With the panel turned, pour on a second ¼" of epoxy. When this dries, you will have a central core of epoxy with glass chunks in bas relief. This makes for an emphatic, clean-looking effect. The problem with doing this is that it ties up a worktable for two days rather than one if you have a commercial studio.

The Hardened Panel

Epoxy takes approximately a day to harden (or cure.) It may then be handled and cleaned up, clay dams removed and kraft paper torn away if you have not used sand. Rubber cement comes easily away from the glass. Acetone may be used to clean any surfaces that remain tacky. Your initial panel may have a defect or two that you will want to improve upon with your next attempt. Chief among these is the "bleed-through spot," where the epoxy is quite thin. There may even be a hole, caused by too much sand in this area. This does not occur if you just pour onto the kraft paper. However, by the time you tear away the kraft paper you may decide to take your chances with the sand after all.

Thinner Pours for Decorative Objects

We have poured epoxy less than ⅛" thick and have had it hold small chunks with no difficulty. Such free-form objects are not very heavy, of course, and may be hung in windows easily. Cement cannot be poured

Fig. 11–12 *A decorative disk of chunk glass and epoxy. This side has been seeded with sand, and the chunks are almost level with the epoxy.*

Fig. 11–13 *Pieces of stained glass held together with epoxy. This material binds well even these ⅛" surfaces.*

this thin without developing stresses that will first crack, then crumble anything made with it. Epoxy can be poured thin enough to accommodate stained glass instead of chunk pieces. Fine or coarse sand may be used to seed the surfaces.

SLAB-GLASS SCULPTURE

Because of their irregular appearance and faceted edges, chunks of slab glass work well as sculpture pieces held together with epoxy. They can be almost hand-carved against the anvil or chipped freehand with a chipping hammer. The result provides an interesting rugged look that embodies the granitic force of stone with the softening colorants of the glass. These pieces are often foiled together rather than epoxied, which allows even freer forms to be designed. Where several pieces are used in overlays, the refracted light is all but blocked out, but reflected light remains. An intriguing arrangement of "positive" and "negative" emphases can thus be presented.

OTHER SLAB-GLASS EFFECTS

Glass chunks from an original slab can be used as decorative breaks, interspersed between pieces of stained glass. They can be glued to an underlying piece of plate glass to add dimension They can be polished on a wet belt so that all surfaces are smooth. In this condition they are gemlike and can be used as jewels. Foiled chunks can be readily incorporated into a stained-glass window for contrast.

Many hobbyists do not purchase slab glass as full slabs but as irregularly sized chunks from studios utilizing slabs. Even these pieces may have to be broken down further for a project. If you do not have a slab-glass wedge, you can make do with a cold chisel in a vise. The edge should be directly uppermost and the chisel held securely. With the edge of the chunk glass on top of the chisel, tap the surface with a hammer. The chunk will fracture. This is by no means a foolproof method, but working with chunk glass is not the same as working with stained glass. The same precision is not expected—or required.

*The danger of giving examples of the most
expert work is that the amateur finds
himself at once afflicted with a justifiable
despair at the bare prospect of attempting
what he can scarcely hope to accomplish.*
NEWTON WETHERED,
**Medieval Craftsmanship
and the Modern Amateur**

PROJECTS

III

12
Traditional Leading: Making a Window

The stained-glass window is fabricated like a stained-glass panel. It may be larger and more complicated in design, but the same techniques are used for both.

At first glance, the designs may appear simple, but you will be surprised when you begin work on them how complexities can suddenly arise, especially if you have not cut glass before. If you have cut glass before, or if you have done some work in stained glass but want to know the correct procedure, follow these mechanics. They will enable you to carry out the process as it is done in professional studios. Beginners should follow the steps given and the designs. Once you acquire the basic techniques, you may apply them to designs of your own.

THE DESIGN

Designing for stained glass involves submitting to the regulations of the material. No matter how beautiful a design may be, if it cannot be cut out of glass, it is useless. Even a design for a square panel, divided into quarters, thirds, or in half, involves difficulties. We make it a point in our classes to insist that beginners start with as simple a panel as possible. That student who came into her first class with a pineapple consisting of eighty-six small pieces was dissuaded. She thanked us afterward.

Where should you go for design ideas?

Artists in other fields—Mondrian, for example—are worth studying. There are many books with pictures of stained glass, old and new, that will give you ideas of line flow. Geometric figurations in themselves can be balanced in a beginning panel. Triangles, diamonds, squares, rectangles, rhomboids, and trapezoids all qualify as grist for your mill. Pattern books are put out for beginners and advanced students alike. As you progress, you will find yourself depending less on others and more on your own imagination.

Sketch, draw, erase, resketch until you have something on paper that looks good to you. Don't be afraid to detail your sketch, but keep in mind that such detailing may have to be summarized in the cartoon by two or three lead lines. Exact and precise detailing on glass can be done only by painting or etching. These techniques are used to complement the basically leaded end result, not to supplant it.

The design should be sketched in charcoal so that extraneous lines may be easily rubbed out. It need not be drawn to scale or size. Once you have a notion that looks as though it might do, concentrate on developing it. When you think it is satisfactory, ink it in with a magic marker. Don't worry for the moment about too small pieces or avoiding curves that look especially difficult to cut and fit. The idea is to get down on paper some informal statement you can build on. A design starts as a

Fig. 12–1 The basic leading procedure for a diamond window. The work drawing is underneath, flanked by the right angle formed by the wood strips. The border leads are against these; the glass fits into these leads and lead is placed against their edges. Note that a separate pattern is cut for each diamond and each is numbered.

Fig. 12–2 As the work progresses, the process is repeated many times, always building from the starting corner in the upper left and fanning outward. Not seen for purposes of clarity are the leading nails, which ordinarily would be holding the end leads against the glass until new pieces are fitted.

preliminary survey and becomes specific as it progresses. Once the design is set on paper in its entirety, you will have realized a beginning, middle, and ending to the progression as you conceived it.

Color choice is going to affect your design strongly. Think in terms of color as well as linear quality. Study pictures of stained-glass windows to get a feel for line flow and color choice of professionals. Don't be afraid to keep changing your design until it's exactly what you want.

Fig. 12–3 The finished window.

THE CARTOON

The cartoon is the stained-glass blueprint drawn precisely to size. Every line in it is either a paint line or a lead line, and every space between lead lines is a piece of glass that must be cut. Some designers make it a point to draw lead lines in one color and paint lines in another, so that the two may be easily distinguished. Only the lead lines, of course, are to be cut. All extraneous lines from the original design are removed

Fig. 12-4 *Diamond window with center break. The basic pattern is thus modified.*

Fig. 12-5 *Kitchen triptych window.*

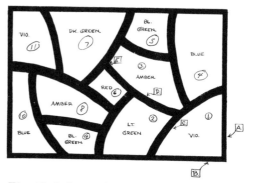

Fig. 12-6 *A typical cartoon for a stained-glass panel.*

Fig. 12-7 *The layout.*

or condensed, while contiguous spaces are divided into individual cuts of glass. Lead lines are indicated as being wide or narrow. Joints are clearly marked.

The original sketch may suffer some radical changes during this procedure. The extent to which it does not depends upon the craftsman's ability to design for glass. You will soon find the more obvious facets of this becoming second nature.

All pieces from the original design involving impossible cuts must be redesigned when transposed to the cartoon. Balance

your lead lines foreground and background so they flow.

Once you have the cartoon inked in, you can begin laying it out to make your work drawing and then your patterns. Number each piece in the cartoon, even though it may be a very simple one and have only a few easily recognizable pieces.

The work habits you learn as a beginner will stand you in good stead throughout more complicated projects in stained glass. Be patient and follow directions.

THE LAYOUT

The layout involves the cartoon, the work drawing, and the patterns. The work drawing, which is made on brown kraft paper, will be used as a guide to lead up the panel. It should be an exact replica of the cartoon. Once you have transferred your cartoon to the work drawing via carbon paper, keep the cartoon in front of you so that you can consult it. The work drawing will show where each piece of glass goes, as does the cartoon, but the work drawing will be on the worktable covered with the pieces of glass placed on top of it. Having the cartoon pinned up before you will help give a quick check where the lead lines are. The cartoon may be used to check against the work drawing during the procedure should the drawing tear or become obscured with flux or solder. Patterns are made of a stiff oaktag and will be used as templates for cutting each piece of glass to the correct size and shape.

The method of laying out the work is as follows: On the worktable, place the piece of pattern paper cut larger than the cartoon. White pattern paper shows up nicely against dark glass. Place on top of the pattern paper a piece of carbon paper, dark side down. Use a heavy, reusable carbon, not an office stationery type, which will not take the wear and tear of the work. If the carbon paper tears, you will have wasted time.

On top of the white pattern paper place your carbon paper. Over the carbon paper, place a piece of brown kraft paper, with much wider margins than the cartoon, then another piece of carbon paper, dark side down. Then place your cartoon on the very top. Having done all this, tack all four corners down on the board or table, allowing no air space. Now, trace firmly with a pencil right down the lines of the cartoon so that it comes through to the underlying white pattern paper. If you have inked in your cartoon with a magic marker, trace down the middle of the wide lines. Next, number each piece that represents a piece of glass. If you have already numbered them on your cartoon, go over the numbers with enough pressure so they will register on the bottom pattern paper. Take out two of the tacks and lift the papers at one end to see if all the lines and all the numbers have come through. If you remove all your tacks without checking, you will have a difficult time getting everything back together again. Once all is in order on the pattern paper, all the tacks may be re-

moved and you can start making your patterns.

To cut glass accurately, you must use patterns. There is no such thing as free-hand work in stained-glass windows. You must also allow for the heart of the lead came when cutting patterns (see Chapter 7). Whether you use pattern scissors or a pattern knife, be sure you leave as equal a space as possible between pattern pieces. If you intend to use wide leads either around the panel or through it, leave an additional $\frac{1}{16}''$ space between the patterns.

When you have your patterns cut, check them against the original cartoon. Each pattern should fit within its predetermined space so that you can see the inked line around it. If you do not see any part of this line, recut your pattern so that the line shows. If you think the pattern is accurate and yet a portion of the cartoon line does not show, check your original design. The pattern must fit exactly. If you don't check, you will find when you cut your glass that the piece will be oversized in this area, which will cause it to butt against its neighbor right over the border of the panel.

CUTTING THE GLASS

Here we reiterate the basic rules of glass cutting: (1) hold the glass cutter properly; (2) work on a flat and steady surface; (3) do not tilt the cutter to the left or the right, but hold it as vertical as you can; and (4) cut standing up where possible, and remember that the pressure you put on the glass should be pressure from the weight of your body and not from the muscle of your arm.

Cut the glass so that it matches the pattern exactly. If the glass breaks improperly and leaves a space where the pattern shows no space, recut the glass, not the pattern. Beginners sometimes try to forget that cutting seven facets on one piece of glass accurately does not make up for cutting the eighth badly. They still have to

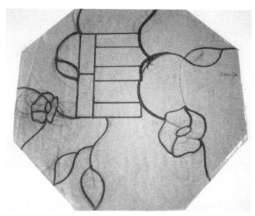

Fig. 12–8 Sketch for a window. The family initial appears in the center. The lines were drawn in charcoal and reworked. They were then inked in.

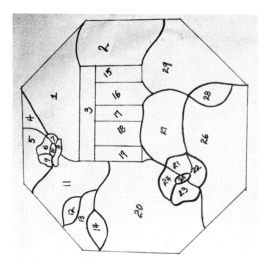

Fig. 12–9 The cartoon of the sketch with every piece numbered.

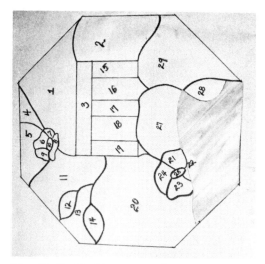

Fig. 12–10 Checking a piece of glass against the work drawing.

Fig. 12–11 All the background pieces are fitted against the work drawing.

redo the entire piece. There is no room for partial perfection.

FITTING THE GLASS

Once you have all your glass pieces cut, they should be resized against the individual patterns. It may surprise you how much off measurement a piece of glass can be, even though it looked good when you cut it. It is easier to be objective about a cut piece after you've let it sit for a while. If the pieces are to be critically close (as with copper foil), sand off all pinhead edges and small chips with abrasive paper. All pains taken at this point will achieve better end results and make your job easier as you progress. So grozz the pieces first, but if the fit is still not good, sand them.

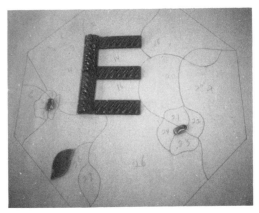

Fig. 12–12 *The foreground pieces selected and checked against the work drawing. Old jewels were used for the initial and small glass globs for the centers of the flowers.*

Fig. 12–13 *Checking the border leads for size and placement against the window border. H leads were used to allow for trim when the window is fitted.*

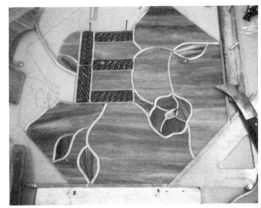

Fig. 12–14 *Leading up the window. Because of the panel's octagonal shape, side braces were employed that would interlock as securely as possible along the outside angles. Note the plastic triangle employed as a brace. Leading nails maintain pressure above the initial, holding the panel together while additional leads are cut and measured. The window is going together from the lower right hand corner fanning outward.*

Fig. 12–15 *The window is fluxed before soldering.*

Once you have the pieces smooth and accurate to pattern, place them on the drawing one more time and check their relationship. If you have large interspaces where small leads are to go, you may have to revise your leading design or recut the pieces. The mistake was probably in cutting the initial pattern. No matter how well the pieces of pattern seem to fit, the thicker glass pieces add a discrepancy. For one thing they may have slanted edges. These provide deceptive space between them for the leading. You may have chipped edges of glass or small indentations. These can seem unimportant when you consider each individual piece. They can become emphatic when the pieces are matched up, fault to fault. The lead may not cover both flaws. So go back to the work drawing before leading up, and stay out of a mess. To rectify a mess, you may either have to cut pieces over again, or, in

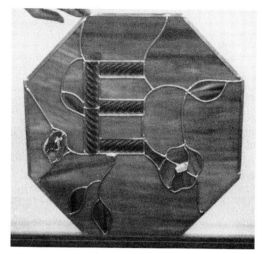

Fig. 12–16 *The finished window.*

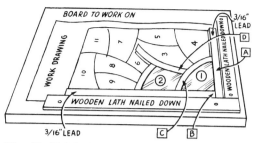

Fig. 12–17 *The leading procedure.*

a more extreme case, take apart the entire panel and rework the design. It is much less frustrating to find out if your glass is going to fit before you get involved with leading it.

LEADING THE PANEL

If all your glass matches and all the spaces seem adequate for the lead, and if you have planned the leading according to the thicknesses of glass, remove all pieces of glass from the work drawing and place them within easy reach. You are ready for leading up.

If your lead cames are bent, straighten them by placing one end in a vise or lead stretcher and pulling slowly at the other end with a pair of pliers. This will stretch the lead slightly. All unstretched lead, even if it is straight, should be stretched. Open the lead cames with a lathkin to allow the glass to fit into the groove easily. Use a lathkin before fitting any strip of came, even if the grooves look adequate.

The correct procedure for cutting came is to place the leading knife on top of it and rock it with a side-to-side motion, exerting only minimum downward pressure to cut through it. The came should be

scratch marked to show the angle of miter. Measure it directly over the drawing space, then cut accordingly.

Leading up is begun by taking your finished work drawing and laying it flat on your board or table (*Fig. 12–17*). Nail two wooden strips, about 2″ wide and somewhat longer than your work drawing, at right angles to each other along the lower right corner of the drawing so that you can just see the outside margin line. You must have enough excess on your drawing paper to allow the boards to grip the edges.

Take a piece of ³⁄₁₆″ U lead, cut it to size so that it is slightly longer than the border line of the work drawing, and place it along one edge of the wood strip, the groove toward the drawing. Put a leading nail through the excess end to hold it in place. Take another strip of this same lead, slightly longer than the border line, and fit it at a right angle to the first along the other strip of wood. Place a nail through the end. The corners where these two pieces of lead meet can be mitered to fit at an angle, or one may fit inside the other, or you can cut the top away from one of the lead cames and the bottom away from the other so the two interlock in the corner. This is perhaps the method that gives the most strength (*Fig. 12–18*).

Pick up your first piece of glass, the right-hand corner piece, and place it into the groove of the leads at their corner juncture and along the sides. Tap it gently with the leaded end of the leading knife to be certain that it is seated properly within the

Traditional Leading: Making a Window **175**

channel (*Fig. 12–19*). The line on the work drawing should be visible around the edge of the glass. It it is not, it means that either the glass is not seated in the lead groove correctly or that there is an inadequate cut somewhere on the glass surfaces. Try to correct this immediately rather than trying to make up the difference in the next piece.

Measure, mark, and cut each piece of lead came to fit exactly into its proper space as you go along. See appendix, *Interweaving Leaded Lines.* Each piece should be slightly shorter than its glass border. Cutting it slightly shorter allows the next lead came room to meet it. If your leads are too long, they will interfere one with the other. If they are too short, you will have a gap between them. *Do not* bridge them with solder, but recut the lead. Even one of these soldered gaps will make your panel look sloppy.

Now we will describe the method in detail. Follow the cartoon in Figure 12–6.

You have put in place leads A and B and glass piece 1. Next comes the first inside piece of lead (*Fig. 12–20*). We arbitrarily chose ¼″ H shaped lead for this. Carefully bend the lead to shape against the glass edge, and cut it off at the proper mitre at one end. Measure it again along the glass and cut it off at the other end. The proper mitre means making the cuts on both sides correspond to the border leads that are running up each side. Again, the leads should be mitered to fit as snugly as possible against the opposing surfaces. If they are not, you will have a gap. Trying to fill such a gap with solder leaves unmistakeable evidence and indicates a poor technique on your part. Place the cut and mitered lead around the exposed edge of glass and fit it into place.

Next, put glass piece 2 into the lead groove. If you can see the lines of the work drawing around it, it is in proper position. If you do not see the lines around it,

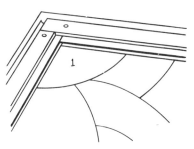

Fig. 12–18 *Interlocking the corner leads. They are flush against the bordering strips of wood.*

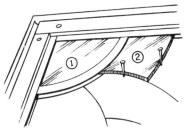

Fig. 12–20 *The first inside piece of lead cut and placed and the second piece of glass placed and held with leading nails.*

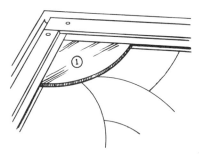

Fig. 12–19 *The first piece of glass fitted into the corner leads. A few tap should seat it properly.*

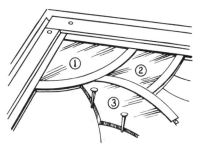

Fig. 12–21 *The pieces of glass and lead fit together like the pieces of a picture puzzle.*

Blue Blazes. *Michael Kennedy. Courtesy of Spectrum Glass.*

A Gallery of Contemporary Glass Work

Lady in Waiting. *Designed and constructed by Joy England, Creative Enterprises, Miami, of Armstrong glass.*

Waterglass. *Paul Marioni. Courtesy of Spectrum Glass.*

Window. Douglas Hansen, Seattle.
18' x 36'', Fremont antique glass.

Silhouette. *Paulo DuFour. Detail of window, constructed of*
Merry Go Round glass.

Glassrolling. *Paulo DuFour. Window, constructed of Merry Go Round glass.*

Earth, *completed in 1977. Joe Castagna, New York Art Glass. 28" x 28", made of Uroboros iridized and drapery glass and Fisher reamy antique.*

Breakfast of Champions. *Ruth Brockmann. Fused and sandblasted glass, with copper foil, lead and brass.*

Starfish Lamp. *Ichiro Tashiro.*

The Great Horned Owl. *Barbara Griffith. See step-by-step project, Chapter 19.*

The Old Western Town. *Barbara Griffith. See step-by-step project, Chapter 19.*

check the glass to make sure it was cut properly. Usually, the most difficult point of entry to the came is at either end where the lead has been cut. Even slight crimping of these ends prevents the glass from properly seating. It's a good idea after cutting came to reopen the ends of the came automatically. This allows the glass to seat without fighting the lead. It is easier to do this with the lead in your hand than resting against the piece of glass on the table.

Once the lead is seated, hammer two nails as shown to hold it in place. A glass piece with more than one exposed edge should be held in place with leading nails, not finishing nails. Leading nails are tapered for ease of tapping and will not press too forcefully against the glass. They can be removed easily from the wood with fingers. Horseshoe nails work well for this. *Do not* use carpet tacks, which are notorious for bent points. A bent carpet tack will probably crack the glass.

Now measure and cut lead D as shown, remembering to cut the one end short at the proper angle at point E. Notice that this lead goes past the piece of glass just placed, piece 2. It may do this because it is continuing the line of the design directly to the line of piece 7. Of course, you could cut the lead between pieces 3 and 6 and put a new lead in, but that would give you three separate pieces of lead and more labor than if you used the single lead to sweep by this particular joint directly to piece 7. See Appendix, Interweaving Leaded Lines.

Glass piece 3 goes into the groove next, again with a nail at each end to hold it in place tightly against piece 2. Fit and form the piece of lead going between pieces 3 and 4, and then place piece 4, tapping it into place from above with the handle of your leading knife, being certain that all other pieces are secured with leading nails so they don't move. It is now a matter of building up the rest of the pieces in their proper places, cutting the leads to fit as you go along.

Pieces are placed consecutively and in

a manner that allows maximum pressure, one against the other, to hold them in place. Obviously, you would not place piece 6 or 8 before placing pieces 3 and 4. As you continue to fit the pieces of glass in position, remove the leading nails one at a time. To ensure that the lead cames fit under the glass already positioned, slightly lift the leads already in place with the point of your leading knife. This will raise the glass. Or you can slide the knife blade under the glass itself to raise it from the table. Remember to use the lathkin often to ensure that the cames are open to receive the glass.

When all the pieces are in place, check the border lines to make sure they show. If they don't, the glass pieces may not be seated firmly. Pieces should be individually tapped into place with the weighted end of the leading knife. However, don't get carried away and tap them too hard, or you will start chipping the edges or break the glass.

Once all your glass is seated properly and the borders are even, take two pieces of wood similar to the two you have already used and fit them securely against the other two sides, first applying U leads as before. Cut all U leads to size. Tap these new boards into position so that they are at 90-degree angles with the two that were already in place. Then make sure that the U lead borders of the panels are flush against the pieces of wood. If they are not, you can back the U leads slightly against them with the leading knife. There may be a slight space left between the channel of U lead and the piece of glass seated within it, but it is better to have an even border with a few pieces of glass not seated all the way to the edge of the lead than to have glass seated well but the border uneven.

When the boards are securely fastened and all four sides of the panel are even you are ready to solder (*Fig. 12–22*). Before doing this, if the panel is to fit into a predetermined space, recheck all measurements to make certain that you are within them. If not, you must rework to the req-

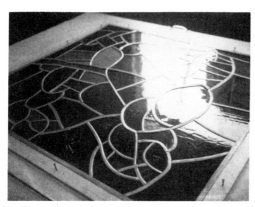

Fig. 12–22 *Prior to soldering, the leads should be tight fitting and the panel bordered by a wood frame held in place with leading nails.*

uisite dimensions. If you have made the window or panel too small, you must build up by changing to a wider bordering lead—even to a wide H if necessary. If too large, you will have to trim down the bordering glass edges. Find this out *before* you solder. There is no reason to be off to any extent, however. If you have followed the lines of the work drawing, and if the drawing was correctly measured to begin with, you should have no trouble with final dimensions.

SOLDERING THE JOINTS

Recheck all lead joints; make sure they are neatly cut and fit well. It may be necessary to clean the joints with a fine wire brush, such as a suede brush, or with steel wool. Lead that is not clean will not solder. If you are not using an iron clad tip, be certain that your copper tip is well tinned so that it will pick up solder.

Flux each joint well with the stiff flux brush. Then lay about ⅛" of solder directly on the joint and apply the iron to it. If your iron is the proper temperature, the solder should immediately melt and form a puddle at the joint. You don't have to cut the solder into pieces. Mold a roll of it in your hand, with the end resting on the joint, and melt it directly as it sits. Don't

hold the iron to the joint any longer than is necessary to flow solder or you may melt the lead away from the glass. Don't lift the iron too quickly either, or the solder will not have time to flow properly and you will have a weak joint.

If your iron is not hot enough, you can "drag" the solder and make a rough joint. As you progress in the craft, you will learn how much time to give the soldering iron to get the solder to puddle over the area. It is not necessary to exert pressure with the iron. Its own weight is pressure enough. Some students think the more pressure they apply, the better the solder will flow. That isn't so. Solder all joints and check the panel for missed joints before removing the pieces of wood. Then, turn the panel over and do the same to all the joints on the other side. Both sides must be soldered securely.

PUTTYING

Once you have soldered all the joints on both sides of the panel, you should putty it. Either black or white putty can be used, depending on whether you want a black or a white line showing beneath the lead came. Puttying is done by hand as described in Chapter 10.

If you apply too much putty, the glass may crack. If the panel has thick and thin glass and your pressure against the one is the same as the other, the thin piece may snap. If a piece of glass cracks, it must be replaced so be careful. Once you have cleaned the putty from the panel and turned down the leads, it is time for the final step, cleaning the panel.

THE CLEANING PROCESS

Sprinkle dry cleaning and polishing compound over the surface of the panel. Then dip a piece of steel wool in some powder and go over all the leads until they are bright and shiny. This removes all gummy oxides from the soldering process and exposes the leads to the air so they can all darken equally. Once the leads are shiny, take a floor scrubbing brush and apply a reasonable amount of force to cleaning the glass itself. Scrub the glass with the scrubbing brush or with the steel wool and then tip your panel up on end and tap it against the worktable. This will knock off most of the remaining powder. The rest can be wiped off with a clean rag or vacuumed. If any pieces of glass are still cloudy, go over them again with the powder. The panel should then be turned on its other side, on a clean area of the table or a clean piece of paper. That area should then be puttied and cleaned.

Now that your panel is finished, you may want to hang it in a window to brighten up a corner of the room. To do so, take two loops of moderately heavy copper wire and tin the loops with solder. Then solder one to each corner of your panel and string fish line through these loops. The fish line will not be seen from any distance. It is strong and will support your stained glass panel nicely. Fishing line

Fig. 12–23 *A decorative window from a church will be refitted in a private home.*

comes in different tensile strengths, and if your work is exceptionally heavy, check the amount of weight the line can bear before using it.

Your first stained glass panel is finished.

WORKING ON COMMISSIONS

As you continue your work in stained glass, word will get around and friends and relatives will begin to ask you to make a "little something" for them. Many beginners, flattered by such requests, give these "little somethings" away as fast as they can turn them out. This is a mistake. Your products should not be casual creations. Put at least a minimum price on your work, if only to cover the cost of materials. To add your time and artistry to the price is to begin to have people take what you are doing seriously enough to pay for pieces made to order. From this, it may be only a small step to a commission for a window.

If you receive a commission and the person does not know exactly what he wants, be prepared to offer advice. A stained-glass window comes into being through an interplay between artist and client.

Guiding the Client

Many people who commission a stained-glass window for their home are not certain what they want. They know they don't want a "churchy" window. They may be completely unaware of what stained-glass windows cost. If you receive a request for a window, find out how large an area is involved. Most professional studios charge by the square footage and by the design. Determine what the design is to be. The more complex the design, of course, the more labor involved and the higher the price. Once the client understands this, you can show your portfolio or sketch out a few quick designs so that you have something on paper that you both can look at and discuss. Without first showing the client something he can work from, no interplay of ideas is possible. If you use pastels, point out that the colors are not accurate for stained glass. We always prefer to use samples of stained glass to show prospective clients what their window will look like. Have a variety of color hues and enough choice of designs so your clients might come to a decision by pointing out a piece here and a color there from which you can fabricate a project for them.

Once the client has decided, get a deposit before doing any further work. After all, you now have to draw the design to scale which will expend a good bit of time and labor. Once you have the final design drawn up, and all the colors indicated, have your client examine it once more. Then any changes can be made before you cut the glass. Specify that once glass is cut, no further changes can be made.

The Work in Progress

Once your client has accepted the final design, get a further down payment. You may want to sign a contract. If you do, surely there will be a stipulation clause in it when the window is to be completed. Whether you sign contracts or not, try to finish the window as soon as you can without putting too much strain on yourself. Most people will want their project as soon as possible; if they press you for a date, try not to be too specific. Always leave some room for something to go wrong.

Try to establish a good working relationship with your client, one that assures him he is getting the best work for his money in a reasonable amount of time, and that allows *you* to feel your creativity is not being suppressed by an inflexible due date and late penalties. Your client may want to visit the workshop to see how the window is progressing, and you may or may not agree to this. We rarely have an objection to clients looking in on the work in progress, providing they realize that nothing can be changed at this point.

Making Acetates

Another method of showing clients what their design will look like is to draw up "acetates" of the finished window. (*Figs. 12–24 and 12–25.*) This involves painting a small, exact replica on clear plastic. It is a time-consuming project, and we do not advise doing it unless tbe project is extensive and a good deal of money is involved. The ordinary window for a private home does not require making an acetate.

Church work, on the other hand, may. If your client insists on seeing a picture of his finished window, and he is willing to pay you for making the acetate, it is not all that difficult to do. It must be drawn to scale and colored in with various paints to give an idea of the projected result. Acetates can be added to your portfolio to show prospective clients. They are much more "stained glassy" than pictures.

All the same, color transparencies of your previous windows are very effective

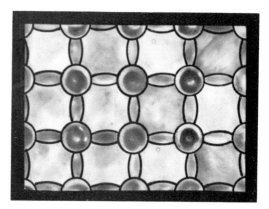

Fig. 12–24 Acetates, drawn to scale.

Fig. 12–25 *Acetates of windows for a restaurant.*

in selling yourself and your designs to a prospective client. We take color transparencies of every window we do as well as our lamps and most of our small hanging objects. Transparencies can also be used in lecturing to groups about stained glass.

Pricing Your Work

How does one price a piece of stained glass? The "rule" is so much per square foot. The square footage is achieved by measuring the length and width and multiplying the two together in inches and then dividing by 144 inches. Stained-glass windows for private homes may be measured in inches rather than in feet. Prices vary with the individual studio from $15 to $20 per square foot for simple designs such as diamonds, squares, or rectangles in a repeating pattern, to $50 to $60 a square foot for more complicated designs involving many more pieces of glass. However, a small area may be more complex than a large area with fewer pieces.

Most beginners during the first year or so cannot work fast enough to justify charging by the hour. You will find as you progress that you work more efficiently, but it is generally more realistic to charge according to the design and the size of the window.

People have little idea of the amount of labor involved in producing even a simple piece of stained glass. They may be surprised at any price quoted. Yet they are not taken aback by the cost of a watercolor or a piece of sculpture. It's a matter of education and exposure. Pricing is a "no man's land," and you will find out whether what you make is under or overpriced by how busy or slow your workshop becomes.

Turning the Window

One side of your 300-piece window is now leaded, soldered, and puttied, and it lies on the worktable in all its glory. It now must be turned and the other side completed. Turning a large window is not the same as turning a small panel. Attempting to raise the window by two corners may fracture it, since it will not be able to take its own weight without bending. It is best to make haste slowly here. Do not attempt to turn any good-sized window by yourself. Work a sturdy piece of plywood between the window and the table. Wriggle the plywood beneath the window while your partner, just as gently, raises it from below. The piece of plywood should be larger than the window and thick enough to support its weight without bending.

Once the window is resting on the plywood, put another board above it, sandwiching the window between them. You can then move the window any way you please. Raise the plywood and the window will come up with it. The weight of the window may be transferred to the back piece of plywood and the first piece removed. Lay the window back on the table with its unsoldered side uppermost and the first piece of plywood beneath it. Once this side is soldered and puttied, the window will acquire a great amount of strength, though it will still require support in moving it.

Barring the Window

If the window is more than 3' by 3', it must be barred. On windows larger than nine square feet, bars should be installed approximately every two feet using galvanized steel straps. Such straps have been coated with zinc so that they are solderable.

When you are making a window that you know will have to be barred, try to work the barring into the design. Otherwise the bar will run straight across the window and may interfere with the design. Where they can be hidden behind lead lines, bars should be. But where they cannot, the bar should not be left out. The window must have support or it will begin to buckle after a time, even in the sturdiest frame.

Bars are placed from border lead to border lead, even though the molding will support the periphery (*Fig. 12–26*). The molding can be sliced to allow the bar to fit into position. To bar a window across the midsection without going to the border leads is to lose the strength of the barring. Cut bars carefully, and solder them to each lead joint they pass over, making sure you press them as close to the joint as possible so as not to have a great gap of solder. Place the bars so the flat side is at right angles to the window. This will make them less obtrusive and provide more support.

We place our bars on the outside of the window, since they are less obtrusive. But inside or out, they determine whether the window stays together or falls apart.

Installation

It is up to you whether or not you install your commissioned window yourself. This may be decided upon at initial talks with the client. We generally do not install the windows we make. First of all, the process is time-consuming and takes us away from the studio, which is where we really want to be. Second, there is nothing creative about installing a window. It's plain hard work. Third, the risks that you take involve possible cracking of pieces of glass, which people tend to think you should replace at no charge. Fourth, there is the matter of transporting the window to the site. Many windows won't fit even into the largest station wagon, and a special truck must be hired for the occasion.

Of course since it is your window,

Fig. 12–27 Any window design begins with the dimensions. To help figure out the square footage of a window, Franklin Art Glass supplies this handy calculator with all the multiplication worked out for you.

Fig. 12–26 Barring a window. The zinc-coated rod runs the width of the window.

you may want to see it through its final phase and not trust the installation to a carpenter or glazier. There is some additional fee to be made from the installation if you have arranged to be paid by the hour. If you have arranged to be paid a flat fee (always a dangerous procedure), you can lose on the job. Many clients like the artist-technician to be on the scene when the window is installed, even if only to oversee. This is probably your best bet.

We have our clients call at the studio for their completed window, which they are responsible for as soon as it leaves our building. We attempt to give it enough support so that it is mobile and it will suffer no damage in transportation. This leaves us free to create other windows rather than spend hours doing a job a carpenter can do more efficiently.

Consider these drawbacks before agreeing to install any window. There is, in addition, the possibility that the measurements given will turn out to be inaccurate. You may then, rather unfairly, be expected to fix them at the site. This involves anything from a little scraping of the frame to a general overhauling. It's a good idea to allow for this sort of contingency by using H lead rather than a U lead on the border of the window. This additional channel may be just the amount of excess that can be shaved away to allow the window to fit properly. If you have not taken the measurements yourself, make sure that whoever has done so gives them to you in writing. If they are off, you don't want to be blamed. Wherever possible, take your own measurements.

THE WORK AREA

The Worktable

The worktable can be made by laying a ¾" thick, 4' by 8' sheet of plywood on top of two saw horses and level it about 36" from the floor. This is about the right height for working while standing without having to crouch over so that you get a backache. Such a table top lasts for years, and then you can flip it over to the other side.

Instead of saw horses, you can make a frame out of 2 × 4s. This will enable you to put storage shelves underneath the table. Be sure that your table is not wobbly; you will be doing a lot of nailing into it and using a lot of pressure against it. The more your table wobbles, the more compensating you will have to do. You can have a table smaller than 4' by 8', depending on the amount of space you have available. But if you possibly can work it in, the larger size will give you room to spread out with one, two, or even three projects going at once. As you continue to work in stained glass, you will modify your worktable to express your own working personality. It's usually best to allow a slight overhang for the tabletop. This makes for a sturdier working surface. The tabletop need not be nailed down unless you have made your frame so wide that the top of the table barely fits it.

The Light Table

A light table should become a permanent fixture in your stained-glass workshop. It may be no more than a piece of frosted glass propped on two bricks with a fluorescent bulb underneath it. The purpose of the light table is to allow you to match various colors of glass. While the best way to look at stained glass is by natural light, this is not always practical. A light table is the next best thing. It is especially useful when choosing colors for a stained-glass window that will involve many pieces. You want to be certain that your colors will blend. Make yourself a good light table. It's not a difficult project, and it will be well worth your labor by sharpening your color sense and allowing your final product to show itself in nicely blended hues and tones.

The larger the light table, the better. A well-supported table is made of 2 × 4s supporting a large piece (or several large

Fig. 12–28 *The light table lit.*

Fig. 12–30 *Glass bins. Smaller bins sit atop the larger ones.*

Fig. 12–29 *A light table with a portion of the glass top removed to show the bulbs.*

pieces) of frosted glass. Fluorescent bulbs are placed about 18″ below the glass top. Use as many daylight fluorescent bulbs as necessary (*Figs. 12–28 and 12–29*) to illuminate all the frosted glass that you have placed. Wire the bulbs together and attach a single switch. Do not use incandescent bulbs. These throw off the colors of stained glass.

Glass Bins
The size of your glass bins should match the sizes of glass you will be using (*Fig. 12–30*). When you are finished cutting up a fairly large piece, you will be left with viable smaller pieces. Allow for smaller bins

to hold these sizes. Otherwise, they will scatter over the workshop and you will never be able to find them when you want them. In our studio we have various size bins for various size pieces of glass. When the glass pieces become too small to be placed within a bin, we use plastic shoe boxes. When we need a glass scrap for instant use, we are able to choose one easily. Not having a small piece means cutting a large piece, possibly breaking it. The key is organization. If your workshop is well organized, you will be able to lay your hand on any color and size of glass as easily as you can find any of your tools.

Storing Tools
One way to store tools is on pegboard along a wall of your workshop, or along one side of your worktable. Your collection of tools will grow rapidly. Nothing is more frustrating than needing a particular tool and not being able to find it. Usually the missing tool turns up when you no longer need it. In addition to pegboard, tool racks on rotating stands are sold in

Fig. 12–31 *Tools kept in a rotating tool rack.*

hardware stores (*Fig. 12–31*). One or two of these should suffice for your beginning tool collection. Glass cutters may be kept in a jar with a pad of steel wool soaked in kerosene at the bottom.

Keep your worktable neat. If the table is constantly covered by slivers of glass, scattered tools, pieces of pattern paper, yesterday's newspaper, rolls of solder, and spilled flux, you will spend more time dodging around the surface than working. Replace each tool as you finish with it. Keep the table free of glass and glass splinters. They will interfere with your glass cutting and probably end up cutting you as well. Food has no place whatsoever on your work table. Aside from taking up

room, it is dangerous to eat while working.

Outlets

Run a multiple-outlet strip to the worktable that accepts as many as three or four plugs. You may not need this many in the beginning, but later on they will come in handy when you want to light a lamp, plug in a soldering iron, and heat wax simultaneously (soldering irons do not usually take enough current to overload such a circuit). It is awkward to have to keep stooping to baseboard sockets. Be careful when extending the baseboard socket to the worktable that you do not place the extension cord where you or anyone else will trip over it. Take time to run it along the baseboard to the table and perhaps up one of the table legs.

Window Space

It's sad that many beginners in stained glass must work in basements. But a basement room is better than no room at all. If possible, try to pick an area of the house that has some window space. You will appreciate daylight, preferably a north light, in organizing colors. While a light table is a fine working tool to get your colors to blend, the only real way to see a finished product is against daylight.

13
Painting on Glass

Glass painting is as old as the art of stained glass itself. Some crafts people feel that painting on glass adds a certain "impurity" to the art and prefer the colors of the glass without any surface modifications. However, adding detail, particularly in a pictorial window, can heighten an artistic statement.

THE FIRED TECHNIQUE

China paint is not ordinarily used for glass. It fires between 1250° and 1350°F, whereas glass paint fires between 1050° and 1080°F. Since china paint is meant to be fired over a glazed surface, there is a difference in the maturing temperatures between it and glass paint. Some china paints can be attempted on glass, but usually the glass melts before the china paint matures, or the paint is not allowed to get hot enough to melt and flakes off when the glass cools.

Glass Stainers' Paints

Fired paints used with stained glass are specific for the purpose, atmosphere-proof and will maintain their color indefinitely. They are classically water-base paints and are affected in their liquid state by weather. If it is too muggy, they will not flow properly; if it is too cold, they will break up along the brush stroke. But used properly they have proved effective for hundreds of years.

The supplies necessary for fired painting are a glass palette, a pestle, several different sizes of palette knives and a supply of special brushes (*Fig. 13–1*). In addition to these brushes, you should have on hand some old brushes to use for stippling or other decorative effects to be worked into the paint. You should also have a supply of toothpicks, quills, or sharp-pointed bamboo sticks for picking away the paint so that the design shows through.

The glass palette should be prepared by grinding sand into its center to provide an abrasive surface for grinding the paint. Many glass stainers' water-base paints must be ground. If you use one of these, scoop a few spoonsful of paint out of the bag to the center of your palette. Grind the paint with the pestle to make it fine enough to utilize properly.

Vinegar Trace Paint

Vinegar trace paint is a dark paint used for figure or design lines. It has no shadowing quality and blocks out the light completely if it is used correctly. Mixed with water, vinegar, and gum arabic, the paint is fairly thick. The gum arabic acts as a sticking or setting medium. The amount of this added to the paint is always questionable and depends on the weather, on the amount of paint you have on the palette, and on your own judgment. If the weather is hot and muggy, too much gum will prevent the paint from flowing smoothly. If the

Fig. 13–1 Basic supplies for fired painting—glass palette, grinder, and palette knives.

Fig. 13–2 Detail from a panel "Bird of Prey" demonstrating fired paint and stick-lighting.

weather is cold, too much gum may break the paint line along a brush stroke, leaving skips or spaces in the line. If not enough gum arabic is added, the paint can flow over the glass but not adhere well.

To mix the paint, pile a small amount on the palette in the center. Grind it thorougly, then scrape it together again into a pile (*Fig. 13–5*). Make a little well or depression in the center and measure in some gum arabic and vinegar. Start mixing with a palette knife (*Fig. 13–6*). If the mixture remains thick, add a little water or vinegar a few drops at a time until it becomes pasty. Try some test brush strokes along the palette occasionally.

Vinegar trace paint is applied with a long-haired brush called a tracer or tracing brush. The paint on the brush must be worked "wet in wet"—that is, wet on the brush and wet on the glass—or it will "fry" when it is fired. This means you cannot go over a dry painted line with more paint or continue to add paint to a stroke that has dried. A trace line must be one complete stroke. If you have painted a stroke that has dried and you are not satisfied with it, you must redo it. If you apply another coating of vinegar trace paint over it, the two areas will separate when heated and the overlying area will bubble up. This "frying" can extend to a general flaking.

Vinegar burns out readily and allows the paint to flow nicely. A small amount of water can be mixed in as well, but we have used vinegar alone with good results.

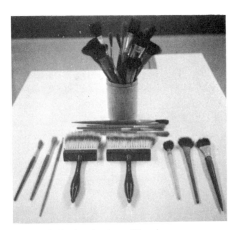

Fig. 13–3 A selection of brushes.

Fig. 13–4 Grinding the paint.

After the trace is dry, it can be scraped or modeled with a quill or a bamboo stick (*Fig. 13–7*). It can be used as either a positive or negative surface, although this technique is more appropriately used with matte paint. Trace paint is fired by sight at about 1100°F. and the kiln turned off when the paint surface looks shiny.

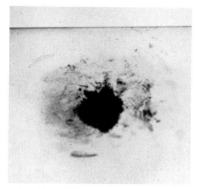

Fig. 13–5 *The paint after its initial grinding.*

Fig. 13–6 *Mixing the materials with a palette knife.*

Fig. 13–7 *Stick lighting areas into the painted (but not fired) piece with a sharp quill or stick to modify and control the light coming through.*

Painting with trace paint requires practice. Make a "bridge" for resting your wrist by nailing two 1" blocks of wood underneath a 12" lathe strip. Before trying any major project with trace paint, practice some strokes on a piece of plain glass to acquire the proper wrist motion. Using the long tracing brush is an experience. Remember it must complete its stroke before running out of paint. Get the maximum consistency to your paint on the palette. Then load the tracing brush by rotating it until all the bristles are covered with paint. If you overload on the brush when you tip it forward to get that neat thin stroke, you'll blot the entire area. Learn how much paint the brush will take. If you don't put enough paint on the brush, you may run out in the middle of a stroke. Since you cannot go back over the stroke or continue it without overlapping some of the dried paint, you'll have to erase the stroke and do it again with a brush containing more paint. As you work the paint on the palette, it will begin to dry out, so constantly replenish it with vinegar and water, but be careful not to dilute the mix too much.

To help keep the mixture fluid, mix it with the palette knife between brush strokes. Get an idea of how fast it is drying out and how much water or vinegar is necessary to get it back to its proper consistency.

Gum arabic is generally purchased in powder form. This dissolves well in water. It will also dissolve in alcohol, but use of this medium allows you less time to work before the paint dries.

When working with vinegar trace, hold the glass up to the light from time to time to see how thick or thin the layer of paint is. If you can see light coming through, it is too thin and your reserve must be replenished with more paint. If the mixture on the glass is so thick that it is ridging, you will have an uneven surface that may fry when fired.

Always thoroughly clean any glass surface before painting on it. Cleaning with alcohol or acetone will leave a thin film on the glass that is difficult to remove. A better way is to smear some of the vinegar trace paint on the glass, then wipe it off with a clean rag or gauze pad. Since the paint contains ground glass, it will clean the surface better than any glass cleaner will do. Remember to clean the bottom surface too. Any dirt on the bottom will fire in and provide unintentional effects.

Once you have the wrist motion under control and the paint at the proper consistency, practice tracing lines onto a piece of glass on a light table. For your first attempt, paint one small piece of glass with a simple design and fire it. Practice different types of lines, curved and straight, while guiding your wrist from the bridge. Fire these different strokes and study which technique and which paint mixture seems to be the most effective.

Place lines of a design you want to duplicate in paint underneath the glass between the glass and the light box. At first, your hand will tremble and globs of paint will roll from your overloaded tracing brush. But as you persevere, you will acquire a "painting hand" and eventually be able to apply the trace paint to follow complicated outlines.

Matt Paint

Matt is made more transparent than trace paint, and it can be applied to the glass thinly or thickly with a soft brush and then "blended." Usually after firing it is somewhat transparent. The base for matt paint is usually water and gum arabic or vinegar and gum arabic.

After it is blended out, matt is sometimes stippled or worked with other brushes or with the fingers to texture it. The amount of gum arabic in the mixture will determine just what is possible with

Fig. 13–9 Delicate matting shows on forearm and hand.

Fig. 13–8 The hair and beard have been painted with matt. Note the highlights and shadowing possible with this paint.

Fig. 13–10 Traced and matted face, hair, and beard. The color is in the glass; the light coming through is modified by the matting. Trace lines block out the light completely. Note the highlights on the cheeks, nose, and forehead.

Painting on Glass **189**

this paint. Matt is applied over the tracing paint either before or after the tracing paint is fired. The use of matt may require two firings—one for the tracing paint, one for the matt. To save a firing, you can apply the tracing paint and then the matt. This is tricky since the spreading of the matt over the tracing paint may blur the tracing paint outline. You may apply matt and then trace over it. Matt also may be used alone. It is fired in the same manner as the tracing paint, but not at quite so high a temperature. Both matt and trace paints fire out to some degree normally, but if matt is over-fired, it will lose a lot of its color and become unreasonably pale.

Matting is used for shadowing and filling in the background of a painted segment. In effect, it is what charcoal is to the artist. Do not mix so much gum arabic into the matt that you cannot work it on the glass easily, but mix in enough so that it will stick effectively. Odd visual effects can be achieved with matt by adding alcohol to it, which causes it to dry out quickly in swirls, or by splashing it with alcohol on the glass after it has dried. Our favorite tool for matt is fingers. Fingers give interesting swirls and lines applicable to flowing hair and beards. The "Pirate" window (see color section) had matt applied to the entire surface of the building. Irregularly shaped thin lines throughout the surface of the matting were removed with a fine wire brush to give the glass a grain resembling wood.

Silver Stain

Glass stains such as orange, red, and yellow contain silver nitrate in different percentages. The word *silver* is somewhat misleading, since the color of a silver stain is golden after firing. Because silver nitrate has corrosive properties, never use the same palette or brushes for the stains as you do for the paints. Quill brushes are best, since silver stain will corrode a metal ferrule brush. The palette for stains should be coarse since stains require more grinding than paints. Grinding stain is a tedious procedure. The grains move out from under the pestle. We do not mix the stain with water before grinding because we find that it gives us less control. When grinding silver stains, use a palette knife made of horn; the material will eventually corrode a metal one.

Stains do not work well from brush to glass, but then the same precision is not required as in painting. Stain changes the glass color unlike paint, which only covers it. Staining is usually done on the opposite surface of the glass from the painting and may be fired with the stained side down, the surface resting on the kiln shelf. This allows you to stain and paint in a single firing. Stains fire at approximately 1000°F. Each time a stained piece is refired, the color gets deeper. Silver stain is affected by light, so store it in a dark bottle. It works well on "white" or clear glass. English glass takes oranges, reds, and yellow stains best. Much German glass will not take stain at all.

Oil-Base Paints

Glass stainers' colors have a limited color selection—in paints, mainly blacks, blues, browns, and greens—while silver stains vary in hue from ruby to yellow. Drakenfield makes oil-base glass paints that are as effective as glass stainers' paints and are easier to work, though perhaps not as long lasting. The palette includes many hues and tones. Drakenfield paints are not affected by atmospheric conditions in the home. These paints must be used with Drakenfield's medium, which contains an oil-turpentine base. No vegetable oil can be used because the carbon content is too great to burn out. Thus, a nonvegetable oil plus a turpentine base is employed. Drakenfield oil-base paints take longer to dry on the glass than their water-base cousins. Gum arabic need not be added. The powder is ground on the palette into a fine consistency and the medium added until the paint becomes a thick paste. A drop more medium is then added so that the paint flows readily from the brush.

Brush strokes may be gone over to a moderate degree with no consequent frying of the paint. Oil-base paints may be blended to different color tones, but you must experiment to determine whether or not these colors will separate upon firing.

The main problem with oil-base paints is consistency. If paint goes on too thick, you will find broken brush strokes where the paint has bunched up during firing. Overfiring will also cause this problem, even if the consistency was correct. Oil paints fire lower than water-base paints—1000°F. to 1050°F. Too much heat beyond this point begins to break up paint lines. Also, oil-base paints, having a longer drying time then water-base, will smear if stick-lighting is attempted too soon after application. If this happens, wipe off the paint and start anew, rather than trying to clean up the smeared areas and making more of a mess.

Stick-Lighting

This technique scratches out portions of the painted surface to allow the glass color to show. If the oil-base paint is allowed to dry well, stick-lighting is relatively easy. Because of the somewhat thicker consistency of oil paints compared to water-base paints, you must be careful in working your sharp quill or stick so that you do not pull away too much paint. Proceed slowly, testing the consistency of the paint before you scratch away any long line of it. It may be a good idea first to take away a little from an outside edge to find how tenaciously the paint is adhering to the glass. One of the advantages of oil-base paint is that you don't have to take the entire design back off the glass and reapply it if you happen to pull away too much paint. With care you can touch up that single area alone.

Stick-lighting is used here as with water-base paint—to emphasize an existing paint line by placing a light line below it, or to use the covering paint as a negative,

scratching away those portions where you want a fine design formation of light to show through. Stick-lighting should never be an intrusive element; it should be subtle, guiding the eye rather than catching it.

Using Oil Colors

Probably the easiest color to use in the oil-base paints is black, whether *intense* or *medium*. The other colors have their idiosyncrasies: difficulty in mixing, difficulty in getting them to flow from the brush, or, most usual, difficulty in firing. Each color should be employed as a new challenge. Yellow, for instance, fires somewhat lower than black. We have fired the black and yellow at the same temperature and found the yellow breaks up or bunches together, whereas the black remains substantial.

Firing Oil-Base Paints

The firing technique for oil-base paint is the same as for glass stainers' water-base paints. Each piece is arranged on the kiln shelf with the painted portion uppermost. Glass stain may be fired on the reverse of a painted piece. If you use kiln wash to cover the shelf, make as flat a bed as possible; at firing temperatures, the glass will take on any irregularities of the surface it rests on.

No piece should touch its neighbor, yet try to use the space in the kiln to best advantage. Make sure the kiln shelf is clean and free of any glass chips or paint from previous firings. Once the glass is in the kiln, turn the heat to "medium" and lower the lid until it is almost closed. Leave it open enough so that the air within may be heated and driven out. Then close the kiln entirely and turn the heat up to maximum.

Watch the pyrometer carefully. If you overfire a piece, you will not be able to salvage it. We fire by sight and check the kiln at approximately 1100° through the door. At about 1150° we turn the kiln off and close it, allowing the glass to cool for about twelve hours. It is possible to cool even fairly large pieces rapidly by opening the kiln and leaving it open until the heat goes down to approximately 900°, then

Fig. 13–11 Ten Commandments—nonfired paint.

Fig. 13–12 Owl of fully stained and fired window glass. (Kay Kinney paints were used.)

Fig. 13–13 Bee ashtray of window glass. This piece was painted with Kay Kinney's Blackline and then sagged into a mold. (Courtesy: Edward Martin.)

Fig. 13–14 Small fired painted panel—a mouse under a mushroom. This quick sketch was done as an experiment in texturing fired paint. Only black trace paint was used.

closing it. But you must watch the kiln. If the heat goes down too rapidly, some of your pieces may crack. It may be best to let the kiln cool by itself. Then you don't have to watch and worry.

THE UNFIRED TECHNIQUE

For the amateur glass painter who doesn't have access to a kiln, glass paints that do not have to be fired and yet achieve some permanency on the glass can be used. In no instance can these be measured against the longevity of fired paint. At their worst, nonfired paints will wash off. At their best, they will be almost impervious to any outside influence, except a considerable amount of scrubbing.

Nonfired Paints

Nonfired paint can be used for touching up decorative objects, such as the faces on small animals or whiskers or eyes, or even lettering names. Black is a popular color for trace lines, but other colors can be used with some practice.

Before applying the paint, make sure that the glass is free from dust and dirt. Stir the paint well and remove any overlying skins of paint from a previously used can. Otherwise bits of the skin will stick to your paint brush. You can dilute the paint according to instructions, usually with turpentine. Softening the brilliance of any colors may be done with the medium provided.

To imitate a leaded glass effect with nonfired paints:

1. Put the sketch behind or between two sheets of clear glass. Then paint the diamonds or rectangles on both sides to cover the sketch in between. When the paint is dry, paint the black lines on the surfaces of both pieces of glass. Allow them to dry, then turn the two pieces of glass to face each other and seal them together. This will give a dimensional stained-glass effect and will also protect the paint.

2. Glue lead tape to make a design on the glass and then fill up the spaces between the paint. Don't apply colors too

thickly, and don't apply them too quickly one on top of the other, which can wrinkle them.

Although some unfired paints are proof against fairly high temperatures, if you are painting on a lampshade, don't use a lightbulb higher than 40 watts.

A striking effect can be obtained by placing a sheet of tinfoil or silver paper behind the piece of painted glass and then placing the whole thing in a frame. This effect can be heightened further if you first crumple the tinfoil.

Painting a Window

Before a stained-glass window can be painted, it must be "waxed up." This permits all the requisite pieces to be held in position so paint may be applied from one to another. If the entire window is to be painted, all pieces are waxed up. Waxing up involves placing the pieces on an easel made of plate glass. The pieces are placed exactly as they will appear in the final window, with space left between them for leading. Each piece is then tacked at its corners to the underlying glass surface with a hot beeswax-resin mixture which hardens almost immediately upon application, and is easily chipped away when the pieces are removed. A glass eyedropper is used to apply the wax, which may be heated in a pot.

Set up the easel against natural light, preferably a northern exposure. Apply the painted lines with the vinegar trace paint and matting as described, from one piece of glass to the next. Copy exactly from your original design. Fire the pieces and re-wax them in the position to be matted. Oil-base paints may be used for trace lines and water-base matting for shadowing and fullness of line. When you remove the pieces from the kiln, examine them for imperfections, then follow the general leading procedure.

The design for leading the painted pieces must be calculated in the cartoon. Painted pieces should not have lead lines

running through them at odd angles. A face is usually painted as one piece of glass, not splintered into three or four different pieces. The same holds true for hands and feet. Garments may be broken up gracefully with lead lines along the line of flow because in most instances these pieces would be too large for most kilns.

For hobbyists painting on stained glass, it is simpler to wax up the pieces over a light table. Rarely will there be so many pieces to require an easel. The pieces must be firmly held in place, especially when you are carrying the same paint line from one piece to another. Otherwise, when you lead up the glass, the painted lines will not match up.

ETCHING

Etching creates a design in glass, changing the color where etch is applied. It presents possibilities for glass effects that can be achieved in no other way.

The most effective way to etch glass is to use hydrofluoric acid. This is an extremely dangerous chemical, and to make it somewhat safe to use several pastes and creams have come on the market. However, precautions must still be taken. All portions of the glass that will not be etched must be masked. Etching requires a well-ventilated room, and clothing and bare skin must be protected. Wear goggles and always work near a water source.

Etching creams such as Armour Etch and Frost'N Etch contain hydrofluoric acid in diluted amounts. So they etch flashed glass quite slowly, if at all, and they work best where the surface to be eaten away is more delicate, as in mirror etching.

Hydrofluoric acid is considered a weak acid chemically, but it is dangerous when it comes to skin. The burn produced is extremely painful and long lasting even when the acid is diluted in its working state of approximately 52 percent. It is used diluted for etching because otherwise it would gnaw large chunks of glass rather than nibbling a fine line. The hobbyist usually

Fig. 13–15 *Etching the wrong side of a flashed piece of glass.*

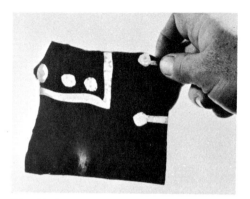

Fig. 13–16 *Careless use of the resist material. The acid has seeped under it and has begun to etch about midway along the bottom surface.*

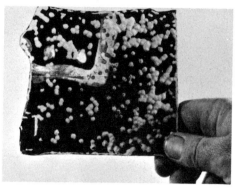

Fig. 13–17 *One side of a piece of glass was left uncovered and placed in the acid. This is what happened to it.*

Fig. 13–18 *The etched piece.*

etches single lines or small designs. If you want to cover a large expanse of glass, the acid fumes—as dangerous as the acid itself—will be stronger, so take the proper precautions. We usually etch outdoors and handle the acided glass with tongs. If you are etching a large area, place the glass in the bath acid side down so that the by-products will fall away. If you are etching only a line or a small area, place the glass acid side up and pour or paint the acid onto the glass. Be careful not to disturb the resist material.

If you mistake the flashed side of the glass, you may sit for several hours waiting for the glass to change color. When you lift it out, you will find deep indentations but no change in color. Always check to see that you are etching the right side. Grozz a corner to check colored side.

Another problem involves careless application of the resist material. Unless it is thoroughly sealed on the glass—and that includes the edges—the acid will seep under the edges and ruin the design.

Materials:

Flashed glass.
A plastic pan large enough to hold the glass.
Plastic tongs.
"Resist" material: Beeswax, asphaltum, or clear Contact paper. This protects those parts of the glass that are not to be attacked by the acid.
Hydrofluoric acid in a plastic container.

Procedure:

Paint the piece of glass with hot beeswax or asphaltum. Smear it liberally over the front and back surfaces and the edges. The design to be etched may then be picked out of the resist. Another method is to draw the design on the glass with a marking pencil and paint the resist material around it. We prefer to wrap the glass in clear Contact paper so that all surfaces are encased securely. As we wrap, we press the Contact paper against the glass to remove any air pockets. The stenciled design is then cut out of the Contact paper. While the principle is much the same as with beeswax or asphaltum, it requires less preparation and is a neater procedure that offers more precision in following the original design.

Dip the resist-covered glass into the acid bath. *Caution:* Don't put the piece into the pan and pour acid onto it. Splashing of the acid will inevitably occur. The glass should be gently placed into the bath with the side to be etched either up or down, depending on the amount of surface under attack. The length of the etching procedure depends on the amount of area to be worked. The process may take anywhere from five or ten minutes to half an hour. You will be able to observe the action of the acid since you can see through the glass. The new color appears as the top layer of color crumbles away. You can use the plastic tongs to move the glass around, but don't overwork it or you may tear the paper resist or lift an edge of it, permitting the acid to seep underneath. Once this happens, all your work is undone.

When the glass has been etched, remove it from the acid bath and rinse it thoroughly under running water. Do not allow splashes to get on your skin. We usually submerse our pieces in a pail of water, then dump the water, and let water run over the piece. The resist material is then taken away. Simply chip off the beeswax, or unwrap the Contact paper. The etching should show in bold impress against the background.

14
Making Stained-Glass Lampshades

THE MULTIPANELED LAMP

The multipaneled lamp may be made in a number of different dimensions by varying the number of panels or making them individually smaller or larger. Multipaneled lamps consist of long panels radiating from a central role and terminating in a skirt. The simplest type is a basic two-piece unit—a single panel and single skirt. This design can be varied in any number of ways. The panel may be broken up into a design of its own, or the skirt may be broken, or both. The basic principles here apply to any type of paneled lamp.

Outfit yourself with the following supplies: a large ¾" plywood board, approximately 4' square, a sharp knife, some leading nails, a good soldering iron, flux and solder, lead came of sizes ¼" H rounded and ³⁄₁₆" U. You should have at least three six-foot lengths of the former and about four six-foot lengths of the latter. You should also have at least 5 square feet of stained glass.

Preparing the Pattern

The basic pattern (*Fig. 14–10*), is for a lamp 16" in diameter:

Panel A—Eight inches tall, with a width at the top of 1⅜" and a bottom with width of 4".
Panel B—*(the skirt)*—measures the same 4" at the top to meet the bottom of panel A, and measures 2¼" at its widest diameter from top to center of curved bottom. Panel B measures 1¾" at either end, from top to bottom. Twelve of these panels will give you a lamp 11" high. Larger or smaller lamps must have the measurements changed accordingly. Cut your panels out in cardboard first to make sure that you will be able to close your circle to the proper dimensions.

Be sure that your pattern is drawn exactly on graph paper before tracing it out on the heavier pattern paper. You will be cutting twelve exact pieces from this pattern, and it is imperative that the material stand up to it. If you are careless with your class cutter and the pattern starts to fray, your pieces will begin to change shape and you will have problems later on. Better to cut another pattern if you are doubtful.

The panel B, or skirt, must match the bottom of panel A exactly for the two pieces to fit later on. Even a ¹⁄₁₆" difference here will multiply drastically as the pieces are being cut, and in the end the top and bottom of your lamp will not fit together. You can make the initial pattern out of a thin piece of sheet metal, but it must be cut exactly with tin snips. Be sure you get a thin enough piece if you're going to do this to allow your glass cutter to ride freely along its rim.

Fig. 14–1 *Multipaneled lamps.* Right: *The long-panel, short-skirt model provides the basic form for almost all variations.* Left: *A variation without the skirt.*

Fig. 14–3 *A large-paneled kitchen lamp with alternating panel strips. The bigger panels are broken into separate elements. Because of the somewhat squat appearance of this lamp a crown was added to give it a finished look.*

Fig. 14–2 *A multipaneled lamp with the panel and skirt broken up into a design. Panels are made as a unit and then folded together.*

Fig. 14–4 *Hanging lamp of stained glass, wood, and metal.*

Cutting the Glass

Cut the sheet of stained glass in twelve exact duplicates of panel A and twelve duplicates of panel B (*Fig. 14–10*). It is best to cut a long strip from your piece of glass, measuring from top to bottom of the panel, with the lines running the way you want them (*Fig. 14–11*). Then lay the pattern on this long strip and cut out the

panels one at a time. Since you are cutting on a bias, the best tool to break out these score lines is running pliers. You can cut panels quickly with little waste by laying the pattern first one way and then the other (*Fig. 14–12A*). The edges of the glass should be as smooth as possible. Very slight irregularities may be covered by the lead. Anything more, however, should be sanded away with abrasive paper or the piece recut.

Next, cut the skirts out of the glass in the same fashion, by cutting one long strip and then laying your pattern along it and cutting out the pieces for the skirt

Fig. 14–5 A small-pieced lamp shade in the Tiffany style.

Fig. 14–6 Panels of a small three-pieced lamp laid out on the worktable to calculate the amount of bending that will be needed.

Fig. 14–7 The panels, now leaded, are soldered together. Flux is applied to a joint surface prior to soldering. Note the leading nails holding the panels in place.

Fig. 14–8 Bending the lamp. Each panel is bent a little at a time to take up the strain gradually.

Fig. 14–9 The finished shade. Small jewels (navettes) have been leaded to the skirt folds to enhance the line of the lamp.

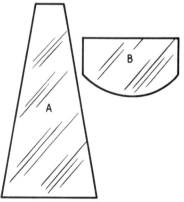

Fig. 14–10 Patterns for panels and skirt.

Fig. 14–11 Using an L square to cut a long piece of glass to start a lamp. Note the position of the glass cutter. The lines within the glass will run up and down.

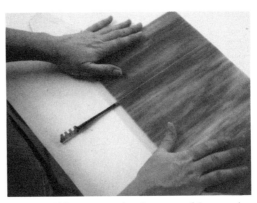

Fig. 14–12B . . . use the glass cutter fulcrum technique, or . . .

Fig. 14–12A Cutting the panels. Keep reversing your pattern. You may use running pliers for this or . . .

Fig. 14–12C . . . break by hand.

(Fig. 14–13). Use running pliers to cut the straight edge and glass pliers to pull away the curved edge. Remember, the pull of the glass pliers is out and down; use the edge of the table as your guide. Sand the panels smooth and lay them aside. Many workers alternate colors from one panel to another or from one piece of skirt to another. We recommend opalescent glass for all lamps because it keeps the bulb from showing, and it allows for an even diffusion of light throughout the surface of the

Fig. 14–13 Cutting the lamp skirts. As always, the pattern is placed on top of the glass.

lamp. Antique glass, or any clear glass, does not treat a bulb quite so courteously.

Preparing the Lead

Cut the ¼″ H lead into twelve strips each measuring 8″ long, and twelve pieces of H lead, each measuring 1¼″ long; the smaller pieces, of course, will be the ribs for the skirt. Make sure the channels are not crimped at the edges from the cutting. If they are, pry them open with your lead knife so that the channel runs completely free along the entire length.

Measuring the Circle

Lay the panels side by side to see how much room they will take on the table. Then you will know exactly where to place the first panel as a starting point. You will notice, when laying them out, that they form an almost complete circle.

Remove all the panels, except the first one, which is your starting point. To the left of the panel, hammer in two nails. These will serve to support the side of the panel and keep it from moving. To the right of the panel, place a strip of ¼″ H lead. Make sure that it fits the side of the panel exactly within the slot of the came. Push the lead firmly up against the panel to make sure there is no extra room for motion and that the lead is indeed seated properly. The lead came should not cover the entire length of glass; a small amount should show above and below. The piece of lead should not be quite as long as the glass.

Now cut approximately 20″ off one of the ³⁄₁₆″ U leads and fit it over the top of the glass panel, making sure the glass fits into the slot of the U lead (*Fig. 14–14*). Start the U lead almost at the end, but leave a little overlap to the left of the panel. Following this procedure, cut another strip of U lead of approximately 60″ and drape it as best you can in a circle so that none of this long length hangs over the table. If any of it does, it will be a drag

Fig. 14–14 *Lamp panels are put together with lead ribs in between and strips of ³⁄₁₆″ U coiling round top and bottom.*

on the portion you're working on, and it will also tangle and twist. Drape it in a rough circle and keep it on the table in its entire length. Fit the end portion of tbe lead into the bottom straight edge of the first panel. This also should fit exactly.

You now have in front of you the basic building block of your lamp. Each strip and each panel will follow successively from this one, and the same procedure will be employed.

Building Your Lamp

Take the second panel and fit its left side into the right open slot of your first long H came. Continue the U lead on the top and bottom, making sure to hold the top and bottom of the first panel as well as the second panel with leading nails. It is imperative that these panels be held securely so that they do not move and throw off your entire effort. The third panel should be treated exactly as the second; remember that you are going to continue the top and bottom U leads concurrently.

By this time, you will see that the glass is starting to bend into the same circle that it took previously, and it is necessary to form the top and bottom U leads to fit into this circle. Make sure they are tightly pressed against the glass and that they are butting against the ribs formed by the H lead cames. They do not have to butt exactly, since a small space between the two leads can be filled later with solder. If the H leads are a trifle too long, cut them down to fit. We do not want them to overlap the top and bottom U leads, as this will create unsightly bulges. Submit all your remaining panels to the same procedure; when you are done, you will have an incomplete circle composed of twelve panels, ribbed with H came and circled top and bottom with U came, all pressed tightly against the glass and all held in place with leading nails.

Note that the last panel has on its right only an H lead, while the first panel has on its left no lead at all (*Fig. 14–15*). It is essential, during the next soldering step, not to allow any solder to flow into the free channel of the H lead on the right. To prevent this, place a scrap piece of glass in the channel and hold it with a leading nail. A small piece of glass top and bottom will do, since it's those areas that will be soldered. You will have trouble melting it out or digging it out, and you might even have to substitute another lead.

Soldering the Panel
Brush flux vigorously on all the joints and run a small amount of solder over each joint, making certain that each is securely

Fig. 14–15 *The panels fanned on the worktable prior to soldering.*

tacked. Be careful that you do not burn a lead rib. If you do, you will have to replace it, because it is impossible to repair it with solder and have it look right. If you have to replace a lead, you must unattach all your leads to that point and remove the offending rib. The further you progress, the more you will have to take apart later on. So, try not to burn any cames, but if you do, replace them then and there.

Solder only the side that is facing you. Do not turn the panel over and solder the other side. Once you have soldered the proper joints, trim the excess lead on the top and the bottom of the lamp and remove all the nails.

Bending the Lamp into Shape
Care must be taken here, or your work to this point can be made useless in one easy step. With one hand, grasp the middle of the top circle of the lamp and bring it away from the board toward you. You should be standing with the open circle facing away from you. Be careful while raising the lamp that the left-hand panel, which has no outer lead rib, does not come away from the rest of the lamp. If it does, push it into position again. It will slide easily into its groove. Very slowly, fold the lamp around away from you, a little at a time, being careful not to crack any of the panels. Try to give each panel a little bit of fold. Each should take the same amount of strain. Should the lamp not fold smoothly, check the nonsoldered side to see if the lead is crimping. This is a critical stage where confidence, not exuberance, is required. Continue to fold the lamp until the free edge of the left-hand panel inserts into the free flange of the H lead of the right-hand panel (*Fig. 14–16*). Manipulate the top, then the bottom, into position (*Fig. 14–17*). Once you get the top seat, solder the two sides together while holding them tightly with one hand. Then fit the bottom to meet and solder that in the same fashion. This way, you will be dealing with one joint at a time instead of trying to fit

Fig. 14–16 Fitting the open glass edge of one panel into the leaded channel of the other end. They should go into place exactly.

Fig. 14–17 Soldering the bottom of the circle together. Hold the panels firmly with one hand.

Fig. 14–18 The skirt lined up and leaded.

top and bottom at once. If the top fits snugly and smoothly, the bottom will too.

The upper part of the lamp is now completed. Do not solder the inside at this time. Place the lamp on the worktable and press to make sure that the bottom of each panel touches the table. This will automatically bring the lamp into proper shape. If a panel or two is not resting on the table, minipulate it gently by pressing around the surface of the lamp. It should settle in. If it still doesn't, check the inside; a piece of lead may be folded in the way.

Making the Skirt

Fasten a piece of wood approximately 4′ long and at least 2″ wide securely to the edge of the worktable. You can either nail it down or clamp it down with C-clamps.

Stretch a piece of ³⁄₁₆″ U lead, open it with a lathkin, and lay it against the straight piece of wood with the channel facing away from you so that the flat end of the came lies directly against the wood. Take the first piece of skirt with the flat side toward you and insert it into the U lead, making sure it seats all the way into the channel. This is a deep channel and may fool you, so be sure that the piece of glass is well in place. Hold the left end of this first piece of skirt with a leading nail. Next, take one of the twelve pieces of H lead, which you have previously cut to a length of 1¼″, and insert the right-hand channel of this first piece of glass into a channel of this piece of lead. Follow this procedure with each piece of the skirt so that when you are done you will have a straight line of skirt pieces—the first one held at the left edge with a nail, and the last one having a lead rib on its right with an empty channel, also held by a nail or by another piece of glass in the channel (*Fig. 14–18*).

Take another strip of ³⁄₁₆″ U lead and, starting at the left, press it firmly against the halfmoon edges of each piece of skirt, making sure it dips down far enough to meet each lead rib between the skirt pieces. This lead is quite malleable and can be pushed into shape with your fingers or a lathkin. Don't be concerned if there is a slight space between the lead rib and the bordering U lead. If a gap occurs, you probably have cut your lead rib too short. It must be recut. Work one piece of skirt at a time, securing each with nails before going on to the next. When you are done, trim the lead margins on either end and solder all joints, making sure that you solder only those joints that are facing you. Do not solder the side facing the table.

Bending the Skirt

Remove all the nails and the strip of wood from the worktable. Stand the skirt line on edge so that the straight edge is uppermost and the curved edge rests on the table. Bend the line inward against the unsoldered side so that the free edge of the left side of the skirt inserts into the empty channel of the lead on the right (*Fig. 14–19*). Solder these two joints, again being careful not to let solder get inside the channel itself. You now have the two parts of the lamp completed.

Putting the Lamp Together

Place the top part of the lamp on top of the skirt, making certain that the panel you are going to solder exactly meets the margins of the underlying skirt. If this is off, all the other panels will be off. Don't worry if all the panels do not seem to meet the underlying skirt at the same time. Work one at a time, and if you are accurate on your first one, all the others must fall in line. If you are making a shade of alternating colors, you should decide now if you want the color of the skirt to match the color of the corresponding panel, or if you want it to match the alternating panel.

The Finishing Touch

Tack-solder all joints, working one panel at a time. Once you are satisfied that the skirt panels meet as accurately as possible, solder each joint firmly. Turn the lamp on its side, solder all the other joints, and run solder in the area between the skirt and upper panel, both inside and out. For a

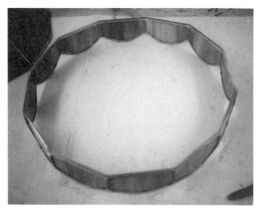

Fig. 14–19 . . . *and bent into a circle.*

Fig. 14–20 *Putting the lamp together. Match up the first skirt and panel as perfectly as possible and the others will match up as well.*

Fig. 14–21 *The finished shade on end showing the lead "belt" that covers the seam between panel and skirt inside and out.*

smooth, finished look, flatten a piece of ³⁄₁₆″ U lead and wrap it around the lamp so it covers the seam between the top and bottom parts. This belt is soldered in place at the joints. Do tbe same with the inside seam (*Fig. 14–21*).

The lamp is completed. Clean it as soon as possible to prevent the glass from clouding; it may already be tacky from the flux. Vinegar and water is a good cleansing agent used with a piece of steel wool. We also use cleaning and polishing powder. Follow this with an ordinary glass cleaner. The leads and soldered joints will darken slowly over time. If you want to antique the leads, they must be tinned (solder flowed over them), then antiquing patina applied with a stiff brush.

Another way to make this lamp is to lay out the panel in a straight line along the table edge, using a long piece of wood as a bottom guide, and place the strips of lead between them. Then, lift the panels carefully, sliding a yardstick underneath, and wrap around and fold down at the same time into the lead channels. This is difficult, however, and can involve a number of broken panels if you are not careful.

THE MOLD METHOD FOR SMALL-PIECED LAMPS

When designing for copper foil, keep a thin margin between the pieces. You may even cut the pattern without the use of pattern scissors, since the copper foil takes up very little room. Your glass cutting must be absolutely precise. If it is not, use pattern scissors.

As a guide for the lamp, you can use a preformed Worden Styrofoam mold, a clear plastic shape as we did, or even a turned-up wooden salad bowl. Keep your initial design simple. Don't try to design a pictorial "Tiffany" shade at the very outset. On the surface of the mold, draw the pattern from your cartoon (*Fig. 14–22*). (If you use a Worden mold, this is done for you.) You need not make the pattern to

Fig. 14–22 Initial sketch for a repeating pattern. Small-pieced Tiffany-type lamp shade.

Fig. 14–23 Laying out the pattern on the clear plastic mold.

Fig. 14–24 Form cut from glass to conform to basic pattern.

cover the entire surface of the mold since your design will be in a repeating pattern around the shade. Once you have traced the design on the mold, transfer the pattern to pattern paper and cut it out. Then cut your glass to match the pattern. As you cut each piece, place it on the mold, starting at the top. Hold the pieces in place with pushpins or with little pieces of plasticene clay (*Fig. 14–25*). The plasticene will anchor the pieces of glass to the mold but still allow you to remove them to check the colors. Work around the top of the mold as though you were knitting a hat (*Fig. 14–26*). If you work down one column at a time, the pieces will start to slip off the mold as it gets heavier.

Once you have covered the top surface of the mold, remove the pieces, check them under the light, and solder them together. Then remove the clay. The next line around the mold can be tack-soldered to tbe previous section as you go. Thus you will build up bit by bit. The pieces of glass must be small enough to conform to the bend of the mold. Don't solder the pieces together firmly, but continue to tack-solder as you go along. Leave a hole in the top of the lamp for the socket and electrical wiring. Don't get so carried way by the creative process that you foil the lampshade directly over the top of the mold.

Once the work is completed, lift it off the mold, solder all the joints together, and bead all seams. Solder the shade on the inside. The lamp will be strong when it is soldered together.

More decorative effects are possible after you have made a few of these simpler lamps. The designing must first be done flat, then measured to conform to the turn of the mold. If you want to make a swan, for instance, you must measure the size of swan against the circumference of the mold. Using graph paper will help. This will give you an idea how many swans you can fit into the space available. Remember to allow some space for the copper foil.

We check our dimensions by cutting designs out of pattern paper and scotchtaping them directly to the form. Another way to compare space to design is to square off all odd-shaped pieces and take the measurement of this square around the form. The square then may be broken internally into any number of configurations.

Fig. 14–25 *Building up the glass pieces in sections on the mold. Other sections to follow are drawn in place on the mold.*

Fig. 14–26 *The lamp taking shape. More and more pieces of glass are being added, working around the top of the mold. Once this is complete, pieces will be added in concentric turns until the shade is completed.*

For a finished edge, line the borders of your lamp with a piece of caming, such as a 3/16″ U. Or apply an extra heavy coat of solder to the ends of the copper foil that form the lamp borders. Finally clean the lamp as before.

Originally, small-pieced lamps were made from molds of rock maple or aluminum, but today they are difficult to obtain and are very expensive. We recommend Worden molds for their variety of design and proven sturdiness. They are not expensive. Salad bowls can also offer some intriguing forms.

Try not to draw directly on a Worden or plastic mold. Don't use a magic marker if you want to use your mold for more than one design; you will get lost among the lines. Don't try to make a lamp without using a mold, as in the flat tabletop method. The copper foil does not bend well, and the small pieces will begin to tear through the foil as you apply pressure.

Apply solder sparingly to the small pieces; only tack a few places. It is frustrating to find that a piece must come out and that you have to use jackhammer blows to loosen it from the rest of the design. If you tack only here and there, you can easily melt away the small bridgings of solder that hold the pieces together.

Test each piece of glass that is going

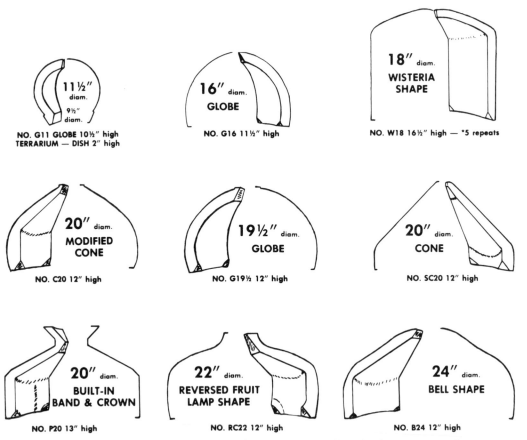

Fig. 14–27 Some shapes from the wide selection of Worden Lamp Molds. The forms automatically arrange a repeat design. Some come with a design already on them. These have revolutionized the fabrication of small-pieced Tiffany-type lampshades.

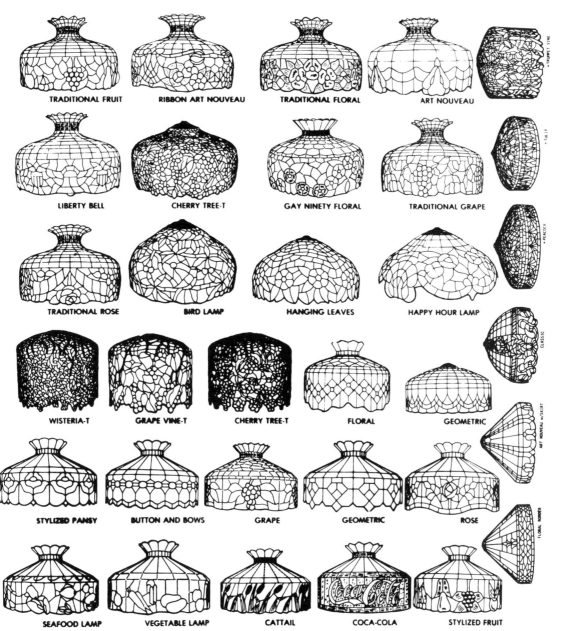

Fig. 14–28 *Styrofoam molds for lampmaking. Styles come in kit form with precut pieces of glass and pre-stamped filigree appendages. It is a long way from the time when rock maple molds had to be turned for forms. These molds can be used over and over and will last a long time.*

to make the curve of the mold at those areas where the curve is most acute. Don't assume the glass will fit simply because the pattern paper does. The paper will bend; the glass will not. Simple as it may seem, many beginners overlook this.

You can combine the small-pieced lamp with the paneled lamp described in this chapter, using small pieces as the skirt. If you do this, make a form out of cardboard or heavy paper and tack the small pieces to this rather than laying them flat and trying to bend them around to form a circle as you would ordinarily do with this type of lamp.

Most small-pieced lamps look shiny and new because of the amount of tinning required. They are generally antiqued with patina to get rid of this effect. This should be done soon after the lamp is finished and before any oxidation has started to form on the soldered surfaces. The more oxidation that is formed, the more difficult the antiquing process will be. For quick action, heat the antiquing solution.

Small-pieced lamps are wired and hung exactly the same as any other type of lamp. They are quite strong, and if you have soldered correctly, you should have no trouble with them coming apart in midair.

Use plenty of solder, but keep the copper-foil edges thin. Solder dripping onto the glass is not hot enough to crack the glass and is easily scraped away. When you bead, turn the lamp on its side so that the solder will not keep dripping onto the tabletop. Put your lamp in a position best suited for you to work. It will not collapse. If the joints are tacked sufficiently, your lamp will maintain its shape, even when it is not supported by the mold.

BENT-PANEL LAMPS

One type of bent-panel lamp (*Figs. 14–29—14–33*) is actually made with flat

Fig. 14–30 The pieces comprising the upper and lower panels are put together and joined as in the skirt-panel lamp.

Fig. 14–29 Basic pattern for a bent-panel lamp. From top to bottom, the pieces are: crown, upper panel, lower panel, and skirt.

Fig. 14–31 The skirt is added, having been put together flat and then bent to shape.

panels that are bent only at the joints. The other type contains bent panels, either in their entirety or as a topping to a small-pieced skirt. This fabrication requires the use of a fairly deep kiln that will go to 1500 degrees F.

Calculating the Circle

Bent-panel lamps take a single or double S-shaped curve. The circle is dependent on the widest portion of each individual panel, regardless of the number of bends within it. Plan your circle from this measurement. If you want a certain diameter, you must divide it by the number of panels you want to employ in your lamp. Bent-panel lamps have an even number of panels, usually eight or more, of similar or alternating colors. They are held in place by decorative brass stripping or white metal or lead came. The hobbyist should start with lead came, since the other metals are more difficult to work with. In our studio, we work mainly with lead came and apply over it brass filigree or decorative strips.

Once you have decided on the diameter of the lamp and have calculated your circle, dividing this diameter among the number of panels, design the panel itself. Your design must taper downward from the widest point of the circle.

Bending the Glass

Transfer your original panel design from graph paper via carbon paper to pattern pa-

Fig. 14–32 The crown is put together flat, then given a slight upward tilt.

Fig. 14–33 The completed lamp.

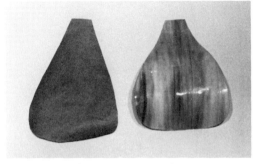

Fig. 14–34 The pattern on the left matches the piece of bent glass on the right.

Fig. 14–35 Putting together a bent-panel lamp. The panels are assembled vertically and supported by plasticene. Once you have three of them tacked together, they will usually support themselves, and additional panels may be added without the plasticene.

Fig. 14–36 *The completed lamp. Filigree has been soldered over the lead borders of the panels and between the panels and the crown to give a more delicate effect.*

Fig. 14–37 *A hanging lamp made of bent panels, each panel individually bent.*

per. You may want to make a few different patterns to prevent a single repeat pattern from fraying from the excessive cutting. You can cut a single pattern out of thin sheet metal as suggested for the multipanel lamp. Cut the glass exactly to the pattern and lay the panels flat, making sure that your measurements are exact.

Making the Mold

Molds are of two varieties—either drape or saggers. We prefer drape molds, but we have used sagging molds as well, especially

for acute bends. Here the weight of the glass blank is used more effectively.

The mold can be formed out of plaster of paris. You can make changes in this material when it is wet, but once it is set it should be allowed to cure overnight undisturbed. Plaster of paris can be used in the kiln as a drape mold. We have had little success using it as a sagger. Before using it to bend glass, it must be heated in the kiln to approximately 1200 degrees and then allowed to cool for twenty-four hours. After it has cooled, you may find tiny cracks developing through its surface. If great chunks of the mold crumble away, the plaster of paris mixture was off. The mixture should be thick and creamy and free of air pockets.

Another type of mold is made of terra cotta, which hardens as it bakes. Whether you use terra cotta or plaster of paris, you must apply a mold release substance to the mold so that the glass will not stick to the surface. Mold releases are sold by ceramic supply stores.

Once the molds are ready and the glass cut, if you are using a drape mold, place the mold in the kiln with the hump uppermost, and balance your glass on top so that it drapes over the mold. If you are using a sag mold, place the glass over the declivity so that it will sag into it. Check for undercuts in the sag mold. These will cause the glass to break when you release it from the mold. Each mold should be coated well with mold coat and the kiln gradually heated. Most stained glass bends between 1150 and 1300 degrees F., depending on color, thickness, and manufacturer. We bend our glass by eye using a toploader kiln. Not all colors of stained glass bend at the same temperature. The cone firing method is of little use here since each piece must be individually watched. Molds may last for five to eight bends before they begin to crumble.

Fitting the Panels

Once the panels are bent, you are ready to fit them together to the general shape of the lamp. The best came to use is ¼″ U round. This follows bent glass with less trouble than any of the other styles. Fit the came to the edges of the bent panels, molding the lead with your fingers, and solder the ends.

Bent-panel lamps should be assembled vertically. A small block of clay makes a good stand for each panel. You should have an even number of panels, usually eight or more, and they should be upright at the angle at which they are to be joined.

Use only enough clay to keep the panels upright. Move the panels so they meet at their juncture points and tack them together with solder. You may have to maneuver them to get them to meet exactly. Make sure that they are all at the same angle or your circle will not close, and if it does, it will appear deformed. With the panels tacked together, you can fill in with solder along the remainder of the lead lines. The panels at the bottom may splay out from one another. Here they must hang free, supported by the juncture lines above. They will be close to the angle point. You can use brass banding as decorative strips over this portion of the lead. If the curved panels follow each other closely all the way down, you can extend your brass or copper decorative banding. This banding should be soldered to the lead from inside the shade so that no solder shows from the outside. When bending brass strips to fit, make a Styrofoam mold as a guide.

When soldering, hold the brass with a protective mitten so the heat does not burn your fingers. It takes only one or two solder points to tack it well to the came. You can solder it through existing areas of solder that are holding the came skeleton together. The solder will puddle against the brass band from the heat of the iron.

THE LANTERN

Compared to multipaneled, small-pieced, and bent-panel stained-glass lampshades, the lantern is easy. Most lanterns consist of four-sided rectangular panels, with a long bulb within that effectively lights up all the corners and angles. The panels can be the same design or alternating designs. (*Fig. 13–38*).

Start by designing the panels. Don't use too many small pieces or you will de-

Fig. 14–38 Lantern composed of four panels broken into an abstract design. One panel contains an old roundel. Note the top supporting bars.

Fig. 14–39 A more simplified lantern showing a small top and long skirt. The trick here is to get the angle right between then. Use a mock-up for this one.

tract from the effect. The pieces need not be as small as in the Tiffany shade, since there is no angle or bend to climb. An old jewel or two or a few chunks can be incorporated into the design. Whether you design a simple four-straight-paneled piece, or a more complex flaring design, or a top-bottom combination that must be fitted together as in Figure 14–39, make a mock-up in heavy cardboard before cutting the glass (*Figure 14–40*). Good cardboard comes from sides of corrugated boxes.

The mock-up should be as neat and precise as possible. If the mock-up is incorrect or ungainly looking, your glass will look the same. The mock-up should show the shape of each panel. Tape the sides together and keep this form in front of you as you work. The mock-up should be slightly smaller than your finished product to allow the glass edges to meet at the proper angles.

Cut the glass panels and place them on the form. Lead (or foil) and tack them with solder. Remove the mock-up and thoroughly solder the panels. Using the mock-up as a guide gives less chance of error in forming the angles between the panels. Ninety-degree angles are difficult to get precisely right and if you attempt to form them without a mold, the lantern will be inaccurate.

The angles may show solder between them. Once the lantern is well soldered, take a strip of ³⁄₁₅″ U lead and flatten it into a belt, as was done with the multipaneled lamp. This belt may be run over the sides of the lantern and tacked top and bottom to form a covering for the seams of any glass sides that were not precisely cut.

Fig. 14–40 A cardboard mock-up for a lamp panel. With this four-sided lamp, first make the form, then match the sides before cutting it in glass.

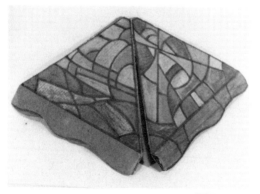

Fig. 14–41 The same lamp panel matched to another cardboard piece with a stained-glass design patterned over the surfaces. The cardboard skirt will be bent down after being sliced from behind.

UNUSUAL SHAPES

Some stained-glass shades are neither square nor circular—for instance, the star-shaped lamp. The "star lamp" is shaped

Fig. 14–42 A vase cap and finial give a finishing touch to the top of the lamp.

with rectangles of glass built up to form a three-dimensional star effect. Although such a lamp looks complicated, as you take it apart panel by panel and see how it is put together, it devolves into nothing more than multiple rows of glass angled together to form the final shape. The mechanics follow closely the making of the lantern, except that the star is an extended and more ornate form. Professional shops that mass-produce noncircular lamps make their molds out of metal so that they are more durable and exact than cardboard. These molds are difficult and time-consuming to make—in some instances, more difficult and more time-consuming than the lamp itself. But they last indefinitely.

THE SHADE AID

The Shade Aid is a unique lampshade positioner that allows comfortable soldering, and anyone who has ever made a small-pieced lampshade must feel gratitude toward its inventor. Shade positioners have made brief appearances on the market but they were either too cumbersome or ultra-ingenious to the point that no one could figure out how to use them. When you make your first small-pieced lampshade, you will find yourself going through many contortions as you try to keep the panels lined up and the solder from dropping onto the table. Burned fingers can result if you let your impatience take hold. The Shade Aid looks like a winner. Here's how it works (*Figs. 14–43—14–48*).

1. To solder the outside segment, place the Styrofoam form so that its center line lies over the joint in the tabletop. Select two holes, one on either side of the form and insert a 6″ threaded rod in each.

Fig. 14–44 *Once the outside soldering is done, the glass can be removed from the mold and turned over, secured, and placed into a comfortable position for soldering the inside.*

Fig. 14–45 *The segments of the lamp are aligned exactly using the guides available.*

Fig. 14–43 *The Shade Aid set up for the first soldering operation. The unit is held securely at a convenient soldering angle.*

Fig. 14–46 *The outside is soldered, again tipping the firmly held shade this way and that.*

Fig. 14–48 *A conversion from table model to floor model.*

Fig. 14–47 *The shade positioned to allow inside soldering. As each area is soldered, the shade is turned to the next area.*

All tacking and rough soldering can be done on the outside of the segment.

2. The panel is soldered on the inside segment.

3. The segments are aligned and the joints between segments rough soldered.

All the segments are lined up in place, tack-soldered, and all seams rough soldered in this position.

4. To finish soldering the outside, you might want to use the shank extension provided. The base must be secured to the worktable when the shade overhangs the base.

5. To finish soldering the inside, use the hole in the top cap as an axis for turning the shade. The ball joint under the unit's table is used to keep the seams level as soldering progresses.

WIRING A LAMP

The Canopy

The canopy is a decorative plate that fits directly to the ceiling and through which the electric wiring passes. Its purpose is twofold: to cover the hole in the ceiling made for the electric box, and to allow the chain to hold the lampshade. Canopies come in all styles, from simple brass bowls to ornately carved, highly polished, or antiqued designs in metal. Select a canopy that will not detract from your lamp. This doesn't necessarily mean the simpler the canopy the better. An extensively foiled Tiffany shade might have an ornate canopy, not a bare metal cap. Conversely, a plain geometric lamp might have a plain canopy.

Canopies come with two types of center holes and with or without small side holes meant for screwing into the underlying electric box. In the latter instance, the center hole runs $\frac{7}{16}''$, and the two side holes are spaced $4\frac{1}{4}''$ center to center. We prefer the single large center hole, which is $1\frac{1}{16}''$ and supports the lamp directly to the electric box by means of a decorative hangar unit. Some popular canopy finishes are brushed brass, black, bright brass, polished copper, weathered copper, chrome, and weathered antique brass.

Swag Kits

If you are not going to place your lamp into a preexisting fixture box, swagging it gives decorative and functional placement. A swag is nothing more than a loop of chain attached from one spot on the ceiling to another. Two swags are enough for most lamps, but three can be used for a large lamp, with equal or diminishing loops of chain. Both the lamp and the loops of chain are held by ceiling hooks with "molly" screws. If your lamp is heavy, try to place the ceiling hook directly into a beam. When swagging, run the chain all the way down the wall to the baseboard socket. It will look unfinished if the chain runs only halfway down the wall.

You can make your own swag kit by purchasing the items separately, or you can purchase a kit with the correct amount of chain.

Die-Cast Loops

Die-cast loops connect the chain to the lamp and hold together the two vase caps that stabilize the lamp. The wiring passes through its center hole. Loops, like canopies, should match the lamp in style.

Fig. 14–49 Lamp hooks of different styles. Each is held to the underlying socket by a brass nipple.

Fig. 14–50 Vase caps of different shapes and sizes.

Fig. 14–51 Two of a kind. A vase cap 9″ in diameter next to a 2″ brother. Lampshades can vary this much in top diameter.

Chain and Chain Pliers

Chain is sold in 3′ lengths, and usually each loop is notched so that it can be opened with a pair of chain pliers. Anyone who has struggled to open decorative chain by gripping the loop on either side and

Fig. 14–52 Parts in wiring lamps: Brass nipples, the top and bottom pieces of a brass socket holder, and plastic line-cord switches.

pulling like mad with regular pliers will appreciate the ease of working with chain pliers (see Chapter 4).

Even if you make only an occasional lamp, you may find that you can't do without them. For anyone producing a number of lampshades that must be wired, they are a necessity. When passing the electric wire through the chain, it is not necessary to weave it through every loop. Every other one or every third one will do.

Sockets

There are a number of kinds of sockets, but we find it best to use those with a set screw in the neck. The set screw allows a definitive measurement to be made along the length of the nipple and holds it firmly in place. Sockets with either a chain or a push-pull switch are awkward. We do not use porcelain sockets simply because they are heavy and add nothing to the fixture. A brass (brass or nickel coated) or bakelite socket is best. The bakelite socket has an advantage in that it is shorter than the brass, although it is a little more difficult to wire. Be sure to get one with a standard base. The base is held by a small screw in the socket, and it is best to take this off before you begin to wire the socket. The keyless brass socket also has a standard

base, which is held in place by pressure locking to the cap. This also must come off before wiring.

Vase Caps

Vase caps are molded discs of brass that rise tentlike from a flat plane to a shallow center peak, where the nipple hole is located. One is placed inside the neck of the lamp and another outside. When the two are then compressed by the outside lamp ring and the inside socket with a nipple acting as a lever between them, they neatly sandwich the neck of the glass and grip in securely all around. Such caps, of course, can be used only with lamps with round necks. They change size approximately every ⅛″, so it is better to first make your lamp and then fit your vase caps to the existing hole, rather than having a specific center hole and trying to force your measurements to conform to it.

Vase caps come in unfinished brass, lacquered brass, and polished brass but it is difficult to get them in any other color. The brass coloring can be changed chemically to an antique copper or a pewter, or you can paint the caps. If you paint them, first remove the lacquer coat from the cap with alcohol or acetone. It is always easier and cheaper to paint an unfinished than a finished vase cap. Use a good quality paint to avoid chipping.

There are those who argue that it is a waste to use two vase caps in a lamp, and that the decorative cap should be used only on the outside. For such individuals, check plates, which are brass-spun round flat plates with an ⅛″ lip, are available. We don't use them ourselves because we believe that a three-dimensional object such as a lamp, which is viewed from all sides, should look its best from every angle.

Furthermore, since a round lamp usually presents a cone-shaped look inside and out, a vase cap that is also cone shaped will fit much better than a check plate, which must of necessity leave an empty space above it to the top of the lamp.

Decorative vase caps are available that have soft fencing in the form of an edge filigree, as well as an additional half-inch edge that tucks in the top portion of the lamp. This is particularly effective if you want to hide a leading job. Remember when calculating vase caps to allow in your measurements for the top rim of lead covering the lamp. The vase cap should fit neatly over it.

Globes

Duralite bulbs are fat and sassy looking and give an air of importance to the inside of the lamp. However, if your lamp's inside dimensions are such that even this bulb will be lost in it, then you would do better with a globe.

Globes have their own problems. They not only require a different fitting operation, but they require a hangar to support them. Hangars are essentially cast brass holders with three thumb screws that grip the lip of the globe. Make certain that these set screws turn easily because they will have to be opened again to remove the globe in order to change the bulb. If you have to use pliers to turn them shut, it will be difficult to open them again without cracking the lamp. When you buy a hangar, check the set screws and make sure they fit. They usually are packaged separately.

Noncircular Lamp Fittings

If you have made a lamp with a square or hexagonal top, there is no reason why you cannot wire and hang it. Of course, you cannot use vase caps, which come only in circular form. Two bars of galvanized steel should be measured across the top of the lamp at the strongest points, usually at two solder joints. Leave enough room between the bars for an 1/8" nipple. This can then be caught from below by a brass check ring and led into the socket. Another check ring and nut will hold it from above and fix it to the bars. You can then apply the lamp

ring and chain. If you don't want to be able to look up and see the ceiling through your lamp, cut a piece of thin sheet metal to fit the top. Drill a hole for the nipple and solder the sheet metal all around the top surfaces of your lamp. This will provide a holding plate and finishing plate at the same time. It is usually not necessary to solder the inside of the plate to the lamp. If your lamp is unusually heavy, consider placing a few galvanized steel supporting rods across the plate at requisite intervals and soldering them to the top surfaces of the lamp.

For lanterns, a flat plate leaves a somewhat unfinished look. Try your hand at bending your own decorative top for such pieces. A sheet of copper and an instrument called a "bending brake" will help you do the job. The bending brake provides a means of bending metal into requisite angles that leave only one seam to solder.

Wiring

Once you have the measurement of the top hole, fit the vase caps top and bottom and measure the size nipple you will need. This nipple will run through the two holes of the vase caps from bottom to top. Enough sbould protrude so that it can be caught by a lamp ring above, and below so that it can screw into the top of the socket. We usually start from below, screwing the nipple into the top of the socket and then tightening the socket set screw. We then place the nipple through the inner vase cap and upper vase cap. The top of the nipple is caught with the lamp ring and tightened so that the vase caps are held securely in place. Once this is done, you can move the lamp in any direction without fear of the vase caps falling off. Measure the amount of lamp wire you will need. Lamp chain comes in 3' lengths, which is the height from the ceiling that most lamps are hung. Measure the wire slightly more than 3'. Pass the end of the wire from the top through the hole in the lamp rings, through the vase caps, and through the top portion of the socket below. Split the wire; take the insulation of the split ends and wire the copper directly against the two screws in the socket. Then tighten the screws, pull the socket up against the top, place the bottom of the socket holder in place, and press it closed so that it snaps into the top of the socket.

With chain pliers, open one of the links of chain, hook it to the lamp ring, and close it. Now weave the lamp wire through the chain at every other or every third link. Be careful not to stretch the chain away from the lamp. The weight of chain can easily pull the lamp to the floor. This is especially true if you are using extra chain to make a swag. Unconsciously you may back farther and farther away from the table as you weave the wire through the chain. Your lamp can topple easily.

Once you have the lamp wire through the chain, split the end of the wire as before, taking the insulation off, and wire on a small lamp plug. Your wiring job is now complete.

15

Suncatchers and Other Creative Shapes

Not everyone comes into stained glass to make a lamp or a window. What draws many people into the craft initially are suncatchers—whether bird, beast, or insect, vegetable or mineral, symbol or emblem, abstract or specific, 3-D, double glazed, or multilayered. One reason why suncatchers are so much fun to make is that they usually can be completed in one session.

Kits are available with precut pieces, but it is far more fun to design your own suncatcher. A whimsical touch is all that it takes to make one lion or one elephant different from any other and give it a life of its own.

CAME OR FOIL?

The technique for making suncatchers is different from that for windows and lamps. You could lay out the pieces and lead them up as though you were fabricating a window, but this is time-consuming and awkward. We use the "wrap-around" method, which is that described in using copper foil. Not only can foil be used in this way, but thin U lead as well. This ¹⁄₁₆″ "back-to-back" variety is wrapped around each piece of glass just as foil would be. If your pattern has many steep angles and corners, it would be better to use foil, since the lead does not conform well. The choice of one metal over the other depends on the effect you want to emphasize. Foil

gives a more delicate, lacy appearance, whereas came is more emphatic and provides greater strength to an object that may be composed of only several fairly large pieces. The rule of thumb is that small pieces generally take foil and large ones lead.

When using ¹⁄₁₆″ lead, stretch it only minimally before use. If you stretch it too much, you will narrow the channel, perhaps to such an extent that you weaken the lead. Excessive stretching will snap the delicate came. If your glass pieces are very thin you might stretch the lead a few times gently rather than once brutally. You can thus lengthen the came a good 6 to 8 inches, narrowing the channel without distressing the surface. The idea is to fit the glass within the channel so that it doesn't rock back and forth like a loose tooth. This can be avoided not only by narrowing the channel, but by wrapping the came as tightly as possible to the glass edges. Use glass pliers to get the came tight around points, but careful not to apply too much pressure with the pliers. This will leave you with more pieces of glass than you intended.

If you choose foil, you can wrap it with a foiler or with your fingers. If you choose lead, our method may be to your advantage. We lay a strip of ¹⁄₁₆″ lead on the table channel side up. Starting at an end, we roll the glass piece up in it, pressing it firmly to the edges as we go. Once

Fig. 15–1 Leading up a suncatcher. The single-groove 1/16" flexible came can take sharp curves and angles with ease. The snail's body is a pressed roundel.

Fig. 15–2 The completed project.

Fig. 15–3 An owl and a bug with copper wire for feet and antennae.

Fig. 15–4 This teddy bear is large for a suncatcher, but it can be hung in a window from the hooks in its back (about the neck for the best balance). Nonfire paint was used for eyes, nose, and mouth. An old jewel lights up the center of the bow tie. The pebble-back opal white glass is used with the texture facing forward to give the effect of fur.

Fig. 15–5 Although this owl is perhaps overly leaded for its dimension, there is an interesting flow of line. Note that the loops are not placed correctly. The weight of the object will pull that top lead away from the glass. Each loop should be soldered where the lead lines from the eyes meet the top.

the circumference is leaded, we cut the excess, press all surfaces firmly to assure a tight fit, solder the end, and place the leaded piece on the work drawing. We calculate where the end will be soldered so that it will match a seam. In this way we do not have soldered spots showing over the outside border. If you intend to tin all surfaces, it is still good technique to keep soldered joints within seams. The tinning

process may reopen these areas, which means extra work for you during what should be a final step.

Some workers use glue in the lead channel, which makes it more like adhe-

Fig. 15–6 The frog's front legs clutching the guitar are three-dimensional. The eyes are dalles chunks. The hanging loops are attached behind the eyes.

Fig. 15–8 A cowardly lion.

Fig. 15–7 A mouse with a mushroom.

Fig. 15–9 Going around a point with 1/16" lead. The initial curve is made wide so that the point doesn't jab through.

sive-backed foil. We do not advise this. Glue makes a mess and adds unnecessary work and expense.

DESIGN CONSIDERATIONS

1. Suncatchers are subject to the same rules as any stained-glass object. Because they are free-form does not mean they can be chaotic. The pieces must bear a proportionate relationship to each other. The pieces should be cut with a pattern scissors if you are using lead. If they don't quite fit the patterns, they should be trimmed or recut.

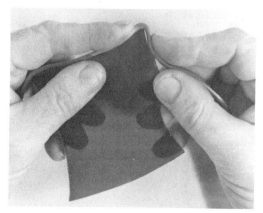

Fig. 15–10 *The lead is pressed against the glass to either side of the point.*

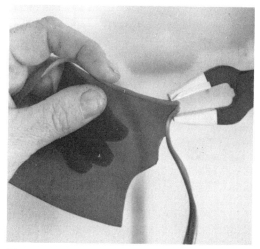

Fig. 15–11 *Pliers with taped jaws are used to get the lead as close against the pointed area as possible. Even minute gaps will allow light to come through.*

Fig. 15–12 *This Japanese lady, made from scrap glass, is a night-light. At left, front view; at right, the bulb in back.*

Fig. 15–13 *A three-dimensional locomotive. The flashlight is functional.*

Workers who are the souls of discipline when making a window or lamp can become careless with suncatchers because they are free-hanging or freestanding. Suncatchers have to be *crafted*.

2. Solder as a filler does not substitute for glass. If the leaded or foiled pieces show gaps between them when they are placed back on the work drawing, recut them. Don't attempt to fill in the empty spaces with solder. This throws off the linear quality of the piece and adds frustration as well. It is not easy to fill in with solder. To spend time on a poor result makes you want to break glass, not cut it.

3. If you use pliers to crimp lead over an area, tape the jaws so that the grooves do not leave an imprint on the lead surface.

4. A common problem with suncatchers is that their weight can cause the lead

Fig. 15–14 *Two girls playing.*

Fig. 15–16 *The smallest stained-glass window we've ever installed is contained in this bronze belonging to the Stained Glass Club. (Artist unknown)*

Fig. 15–15 *The "minilamp" measures approximately 9" high and about 5" wide. It makes a nice night-light. (Courtesy: Heirloom Lamps)*

Fig. 15–17 *A Christmas star, foiled and with each leg angled to provide depth.*

or foil border to separate from the glass. Where a border is involved, especially an area that is a suspension point, strutting to underlying joints must be provided in the design stage.

5. Don't overdesign. A suncatcher of 400 pieces may make an artistic statement, but it would have been better to turn it into the window it really is.

6. Loops for hanging should be placed at the juncture of several lead lines to provide the maximum support. Make certain that the loops are properly affixed. Don't be careless with this last step.

7. If you intend to sell your suncatch-ers, make as many as possible of the same kind at one time. A pattern-cutting machine can help cut down your time. These machines cut each piece of glass to pattern. There is nothing unartistic about using them. The artistic achievement is already inherent in the design.

Fig. 15–18 *A standing angel. Stability is furnished by the triangular shape. (Courtesy Glass House Studio, St. Paul, Minnesota)*

Fig. 15–20A *An aviator. Two small washers were used for goggles. The paint is nonfire.*

Fig. 15–19 *The runner of the sled is a piece of lamp filigree. Being brass, it solders well. The painted bows and ties are nonfire black.*

Fig. 15–20B *The aviator's airplane. We curved the propeller and provided a few other touches, such as the flames coming out of the engine and the fancy spoked wheels. The strutting for the wings is made from brass rods. The entire piece is foiled except for the lead came "tires."*

THREE-DIMENSIONAL EFFECTS AND DOUBLE GLAZING

Most three-dimensional effects are best done using copper foil. Came does not have the mobility of the foil, and its bulkiness, even at its thinnest measurement, gets in the way. Hold the foiled piece to be soldered with pliers. Heat from the soldering is quickly transmitted to the foil and

Fig. 15–20C *The completed project. The aviator fits into, but is not soldered to, the plane. This is a good project to take a flyer on.*

then to your fingers. Avoid overbracing 3-D objects. If your piece needs excessive bracing, redesign it. 3-D effects should appear as natural extensions of the project, not tacked on afterthoughts.

Double glazing is the process of employing one piece of glass on top of another. Since suncatchers shouldn't be heavy, use this effect sparingly. Extra wide leads are available to fit two width glasses, although you can foil or lead them individually and solder these borders together. What you achieve in double glazing, if you do it properly, is depth. This is produced at the expense of color, which becomes duller. Tiffany used double and triple glazing extensively in many of his windows. The effect can provide an interesting emphasis to a portion of your suncatcher. Before cutting any colors, however, hold them up to bright sunlight and see how they act one atop the other. It is much easier to find this out before you double glaze them.

MOBILES

Mobiles are a great way to use up stained-glass scraps. Almost anything goes here so long as it can be balanced. Mobiles, in effect, are three-dimensional graffiti. We have made all kinds, some of our favorites employing long strips of glass mixed with bamboo or driftwood. The holes that must be drilled in the glass are easily accomplished with any of the different grinding bits available. Hang mobiles with fish line.

FREESTANDING OBJECTS

Since the purpose of stained glass is to reflect as well as refract light, standing objects are perfectly valid expressions of the craft, are fun to make, and provide many novel exhibits. We provide some here, from the simple standing owl and bug to the complex airplane and pilot. The fabrication of freestanding objects provides different challenges than anything we have discussed so far. The main problem is balancing the piece so that it can maintain delicacy without falling over. This is nicely accomplished in the Glasglo Angel, where the triangular shape allows the piece to sit firmly while actually being a part of the design. In the case of the airplane and pilot, the weight of the airplane had to be divided among the different pieces, mainly the wings, so that it wouldn't collapse. Glass will not take the strains that metal will. We once used this piece, with different supports, in a lecture. As we demonstrated its stability, it began to self-destruct. The fault was in the fabrication, which had been compromised to an extent the material would not allow. It is an embarrassing way to be taught a lesson, but that is sometimes what it takes.

16
Gluing, Cementing, Fusing, Torching, Crushing, Embedding, Filigree, and Framing

Working with stained glass provides quantities of leftover material. In this craft, you will soon learn to throw nothing away, especially after watching more experienced workers retrieve your "debris" from the wastebasket and turn it into little treasures. Odds and ends of solder can amount to several pounds after a while. Dalle and came pieces and even a few inches of copper foil can find new life elsewhere. As for pieces of glass—they can be used almost to dust. The possibilities for all these scrappy remnants are all but endless. Here are a few ideas.

GLUING

A Mosaic Window

On a piece of double-strength window glass, draw a design, not too simple but not too complicated either. Sketch the design on paper first or draw it directly on the glass with a glass marking pencil. Be sure the glass is clean. Once your design is set, use pieces of scrap stained glass to fit portions of it. Your design should not involve pieces of glass any larger than those in your scrap pile. That is why we refer to this as a "mosaic" window. In fact, the smaller the pieces, the better. Try to fit the pieces to the design as accurately as possible. Then glue each to the window glass using a clear-drying glue such as Bond's #527 or Duco Cement. In essence, this is similar to working with mosaic tile. In fact, you can use glass nippers to make your glass pieces even smaller, carving them roughly into different shapes.

A mosaic design can cover all or part of the window glass. The clear glass acts as a negative space where it is left open; where the stained-glass pieces cover it, the light is modified into colors. Not only is the technique fun, and not only are the materials "found" pieces, but the effect is striking. Take your time here; don't assume that just because you are working with scrap pieces of glass and glue that you can be slapdash.

After gluing let the project sit for several hours; overnight is always a good measure. Don't worry about any excess glue that seeps between pieces. When the pieces of glass have hardened in position, use grout or liquid lead such as Met'l Bond Liquid Lead to fill in between them. Your choice depends on what sort of a finish you want the border line to have. Grout (which is mixed with water) provides a smooth, even surface; liquid lead gives a rough, more soldered or "tinned" appearance. Avoid getting liquid lead on the glass; if you do, wipe it off immediately or you will have to chip it off when it dries, possibly loosening the piece of glass in the process. Squeeze the tube of liquid lead from the bottom; these tubes have a habit of bursting through the bottom if you squeeze from the middle.

Drinking Glasses and Candleholders

Measure your stained-glass pieces against the curvature of a clear drinking glass. Then glue them as described for the mosaic

Fig. 16–1 A rose by any other name is a stained-glass rose. The glass pieces are attached to a brass rod.

window. Since you are working against a curve, lay the glass on one side and prop it in position. You will have to wait to turn it before doing the other side. Don't turn it too soon or the pieces will fall off or slide out of position. If you use a quick-setting glue, you can actually allow the glass to maintain an upright position and glue in layers from the bottom, since each layer will, to an extent, support the one above. We find this method is good when working with children. Finally, grout the peices.

CEMENTING

Small plastic containers of cement are available in hardware stores. All you need to do is mix the powder with water to a proper consistency. Place the cement mix in a wooden frame within which you have placed pieces of scrap dalles. Once the cement sets, you will have a firm panel sparkling with faceted jewels. You can make small, shaped objects by using cookie cutters as molds.

FUSING

Access to a kiln broadens the possibilities of scrap use. Try this: Take a wall tile (preferably a white one) and place a few

Fig. 16–2 A "mosaic" window in process of construction. Stained glass is glued to underlying window glass according to the pattern marked on the glass. The pieces will stand out in bas-relief against the clear glass.

Fig. 16–3 *A drinking glass with small pieces of stained glass as decoration. Grout or liquid lead will be placed between the pieces.*

Fig. 16–5 *A stained-glass upright piano is an interesting freestanding object. A music box is glued on the back.*

Fig. 16–4 *Stained-glass candleholders made from scrap pieces, glue, and grout.*

Fig. 16–6 *A kangaroo planter.*

scrap glass chips on it. Fire to about 1450°F. and cool the kiln overnight. The glass will melt into the tile and form an interesting pattern. It may take a lot of these to do your bathroom wall, but you will have one of the most original walls around.

TORCHING

Using a butane torch, small pieces of glass can be heated and bent into twists and turns to suit your fancy. For these creations to cool without fragmenting in the process, it is necessary to anneal them. One way of accomplishing this is to place them into a kiln directly after torching.

Here the temperature is maintained about 900°F. Allow the torched pieces to cool overnight.

Less cumbersome for small pieces is placing them on a wire grid heated from below with a Bunsen burner. Alternatively, you can use a piece of metal that is

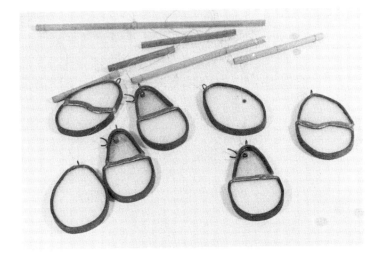

Fig. 16–7 *The chick and egg mobile.*

Fig. 16–9 *A wall tile with pieces of stained glass fused into it.*

Fig. 16–8 *A locomotive.*

kept heated on a hot plate. This type of annealing is somewhat hit or miss because the pieces cool unequally. If you keep them small enough, however, they should be able to take the stresses of torching.

Torched pieces of glass come in handy for stems for leaves, flower parts, glass filaments for twists, abstract shapes and glass overlays. Stems and other thin parts may need no annealing; you can cool them directly on a heat-resistant pad or block. They are small enough to be self-annealing.

When torching small pieces of glass,

use needlenose pliers to hold them in the heat of the flame. As the center melts, pull to either side as though pulling a piece of taffy. The more you pull, the thinner the bridge of glass becomes until it develops into a thread. If you continue to pull, it will come apart. It takes considerable practice to get a requisite size and shape from such a guided melt. However, it's fun to practice. Torching glass is an entire field in itself and one that is extremely rewarding.

Scrap Lead

You can also use a torch to melt scrap lead. If a piece of came is less than 2 feet, we melt it. Melted came has a number of uses—for lead knives or other tools that

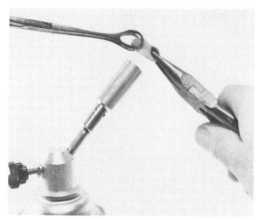

Fig. 16–10A *Torching glass. The piece of glass is held in the flame until it begins to soften.*

Fig. 16–10B *As it softens, pull it gently apart and it will begin to stretch in the center.*

need weighted handles, bases for glass sculpture (chessmen, for instance) and miniature lamps, and to make decorative lead objects from molds. At the very least, accumulating scrap lead provides a quantity to sell eventually to the scrap metal collector, who will give you the going rate per pound.

Other Metals

You can use your torch on brass, copper rods, and filigree if you want to take the

Fig. 16–11 *Lenk's new miniature butane torch might be ideal for "drawing" scrap glass into melted objects for suncatchers or as ancillary touches for a larger project. It burns up to five hours, is lightweight and easy to handle, and produces a hot, clean flame up to ¼" × 2⅛".*

Fig. 16–12 *You can melt scrap lead on a ladle and pour it into a mold, as shown, to make stands for stained-glass objects.*

temper out of the metal and bend it to shapes that it will not otherwise hold. To do this play the flame of the torch over the metal, pick it up with tongs, and plunge it into cold water. It will hiss a bit, and when

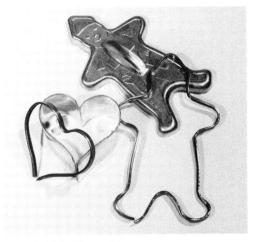

Fig. 16–13A *Two cookie-cutter patterns . . .*

Fig. 16–14 *Glue is flowed from above and allowed to percolate through the glass. Make sure you have wax paper underneath. When dry, these medallions will glitter and sparkle in the sunlight.*

Fig. 16–13B *being filled with crushed glass.*

it cools you will find it quite pliable. This technique is used to bend the decorative filigree of lamps over a curved-panel lead. The torch is a handy item for other processes as well, but a word of caution here: Never apply the torch to a large sheet of glass. The coefficient of expansion can shatter the sheet and you could injure yourself badly. Large pieces of glass should be heated only in the kiln, where uniform heating and cooling is provided.

CRUSHING

Crushed glass is sold in various color in hobby shops and in some glass distribution centers. Blenko Glass is a good supplier of much crushed glass. However, you can make your own easily enough. Wrap a number of scrap glass pieces in a heavy rag, tie the neck of the rag, and beat the pieces with a hammer. Do this on a firm surface, preferably metal. We use a portion of an old girder. Do not do this on a wooden floor or even a cement floor since the glass can score it. A brick (not a firebrick) makes a good rest; its roughness contributes to the crushing. Look inside the rag from time to time to see just how small your glass particles are getting. If you hammer too much, you will end up with glass powder. Quite a bit of crushed glass can be made very quickly. You needn't slam the hammer down with a lot of force; tapping is usually sufficient.

Acquire a few cookie cutters of various shapes and wrap 1/16″ U lead around them. Solder the joint and lift away the cookie cutter. The lead will maintain the shape of the cutter. You may have to compensate a little by hand to finalize the shape. Place the lead on wax paper and fill the bottom of it with a clear-drying glue

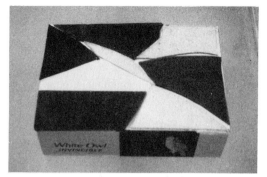

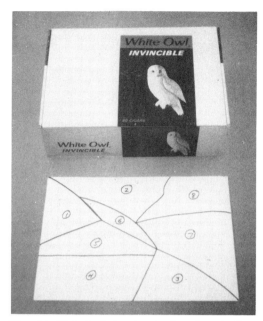

Fig. 16–15 *Stained-glass jewelry box. Step 1. Get a cigar box in good condition, cut a piece of pattern paper to the size of the top, and draw a pattern. Children may just trace the shapes of some scrap glass pieces to fit the existing area.*

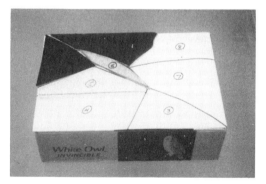

Fig. 16–16 *Step 2. Glue the pattern to the top of the box and glue the glass pieces to it with a clear, quick-drying glass cement.*

Fig. 16–17 *Step 3. All the pieces are glued to the lid of the box. Move them as close to one another as you can while the glue is still workable, but remember to line them up with the borders of the box.*

Fig. 16–18 *Step 4. A plastic filler (liquid lead) is used to fill the cracks between the pieces of glass. Use enough to form a definite ridge between the glass patterns.*

Fig. 16–19 *Step 5. Cut a piece of glass to size and glue it to the front panel of the box. Repeat this process for all other panels.*

(Duco or Bond 527 or Bond Grip.) Pour some crushed glass into the center of this mold and spread it with a toothpick. Add more glue, then more glass, to the top of the lead. Spread glue and glass evenly over the surface. You can make several of these

Fig. 16–20 *As a finishing touch, place some glass globs or chunks in a free form or figurative design.*

Fig. 16–22 *A stained-glass lamp showing filigree overlying all the panels. (Courtesy Jefferson Art Lighting, Inc. Ann Arbor, Michigan)*

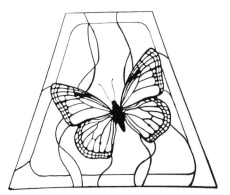

Fig. 16–21 *A filigree butterfly for a lamp panel. (Courtesy Ed Hoy Co.)*

items at a time. Put them aside to set. When the glue matures, peel away the wax paper. You will have a stained-glass medallion. The process may not sound very "artistic," but it is fascinating, especially to children.

Crushed Glass Greeting Card

Cut a piece of clear or stained glass (a light color) into a small rectangle. From a stationery store, get several sheets of lettering stencil. Scotch-tape four or five of these sheets together for thickness. Cut out let-

ters to form some simple greeting and arrange these on the glass surface, using scotch tape to hold them secure. Squeeze glue into these little letter "wells," then pour in small pieces of crushed glass. Spread them with a toothpick so that they are even, then add more glue. When the glue dries, remove the stencil and you will have crushed glass in bas relief forming your greeting against the stained or clear glass "card." Simple designs can also be stenciled against the glass and filled in this way.

EMBEDDING

A Stained Glass Jewelry Box

Start with a cigar box. Cut and glue measured pieces of white paper over it to cover its design. Create your own design on this covering paper. Take a pattern from this and cut pieces of glass to fit. In addition to the glass pieces, you may use crushed

Fig. 16–23 *A more ornate filigree pattern.*

glass, millefiore, glass chunks and glass globs. Once all your items are glued into place and the glue has dried, fill in between them with grout or liquid lead. This will raise the surface and make it appear as though the glass was embedded in the box itself.

The Globe Lampshade

Use a regular glass globe, one with a lip around the hole. Affix over the surface pieces of stained glass or globs, and glue them in place. Grout between the surfaces. You can draw your design right onto the globe. The pieces of glass must be small enough to take the curvature of the globe.

FILIGREE

Metal filigree is not new to stained glass. Tiffany used it for lampshades as well as in his inkwells and other objects. Filigree furnishes an alternative to painting details as well as an overlay to set off the glass beneath. It is not meant to provide amateur shortcuts, but to add another di-mension to the craft—one that can be at the fingertips of the least experienced student as well as the most experienced professional. Like any other stained-glass aid, filigree must never overwhelm the glass proper. It can be used effectively with scrap pieces of glass as well as in basic window or lamp designs.

FRAMING

Framing a panel in wood provides a fin-ished border to the work. Frames are avail-able in all sizes and shapes to match almost any glass design. For large panels, oak is our preference. It is strong, finishes well, and is stable. If you make your own frame, 1¼" oak finished to 1" rather than 1" fin-ished to ¾" is best for strength and ap-pearance. Make your frames from four pieces so as to "run" with the grain. This eliminates shrinking of the wood over time. Wood shrinks more across the grain than with it. Wood also "cups" with age. The greater the width, the greater the cup. For heavy (large) panels, all joints should be doweled and glued.

Fig. 16–24A *Filigree suncatcher. The pattern pieces are ready to be fitted on the work drawing.*

Fig. 16–24B *The pieces on the work drawing.*

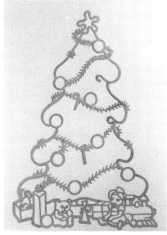

Fig. 16–24C *The foiled pieces placed on the work drawing.*

Fig. 16–24D *The filigree for the project.*

Fig. 16–24E *The glass pieces placed on the work drawing and the filigree laid over them to show how the completed suncatcher will look. (Courtesy of Ed Hoy Stained Glass)*

Fig. 16–25 *A pattern combining filigree (the owl) and stained glass. (Courtesy Ed Hoy Stained Glass)*

Fig. 16–26 *The completed stained-glass design made into an octagonal window. The gibbous-moon glass is by Uroboros.*

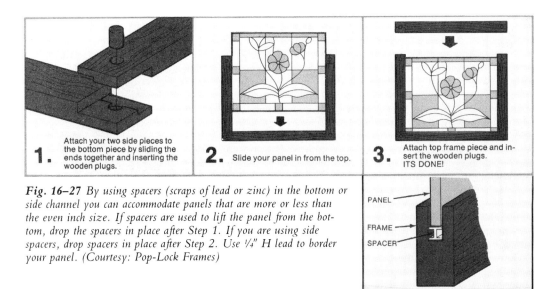

1. Attach your two side pieces to the bottom piece by sliding the ends together and inserting the wooden plugs.

2. Slide your panel in from the top.

3. Attach top frame piece and insert the wooden plugs. ITS DONE!

PANEL

FRAME

SPACER

Fig. 16–27 *By using spacers (scraps of lead or zinc) in the bottom or side channel you can accommodate panels that are more or less than the even inch size. If spacers are used to lift the panel from the bottom, drop the spacers in place after Step 1. If you are using side spacers, drop spacers in place after Step 2. Use ¼" H lead to border your panel. (Courtesy: Pop-Lock Frames)*

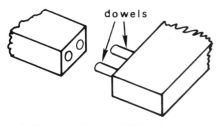

dowels

DOWELED BUTT JOINT

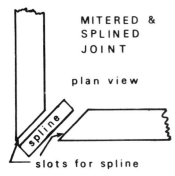

MITERED &
SPLINED
JOINT

plan view

spline

slots for spline

Fig. 16–28 Two types of frame joints. (Courtesy Emerson Wood Works Inc.)

Fig. 16–29 The Fletcher No. 5 gold-tip point driver.

Fig. 16–30 Using the Fletcher point driver to stabilize a window within a frame.

Fig. 16–31 The framed window.

Gluing, Cementing, Fusing, Torching, Crushing, Embedding, Filigree and Framing **237**

Use spacers (scraps of lead or zinc) in the bottom or the side channels provided to accommodate panels that are less than the "even inch" size. Use ¼" H lead to border a panel you intend to have framed. Such companies as Pop-Lock can accommodate any size panel. The panel does not have to be made to fit the frame because the Pop-Lock frames have been designed to fit the panel. A package marked 10" will accept a panel from 9½" to 10⅞". If you want to remove your panel from the frame, you can do so without destroying the frame or the panel. Emerson Wood Works of Denver, Colorado, will custom-frame almost any size or shape up to eight feet.

Many workers find that a framed panel presents a finished appearance that sells itself better than a panel framed merely with lead. And it is easier to move around. Even small objects can be framed with small commercial frames.

To hold the glass in position, we recommend the Fletcher point driver and its No. 2ST stacked triangle points (Fig. 16–29). This new model of an older unit assures the correct depth of penetration into wood of any type. Even small oak frames can be used. The advantage of a point driver over hammering in nails to hold the glass, aside from ease of operation, is the single as opposed to multiple blows against the frame. There is also no chance of hitting the glass with the hammer as when applying nails. The points are small enough not to show but large enough to grasp wood and glass securely. Together, wood frames and the point driver add another aesthetic facet to your finished work.

A well-known artist and craftsman once stated that no art could be taught through the medium of a textbook. With this view I quite agree, but I think the statement may be qualified to this extent, that if pure art cannot be so taught, there is no reason why instruction cannot be given through the medium of written material in the practical application of an art.

E. W. TWINING,
The Art and Craft of Stained Glass

ARTISTS
AND THEIR WORK

IV

Portfolio / David Hammang and Mark Capelle

In the Best Taste. *Cabinet doors demonstrating pictorial use of Armstrong glass. Because of the nature of the placement, opalescent glass was used almost exclusively; features are hand-painted. David Hammang, designer; Mark Capelle, artisan: Old World Glass Co.*

Portfolio / Saara Gallin

Photographs by James Mejuto,
except where otherwise noted.
Saara Gallin discusses her work
in Chapter 20.

Profiles in Glass. *Three screens: slumping,
wire, crackle glass.*

The Three Musketeers, *"What If" series, #2. Slumping,
fusing, wire.*

Muted Tears, *"What If" series, #3. Slumping, fusing.*

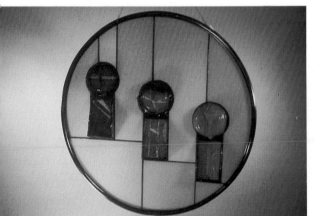

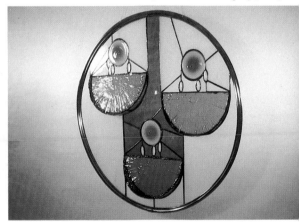

All of Us. *36" round; slumping, copper foil. Photograph by Vacha.*

All of Us, *detail. Photograph by Vacha.*

Profiles in Glass. *Faceted glass inserted into giant cut-up roundel.*

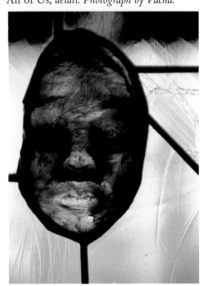

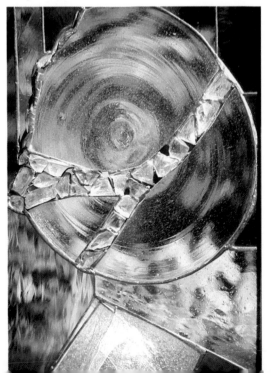

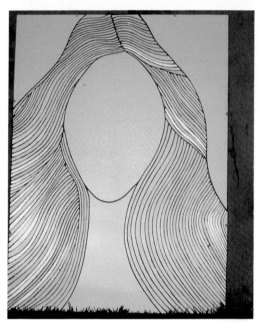

Woman #1, *1980. 48″ x 36″ x 3″ mirror.*

Portfolio / Jeffrey Franklyn Glick

Photographs by Diana Bond, except where otherwise noted. Jeffrey Glick discusses his work in Chapter 22.

Lycaste Longipetala.

Buddha. *Photograph by Stuart Arrow.*

Enchanted Forest. *Mirror imagery.*

Coconut Grove, *1977. 53" x 75" x 4" mirror.*

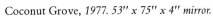

Rose.

Winter Tree.

Dorothy Maddy discusses her work in Chapter 17.

Rose oval, 1982. 6¼″ x 9″; silkscreening and glue-chipping.

Ramblin' Rose, *hand-painted detail.*

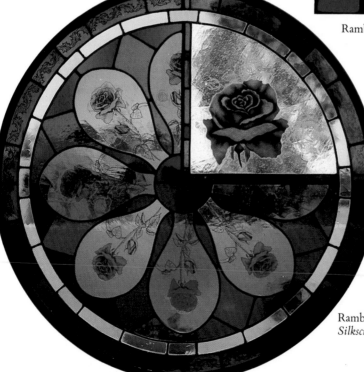

Ramblin' Rose, *1982. 24″ diameter. Silkscreened and painted glass.*

Indian Head, *1982, 12" high; hand-painted on glass.*

Nativity, *1982. 4" x 5½". After a 14th-Century French window; silkscreening requiring six screens.*

Window, Chapel of Evergreen Baptist Senior Citizen Home, White Rock, British Columbia. 6' x 5'6''; Fremont stained glass.

Portfolio / Lutz Haufschild

Detail of window, Scotia Place, Edmonton, Alberta, 32' x 32', Fremont stained glass.

17
Silkscreening and Glue Chipping

Dorothy L. Maddy

Dorothy Maddy is an artist of considerable renown who has developed primary interests in the glass surface techniques of painting, silkscreening, and glue chipping. Her Tree Top Studio is located in Scottsdale, Arizona. In addition to turning out commissioned pieces and teaching, Ms. Maddy enters her work in numerous shows around the country. She also lectures and writes articles about glass.

SILKSCREENING

Silkscreening is a printing process that can also be used on glass to create unusual design elements. For instance, a pattern that is extremely complex for handpainting can be applied to a screen photographically and then transferred to the glass. And all with one pull of a squeegee. You can reproduce such delicate tracery as lace, ferns, and leaves, and the screen can be used once or many times to re-create impressions that stay crisp and precise. Understanding the basic nature of silkscreening opens up unlimited possibilities for creative expression. To add to the joy of the work, the materials and supplies are readily available and inexpensive.

Materials

The Frame
You will need at least one silkscreen frame, and may need more depending on how many designs or colors you want to print. You can either make a screen or purchase one. If you make your own, buy choice-grade white pine lumber. This will resist warping and have the least amount of knots. For a maximum screen size of 18″ × 24″, you can use a 1 × 2. Larger screens will require a 2 × 2. Cut these boards to the proper lengths, bearing in mind that the fabric area should have a 2″ border all around the design to accommodate the paint and the squeegee. Butt the corners firmly and glue them, fastening one or two screws at each corner. The frame must be absolutely flat and straight. If you are careful with the placement of the screws, you can run the top of the assembled frame through a router, making a ⅜″ deep channel with a ⅛″ router tip. This channel will be used for fastening the fabric with cord. You may also purchase boards in various lengths that are already routed, but this will be more expensive if you are making many screens. If you staple the fabric to the frame, the channel is not necessary.

The Master Board
The master board is used for fastening the silkscreens when printing. You could use your worktable as the board, but it would be better to use a specific master board so that you can store it when not in use. The board should be made from at least ½″ plywood or particle board that will not warp, and should be made larger than your

Fig. 17–1 A corner of the assembled 1 × 2 with the holding screw and the routed groove. A 2 × 2 would need two screws to provide more stability.

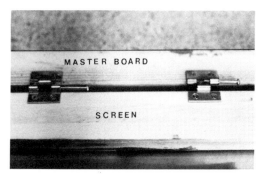

MASTER BOARD

SCREEN

Fig. 17–2 The master board and the screen. Note the loose-pin hinges.

largest screen. For example, if your screen has an 18″ × 24″ opening, the outside dimension of the screen would be 22″ × 28″. This would require a master board of about 24″ × 28″. The 24″ width gives you 2″ over the screen width in order to mount a strip of wood the same size as the framing of the screen. On this piece of wood you fasten the two opposite parts of a 1″ loose-pin hinge. Another pair is used on each screen in alternate positions to attach the screen to the master board. By removing the pins, the screens are made interchangeable. A small "leg" screwed on the side of each screen is necessary to hold the screen in a raised position when you are not printing.

The Squeegee
A 6″ and a 12″ squeegee should take care of most designs. The squeegee must cover the

width of the design with some additional leeway. Of course, it must fit into the screen frame. The smaller size is better for a small design because it requires less paint.

The Fabric
Today, silk is seldom used since synthetics are cheaper and more durable. Of these, polyester is more stable than nylon over an average work range. Both polyester and nylon are available with a weave of either multi- or monofilament threads. For fine detail work and easier clean-up the monofilament is better. Fabric also comes in various thread counts. The higher the number, the finer the mesh. The finer the mesh, the better the detail and the less amount of paint that will be printed on the glass. I use a 200-mesh polyester monofilament fabric. If your design has broad areas and you want more paint on the glass, use fabric with a smaller mesh number. However, too small a mesh number will produce on the edges of the screen a "checkered" effect from the weave.

Fastening Fabric to the Frame
There are two ways to fasten the fabric to the wood frame. I use both, depending on the availability of a routed frame. If your screen frame has the channel routed into it, or if you intend to replace the fabric often, you can use the cord method. Here you will need a roll of cotton silkscreening cord. Measure a piece of fabric so that it overhangs the outer edges of the screen frame by about 1″. "Tearing" the fabric to the size is best because this keeps the mesh lines straight on the frame. Wet this piece of fabric to help keep it in place. Partially inserting a thumbtack in each corner will also help hold the fabric at this stage.

Begin laying the cord in the groove, working it down lightly with a hammer so that it will attach firmly. Move around the screen, keeping the fabric tight but not taut. Cut the cord at the end. With a 3″ flat-angle iron or any other tool that will fit the groove, hammer the edge against the cord so that it depresses fully into the

Fig. 17–3 *The silkscreen cording process. The empty groove is seen above and to the right. Below and to the left, the cord is being pressed into the groove.*

Fig. 17–4 *The stapled screen showing two methods of stapling: diagonal staples in a single row, and doubled stapling, alternating the rows.*

groove. With this maneuver the fabric will be stretched very tight. Work slowly and carefully here, alternating sides so that the fabric does not pull out of any areas before all of the cord is fully depressed. When you are finished, the fabric should be evenly firm and tightly stretched like a drum.

The second of the two methods of fastening the fabric to the wood frame is to use a staple gun rather than a routed groove and cord. The problem with this method is that although it may seem simpler to lay the fabric, it is difficult to replace it when necessary. This problem can be overcome by using a special tape under the staples. To start, tear the fabric to size, wet it, and anchor the corners with thumbtacks. Start stapling in the center of each side, working toward the corners, and keep alternating from top to bottom and left to right, pulling the fabric tight as you go. The staples will hold best if they are fastened diagonally to the frame. They should be spaced closely enough to provide a good tight, flat surface to the fabric without any ripples.

Once the fabric is in place, wash it with vinegar to remove any traces of sizing. After it has been rinsed and dried, the raw edges of the fabric should be fastened with wide masking tape. Be sure there are no loose threads that might get in the way of the stencil. If you expect to use the same

screen for a long time, you will want to tape it on the inside as well as the outside and then cover it all with two or three coats of white shellac.

Making a Stencil

The screen is now ready to receive a stencil of your design. Although there are many ways to make a stencil, two methods fill most needs and give dependable results. One is the direct-photo stencil, which is excellent for details and very versatile. The other is a lacquer film, which is good for large designs or for geometric shapes such as the circle shown in Figure 17–14. It is also possible to cut detail with this method, although it is more tedious than with the direct-photo method.

The Direct-Photo Stencil

If you use a direct-photo stencil, your finished design must be a positive. This is the opposite of the usual negative film, so the image will be black (no gray tones, please) on a clear or translucent background. You can have your design made into a negative, then a positive on Mylar, at a blueprinting shop. You can use the negative design as well if you want the painted areas reversed. Shops charge by the square foot, so get as much as possible on each square foot of film. Later, you can cut the film for specific areas and reposition them for the silkscreening process. It is somewhat cheaper to have two acetate copies run off on a duplicating machine. A single copy is not dark enough, but with two copies overlapped carefully a good impression will appear on the screen.

Designing on Translucent Paper

Instead of using a Mylar positive, you can make a design directly on translucent paper. Clear acetate does not have enough "tooth" for most drawing materials, but there are many translucent drafting papers that are excellent for both the drawing and the exposure. Various drawing tools can be used so long as they are opaque. Among these are drawing ink, red photo-opaque felt markers, and lithograph crayons. For good detail work Rapid-o-Graph pens are excellent. Make sure that all of your marks are completely opaque by checking them over a light box or holding the design up to the light. Any halftones should be darkened to solids because they do not print well. Used with discretion, transparent graphic aids such as Formatt, Chartpak, or Lettraset are also useful. Strips of opaque tape will make lines and borders.

Applying Emulsion to the Screen

Once your positive is ready, you are now ready for the next step, which is applying the emulsion to the screen for the photo stencil. I use a Diazo-type emulsion with a liquid sensitizer. It is available at a local silkscreen supplier, but crafts supply stores also carry these items. Follow the manufacturer's instructions for mixing. Once mixed, the emulsion should be kept in an opaque plastic or glass container in the refrigerator, where it will last for several months.

Once painted on the screen, until the screen is exposed to light, the emulsion must be kept from sunlight or even from fluorescent lights. A low-wattage incandescent light or low daylight will not expose it while you are mixing or working with

it. So it is in this low-light situation that you apply the emulsion to the fabric.

With the screen held almost upright, I run a bead of emulsion along one end of the screen. With a squeegee or a stiff piece of cardboard the width of the screen opening, I pull the emulsion tight across the fabric, going in opposite directions on both sides of the fabric. I cover the entire screen, carefully but quickly, laying on a very thin coating. You will find that you have to go over each side a few times, since you want to push the emulsion not only over but *through* the fabric each time. When the emulsion is thin and even, put the screen in a dark area to dry overnight. The screen should be in a horizontal position with the fabric side up. If the area is humid, allow more drying time. Drying can be speeded up with a fan. You can also use a blow dryer if it's set on "cool" and if you don't hold it too close to the screen. Once the screen is dry, use it within a day or two; otherwise the emulsion will continue to harden and diminish the degree of exposure.

Time Out for a "Sandwich"

It is now time to build up a "sandwich." Start with a flat, sturdy board for support that is larger than the screen. On the board place a piece of 3"-thick foam the size of the interior of the screen. Cover the foam with a piece of black paper cut to the same size. (This will prevent any light from entering under the screen and causing overexposure.) Place the screen over the black paper with the smooth side (top side) of the screen facing you. Place your positive design face down on the screen. This is important, and in the heat of getting on with the job you may forget to do this. If you do, your design will be printed in reverse. If your design has letters on it, or if you are doing several stencils of one design with various colors, your design will be ruined.

It is helpful when assembling several separate pieces for one design to tape them

Fig. 17–5 The basic "sandwich": (1) The support board, (2) foam cushion, (3) black paper, (4) screen with emulsion, (5) design taped to clear window glass lying face down, (6) plate glass, and (7) black paper protects the screen until it is ready for exposure.

with transparent tape onto a piece of single-strength window glass cut to the size of the fabric opening. The edges of the glass should be smoothed to protect the fabric and your fingers. Tape them to the glass as you want them to appear when printed. Lay the glass face down so that the positive design is next to the prepared screen. On top of the glass place a piece of ¼" plate glass that is larger than the whole screen. The purpose of all of this is to ensure a tight fit of the design on the screen so that light will not enter around the edges of the design. When exposing, push down on the plate glass to depress the foam, keeping it as tight to the screen as possible. To protect the screen, put a large piece of black paper over the sandwich until you are ready to expose the screen.

The Exposure

I live in an area where the sun is very bright and very dependable. So I use it to expose my screens. If you want to use the sun, simply place your "sandwich" on a table outdoors and remove the black paper. Hold the glass down against the screen for the calculated exposure time, keeping your hands away from the area you want exposed. Then replace the black paper and bring it all inside.

Exposure times vary. If your design has a great deal of fine detail, expose it for about 8 seconds. If there are large areas, try it for 12 seconds. However, no matter what your light source, definitely test a screen before you do your regular screen. This will save you a lot of frustration, and once you know the exposure time, you can reclaim the test screen by washing it with Clorox and reapplying the emulsion. It is a good time-saving idea to make a test screen. Once you have established the proper developing time, you should not have to retest unless you change the design, materials, or procedure.

For the test, assemble the "sandwich," but then expose it in steps. Do not pull the black paper completely away; pull it away in portions, perhaps in five or six steps of gradually longer time periods. This should create strips on your design of the varied exposures, say 4, 8, 10, 12, 14, and 16 seconds. If you use an indoor light source for exposure, these time intervals will be in minutes. That is how great the variable is from sun to artificial light.

When I expose screens indoors, I use a #2 photo-flood bulb hung from about 18" above the top of the screen. Then I expose the screen for 5 minutes. To expose the screen evenly, hang the bulb at a distance from the screen equal to the diameter of the screen, but never closer than 12".

Developing the Screen

As soon as the screen is exposed, wash out the design. The transparent or translucent areas that have been exposed to the light source are now chemically changed and no longer water-soluble. However, the opaque design areas are still water-soluble. In a low-light area, rinse the screen with warm, not hot, water. A soft spraying for half a minute will soften the emulsion. Increase the pressure of the spray on the design areas and you will see the emulsion begin to wash away. This is the exciting part, because the design starts to appear. Keep turning the screen from one side to the other. When you think the design areas are clear, hold the screen up to a light source for a few seconds to check the design. Re-wash any areas that are not clear. If any areas are stubborn, wipe them carefully with a chamois. Do not rub too hard or you may rub away the background emulsion and ruin the screen. If the background areas wash away readily, you can assume the screen was not exposed to light long enough. If the design areas do not wash away easily, the screen has been exposed too long. These are the incidentals you should look for on your test screen.

When all the design areas are clear, blot the screen carefully with clean newsprint, first on one side and and then the other. This will prevent any wet background emulsion from running onto the design areas. Let the screen air-dry horizontally, fabric side up. When the screen is completely dry, use masking tape to seal any areas along the edges of the screen that were not completely covered with the emulsion. This will keep the paint from overflowing and causing a mess when you print. If any areas of the design are scratched or if there are any pinpoint holes in the emulsion, block them out with a screen block-out material. This is a liquid that you apply with a small brush. If you do not plan to use any water-soluble materials such as Screen Etch, you can block out such areas with muscilage or white glue. Do this also on the inner side of the screen and let all materials dry thoroughly.

Using Lacquer Film

The other stencil method involves lacquer film, which can be bought by the foot in varying widths. This is a thin green film applied to a heavy Mylar base. The design is cut into the green film without going through the Mylar base. An X-Acto knife or loop cutters are good here. Loop cutters come in three sizes and have a sharp edge at the end of a metal loop. They cut lines of different widths and are easy to use and available at most art supply stores. For taking out larger areas from the film, the out-side borders are cut with the X-Acto knife and the inside film area is lifted out and away. The circle shown in Figure 17–19 was cut with a divider compass. Two circles were made, then the inside area was lifted out. A piece of the scrap green film was used to patch the hole in the center made by the compass point.

To attach the film to the screen, place the cut lacquer film with the green film up on a firm flat surface. Then place a clean screen with the smooth fabric side down over the green film. Dampen a cotton ball lightly with lacquer thinner and wipe it gently and quickly over the inside of the fabric. A clean cloth is used to blot this same area. Remember to *blot*, never rub. Do no more than a 6″ area at any one time. The object is to soften the green film enough so that it will adhere to the fabric but not completely dissolve it. If you use too much lacquer thinner or rub too hard, the film will dissolve. If you wipe too lightly, the film will not adhere to the fabric. As you blot, you should begin to see a difference in the appearance of the film; use these changes as a guide. Once the film adheres to the screen, let it dry for 10 to 12 minutes. Then turn the screen over and gently peel the Mylar backing from the film. If at this point the green film pulls off the fabric, stop and reapply lacquer thinner to this area. Once this step is completed and you have taped any open areas at the outside edges of the film, your stencil is ready to use.

Preparation for Printing

Attach the screen to its master board with the pins inserted in the hinges. Tape your original drawing to the master board. Move it around very carefully while looking through the design in the screen until you have it perfectly lined up Then tape it down securely. This will now act as a guide to place your glass. If you are screening onto square or rectangular pieces of glass, it helps to tape the original drawing to a piece of graph paper. This can then be marked where you want the pieces of glass to be in relation to the design. Then line it up under the screen.

Paints for Silkscreening

The paint for silkscreening should have an oil base. I use L. Reusche & Company glass paints mixed with its number 175 Squeegee Oil. Both opaque and transparent colors are available. A beginning palette might include transparent blue 2867, transparent green V–554, and transparent yellow 2865. The transparent reds are a bit expensive for silkscreening. The opaques might include 7882 MB Blood Red, 7870 MB Dark Green, 7872 MB Yellow, 2877 Black, and 20–511 White. These colors are listed as having a firing range of 1,050 to 1,100°F. However, if you use any tracing blacks or matting browns for glass painting, you can use these and fire them all to 1,200°F. The higher temperature paints should be printed first, with the lower fire paints on top. Remember that the colors generally do not mix or overlap well. Results are far more satisfactory if you use them singly. Always make test strips of all your paints before using them in a finished work.

Each color must be mixed on a ground-glass palette using 3 parts of powdered color to 1 part of oil by weight. It is best to weigh for proportion, but if you use 1½ ounces of color to ½ ounce of oil—that is, about 3 level tablespoons of powdered color to 3 teaspoons of oil—you should come out alright. This mix should be creamy thick. If you weigh the first batch you mix, this will give you a good idea of the workable consistency. This will guide you later when you mix by eye. Mix only the amount that is easy to handle with a spatula on a 14"-square palette. Don't stint on the mixing. Mix paint powder and oil until you have saturated all the powder with the oil and the end result is smooth. Then put the mix in a small jar with a tight lid. This will keep almost indefinitely. If you need more, mix this same amount again. Clean up with turpentine.

Fig. 17–6 *The powdered paint on the palette and the oil for mixing.*

Fig. 17–7 *Mixing the paint.*

Keep in mind that a small amount of paint will screen a great many items. If you need large quantities, you can use an old Kitchen-Aid mixer. I also use Amaco's Versa-Color, which comes already mixed, but the color palette is limited and, except for the blue, the paints are all opaque. L. Reusche also carries premixed paints for silkscreening.

Preparing the Glass

Your glass should be as flat as possible to get a good screening. Single- or double-strength window glass works best. Antique and especially semiantique glasses also work well if they are even in thickness. Some cathedral glasses that are textured only on one side are also good for printing. Watch the temperature on the reds, though; many will change color at 1,200°F. Opalescent glass will also work well, but some opalescents tend to lose their gloss at 1,200 degrees. Always run tests before printing on any glass that is new to you.

The edges of whatever glass you use must be stoned smooth so as not to tear the screen fabric. The glass should be absolutely clean, and once cleaned it should be handled only by the edges. One cleaner that works well is Glass Plus. For a large run of glass, don't overlook the dishwasher. It is a real time-saver.

Fig. 17–9 Pouring the paint onto the screen.

Printing

Before you start printing, make sure that you have everything lined up and ready to go. If you have to spend too much time searching for things between printings, the paint will dry in the screen. If this happens, you will have to wash it carefully on both sides with a cloth dampened with turpentine. So have all your glass cut, cleaned, and the edges stoned. Have the pieces within easy reach. Lay the first piece of glass carefully in place on the graph paper or design outline. Lower the screen

Fig. 17–10 Running the squeegee for the first piece of glass.

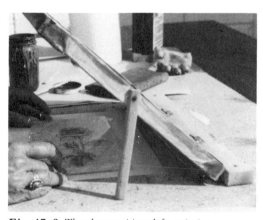

Fig. 17–8 The glass positioned for printing.

Fig. 17–11 After running the squeegee, lift the screen.

over the glass. Run a bead of paint along one edge. (You can pour directly from the jar or use a spoon.) The amount of paint you will need will be determined by your design. If there are large areas of open screen, you will need more paint, but don't use so much that it runs all over the edges of the screen. At the same time, be sure to

Fig. 17–12 *The opposite pull of the squeegee on the second piece of glass.*

use enough to get a few complete screenings each time. It's a good idea to lay a short piece of a yardstick along the front edge under the screen. This will help the screen to pull away from the glass after it has been squeegeed.

Using a Squeegee

As you learn to squeegee, you will develop a natural rhythm as you go along, although it may seem awkward at first. Holding the squeegee at an angle, not straight up, pull the paint firmly across the design. You should cover it with the single stroke. Now raise the screen off the glass. Remove the printed piece of glass and replace it with a clean one. Lower the screen and print in the opposite direction. Continue this procedure until you have finished all pieces of glass.

Cleaning

Clean the screen as soon as you finish printing. The best way to do this is to

Fig. 17–13A *The rose on a clear oval of pink glass surrounded by a glue-chipped border. This is the first screening of the brown outline.*

Fig. 17–13B *The printed rose in yellow with green leaves.*

Fig. 17–14 *A circle design on green film.*

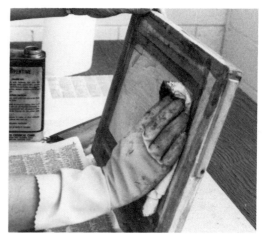

Fig. 17–16 *Cleaning the bottom of the screen.*

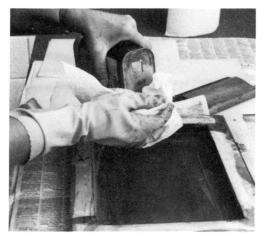

Fig. 17–15 *Cleaning the screen with paper towels and turpentine.*

place several sheets of newspaper under the screen on a workbench or on the master board. With the squeegee, remove as much excess paint as possible and put it back in the paint jar. Saturate paper towels in tur-

pentine (using mineral spirits is cheaper but slower) and start cleaning the screen. After you have worked most of the paint off the inside, turn the screen and do the underside. Don't forget this part. Keep changing the paper towels and the newspaper. It is a good idea to protect your hands with rubber gloves. Hold the screen up to the light to make sure it is absolutely clean. Any paint left on the screen will affect the next screening or the reclaiming of the screen. Rinse, dry, and store the screen if you intend to use that design again. If you do not intend to reuse the design, wash the photographic stencil clean with Clorox. It may take a few soakings to remove all of the emulsion. If the emulsion is hard, you may have to replace the fabric. Lacquer stencil film can be removed with lacquer thinner and the screen rinsed and air-dried.

The Firing Process

The printed glass must be dry before you fire it. In an area of average humidity this will take at least overnight to accomplish. The drying process can be shortened, which is especially necessary where more than one color screening is involved, by setting the printed glass in the sun or in a vented kiln at a low temperature. You may find it is not necessary to fire each and every color, particularly so long as each color is dried completely and the high-fire paints are applied first to the glass. The paints are all put on the one side of the glass. Once the paint is dry, you may hand-stipple the design. This is easy to do with a fairly stiff-bristled brush. Be careful that you don't remove too much paint in the process.

As far as your kiln is concerned, everyone must discover the idiosyncracies of his or her own through experimentation. As a guide, I fire my pieces on medium for a half hour at 600°F with the door vented. By this time the oils are burned off. You can tell this by the odor and watching that no further fumes are being produced. This effect must take place before you close the kiln. If the process is not over in a half hour, fire for 5 or 10 minutes more or to 800°F with the kiln door vented as before. You should also vent your room with an exhaust fan.

Once the oils are burned out, close the kiln door and fire on high until the proper temperature is reached for the specific paints. Turn off the kiln, vent it for about a minute, making sure the pyrometer does not go below 1,000°F and close the door until the kiln is cold.

Leading Up

When leading the finished printed glass pieces, it is a good idea to use flux sparingly when you solder. Acids will dull the paint. You don't want to come this far only to diminish the glory of your end result. Chemicals such as copper sulphate used to antique copper foil or soldered joints will also dull the paint. If necessary, protect your painted area with masking tape and clean it carefully before removing the tape.

GLUE CHIPPING

Although glue chipping is now done on a commercial scale, it is fun to chip your own glass. The process is simple and inexpensive. You can achieve consistent results if you control your variables rather strictly. Humidity and temperature should not be extreme, but even without controlling these conditions precisely, you can usually come up with exciting results.

Glass chipping results from a chemical action between the glue and the glass. After the glue is applied, two drying procedures are necessary. One dries the top surface and the other the interior of the glue. At this stage the glass is literally pulled apart and chipped patterns formed on its surface. By adjusting the amounts of glue and water, you can achieve many patterns.

Almost any glass can be glue-chipped. Since the objective is to catch the transmitted light, opalescent glasses are not effective. Window glass is exceptional, and it is a good one to start with.

Supplies

The most important and sometimes the most difficult item to obtain is the animal-hide glue, sometimes called "rabbit-skin" glue. It is the only type of glue that will bond securely with the glass. It comes in flakes or granules. You can find it in some art supply stores, since it is used by many artists to prime their canvases, and it can be ordered from glass suppliers. One pound of glue goes a long way, so don't overorder.

If you are frustrated in your quest for glue, try unflavored gelatin. This is a similar though more refined product. The results are not as effective, but you can use it on small pieces of glass when you can't get glue. The procedures for glue and gelatin are the same.

You will need a small scale to weigh the glue and water, a candy or wax-making thermometer, an inexpensive 1″ natural bristle brush (synthetic bristles will melt in the hot glue), a double boiler for heating the glue, and your glass pieces.

Fig. 17–17 Dry glue on the scale and soaked glue in the pot.

Fig. 17–18 Glue after soaking in the pot. Other equipment: Hot plate, double boiler, scale, weights, brushes, thermometer, and paper cups for measuring.

Preparing the Glass

The area of the glass you intend to chip first must be abraded by sandblasting. Hand methods are tedious, but the abrading also can be done on a wet-belt sander or similar grinding machine. Some glass will chip after being abraded with three coats of Screen-Etch. Brush this on heavily, alternating directions with each coat. Don't worry about brush marks. The results of the chipping are not as predictable as with sand blasting, but they are usually more brilliant.

Designing the Chip Area

If you plan to use a design and to glue chip only certain areas of one piece of glass, you must protect the negative areas before you sandblast. Attach a piece of Contact paper to the front and back of the glass. Cut out the design with an X-Acto knife or a loop cutter. Remove those areas of Contact paper that cover glass to be abraded. Only a light blast is necessary. If you are using flashed glass, make sure that the blast is light enough so that you retain the flashed color. Leave the Contact paper in place

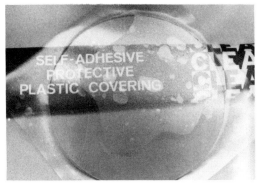

Fig. 17–19 *A random design on a 9" circle of double-strength window glass is prepared with Contact paper prior to sandblasting.*

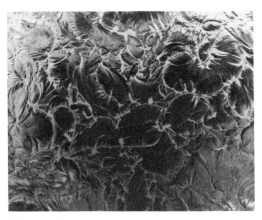

Fig. 17–20 *Fern chip on glass.*

during the chipping process and wash the glass.

The Chipping Procedure

Cover the work surface with newspapers. Elevate the glass and make sure that it's level. You can rest it on an inverted paper cup if it is a small piece or on a tin can for firmer support. If you don't elevate the glass, any glue on its edges could bond your glass to the working surface. If the glass is not level, the glue will not be able to maintain an even depth and will chip erratically.

A good ratio for the glue mixture is 1 part glue to 2 parts water by weight. For 1 square foot of glass, a mixture of 2 ounces of glue to 4 ounces of water will give you a surface thickness of about 1/16" on the glass. This will usually produce a chip with a fern pattern. As the glue dries, this thickness will slump down to half that. If you want to change the type of chip, you must either reduce or increase the 1/16" thickness. However, if you use too thin a coat of glue, by the time it slumps there will not be enough thickness to allow for the two drying stages. It will be completely dry from a single drying, and this is not what you want.

A tighter chip than the fern pattern is called a *snail chip* and this can be achieved

Fig. 17–21 *Snail chip on etched glass.*

Fig. 17–22 *Closeup of an iceberg chip.*

Fig. 17–23 *Applying the glue to the glass with a brush. Dab it on rather than pouring it. Note the thermometer in the pot.*

Fig. 17–24 *Pouring the glue onto a fleur de lis design on the prepared glass.*

Fig. 17–25 *Pouring and spreading the glue with a brush.*

with a mixture of 2½ ounces of dry glue per square foot of glass. This means 2½ oz. of glue to 5 ounces of water per square foot. These proportions will put about a ⅛″-thick coat on the glass. If you use more than this, you will create an *iceberg* chip. Such a chip cuts deeply into the glass and can be very dramatic.

The ratio of glue to water stays the same for the different chip effects, but the amount of dry glue that is used varies, as does the thickness of the mixture on the glass. The proportions given here are only a guide.

If you work in a very humid area, you may want to try a 50/50 glue/water mixture. This will be very thick to work with, but it can be dabbed on the glass with a brush. If your humidity is below 30 percent, you will have to add more water to the mixture to help slow down the first drying time. If the glue mixture dries out too fast, it will start to pull away from the glass before it has a chance to chip it. If you increase the amount of water, you will have to build a dam around the glass to contain the glue. Tape the outside edges of the glass with masking tape, and make sure that the tape is snug so that the glue does not leak. Remove the tape as soon as the glue jells so that the glass edges can dry as well.

After you weigh the glue, soak it with the weighed amount of cool water. Cover it to prevent the water from evaporating and leave it for at least an hour. If you do not soak it, the glue will not dissolve properly when it is heated. It should look very fluffy after it has absorbed the water. Heat the glue in the top of a double boiler. It will begin to melt as you stir it. Use the thermometer and watch the temperature carefully because the glue rises to 145° rapidly. You want the glue to be between 140° and 150°. If it is not hot enough, it will not bond with the glass. If it is too hot, the properties in the glue will become inactive. Remove the pot from the burner to stop the rise in temperature; the hot water in the bottom will still maintain the

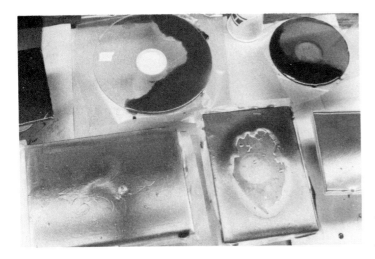

Fig. 17–26 *Pieces of glass covered with glue for the chipping process.*

temperature where you want it. Let the bubbles settle, then apply the glue to the glass. It helps to warm the glass before you do this. Set the glass in the sun or on top of a warm kiln before you apply glue.

The glue can either be poured on or dabbed on with the bristle brush. The size of the area to be chipped and the thickness of your mixture should determine which method you use. Sometimes a little of both—pouring and dabbing—works well too. The important thing is to pour or dab while the glass and the glue are warm. Once the glue starts to jell on the glass, you will do more harm than good if you add more glue or disturb it with the brush.

Any leftover glue can be poured onto a sheet of plastic and allowed to dry, or it can be left in the covered pot for a day or two. After that time, however, it will become moldy and gain an unpleasant odor. Don't leave the glue in an uncovered pot, since it could harm it. Soak the pot and brushes before they dry.

The First Drying Stage

The glue should take at least overnight to dry. You can slow up the drying by putting the glass in a closed cupboard and adjusting the door opening. In a humid area it could take several days to dry com-

Fig. 17–27 *Glue chipping away from the glass in an iceberg chip. Note the chips of glass coming away in the layer of glue.*

pletely. When it is dry, the glue will no longer look cloudy, and you will not be able to cut it with your fingernail. At this stage the glass is under a great deal of tension, so handle it carfully. Don't attempt to chip pieces much larger than one square foot.

The Second Drying Stage

The easiest way to accomplish the second drying stage is with the sun. If this is pos-

Fig. 17–28 Silica gel to be used as a drying chamber.

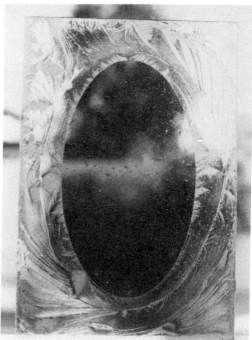

Fig. 17–31 Pink flashed oval with iceberg chip surrounding it.

Fig. 17–29 The glass, covered with glue, inside the silica-gel drying chamber.

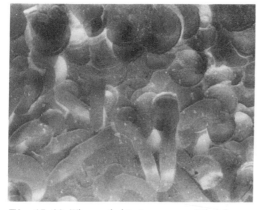

Fig. 17–30 The snail chip in progress. The glue has pulled away in part, taking chips of glass with it.

sible, choose an area where no one will walk barefooted. The glass and the glue chips will fly in all directions during the chipping process, and these fragments are extremely sharp. Set the glass on newspapers on a table since the humidity from the ground will remelt the glue. The sun will dry out the inner area of glue. As this dries, it tears the surface of the glass and reveals distinctive patterns. The surface of the glass will get hotter than the outside air, but make sure that it does not reach a temperature above 120°. In about an hour, depending on temperature and humidity, you will begin to hear the glue chipping. The process can take two hours or the whole day. The thickness of the glue will also affect the drying time. Just let the glass sit in the sun, checking it every so often.

When the process is complete, pry off any loose chips with a small stick. Never use your fingers. Most of these loose chips

Fig. 17–33 *Detail of a snail chip.*

Fig. 17–32 *Flashed glass, red on green with snail chip border and matt-painted design in the center.*

will fall off when you tip the glass onto the newspaper. If any chips remain, they can be removed easily by soaking the glass in water. Gather up the loose chips in the newspapers and carefully dispose of them. The glue from these chips can be recovered by remelting, but this is not advisable unless you are working with large quantities. It is more work than it is worth, and you no longer have any control over the glue/water ratio.

Instead of drying the glass outside, you can place it in a sunny window. Set it on the newspapers on a shelf or tray and proceed as above. If this is not practical, you can use a drying chamber. That is easily done using silica gel, a desiccant that is also used for drying flowers. The gel

changes color as it absorbs moisture from the air. When the crystals are blue, they are very dry, but as they absorb moisture they turn pink. They can be reconstituted by setting them in a pan in a 400° oven or kiln for about 20 minutes or until the crystals become blue again. The gel must be used immediately or kept in an air-tight container.

The amount of silica gel you use depends on the size of the glass to be chipped and the air space in the chamber. A good rule of thumb is 3 cubic inches of silica gel for each square foot of glass surface. Spread the silica gel in a flat pan and cover it with cheesecloth to keep the glue chips from mixing with the gel. Set a rack over the pan or put the glass right on the cheesecloth. Slip this arrangement inside a heavy, airtight plastic bag. Fasten it tightly, removing any excess air as you go. Set it aside and you will begin to hear the characteristic snap, crackle, and pop.

18
Sandblasting

Kathy Bradford

Kathy Bradford's cut, sandblasted, airbrushed, and etched glass pieces are a unique blend of art media. She has a long-standing tradition of breaking with tradition, using things that others consider taboo. Bradford treats glass like a transparent canvas and much of the strength of her work rests in her talent and background in graphic arts and watercolor painting.(Portions of this chapter are reprinted from "A Discussion on Sandblasting Glass" by Kathy Bradford, in Who's Who in Stained Glass. Carl Hungness Publishing, 1983.)

Sandblasting on glass creates an etched surface. The technique is the same as any sandblasting activity. A compressor is used to blow compressed air and sand (or some other grit) onto the glass. The grit etches away an outer layer and makes the glass appear frosted. The artist can control the frosted design by setting up different kinds of resists on the glass surface. A variety of exquisite results are unique to the technique and cannot be duplicated by any similar technique, including chemical etching.

There are no rules or regulations that should dampen your natural curiosity as to what effects you can produce with sandblasting. Whatever works the best for you is the best way to work. Many craftspeople shy away because of the cost of the equipment. Don't let that stop you from at least exploring the technique, even if you do this just by renting time on someone else's equipment. By no means should you think that you must invest a lot of money in equipment in order to sandblast. The fanciest and most expensive equipment does not produce good art. Only you can do that.

UNDERSTANDING POSITIVES AND NEGATIVES

Sandblasting is really a graphic technique. Setting up a resist for a sandblasted panel is similar to setting up resists for airbrushing and silkscreen or stencil printing. The object is to block out what you do not want the sand to etch.

It is important to develop a habit of thinking along the lines of positives and negatives just as you would if you were printing photographs. On sandblasted clear glass, the frosted glass, or positive, will read the whitest. The clear, or clearer areas of glass, will read as dark, or negative. When you shade a particular form, you must remember that the white areas will advance and the darker values will recede. The idea is the same as in a rendered pencil drawing, except on clear glass the frosted area advances and the clear areas recede. Before sandblasting anything, you take the time to render—that is, shade—your pencil drawing accurately. As you shade the various forms, your mind should be thinking through the process you will repeat in the sandblast booth. Mistakes are sometimes very difficult to correct. Instead, make your mistakes in pencil and correct them

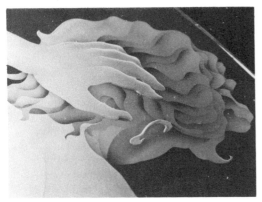

Fig. 18–1 *Some subtle effects in sandblasting. Note the flow of the lines of the hair and the way the hand stands out above them. (All photos in this chapter by Norbert Hennecke, except where otherwise noted.)*

Fig. 18–2 *Sandblasting on the front of the glass makes the object look as though it were coming right out of the glass.*

then. Remember that the values on your drawing will be reversed on the glass. The shaded areas of a form would appear in heavier pencil on white paper, whereas on the glass they would be the clear areas. The possibilities of rendering on glass are no more limited than with pencil on paper.

FROSTING

If you include light frosting as well as deeper-cut details, the details should be cut or blasted first. Then the rest of the resist can be peeled away and a light sandblasting can be done. The sand will continue to frost the surface on a flat plane, so the detail, so long as it is cut deeply enough, will not disappear because of the frosting. Only the edges of it may smooth out. However, this makes them blend in better within the pattern.

SUBTLE GLASS EFFECTS

Even when glass is lightly frosted, it will react to light. But this effect depends to a great extent on which side of the glass is blasted. For instance, if you want an object to appear to be coming forward, blast on

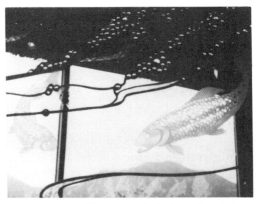

Fig. 18–3 *Sandblasting on the back surface of the glass provides a depth and a hazy effect.*

the front of the glass—that is, on the surface facing you. If you want the object to appear to recede, blast on the back surface. A fish swimming underwater, as in Figure 18–3, will be more emphatic if it is under the front surface and blasted onto the back. Sometimes the true effect is achieved by blasting on both sides of the glass. Clouds done on both sides of the glass, even on ⅛" clear glass, will give the illusion of space. The thicker the glass, the more distance will appear between the two surfaces. Usually the smooth side of the glass—the unblasted surface—gives the piece a more finished look. The light is enhanced as it

Fig. 18–4 It's those blasted Isenbergs! A sandblasting "sketch" done by Bradford during a visit by the authors to her studio.

SPATIAL ILLUSION

The thickness of the glass can have an important effect on a piece of sandblasted art. Spatial illusion can be heightened by using several layers of glass together within one frame. The sandblasted surface also can serve as a ground for other media such as paint, ink, or shoe polish.

Sandblasting mirror differs in two ways from sandblasting clear glass. It makes even more of a difference which side is blasted than when clear glass is used. If the blasting is done on the front, mirrored surface, a double image will result. If it is done on the back, where the mastic is, the mirroring effect is removed and the blasting shows white from the front of the mirror.

COMBINING SANDBLASTING AND STAINED GLASS

The combination of sandblasted glass and constructed stained glass is something that must be done with extreme caution and finesse. Even beautiful sandblasting combined with beautiful stained glass can sometimes cancel one another, making the end result chaotic. Sandblasting should never be used as a gimmick or shortcut or as an excuse to camouflage poor workmanship. To be effective it should be compatible with all the other glass in the panel. Sandblasting at its best is lightweight, ghostlike, clear on clear. The glass that you choose to go with it in a stained-glass panel should not overwhelm it.

passes through the sandblasted areas and out through the smooth surface facing the viewer.

DEEP CUTTING

Sandblasting can be carried to many extremes. If an area is blasted for a long time using several layers of resist, the result is a deep cut, almost a carving. It's possible, in fact, to carve a bas-relief figure into glass. The direction here is sculptural, and it is particularly beautiful when it is viewed from the smooth side of the glass. When deep cutting is desired, usually several layers of Contact paper will suffice as a resist. A thicker opaque, rubberlike material called Buttercut is also often used as a resist for deep cutting. Buttercut has a peel-away backing and will stick on glass like Contact paper. A surprising amount of detail can be cut into Buttercut, and sometimes the stencil can be used over and over, depending on the design. The only problem with it, other than not being able to see through it, is that it is fairly expensive.

USING THE RESIST

One of the most common resists is Contact paper. Clear Contact paper is heavier than the plain opaque type, and a fairly detailed design can be created with an X-Acto knife, similar to cutting a silkscreen stencil. It also allows you to see through to the rendered drawing. If an even more detailed design is desired, then perhaps another technique such as photographic etching should be employed. You should develop a skill for stencil cutting or resist cutting because you will be imparting your most perfect drawing directly onto the Contact paper with the knife. Your drawing should eventually serve only as a guide, with your focus of attention jumping from pencil drawing to the surface of the resist material to the surface of the glass. The pencil drawing should be followed as accurately as possible, and it's a good idea to take it into the sandblast booth with you.

If you want a deep cut, you will need two or three layers of Contact paper. The number of layers will depend on how deep you want to cut into the glass. You can usually tell if you do not have enough layers of resist, since the first layer will blow off before the second. If you pay attention, you will have plenty of notice in order to repair the resist. Make sure the resist is firm against the glass before you start to sandblast. Small air bubbles in the Contact paper will enable the sand to blast through the resist.

Blasting on mirror requires that you transfer the original drawing, since the mirror, being opaque, will not permit you to see the guide. Transfer your design with carbon paper onto a solid, light-colored Contact paper. Remember to reverse your original drawing, especially letters and numbers, when working on the back surface.

Another good resist material is Elmer's glue, which is easily painted onto the glass directly out of the container. A little experimentation will prove how thick it should be to be effective, but even a thin bead will resist the sand if no especially deep cutting is required. Elmer's glue allows you more "painted" effects. Sometimes a particular effect may be obtained by first applying Elmer's glue, letting it dry, and then going over it with a Contact paper resist. At the completion of the project, the glue can easily be washed off with warm water. Greasy fingerprints and greasy dirt are excellent resist materials, so be sure to keep your glass clean.

Other materials such as fabric, lace, wire mesh, or coarse screens can serve as a resist when glued lightly to the glass. A piece of fabric, even one so fine and delicate as lace, will resist the sand nicely if it is first immersed in a watered-down solution of glue and pressed down and allowed to dry against the glass. Interesting patterns can be achieved by stretching and pulling the lace before the glue dries. A whole world of things can function as resist media. Be inventive and experiment.

SANDBLASTING EQUIPMENT

The Compressor

Probably the most expensive or most difficult to find piece of equipment for sandblasting is the compressor. The compressor releases a continuous stream of air under pressure. A sandblasted surface will result with a small amount of pressure, but it's better to have a large amount of pressure, say 90 pounds or so, over a long period of time to ensure full control of the work process. To obtain that much pressure for

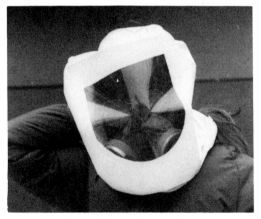

Fig. 18–5 A respirator and safety glasses go on first. A paper hood with a plastic face mask keeps the sand off the head and saves the safety glasses from being blasted.

Fig. 18–6 My "free form" sandblasting booth of black plastic and two clear plastic shower-curtain liners. I don't wear gloves, and I hand-hold the glass.

Fig. 18–7 Pulling off small pieces of resist while doing progressive shading. This gives an uninterrupted flow to the work.

even several minutes, you will need a fairly large compressor, hence a fairly expensive one. The key to having a large quantity of pressure is to have a compressor with a large tank. A compressor with a two-horse-power engine but with a large tank, say 100 gallons, will produce an adequate amount of pressure for several minutes. A compressor with a three-horse-power engine but with a smaller tank will produce the same amount of pressure for about the same amount of time.

There are several ways to get around

the cost of a compressor. Many places will rent compressors, or rent you time on their compressor. There are numerous sources for picking up used compressors, such as gas stations going out of business, farm or ranch auctions, companies who are selling their equipment, as well as air-equipment dealers. You may find a situation where you could rent a corner of a shop and quick-connect into their compressor when it is not in use. Perhaps you could find an old compressor with a burned-out engine. It it is otherwise in good condition—and most tanks last practically forever—you could have a rebuilt engine installed. An old compressor, if it has been taken care of, will probably work just as well as a new one. One hidden cost to be aware of, however, is that any compressor must be properly wired in. To save on electrical costs, look for single-phase wiring. Most large compressors run on 220 current, and this can be expensive to wire. Also, a safety feature that all compressors have is a drain valve. Moisture builds up inside the tank, and it must be periodically drained. Otherwise the moisture can rust the tank and the compressed air could blow up the tank—not to mention you.

The Pressure Pot

One piece of equipment that provides a larger amount of pressure from a comparatively smaller compressor is a pressure pot. This is a second piece of machinery that is hooked onto the compressor. Sand and pressure go in it together and are released together. A pressure pot can be very effective for deep cutting. However, the pots do not hold much sand, and the pressure is released with so much force that it can blow off the resist with frustrating ease. It offers little control over shaded and softened areas, but it may suit your particular needs.

The Sandblasting Gun

The sandblasting gun resembles a small pistol. One hose supplies air and another supplies the sand. Air and sand are mixed within the gun and released together. The air hose must be a pressurized one, similar to those in gas stations. Most hardware stores carry these air guns. The gun has a trigger, and with a minimum of practice you will be able to modify the pressure to whatever degree you want. Eventually the tip of the gun wears out, but it is easily replaced.

The Sand Hopper

A container for the sand, or hopper, is a must. An adequate size hopper will hold approximately five gallons of sand. It is best to situate the hopper above the working area, since the sand will feed by gravity into the gun. A sandblasting outfit that includes a hopper, sand hose, and gun is available from Montgomery Ward and Sears for about $50 or $60.

The Respirator and Safety Glasses

A respirator is an absolute essential in sandblasting. Breathing sand and powdered glass can be deadly, so be certain that the respirator you buy is a good one. Pinching pennies here is not common sense. The same rule applies to safety glasses. Use them whenever you sandblast.

THE SANDBLASTING BOOTH

Where is the best area to sandblast? It is nice, but not necessary, to have a completely enclosed sandblasting booth with a viewing window and arm holes to work through. These booths can be expensive to buy, although you could build one yourself readily enough. For more than a year I sandblasted inside a large cardboard refrigerator box. It worked just fine. Naturally I used respirator and safety glasses. When working within the confines of a studio, however, perhaps an enclosed booth would be the best idea because little sand will escape. Unfortunately, an enclosed booth tends to be limiting and inhibiting. It is difficult to see the work up close or to re-

move small pieces of resist in the middle of the sandblasting procedure. This is especially true if you are wearing those heavy rubber gloves that generally go in the arm holes.

I prefer to be inside a booth with my piece of work. The propinquity is comforting—I can see close up exactly what I am doing, feel the glass, check it out from

Fig. 18–8 *Rendering the drawing. There is no time limit here. Every project requires patience.*

Fig. 18–9 *For this project, I selected two drawings of the Globe playhouse, the Chandos portrait of Shakespeare, and a rose to commemorate the history plays based on the Wars of the Roses.*

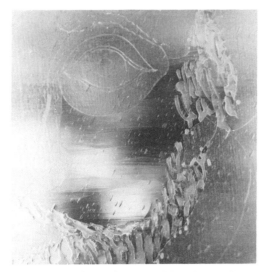

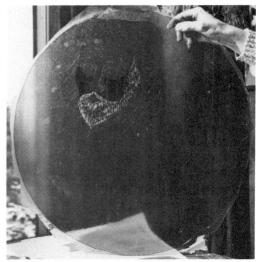

Fig. 18–10 *Elmer's glue painted directly out of the bottle onto the glass, I used here in combination with a Contact paper resist.*

Fig. 18–12 *The last panel to be blasted.*

Fig. 18–13 *A detail from the completed and assembled piece.*

Fig. 18–11 *Sections of the piece before completion. The front piece shows blasting over a Contact paper resist and over a section with glue resist.*

both sides, remove tiny bits of resist as I work from one side of the glass to the other. I remove bits of resist to enable shading to occur during the sandblasting process. The only problem with this cozy arrangement is that you get sand all over

yourself. So long as I have respirator and glasses, I am quite at home inside this sandbox. I follow up a sandblasting session with a long, relaxing hot shower. If you use too much Elmer's Glue as a resist, you may take your piece of glass to the shower with you.

My sandblasting booth is very free

Fig. 18–14 *The completed project. There are four individual panels of glass, each sandblasted, arranged one behind the other within the frame. This provides depth and overlay. (See Color section.)*

form and consists of a corner of my garage. This area is draped on two walls and the floor with one large piece of black plastic. Black plastic offers a good contrast to the glass as I hold and sandblast it. The two outside walls are draped with clear shower-curtain liners, which allow natural light in. I also have one fluorescent light suspended from the ceiling, but I often bring a secondary light with me for extra illumination. A fair amount of sand does manage to escape into the garage, and about once a year I sweep it all up, run it through an 80-grit sieve, and pour it back into my sand supply. I have found that a 100-pound sack of sand will last at least a year, maybe two. Since the entire "booth" is made out of draped plastic, it is easy to expand it for a large project or shrink it for something small. The whole thing couldn't cost more than $10, unless you use an extra expensive fluorescent light.

SAND

A number of different types of sand can be used in sandblasting. Even playground sand will cut glass. Look in the Yellow Pages under Sandblasting Supplies or Abrasive Equipment. Some lumberyards also carry sand for sandblasting. Most monument dealers sandblast their headstones, and they can also be a source of sand. Silica sand is inexpensive and may be the best sand to try at first. It will work well for a time; the trouble is it eventually wears out because the individual grains become rounded with reuse. Many people who sandblast outside use silica sand.

For most sandblasting, an 80-grit sand will work just fine. The higher the number, the finer the sand, hence the smoother and whiter the sandblasted surface will be. However, the finer the sand, the less cutting force it will have. For deep cutting, use a coarse sand. Experiment with differ-

Fig. 18–15 The Cyclo-Blast Jr. sandblasting machine leaves no mess and needs no cabinet. The unit weighs approximately 170 pounds and is on wheels for easy movement. The vacuum-recovery blast-gun system recovers the abrasive dust and debris, so you can blast without wearing a respirator or protective clothing. (Courtesy the Grady Company)

ter lid made to cover a frying pan has a screen of about 80 grit and works just fine.

TECHNIQUE

One technique that I use in sandblasting is what I call progressive shading. This is a method in which a contrast is made between different areas by light blasting against heavily blasted areas. Imagine a group of shapes, such as clouds, one overlapping another. If the resist of the first cloud is pulled, but only that one section, then you can blast heavily along the edge that will contrast with the next cloud. The area can be shaded from a heavy blast at the top edge, to lighter blasting as the edge goes down to the bottom. Then the next cloud section's resist above is removed. Heavier blasting is done at the edge tip and gradually shaded down the bottom of the section, leaving a contrast between the lightly shaded area and the former heavily blasted edge of the first section. Each section can be done in such a progression, the contiguous edges being treated as you go. Small sections can be blasted in contrast to create fine detail. The progression may be done from side to side, top to bottom, or bottom to top, depending on what you want to achieve. The same method can be used with deep cuts in glass, only be sure to use several layers of resist here.

Occasionally, I deep-cut detail lines that will not be affected by soft blasting. Then I do some progressive shading over the detail lines to give them a softer value. With experimentation you will soon realize that a very slight hand can create stunning effects on glass, whereas deep cutting can be almost violently dramatic.

Don't be afraid of sandblasting. Try out different sands, different resists, and different techniques until you discover your own way of working. Then you will find that sandblasting is a kind of magic—like glass itself.

ent grits to see which works best for what you have in mind. Some particularly sharp sands will do a great job on the glass, but they will also tear your resist to pieces.

A fairly expensive sand, but one that is long-lasting, is Aluminum Oxide sand, a reddish sand that comes in several grits. Aluminum oxide has a good cutting edge and the grains of sand actually become sharper with use instead of duller. Because of its price, try to recover as much of it as possible. It will last forever if you can continue to recover it.

Different types of sand will give different textures to the glass surface. However, be careful not to mix sands in the sandblasting booth. It is horribly time-consuming to sift them apart. An 80-grit sieve, found in a ceramic supply house, can be a fairly expensive item to add to your sandblasting equipment. However, a spat-

19
Three-Dimensional Patterns and Designs

Barbara Griffith

Barbara Griffith of the Glass House Studio (125 State Street, St. Paul, Minnesota 55107) has allowed us to reproduce several of her unique, provocative patterns in order to demonstrate yet another way of designing for stained glass (finished pieces are shown in the color section). By making these items, you will begin to appreciate the ingenuity of their construction. Once you acquire the skill, you can produce your own three-dimensional designs.

THE GREAT HORNED OWL
Materials:

3/16" copper foil
5-ounce solder
16-gauge wire
Glass
Easy solder tin
Testors paint
Old stump, drift wood, or barn wood
Heavy brass rod for mounting

All pattern pieces are 75% of original. *Do not allow foil space between pattern pieces,* so cut out the pieces with ordinary scissors. Foil and solder together all the pieces and the wire stems on the leaves. Patina and paint them as shown. Drill holes in the wood for the brass rod and pound in the brass rod. Hold the owl next to the brass rod and solder it to it. Drill a hole in the wood for mounting the leaves. Pound in the brass rod to get the proper angle; then take out the rod and solder it to the back of the leaf at the proper angle. Put the leaf-rod combination back into the hole. Solder the stem to the owl and curve the back of the stem up behind him as shown.

THE FARM SCENE
Materials:

Glass
1/4" copper foil
Copper sheeting
Brass sheeting .005 gauge
5-ounce solder
20-gauge wire
16-gauge wire
24-gauge copper wire (optional)
Copper rod (small)
Tin .008 gauge
Copper patina

Enlarge pattern and cut glass and foil as shown in the diagram. Cut hay, haystacks, and birds out of brass. Cut the barn door, silo roof, and bird nest out of copper. Cut the swing out of tin. Solder the tree together and add the bird, nest, and swing. Solder the barn together and outline the copper silo and the copper door in 20-gauge wire. Use the same gauge wire for the window and sill. Solder on the hay.

Solder the background together and angle out the rays of the sun. One ray touches the barn roof and the tree as an active top support.

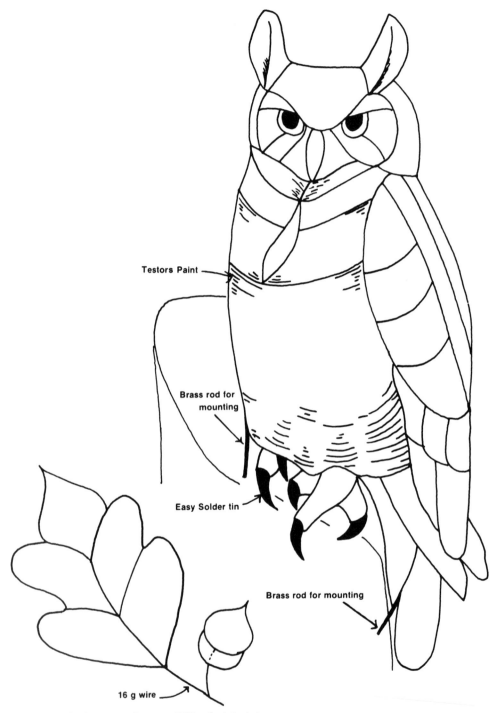

Testors Paint

Brass rod for
mounting

Easy Solder tin

Brass rod for mounting

16 g wire

Fig. 19–1 Owl pattern, shown at 75% of original size.

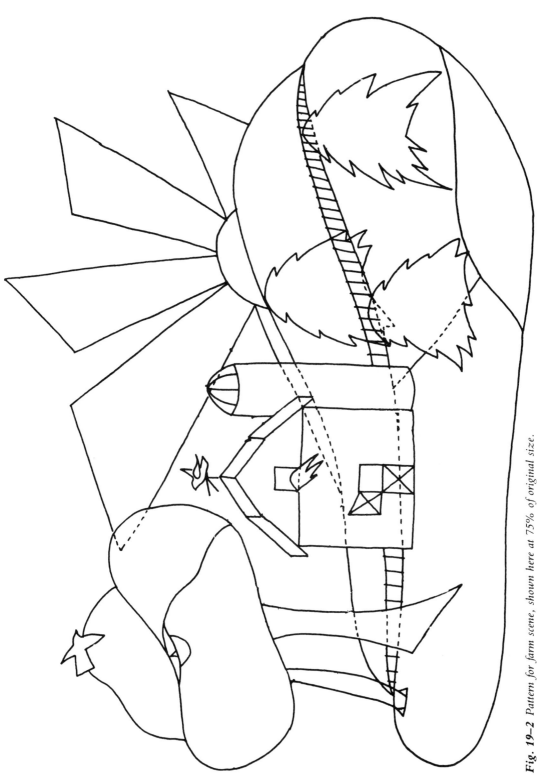

Fig. 19–2 *Pattern for farm scene, shown here at 75% of original size.*

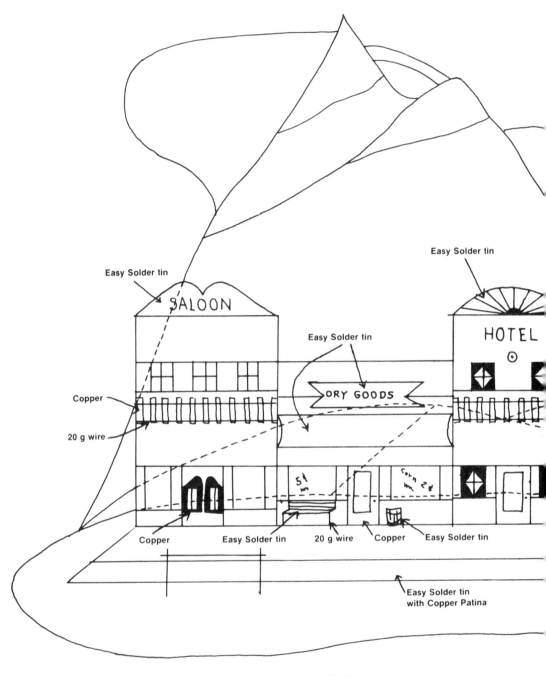

Easy Solder tin

Easy Solder tin

Easy Solder tin

SALOON

HOTEL

DRY GOODS

Copper

20 g wire

Copper   Easy Solder tin   20 g wire   Copper   Easy Solder tin

Easy Solder tin
with Copper Patina

Fig. 19–3 *Pattern for Old West setting; pattern shown is 75% of original size.*

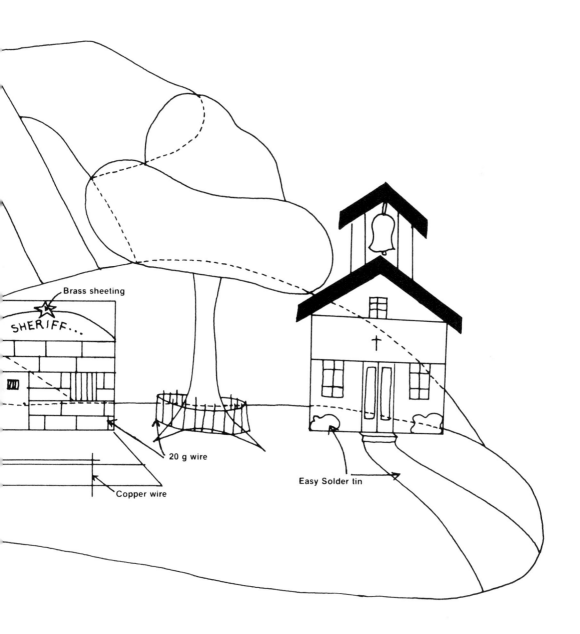

Brass sheeting

SHERIFF...

20 g wire

Copper wire

Easy Solder tin

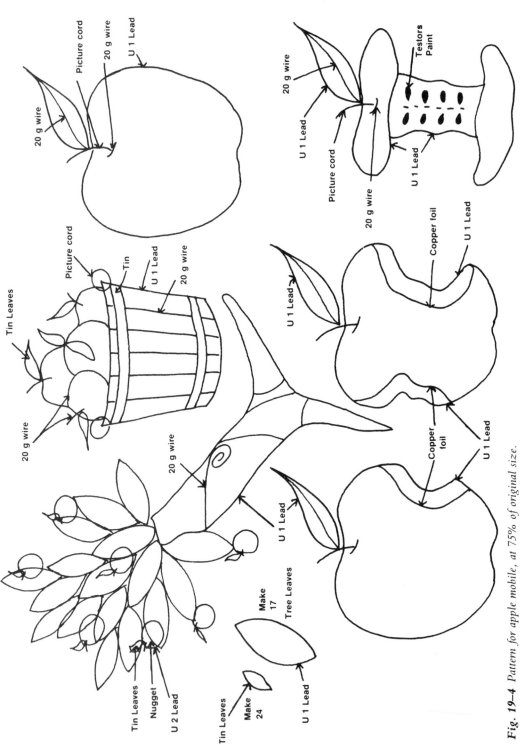

Fig. 19–4 *Pattern for apple mobile, at 75% of original size.*

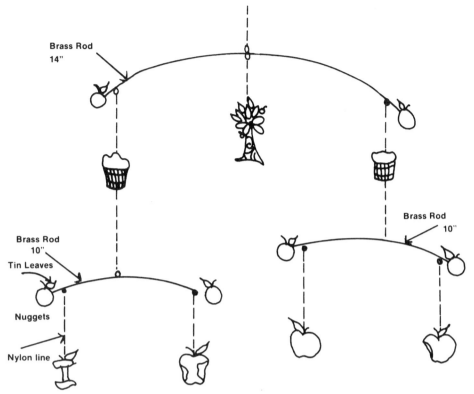

Fig. 19–5 *Assembling the mobile.*

Cut the copper rod in three 1″ lengths and four ½″ lengths. Solder the 1″ pieces to the side of the tree down to the foil. Solder the ½″ pieces to the side of the barn down to the foil. Solder on the back haystack and the fence with 16-gauge wire. Solder on the other haystacks. Turn the piece over and on the center back solder the tin for support of the hangers. Solder the wall hanger to the tin, the foil, the back of the sun, and the earth behind the barn. This will give the piece plenty of support.

OLD WESTERN TOWN
Materials:

Brass sheeting
Copper patina
¼″ copper foil
20-gauge wire
6 oz. solder
Easy solder tin
Glass
Thin copper
Brass or copper rod (small)
Testors paint
Small bell

Enlarge all pieces for full-size pattern. Cut all the pieces out of glass and foil them. Foil and tin the edges of all the buildings except the church. Complete each building and tack-solder them from the front. Turn them over and tin all together on the back side.

Solder the background together.

Use ½″ rods to raise the buildings. Solder them from the sides of the buildings to the foil on the background. For the tree, use 1″ rods from the sides of the tree to foil the background. Make the fence out of 20-

gauge wire. Foil and tin all parts of the church. Solder them together and wire in the bell. For a copper look, patina the solder tin of all the soldered surfaces. Solder 20-gauge wire to the seams on the back of the background. Paint the designs with Testors paint.

APPLE TREE MOBILE
Materials:

Glass
Copper foil
Solder

³⁄₁₆″ U leads
Solder
Brass rod (large)
Testors paint
Nylon line, 8-pound test
20-gauge wire
Nuggets (preferable red)

Follow the instructions on the pattern.

THE 3-D STRAWBERRY
Materials:

Green glass
Red glass

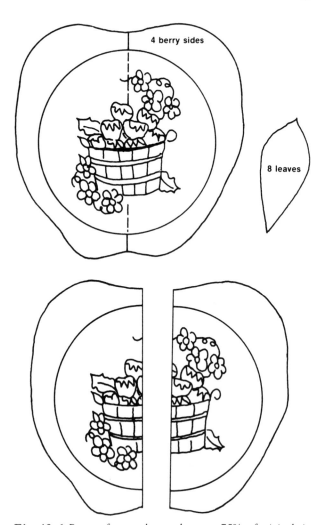

Fig. 19–6 *Pattern for strawberry, shown at 75% of original size.*

Clear antique glass
20-gauge wire
¼" copper foil
4 oz. solder
Acrylic paint
Testors paint
Epoxy glue
Replacotta (clay)
Black patina
3½" wood circle for base (optional)
Ribbon (optional)
Nylon line, 8-pound test for hanging
(optional)

Enlarge pattern to full size. Cut out four circles and divide two of them in half. Cut out the four strawberry sides. Paint the picture on one whole circle. Paint the picture on two of the half-circles as shown by taping the glass over the pattern. If you use acrylic paint, do not wash the glass after painting. If you use Testors paint, you can wash the glass after the paint dries. Put the other glass circles over the painted side of the glass, hold them together, and wrap the edges with ¼" copper foil. Leave the straight edge of the ½" circle without foil. Copper foil the strawberry sides. Solder two strawberry sides around the whole circle, one strawberry side around each half-circle. Center the half-berry on each side of the whole berry. Solder the top, bottom, and seams. Use epoxy glue on all sides of the unfoiled center seams. Let dry.

Cut out and foil eight glass leaves. Make one wire stem and two vines of 20-gauge wire and solder to the top of the berry. Solder on the thinner leaves—four at angles down, four straight out from the stem over the side seams. Clean the glass. Patina. Paint white dots on the glass with Testors paint. Mold the flowers out of Replacotta, bake and paint with acrylic paint. Glue on the berry top.

20
Stained-Glass Sculpture

Saara Gallin

Of her starting off in stained glass, Saara Gallin says: "Stained glass had been around for centuries, but the Isenbergs had not. Instruction was hard to come by. There was some literature, but the Isenbergs' was the only book that became a fixture in the workshop. I followed their instruction in basic techniques and then developed my own ideas." Her contribution to the second edition of this work is therefore only logical. Of Saara Gallin it has been said: "In the realm of innovative, experimental, and often avant garde work, there are few whose work demonstrates these directions more than that of George Sell and Ed Gilly in their dimensional work, and that of Fredrica Field, Saara Gallin, Paul Marioni, Kriston Newton, Narcissus Quagliata and James Hubbell." (Glass Digest, March 15, 1981.)

Art, like sin, is a matter of opinion. Opinions are what I was most freely given when I first became interested in stained glass. Since advice costs nothing until you act upon it, I would have made suncatchers and very little else had I followed the notions of my well-intentioned counselers. The price would have been my own freedom as a designer-artist.

When I started working in stained glass, I was told in a course on selling crafts, "Make multiple items." Other advice was just the opposite: "Do commissions. Then you will be a true professional." I wanted to do neither. Instead, I decided I wanted to make things I had never seen. I wanted the adventure and challenge of discovery and the uncertainty of trial and error. The first questions I ask myself when beginning a project are: How will it stay together? What will be the supports and how to place them? How will it be framed? How will it hang? Can it live with people in their homes? How will it find itself in the spaces generally available for exhibit?

It may seem that my primary anxiety is how to support my pieces. I do not like heavy, clumsy, earthbound frames. I prefer to have the glass appear to be floating. Flexible copper tubing from a plumbing supply house formed around a template is useful in this regard. I always begin with the frame. Never do I try to fit the frame to the glass. This is as important practically as artistically, especially when using antique wood frames, which warp with time. Even if this warp is ever so slight, it can create a problem.

My affinity for the sculptural expressed itself first in giant mobile butterflies. Skyscrapers fascinate me, and my abstract work has strong ties to these commanding elements. Most of my ideas develop out of the material. I work out ideas first by choosing a glass that particularly fascinates me at the moment. Then I glean some of the forms that seem consistently to sift through my mind. Sometimes these are made more concrete by making a cardboard model of the projected work. At

Fig. 20–1 *Saara Gallin at work in her studio.*

other times I just proceed to build directly out of the glass. Once I lay out a group of forms, I arrange and rearrange. This is the point where the work takes on a life of its own. Once these dimensional forms relate one to another, I draw in the background, make the cartoon, and cut the background glass. It is most important to my work process that I completely construct the pieces that are to be in relief before I ever work on the background glass. Only in

this way can I avoid unforeseen spaces between the background glass and the sculptural elements.

The copper-foil technique seems to be the most suitable for my particular designs and desires. All of my experimentation has been with this method. I foil and tin each piece of glass before putting the pieces together. This makes the soldering process much easier. I love using the kiln with all its possibilities of exploring those ambiguous glass shapes that arise from slumping and fusing glass. I am interested in the effect of gravity on glass when glass is exposed to heat. I have another ongoing interest in faces. I work with clay or plaster as a preliminary medium for faces because it allows more mobility for making them out of glass. The faces for "Profiles in Glass" (shown in the color section) were done with the slab method of working in clay. Firebrick, dental investment, plaster, and corregated paper shell-backed and filled with plaster have all served as useful molds for slumping.

I think of my work as sculpting with light. My fascination with the effect of light on the transparency and texture of antique glass keeps growing. I work because I have a drive to see what an idea will look like. The creative impulse concerns itself with the evolving nature of the work. Will it be any good? Will it meet my specifications? It has been said that each new work is a voyage of discovery. For me that voyage begins with the words *what if*?

The best advice I was ever given was from a fellow artist. He said, "Make it; don't worry about selling it." This advice I have heeded.

21

Surface Treatment of Metal Cames

Susan Dodds Stinsmuehlen

Susan Dodds Stinsmuehlen developed her unusual leading techniques over a ten-year period as a partner in the Renaissance Glass Company, Austin, Texas in order to achieve a particular feeling and to emphasize that possibilities are unlimited.

The sensibility of glass construction can be melded with the open-ended possibilities of painting and collage. Traditional stained glass is perfectly suited to set off the contradictions of these unlikely juxtapositions. To go against the conventional approach to stained glass—to treat it is an object whose main purpose is to modify light passing through it—is often lost in my work. I do not believe there need be a single focus or interpretation of stained glass. Meaning in my work comes to light through metaphor.

My figures and forms interact with the surface differentiation. The patterning and garish coloration is not limited to glass. The structural lines become linear spaces. Their relationship to the glass is minimized or maximized by the liberties I take with color and texture. A free combining of such materials as diffraction gradings, fabrics, plastics, jewels, glitter, paints, brass findings, etched and painted mirrors, nail polish, bevels, and burnished metals reveals an unrestrained world. Here is a precious facade at once kinetic, glittery, glasslike. The abstract and realistic images add to the effect and the whole takes on mythic proportions. I feel that the underlying tone, both in the making the piece and in its fi-

nal impact, is one of hovering chaos simultaneously projecting its own resolution.

Almost any paint can be used on lead and zinc came, but the came should be rubbed with steel wool and cleaned with solvent first. When using a smooth enamel, the finished surface will look better if the solder joints are ground down with a Dremel tool and abrasive wheel before painting. The choice of paint must be sympathetic to the feeling of the work. Paints that can be used include Testors enamels, acrylics, oil pastels and paints, nail polish, Deka paints, and even auto paints. Coat all painted surfaces when dry with clear polyurethane to protect the surface from chipping or weathering. If a gloss polyurethane is used, the shiny quality of the painted lead will better relate to the glass surface.

If you want a more baroque or collage effect, try using pearls, glitters, beads, or pressure-sensitive tapes. Except for the tapes, these materials can be applied with glue.

Another way to add texture to the came is by soldering directly to it such things as findings, cutout metal forms, wire, metal grids, chains, or jewelry. There are no limits on the kinds of material except to consider where a piece is to be installed and how it will wear with time.

For a nice variation, use the natural qualities of brass or copper came by polishing with a Dremel tool and grinding wheels. This creates a shimmering surface. Coat the metal with gloss polyurethane to prevent tarnishing.

Fig. 21–1 *"Man In Nature." Handrolled glass, lamination, etching; brass and zinc with painted lead.*

Fig. 21–2 *"Thor Medallion." 20″ by 20″. Laminated diffraction grading; etched and painted mirror; brass, fabric, oil pastel. Photograph by Will Van Overbeck.*

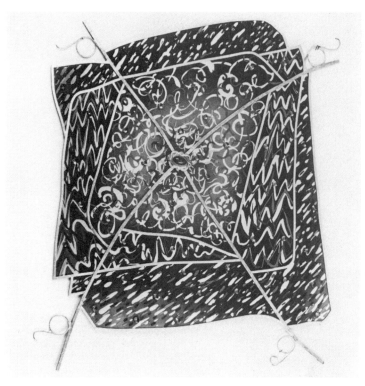

Fig. 21–3 *"Xcited X." 36"*
by 36". Etched and painted
mirror, jewels and painted
zinc.

Fig. 21–4 *"X Poodle Bub-*
ble Memorial." 26" by 26".
Laminated diffraction grad-
ings; jewelry, etched and
painted glass, brass.

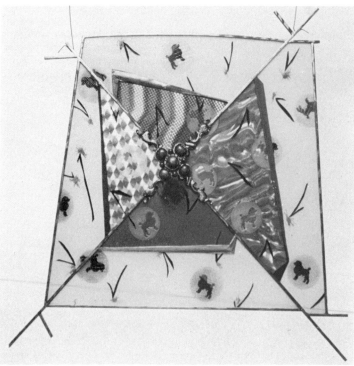

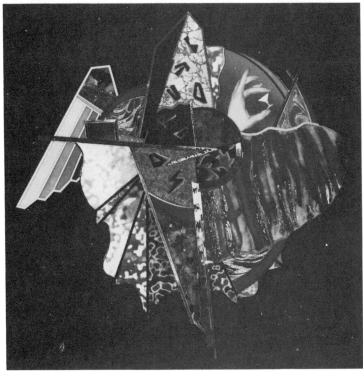

Fig. 21–5 *"Composition J," from Uroboros Triptych. 30″ by 30″. Handrolled glass; etching, painting; brass, copper, zinc, lead.*

Fig. 21–6 *"Alchemical Resolution." 42″ by 42″. Commissioned by Uroboros Glass Co.; constructed by Renaissance Glass Co. Handrolled glass; etching, painting, lamination; brass, copper, zinc plating.*

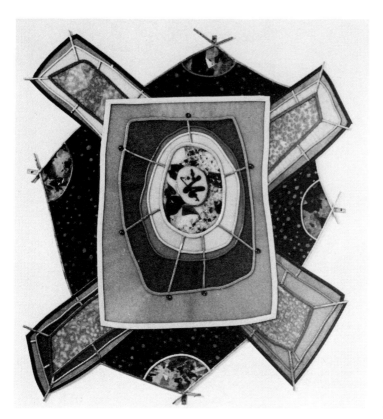

Fig. 21–7 *"Another Pretty Face." 40' by 40'. Painted lead; etched and painted glass; Plexiglas jewels and brass.*

22
Mirror Images

Jeffrey Glick

Born in New York City, Mr. Glick attended the Pratt Institute and the School of Visual Arts. His early works were electroluminous kinetic sculptures, which brought him a reputation as an experimenter in nontraditional art forms. The acclaim given his work on both the East and West coasts gained him a joint show with Salvador Dali at Lincoln Center in the mid-1960s. For almost fifteen years he has worked with mirror sculpture, which is similar in technique to stained-glass fresco but radically different in concept and effect.

The sign on the wall of my studio reads: "Sight is an ability. Seeing is an art." My medium is light, dimension, and space. Each of my mirror sculptures is constructed of hand–cut pieces often numbering in the thousands. The largest of them, "The Buddha," is 5½ feet by 6½ feet. The price tag is $50,000. The headpiece alone contains 90 glass shards.

The technique involved in working with mirror is the same as working with any other glass, stained or clear. Once cut, the glass pieces are sanded, framed in copper foil, angled in a variety of refractory planes, joined, and lead-soldered. Construction of each sculpture begins only after hours of painstaking drawings that can take from a few days to a few months. "Buddha" took five months to complete.

I never duplicate a piece. I guess one reason I like working with mirror is that I like mathematics—angles and elevations, multidimensional effects. My mirror pieces are carefully designed to play with light, to evoke a dance of colors and reflections. Hidden in the design are new colors, new impressions. In these elements are the glory and the test of working with mirror. I polish the mirror again and again for highlights. It comes out diamond-faceted, shimmering. As I work, the mirror becomes fluid, warm, and soft. I use only the finest glass, only clear mirror to reflect the colors of the environment. In a strong sense, I guess it is my own reflection there on the line.

Fig. 22–1 *Jeffrey Glick in his studio. (Photo by B. J. Perkins)*

Fig. 22–2 *Glick's designs and ideas, individual and striking by themselves, are made even more dramatic through his use of mirror. (Photo by Diana Bond)*

Fig. 22–3 *"Enchanted Forest." (Photo by Diana Bond)*

. . . bright is the noble edifice that is pervaded by the new light.
ABBOT SUGER,
c. 1144, on his Church of St. Denis

THE COMMERCIAL GLASSWORKER

V

23
Stained Glass Classes: Teaching and Learning

FINDING A TEACHER

"Where do I find a good teacher?" This is a constant query. While the reply must be qualified by saying it is less difficult to find one today than when the first edition of this book appeared, your success or failure will still depend to a great extent on what part of the country you live in and how desperate you are. Most serious stained glass teaching occurs on the coasts, with isolated pockets of instruction scattered generally in the major cities.

Unfortunately, some craftspeople get involved in teaching almost as soon as they have learned the basics themselves. This has been a source of confusion. Students often have to unlearn what they have been taught under these circumstances. This book should give you an idea of the breadth of the craft, as well as a measure of a teacher's capabilities and qualifications.

Teachers, good and bad, often have shops or studios where they sell supplies. This can be a great convenience to the student, providing the pricing is fair. You can usually discover whether it is or not by checking prices either in mail-order catalogues or in other retail outlets. Some teachers provide tools for their students to use, others insist you purchase your own and come to class fully equipped. You may find your choice of teacher hinging on such a requisite. You may want to investigate the type of work your teacher has done, provided such is accessible; however, skill in the craft does not always mean skill in teaching the craft.

In the long run, of course, selecting a teacher is a matter of how much you have to learn and the amount of knowledge and capability the teacher has to share. While this textbook is not meant to take the place of a teacher, it can effect the purpose where circumstances make it necessary.

It is likely that when friends discover you are working in stained glass they will ask you to teach them. This is fine if you just do it as a favor for the sport of the thing. If you start to do it for payment, you should begin considering your options and your capabilities. These may need expanding by experimenting and studying— either on your own, or with professionals. Either way, teaching takes you out of the category of "hobbyist" and places you in professional status (in our opinion, at any rate) and places on you responsibilities you should be prepared to assume. If you are not ready for them, don't teach.

THE GLASTAR SURVEY

A recent survey of 100 stained glass shops across the country conducted by the Glastar Co. came up with the information that most teachers of stained glass classes charge $40 for 14 hours of instruction and have an average of 9 students. Most students learn copper foil rather than lead came. Probably the most effective new piece of equipment for the craft in recent years has been the glass grinder.

THE VILLAGE HOBBY MART: EXAMPLE OF A TEACHING SHOP

Barney Welborn at The Village Hobby Mart in Houston, Texas, offers classes in 6-week sessions. Each class is 3 hours long. Special classes are offered in sandblasting and box and terrarium construction. The sandblasting equipment is available for use at any time. A fee is charged for sandblasting time which is waived when the equipment is in conjuction with a class. Classes are divided into beginning and advanced students. Th beginning student constructs a 50 to 100 piece panel with copper foil. The advanced student either learns leading technique or gets into Tiffany-style lampmaking.

Classes begin with a general introduction to types of glass and their manufacture. Basic tools are introduced to beginning students; they learn to break and score window glass. Students are encouraged to buy their own equipment and to continue work at home, rather than rent or borrow. Progress is at individual pace throughout the 6 week session. The instructor is available at all times to teach specific skills, help with special problems and give instruction as needed. If a student needs extra help or additional time to complete a project, the classes can be extended to suit these individual needs. This may involve one extra night at class, or the student may attend additional sessions with a new beginners' class at no extra charge.

SOME STUDENT COMMENTS AND EXAMPLES FROM THE STAINED GLASS SCHOOL, DENVER

"Like most people, I've walked by a store and my eye has been caught by a stained glass window. The colors always looked

Fig. 23–1 Pam McDowell and her panel.

beautiful, but so was the price. I decided to take a few lessions. Now I know, having finished my first project, why those prices were so high. As for my own first panel— I couldn't even put a price on it."—Pam McDowell

"My wife and I were looking for a joint activity, so we enrolled in a beginner's class working with leaded windows. Since I possess a limited amount of patience, and my wife has never done any type of glass or woodworking, we started the classes with apprehension. After a short period of familiarization with the glass and tools, we discovered that were able to construct some simple yet satisfying projects. Soldering the window as we constructed it, piecing and adjusting the paper pattern within the window before cutting the corresponding piece of glass, and continually sharpening the lead knife proved to be practices that were most beneficial. My wife experienced the most difficulty in cutting and placing the lead, whereas I experienced a considerable amount of frustration

Fig. 23-2 *Smitty and Diane Grayson and their panel.*

Fig. 23-3 *Jerry Shennan and his panel.*

when attempting to place exceptionally small pieces of glass. Ironically, the thing we feared most proved to be rather simple, and that was cutting and breaking the glass. Our eagerness to complete the project grew with each piece that was added to the window. We both experienced a real sense of accomplishment and pride the moment the finished panel was held up to the light."—Smitty and Diane Grayson

"What motivated me to work in stained glass was basic curiosity. I have worked with wood all my life. Glass, I thought, would be a new challenge. On my first piece, a window, the actual construction came fairly easily. I didn't have too much trouble cutting glass or leading. I had done soldering before. For me the greatest challenge was picking and mixing the colors and textures of glass. When did one use cathedral and when opaque? What effect would one texture have over another? Is there too much contrast? These questions came up repeatedly. To get a window that is pleasure to the eye was a main object. To get a final result that stops one in one's tracks with its beauty is my basic goal."—Jerry Shennan

SOME STUDENT EXAMPLES FROM THE STAINED GLASS SHOP, SUN CITY, ARIZONA

Fig. 23–6 A. L. "Bud" Larsen and his rooster.

Fig. 23–4 Selecting glass at the Stained Glass Shop. Carolyn Werbelo decides on colors and texture.

Fig. 23–7 Mim Grumstrup's greenhouse.

Fig. 23–5 Nancy Dittbrenner uses the copper foiling technique.

Fig. 23–8 *Krystyna A. Chobot's "Indian Woman" was inspired by a large scrap of opaque glass that looked like Indian blanket.*

Fig. 23–10 *Gene Pulhamus's "Ship of the Line."*

Fig. 23–9 *Roy V. Arndt's mixed-media glass and driftwood.*

Fig. 23–11 *Doyle G. Gladon's "Figure and Sunburst."*

24
Repair
and Restoration

Repairing stained-glass objects involves different techniques from those required to fabricate the piece itself. In many cases, it's easier to rebuild an item completely than to repair it even partially. This holds true whether the piece is a panel with several broken portions or a lamp with a missing panel. Not only is the work tedious and difficult, but most objects brought in for repair are dirty. As you clean the glass and scrub the corroded leads, you may abruptly peel them from the glass, and then you must replace them. With all this you can't even charge as you would for a new creation.

It's not true that it costs more to rebuild than to repair. More time may be spent trying to repair, and if you are paid by the hour, more money too, although it's never enough. It's the end result that matters, and the best end result for a thoroughly battered window or lamp is rebuilding. Anything short of that is a poor compromise. Unfortunately, your customer may compromise by lessening your fee but not on your labor. And repairs on stained-glass objects, like surgery, leave scars. If subjected to careful scrutiny, the piece will always look repaired.

The beginner is often tempted to quote a low price to get the job. Unfortunately, he then has to take shortcuts in order to match the fee, and the piece may look worse than it did when it was brought in. Always tell the customer that a repair job is not a restoration. Restoring something implies that it will be brought back to a state of pristine creation, while repair involves merely replacing a portion of the object so that it will once again be functional and decorative. But it will not necessarily be perfect. People may be willing to pay the price of repair, but they too often expect restoration for their money.

REPAIRING WINDOWS

The easiest windows to repair have pieces that are broken out near the borders. If the window is brought in with its wood frame, it must be taken out before any work can be done on it. Never accept a window in its frame. Getting it out takes time and involves the risk of cracking more glass, which you will then have to replace gratis.

Clean the glass with Windex, and be careful when passing a rag over the surface of any old panel that you do not inadvertently stick yourself on a piece of turned-up lead or an old copper wire that was used to join a reinforcing rod. You can easily cut a finger by cleaning a piece carelessly. Once the window and the leads are clean, cut away the border lead surrounding the broken piece. The broken glass should be pulled gently out of the surrounding came with glass pliers and the point of a lead knife passed through the channels to make sure that no small pieces

Fig. 24–1 *Repair or restoration? You tell us.*

For windows or panels that have pieces broken out in their centers, the repair is considerably more complicated. Several methods may be applied here.

The Tinker-Toy Approach

The tinker-toy approach involves taking the entire window apart to the point of the missing piece or pieces. You must cut away the border lead and work your way through all the sound pieces of glass between the border and the area you must fix. In complicated windows, this can involve a great number of pieces of glass and a great number of pieces of lead, for all the lead must be cut away as the glass is removed. There is the additional risk of breaking a number of these glass pieces. There is also a lot of putty scraping involved, since before any of the pieces of glass can be removed, you must pass the point of your lead knife under all surrounding caming to break away the hard putty. This must be done on both the front and the back of the panel, and the more pieces you get out, the more difficult it is to turn the panel back and forth. It's a cumbersome method, but once you get to the area of the break, you can fit the new glass exactly. You then back out the way you came in, replacing leads, glass, and putty as you go. As with most repair jobs, the most difficult portion is preparing the object for repair, not the actual repair operation itself.

This approach involves time and effort, and you should get paid according to the complexity of the work. Usually, we use this technique only on windows that we pick up in an antique shop and are repairing for our own use.

The tinker-toy approach requires a good craftsman with a steady hand. If the window has a fairly complicated design, make a pattern before taking it apart so that you will be able to fit the pieces together again. An easy way to make a pattern is to hold a piece of brown kraft paper over the panel and press your fingers along the lead

of glass and putty remain inside. Place a piece of pattern paper beneath the opening, and with a sharp pencil follow the design exactly. Do this precisely to the point where the border lead has been cut away, and use a ruler to join the two ends of the design to take the place of the border lead. Then enlarge your design very slightly to allow for the leads covering the two neighboring pieces of glass. Cut out the design and check the pattern in the space. Then cut a piece of glass to shape. The glass should fit exactly into the empty space, snapping into the empty channels of the lead with the least bit of tapping from a lead knife handle. You can then replace the missing portion of border lead and solder it to the lead on either side.

In many cases, you will find old putty within the empty leads surrounding the broken glass. This should be thoroughly cleaned out with the lead knife blade, and once the new glass is back in place, new putty should be applied. Never skip this step. It is one of the most important guidelines in repair—all replacement pieces of glass must be puttied, even in lamps. The putty helps fill in areas that are not exactly to dimension, and it also helps strengthen the repaired area.

lines. This will indent the paper, and when you lift it, you will have a rubbing of these lines that will give you the design and the exact spacings of the glass as well. You can then darken these lines with a magic marker.

Be gentle when removing sound glass. If you break a piece, you may not be able to match it. Keep scraping your knife into the leading, sinking it progressively deeper to get the putty out so that the piece can be wiggled free. Be careful that the old glass doesn't suddenly snap and your hand flies back against a neighboring piece of glass. This is one of those all too frequent accidents that accompany repair work. Another is having your lead knife slip into a carelessly placed bracing hand.

The Lead-Flap Approach

The lead-flap approach is also used in repairing central portions of broken panels. Flap up the edges of the surrounding lead came as best you can so that the top flanges are at right angles to the surface and fit the glass as closely as possible, approximating it to the space left for it. This procedure works best for diamonds, squares, or rectangles. It will not work with free-form pieces, and especially pieces with sharp points or acute inner or outer curves. The specific technique is as follows:

1. With the point of a lead knife, thoroughly explore all channels of the surrounding came that are still reasonably intact. If any of the channels are torn or if the leads are in poor condition, they must be cut loose from the glass and replaced. This must be done before any glass is cut. When cutting old leads away, be careful not to crack any of the glass they adhere to. Very gently with the lead knife, first cut one surface to the glass and then turn the panel over and cut the other. Then, pushing the came from behind with your knife blade, you should be able to pry the old lead loose. With the lead knife, scrape

the piece of glass to remove all putty from its surface, and replace the lead with a new piece, soldering it to its neighbors. Make sure all the leads are firm and the channels completely empty.

2. With glass pliers, bend the flanges of the leads upright so that they end up as close to a right angle to tbe surface as possible. Cut all soldered joints. It is necessary to do this only on one side of the panel. The came on the other side should be left alone to form a shelf for the glass to rest on. You then have a hole surrounded by came, which has sticking out below a small flange in a horizontal position, with the flange above in vertical position. This should allow you enough room to wiggle the glass back into the space.

3. Place a piece of pattern paper underneath the opening. With a sharp pointed pencil, make a pattern of the existing space. You must enlarge this pattern to compensate for the horizontal shelf of lead below so that the glass will be about $1/16''$ larger than the pattern.

4. Cut the glass to shape after enlarging the pattern and smooth all edges with abrasive paper. If you have cut your pattern correctly, you should be able with the help of the lead knife to wiggle and pry this new piece of glass into the opening. It should sit firmly on the bottom flanges of lead.

5. With the lead knife, check to make sure that the glass is sitting properly. Then, using the blade of the knife or a putty knife, smooth down the raised flanges of lead so that they now cover the upper edges of the glass. The area should be soldered where the leads meet. Once this is done, the piece should be seated firmly back in the leads. Try to use smooth glass pliers when bending the flange; otherwise the grozzing teeth will leave their marks in the lead, and these are impossible to remove.

The difficulties with this procedure are manifold. The glass cutting must be absolutely precise, and no matter how precise your glass cutting is, if your initial pattern is not correct, you will still have trouble with the glass. While the paper pattern may seem to be sitting properly, this is only an illusion because of its thickness as opposed to the thickness of the piece of glass that is to follow it. So don't be discouraged if you've cut your glass precisely to pattern and it still doesn't fit. You will have to back and fill, placing marks on the glass with a glass pencil at the areas of contact and grozzing these until the glass finally fits.

Don't overgrozz. The grozzing must be done a bit at a time. If you do too much grozzing in any one space, when the glass sits in, you will have a hole between the glass and the lead at that point, and the whole piece will have to be redone. Grozz and fit, grozz and fit, and eventually the glass will go into the space. However, this may still not be the end of your troubles, for the lead rim that has been dislocated upwards may not want to come down again without looking crumpled. Lead so treated tends to look somewhat ragged when placed back over the glass, and to the extent that it does your repair will be noticeable. You can avoid this ragged appearance by bringing the lead both up and down very gently and a little at a time. Patience is the key.

All the same, you may find that no matter how much patience you exercise you're left with a piece of lead that looks tattered and worn. This is one of the difficulties of this technique, and you can try to ameliorate it only by smoothing the surface with a lead knife or putty knife blade over and over. Watch the amount of pressure you apply. When you bend the lead up, cut it with a lead knife at the corners where the tension is at its worst, rather than letting the lead tear away at these areas. This not only will allow for a neater solder joint at the site when you are done, but it takes a lot of the strain off the central portion of the flange so that the whole flap can move as a unit. Above all, do not use any tool other than wide-jaw glass pliers to bend the lead upward.

THE HALF-A-LEAD REPLACEMENT METHOD

A third technique of replacing these difficult central portions of glass starts by taking a lead knife and cutting away all the leads surrounding the space to be replenished. This leaves the empty space surrounded by borders of glass. Pattern paper, is placed beneath the space to be filled and a sharp pencil used to trace the pattern upon it. However, here the pattern need not be enlarged since you don't have to compensate for existing lead. Once the pattern is cut, fit it into the space to see how closely it matches. If it does not match, mark where it is off and cut a new pattern. Once the pattern fits accurately, cut the glass to match. Holding the glass from beneath, push it up into the space. It should fit as closely as possible to the bordering surfaces of glass, leaving only the space for the lead heart between.

Make a plasticene-clay bed underneath the glass space to support the surrounding pieces. It should be thin enough so that it doesn't lift the panel away from the table surface, but it should keep all pieces of glass from moving. Press the new piece of glass into the space and onto the clay bed. With a toothpick, remove any plasticene that oozes up between the pieces. Measure the leads, always remembering to match them to the type of lead used throughout the rest of the panel. Cut the leads to size, then cut them in half through the heart. Don't mix up these matching halves. Mark them so that you can match the top and bottom surfaces. On half of each piece of lead, run some glass glue down its side. Then place each piece on the panel covering the spaces between glass. Press each piece down firmly and allow a few moments for the glue to hold. Solder the ends of the lead together and wipe away any glue seeping out from beneath the channels immediately.

Allow an hour for the glue to set, then turn the panel upside down, remove the clay bed, and clean the sides of the glass. Carefully place each remaining half lead on top of its neighboring piece in the same direction as it was cut, and repeat the process of the leads. You will have a neat surface that has a single H lead holding two pieces of glass together. This type of repair gives the best appearance for the least amount of work.

You may have some difficulty shaving the old lead from the glass. Make sure your lead knife is sharp. Lead will come away if you nick a corner and run your blade through the heart along the surface of the glass. The major problem is mixing up the two halves so they don't match, leaving one side standing out from the glass.

Another source of difficulty can be the glass itself. If the cutting has been so close that one surface of glass touches another, you will not be able to force the lead heart between them. Conversely, if the glass edges are too far apart, you may find that the lead came is not wide enough to cover the space. You have no choice here but to recut the glass. Make sure that you size your cut piece of glass against the space provided before beginning the leading process.

Repairing Buckled Windows

In a buckled window, the bracing has given way and the leads have allowed the glass to buckle forward. Leaning on the buckled portion to push it back into shape is not sufficient. Windows that are badly buckled must be taken apart and completely releaded. There is no other way to fix them. If the buckling is just beginning, you might get by with a new reinforcing rod, pulling the old lead cames back into place against it. However, chances are that once the window begins to buckle in one area it will probably begin to buckle in another.

Releading any window involves a certain amount of initial unleading. This is the most extensive part of the repair process. When you quote a price, don't neglect this. Consider how much you will have to do

before you can actually start the work that the customer feels he is paying you to do.

REPAIRING SUNCATCHERS AND MOBILES

Repairs on suncatchers and mobiles are usually simple. The back-to-back lead allows for a good deal of mobility in moving pieces around. Just cut the outside lead and all struts to the broken part, bend them aside, slide the broken pieces out, and replace them. Then bend the piece back into shape and solder the bordering leads. If the object is smashed in several areas, it is not worth repairing.

REPAIRING LAMPS

Straight-Paneled Lamps

Repairs may be necessary for long pieces of a skirt or paneling or for some of the small pieces within the skirt. Small pieces must be removed and replaced, which means also removing and replacing the surrounding pieces. Since most of these pieces are foiled, you must take the area apart and rebuild it. Such skirts are not deep, and usually there are only a few pieces of sound glass between you and the fractured area.

Repair of lamp panels can be accomplished best by stripping away the top surface of two adjoining H cames. This allows you to remove the broken glass. Then cut a new panel to the shape of the space and place it on the half-leads remaining below. Cut away as much of the heart of a new half-lead as possible, cutting with metal shears right to the flat surface of the lead. Put the half-lead over the edge of the new piece of glass. It should match the half-lead below, whose lead heart projects upward between the new panel and the neighboring panel. Before replacing the new half-lead, stretch it so that it will be firm and straight. Run some glass cement under it so that it will firmly adhere to the glass.

This type of repair usually is easy, and the heat of the bulb will not disturb the glass cement, which can take high temperatures.

Bent-Panel Lamps

Bent-panel lamps are the most difficult to repair. The problems vary with the number of curves involved in the bent panel, whether it is a U-curve or an S-curve, and whether the piece of glass is held to the frame by metal clips or channels.

Clip-type panels are the easiest to repair. Make the new panel using one of the existing panels as a guide and fit it into the clips. It should fit accurately if your mold was made correctly. Even S-shaped panels will fit well into a clip-in frame. However, S-shaped panels held in a metal groove frame are difficult to work with, and repairs should be done only with the understanding that the end result will not be perfect. In addition, any soldering that must be done on the old brass may show no matter how you try to disguise it chemically.

If the lamp's panels are channeled in, your molds and pattern must be made as accurately as possible. You may have to cast four or five panels before you get one that will come close to fitting. Even at that you will probably have to grozz the panel here and there to get it right. Grozzing a bent panel, especially a newly fired one, is a risky business because of the stresses within the glass from firing. You may try to grozz off the smallest amount from one edge and find that the panel has broken in half. Without grozzing, you probably will not get the panel to fit. One of the reasons bent-panel replacement is so expensive is

because of this fragility. When the lamp was originally made, its panels were bent on steel molds and any variations in the glass could be made up in the channeling. There is no way to move the metal around now to allow for modifications in the glass. And chances are that your glass will not fit perfectly within its groove. To alleviate this, copper-foil the panel after smoothing the edges. Widen the brass space to take the copper-foiled edge. To enable the metal to accept solder, rub it with a stiff brush until it shines. Flux and run solder between foil and metal so that the panel is locked in.

The soldered surface must be aged to match the other metal. This is done either with copper sulphate solidifier or a mixture of hydrochloric acid and sulphur, a noxious concoction that should be used only in a well-ventilated area. Don't do this until you finish soldering; once the color has been changed, you will no longer be able to solder along this surface. With S-shaped panel repair, the best you can hope for is a panel that will not stand out too badly from its neighbors and that will be held in place by the pressure of the lamp frame.

Stained-glass repair should be reserved for fixing your own stained-glass objects or as favors for friends. You can probably only make money repairing if you work on several jobs at a time. Split the time among several projects. Each procedure involves waiting periods—for instance, waiting for the glass cement to dry when using the half-lead method—and this time may be spent on another repair job. In this way you will be able to make such jobs pay, thus financing your more creative endeavors.

25
Selling
Your Stained Glass

THE GIFT SHOP

Unless you are a craftsman of long experience with an extremely good reputation, most gift shops will not buy your items directly from you. Instead, they will take your work on consignment, displaying it for a certain length of time. If the items are purchased, they will take a percentage of the purchase price.

Most gift shops consider 20 percent to be a fair price for each item. We consider this reasonable. Some shops take 25 or 33⅓ percent, which is too high. Consider the consignment percentage when you decide on a price for your items. If the percentage is high, your overall price will be high, and your items may not sell. You should make 50 percent profit on small hanging objects—the gift shops' specialty. If you cannot make at least that, then it's not worth it. Either find another gift shop or redesign that particular item so that is is less expensive to make.

Consult with the owner of the gift shop periodically. He should know how much interest has been expressed in your pieces. He may feel that after two months they should be changed, since they have not sold and people are getting used to them. Individuals who frequent gift shops and see the same stained glass hanging there month after month will tend to think the artist is not selling. This may be the truth, in which case it is wiser to put in a whole new display. Even a successful display should be changed at least four times a year; add new items and remove less successful ones.

Your work should be signed so that anyone buying it will know that it is a piece from your studio. Carbide scribers are available for this purpose. If you can arrange to have an attractive little label printed, describing your work with a short description of stained glass and how to care for it, you may find that this, will attract attention and will become an additional incentive for purchase. People may not read about what they are buying but a label makes them feel their purchase is important. Printing small labels can be done at minimal cost.

When you place your stained glass in a gift shop, it is best if you do not have to compete with another artist. However, you may have to compete on a consignment basis. If you cannot get an exclusive for your work, at least make sure your glass is very different from what is there. If a shop has been carrying your work and the owner feels that he would like to try somebody else as well, he should inform you. You should then check carefully to see how it will compete with yours. You should try for an exclusive, at least for a reasonable length of time.

There should be a working arrangement with the shop that if someone wants a piece of stained glass fabricated, the request be referred to you. The shop still

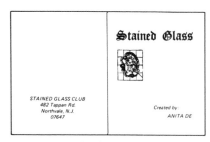

Fig. 25–1 Label for gift-shop items.

Fig. 25–2 Small stained glass kits—mass-produced and ready to go. In order to make a profit on such items you have to sell a lot of them and be able to turn them out at a rapid rate.

gets its discount on the item and you get the commission.

Mail Orders

An agent, having seen your work in individual shops, may contact you with a view toward displaying your special glass at gift shows and you could find yourself deluged with orders and an instant business. *Do not accept consignment terms.* Be sure to check the list of your prospective customers. Your agent is taking the orders for a commission. You must pay this whether or not you get paid from the gift shops. Make sure you are dealing with reputable shops who will pay you. Before agreeing to fill an order, write to the firm and ask if it is

rated in Dun and Bradstreet. If it is, check its credit rating in the Dun and Bradstreet volumes at your local library. If it isn't listed, ask the firm for credit references. If it won't do this, insist on payment in advance (pro forma). Some shops will refuse, and you will lose the order. It is worth it; otherwise, you may end up losing your labor as well. We never deal with any shop that is not rated in Dun and Bradstreet or that will not furnish several good credit ratings. Even if you do get a good credit rating, most shops do not pay before 90 days. You will wait for some time before you get your money, but your agent will want to be paid right away. The gift shop business is tricky. Sometimes your agent, for an additional percentage, will agree to do the billing for you and accept the loss of his commission on accounts that do not pay.

When you are making up your invoice and the order is packaged and ready to go, add the charge for postage. If you do not add it to the invoice, you will not be paid for it. Reputable gift shops expect to be billed for postage. If you are sending items via UPS, be sure to add in the UPS charge.

We have sent items via UPS, Railway Express, and parcel post and feel UPS is best. Items sbould be insured so that if they break you will get your money back. Try to avoid sending *any* glass through the mail. *Fragile* notices have no effect. The glass in these packages breaks twice as fast. You will never know if the mail or the gift shop dropped it. Unless you have insurance, you will find mail orders are more trouble than they are worth.

Billing Procedure

If your items are in the corner gift shop, you will not have to bill; the shop should send you a check each month for whatever it sold, plus an itemized list of what went out. However, if you are sending items to gift shops across the country, you must bill them each month or you will not get paid. No gift shop will send you money without an invoice. Have a standard invoice printed up with your name and the name of your studio on it. Your invoice should include the date, the items sent, to whom they were sent and where the order was placed and with whom. A copy of this should also go to your agent. List the items that were ordered and when the order was shipped, the total plus postal charges, and then list the amount on the bottom. It is not necessary to go through this type of invoicing each time. You may send a "balance due" statement thereafter. You will probably have to follow up. Of course, if you run into gift shops that are slow payers or do not pay you at all, notify your agent not to accept any further orders unless they are paid in advance.

Mass-Produced Items
If you have worked up a successful business making items for gift shops, you may want to start mass production. You may require some help in this. To do items on a mass-production scale, you must cut out at least 30 or 40 of each. Do all the glass cutting first. Then foil and solder each piece on an assembly line. Pieces are soldered as units, then turned over and soldered. Investing in special glass-cutting jigs helps considerably in getting your items turned out rapidly.

Packaging
Package all items carefully to avoid breakage. Straw or bubbled plastic is best for protecting glass because it seems to absorb shocks well. Crumpled newspaper is also good. Do not send more than two or three items in a package, for if a package gets roughly handled, all the items will be broken. Have boxes made that will fit the size items you are going to ship. The boxes should be large enough to allow space for a generous amount of packaging material.

Pack these boxes in a carton. If items that manage to get through safely month after month suddenly start returning broken, you might want to check and see if some new postal employee or some new UPS driver is handling them too roughly.

THE CRAFTS SHOW
If you are interested in developing your craft and in having people know what you

Fig. 25–3 *Advertising in stained glass. We have used this sign at craft shows for almost twenty years. It consists of an opalescent glass border surrounding a large piece of opal white glass. The panel is leaded. The letters are cut to fit and glued to the underlying glass.*

Fig. 25–4 *Another way to advertise is with a stained-glass calling card. The lettering can be painted and baked on the glass rectangle or mass-produced by silkscreening.*

are doing, you might well attend a crafts show. After your work becomes known, you may be invited to participate. Here are some tips:

1. *Location.* Try to visit the site of the show to check how much space you will have and important details such as lighting. The exhibitor information sheet should state the size of each booth and the cost for the space as well as the conditions of sale and awards.

2. *How to display.* We display on mobile racks that may be put up and taken down quickly and stored in the car. These are made of ¾" pipe and screw together at elbow joints for stability. The foot of each has a T connector from which two lengths of 12" pipe spread for balance. The racks stand approximately 4' high and measure 4' across.

3. *What to Display.* Bring only your best works for display, and bring work that not only shows off your capabilities but also enhances the medium. If you have several different types of work, don't leave out the experimental.

4. *The Demonstration.* Some craft shows have spots in the program for demonstrations. This may be noted in the questionnaire accompanying your petition for space. We have found it a good idea to demonstrate. Don't worry about feeling awkward and don't worry about not knowing enough. You are trying to pass on information, not setting yourself up as an expert.

Don't make your lecture or demonstration too complicated. A good demonstration should take no more than twenty minutes. Include some techniques of glass cutting, tell a little about what stained glass is, and show quickly how the pieces are put together.

5. *Pricing Your Work.* There is no hard and fast rule for pricing your crafts. No matter how long it may have taken you to make something, most people are not prepared to pay what you think it is worth.

You may not be able to afford to sell one-of-a-kind items. Better to make up five or ten of a given item so that you can price more cheaply and end up with a good return. It's not as difficult to mass-produce handicrafts with the new devices, but if you make all your pieces complex, you will probably not be reimbursed for the time spent. Design so that you can cut pieces quickly and lead quickly. Avoid extreme inside curves and difficult leading areas.

People tend to admire things vociferously until they discover the price. If this situation keeps repeating itself, consider redesigning the piece, cutting down on the number of pieces and the intricacies of the leading. Then sell it at a lower price. If you feel that your creation is worth the value that you have put on it, stick to your guns.

6. *Advertising Yourself.* Most exhibitions are advertised in the local newspapers or if the show is a large one, in national arts and crafts magazines. Specify when sending in your application that you will allow your work to be included in the publicity. Inform your local newspaper that you're going to be in a show.

At the craft show you should have a sign to advertise your presence. You can make a sign out of stained glass with letters cut out of wood and glass placed behind it, or glass can be cut to shape and glued with glass cement to an underlying stained-glass panel to stand out in bold relief. If you have any particular large piece of work, place it so that it will be seen over everyone's head. If you have any printed material that tells about your studio or your work, put it on the booth in front of you. You will be surprised how rapidly it will disappear.

THE EXPO

Another type of exhibit that has become even more important than the mixed craft show is the trade show. Chief among these is the International Glass Craft Expo, presented by Hank Siesel & Associates. This four-day meeting is held annually in a different city. To it come all the important distributors, wholesalers, manufacturers, and retailers. By attending the show, you can update your techniques and view the latest developments in tools and equipment. The most recent teaching developments have been the advent of video tapes as well as hands-on workshops in sandblasting and slab glass.

APPENDIX

Glass
Manufacturers

FREMONT

Femont antique glass is free blown, so many decorating techniques are possible. Fremont makes transparent flashed and opal flashed glass, crackles, reamies, and several styles of streakies. Cuts easily. The company also works with artists and designers who need custom glass for specific projects.

ARMSTRONG

Armstrong's glass is hand mixed and machine rolled and is available in irridescent finish, smooth, seedy, or granite. The company offers more than 70 colors in cathedral and opalescent glass. The sheet sizes are 30″ × 40″ or 1′ squares. The wood cases hold 60 sheets and Armstrong will mix colors within a case. Orders are filled within three weeks from the date of the order.

CHICAGO ART GLASS

Chicago Art Glass manufactures mottled glass in 34 different colors or color combinations including many three- and four-color mixes; ripple glass in 30 colors and combinations; smooth glass in 40 colors and combinations; hand-cast glass, including drapery, streamer, confetti, and herringbone available in 104 colors; gold pinks; and cast jewels from original Tiffanys.

KOKOMO GLASS

Kokomo makes cathedral and opalescent glass and two five-color streakies. It currently makes 540 colors and color combinations for "original" repair and restoration of the works of Louis Comfort Tiffany. Colors are never con-

taminated. The oldest makers of stained glass in the country.

MERRY-GO-ROUND GLASS

Merry-Go-Round makes rolled, colored sheet glass, hand mixed, in 8′ sheets that are then cut into three sizes—24″ × 42″, 18″ × 26″, and 10″ × 10″. More than 150 colors in four different textures; as well as opalescent, cathedral, seedy, streaky, and iridescent.

Easy-to-cut streaky red, orange, and yellow glasses. Franchises stained glass centers all over the country. Artist-in-residence Paul DuFour is available for lectures and workshops on a no-charge basis.

UROBOROS GLASS

Since 1974, Uroboros Glass Studios has created some of the most exotic special-effects glass in the world. Reinvented ring-mottled opalescent glass, a glass-making secret thought to be lost with Tiffany. Its research into the use of gold as a colorant has now opened up a rare color range that includes fuschias, purples, and hot pinks. Uroboros also makes fracture and streamer glasses, traditionally used to suggest foliage or floral backgrounds, but also exciting in contemporary works.

HERITAGE GLASS

A major producer of dalles—tbe sole product of this company. Well-annealed product which cuts well, so less waste, more usable glass. Sizes are 8″ × 12″ × ⅞″. Many colors available. Sample boxes can be had: sizes are 3″ × 3″ of colors and intensities in current production.

BLENKO GLASS

The founder, William J. Blenko, came to America from London to produce handblown glass for use in windows. Still unique in the field of traditional handblown glass and glass products. Invites visitors to watch the manufacturing process from beginning to end. A lively selection of these glasses, as well as a large color range of dalles, is produced.

SPECTRUM GLASS

Offers 130 different glasses, ranging from double-rolled cathedrals and seedies to variegated opals and multi-color mixes. Utilizes large electric furnaces to feed molten glass in a continuous ribbon through annealing lehr, assuring uniformity of composition and therefore good cutting capacity.

Avoiding the Spotting of Mirror (Black Edge)

Spotting of mirror, especially at soldered areas, is a common and frustrating situation. Called "black edge" by glaziers, it means the backing of the mirror is showing through the glass; it can happen at any time, from two weeks to two years after installation. The spots gradually enlarge.

Black edge is really a tarnish of the metals used to make a mirror. When a mirror is produced, after the glass is cleaned, a thin layer of silver is applied, then a layer of copper over that. Finally, the silver and copper are coated with a dark paint backing and the whole is baked. The backing keeps corrosive material away from the copper and silver, but once the mirror is cut and the exposed edge comes into contact with corrosive agents—such as glass cleaners containing ammonia, or flux—the metals react and black spots are the result. Some fluxes can eat right through a mirror's paint backing without any cutting having taken place. Other culprits are the adhesive backing on copper foil; DAP 1012, used to cement a leaded panel (never use this with mirror); and patinas.

The best way to avoid spotting is to protect the exposed edge as soon as it is cut—before foiling or leading. A good quality varnish or unbleached shellac will do; so will nail polish or Pittsburgh Plate Glass's special Mirror Edge Sealant. Paint the edges of all mirror pieces with one of these substances before leading or foiling.

Interweaving
Leaded Lines in
Geometric Panels

When using the lead came method, there are a number of ways to produce an effective linear arrangement. These are only meant for the geometric panel; an abstract must be constructed in situ, as it were. The choices are two: where to cut a particular lead against its fellow and which particular lead to cut.

If you are leading a diamond panel, for instance, from a corner upward, you have certain design choices. Do you want to cut your left lead at each joint (Fig. A–5) or interweave right and left leads (Fig. A–7) or cut separate pieces of lead for each diamond side (Fig. A–11)? The choice is not one merely of aesthetics, but of practical placement of glass pieces, as seen in Figs. A–2 and A–3. We hope to make the lead-ing up operation more understandable through these schematics.

Keep in mind that it makes a decided difference to your solder joint and window strength how many separate pieces of lead are to be incorporated in a single joint. Where four pieces are involved, the joint needs to be heavier and more outstanding than where you deal with two pieces butting against an uncut third (interweaving). All solder joints should be as unobtrusive but as strong as possible. One way to make them so is to try to interweave uncut against cut lead line. Planning out the design of such a leading-up procedure in advance of doing it will also make your work more efficient. Time is the enemy of us all.

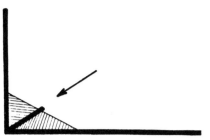

Fig. A–1 *Work begins in the left lower corner with two half diamonds.*

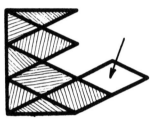

Fig. A–2 *The arrow indicates a pane leaded "in air," attached only on one side. The bottom piece should have been placed first—a common beginner's error.*

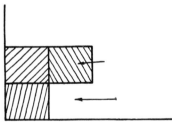

Fig. A–3 *The same problem with rectangular pieces: the top arrow indicates a piece leaded "in air"; bottom arrow indicates space where the glass must first be set.*

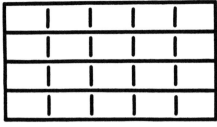

Fig. A–4 *Connecting rectangles in rows; here all horizontal leads are uncut, all vertical leads are cut to meet them.*

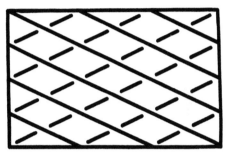

Fig. A–5 *Connecting rhombic pieces in rows; leads are handled as in A–4.*

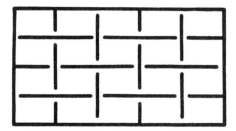

Fig. A–6 *Rectangular interweaving in an alternate format. A pleasant design flow.*

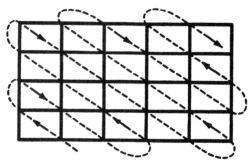

Fig. A–8 *Zigzag square-piece placement. The first piece is at lower left, the second directly on top of it, the third to the right, the next to the right of that, providing a solid base for the upward flow.*

Fig. A–7 *Rhombic pieces in the same alternate format as A–6.*

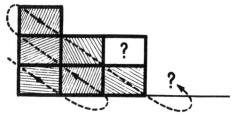

Fig. A–9 *Which piece would you place next? Our choice would be the bottom, again to provide stability.*

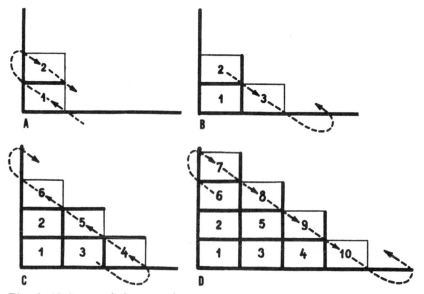

Fig. A–10 *Sequential placement of pieces.*

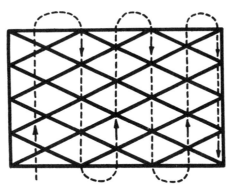

Fig. A–11 *Diamond panels can be placed straight up and down, since they interlock.*

Three Methods of Cutting Lead for Hexagonal Buildups

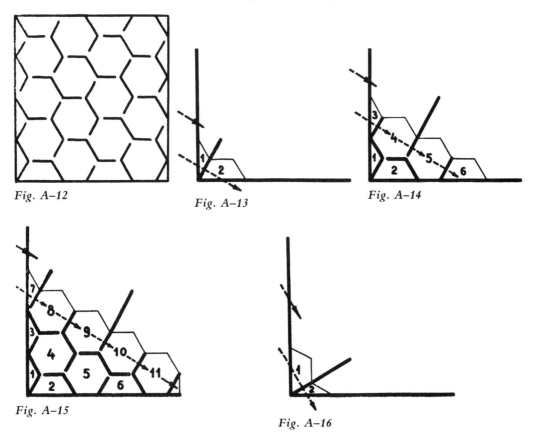

Fig. A–12

Fig. A–13

Fig. A–14

Fig. A–15

Fig. A–16

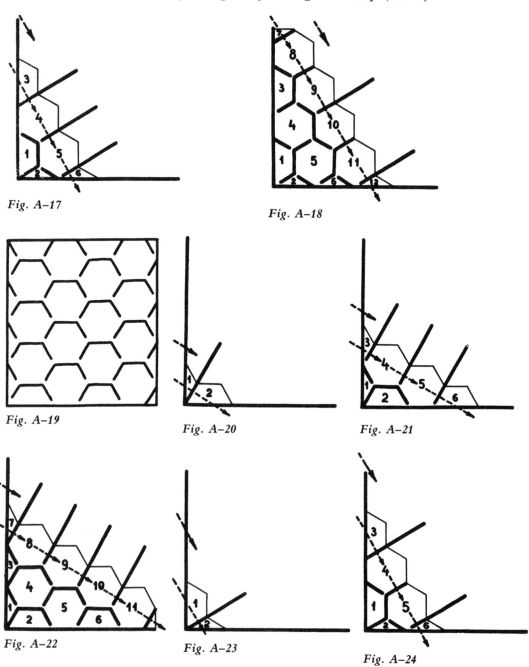

Fig. A–17

Fig. A–18

Fig. A–19

Fig. A–20

Fig. A–21

Fig. A–22

Fig. A–23

Fig. A–24

Safety First—and Last: A Checklist

TOXINS AND FLAMMABLE SUBSTANCES

The degree of risk from exposure to toxins depends on the material or substance used, length and frequency of direct contact, and personal sensitivity; risk is exacerbated by careless handling or improperly arranged working areas. Skin irritation is the most common problem experienced by glassworkers, with respiratory trouble and poisoning next.

Warning: We urge pregnant women to consult with an obstetrician before working with stained glass. The first three months of pregnancy are the most critical period of exposure to possible toxins; this is the time of greatest sensitivity for the unborn child.

Always use utmost caution when working with solvents such as toluene and xylene, benzene and other hydrocarbons, or with lead. Don't breath fumes during the soldering process. One way to avoid potential health risks is to use a less dangerous substance that will do the same job, even if the product is more costly. The same applies to the choice of process or technique. If two methods are available, choose the less dangerous. For example, wet grinding is preferable to dry as it does not throw off large amounts of dust into the air. Never use any material that is not well labeled. Read labels for a complete list of ingredients, easily understood instructions for handling and descriptions of safety hazards. In general, if a product smells bad, burns the eyes or causes tearing, irritates or bleaches the skin, or causes an itchy nose or coughing, assume it to be dangerous.

Handle Things Thoughtfully

You can always obtain information about ingredients by writing to the manufacturer for a Safety Data Sheet and product description. But certain things should be self-evident. For instance, flammable substances should be kept away from heat. Hot objects should be allowed to cool before picking them up. Disposal of waste chemicals should be performed immediately after they accumulate. Always follow the instructions provided when mixing chemicals. All spills should be cleaned up immediately. A leaky container should be replaced, not patched. Where possible, unbreakable containers should be used.

Good personal hygiene is essential, as we have stressed throughout this book. Eating, drinking, smoking, or applying cosmetics should never be done in the work area. Accidental splashes on the skin should be washed with water immediately. Eye splashes should be flushed with water for at least 15 minutes and a doctor consulted.

Styrofoam

Styrofoam presents the greatest fire hazard of all the polymers. If methyl chloride has been used as the foaming agent, sawing or cutting the foam may release methyl chloride vapors and produce serious bealth effects, including damage to the liver, kidneys, bone marrow, and central nervous system. Heating Styrofoam for any purpose (molding usually) is extremely dangerous because it releases noxious vapors. *Never heat a polystyrene.*

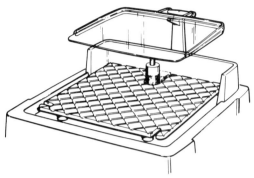

Fig. A–25 *A new safety feature, the grinder eye shield has been added to Glastar grinders. The eye shield's swingback transparent protector guards against flying chips of glass kicked up by the grinding action. It is easily installed or removed.*

Fig. A–27 *Soldering with the Vacu-Lite. It can be vented through a large hose either through the wall or a convenient window.*

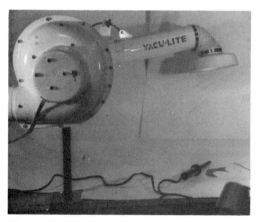

Fig. A–26 *The Vacu-Lite evacuates fumes and smoke at the source while illuminating the work. It clamps to the table and uses less electricity than a large fan. The arm swings from side to side and up and down, bending in the middle like an elbow. (From De Groot Fabricating, 6 Washington Street, Frenchtown, N.J. 08825.)*

Epoxy Resins

Wear protective clothing when working with resins. Curing agents, or hardeners, can cause serious skin irritation or even burns if you get splashed and pay no attention. In addition, these resins are flammable. Smoking increases the inhalation effects of any exposure to these materials and also creates a potential fire hazard.

Lead Came/Soldering

Soft soldering, which employs an electric iron, as opposed to hard soldering, or brazing, does not present a significant lead exposure if proper ventilation is provided. However, the lead itself *is* poisonous. When working with it, keep fingers out of your mouth, wash your hands before eating, cover any cuts or sores, and store lead and other dangerous materials away from children or pets.

A SAFE WORK AREA

The kitchen is a bad substitute for a workshop or storage area. Contamination of food is inevitable. Your work area should have built-in safety features, such as a source of running water, an eye-wash kit, a first aid kit, and a fire extinguisher. Physical hazards such as cluttered walking space, floor spills or inadequately grounded or overloaded electrical equipment should be eliminated. Be careful of long hair, loose sleeves or hanging jewelry that might catch in equipment.

Ventilation

Adequate ventilation is absolutely essential in the workshop. *Adequate ventilation means that fresh, uncontaminated air moves past your face and away from you with sufficient strength to clean the toxic fumes from your breathing zone.* As a test for proper amount of moving air, a wet finger should be dried by evaporation within 2 to 3 seconds. Properly placed window fan or exhaust and blower fans may do the job in conjunction with an open window.

GLASS

To reiterate a point we keep making: Glass is no more dangerous than the individual working with it. Glass does not cut; it reacts. The simplest way to avoid having it do so is to think before you act upon it. Any large piece of glass should be tapped lightly with a knuckle to test for vibration before it is lifted or carried. A rattle is a warning, a solid ring means the piece is safe to handle. Small pieces should be checked for beginning fractures, not against an overhead light, but by supporting them with two hands in front of you before a window or good light at eye level.

Be careful how you store glass. It should never be stored above shoulder height. If you have to reach over your head to a glass bin—or worse, climb a ladder to reach it—you are asking for that reaction we mentioned above. The best way to work with glass is to keep both feet on the ground, literally as well as figuratively.

The purpose of pointing out hazards is not to discourage anyone from working in stained glass. Just the opposite: to know your materials and use them intelligently is as much a mark of sophisticated purpose as the product that comes out of them. Our point is that unless you heed the first part, you may not get to the second. That would be a shame, considering how much fun you'd be missing.

Sources of Supply

Allnova Products Corp
PO Box 18842
Seattle, WA 98118
Patinas

Anderson's S/G Studio
21243 Pacific Coast Hwy.
Malibu, CA 90265
Lead choppers

Cline Glass Co., Inc.
1135 SE Grand Ave.
Portland, OR 97214
General glassworking supplies

D and G Supply
4919 N. Broadway
Boulder, CO
General glassworking supplies

Diamond Tool and Horseshoe
PO Box 18326
Jacksonville, FL 32229
Pliers

D & L Stained Glass Supply
4919 N. Broadway
Boulder, CO 80302
General glassworking supplies

ESICO
West Elm Street
Deep River, CT 06417
Soldering irons

Fletcher-Terry Co.
Spring Lane
Farmington, CT 06032
Glass cutters

Franklin Glass Art Studio
222 East Sycamore St.
Columbus, OH 43206
General glassworking supplies

Glass Accessories INT
710 Joshua Green Bldg
Seattle, WA 98101
Glass cutters

Glassart Studio of America, Inc.
510 S. 52nd St., Suite 104
Tempe, AZ 85281
General glassworking supplies

Glass House Studio, Inc.
125 State St.
St. Paul, MN 55107
General glassworking supplies; finished glass products

Houston Stained Glass Supply
1829 Arlington
Houston, TX 77008
General glassworking supplies

Ed Hoy's Stained Glass
999 East Chicago Ave.
Naperville, IL 60540
General glassworking supplies

Inland Diamond Products
1470 Temple City Drive
Troy, MI 48084
Glass grinder

Jennifer's Glassworks
2410 Piedmont Rd., N.E.
Atlanta, GA 30324
General glassworking supplies

Mad Dog
18615 Topham St.
Reseda, CA 91335
General glassworking supplies

Morton Glass Works
170 E. Washington
Morton, IL 61550
Portable Glass Workshop

Nervo Distributors
650 University Ave.
Berkeley, CA 94710
General glassworking supplies

New Renaissance Glass Works
5151 Broadway
Oakland, CA 94611
General glassworking supplies

Oklahoma Stained Glass
2606 N. Moore Avenue
Moore, OK 73160
General glassworking supplies

Pop-Lock
Bruce D. Olson
6814 Humbolt Ave. N.
Brooklyn Ctr, MN 55430
Framing

Simon Industries Inc.
PO Box 125
Evergreen, CO 80437
Electric pattern cutters

Stained Glass Design Inc.
309 Boulevard
Hasbrouck Hgt, NJ 07604
Copper foiler

Stanford Art Glass
513 Manitou Ave.
Manitou Springs, CO 80829
Glass cutters; lamp kits

Ultima Industries Inc.
1702 Swann St.
Fayetteville, NC 28303
Glass cutters

Village Hobby Mart
2414 Bolsover
Houston, TX 77005
General glassworking supplies

Glossary

abrasion The process of grinding away the top surface of a piece of flashed glass. A grinding wheel or burr may be used.

acetates Scaled down treatments of windows of stained glass done with special paints on heavy plastic to get a "see through" effect.

antique glass Glass that is made by the old method of hand blowing. The glass is blown into cylinders and the cylinders cut and flattened into sheets.

breaking the score Separating a piece of glass into planned sections along a marked line.

breaking and entering It is more difficult for a burglar to get into a home through a stained-glass window than through one of window or plate glass.

cartoon The blueprint for a work of stained glass containing all cut lines and possibly all paint lines.

cathedral glass Machine-made, transparent stained glass. Uniform in thickness; about ⅛".

composition The overall design of a finished piece containing the proper balance of color and linear flow.

cut line The borders of cut edges of glass demarcated in a cartoon.

cylinder One of the steps in the production of antique glass sheets

dalle A thick slab of stained glass for use with epoxy or cement. Broken pieces of dalles, or "chunks," may be copper foiled into windows or lamps to give a faceted effect.

epoxy Clear, fast-drying glues for joining glass to glass.

etching This process is done with hydrofluoric acid, the only acid that attacks glass. The purpose of etching is to save cutting and leading of tiny pieces. Etching can be done only on flashed glass.

Favrile® A word coined by Tiffany to describe his glass. His methods of production of this glass are still unknown.

flashed glass A sheet of glass where one color is laid on top of another. Any color may be flashed on top of another provided the two are not mutually exclusive of light. Such glass is used extensively in etching, but it can be used as is for the particular hue it presents.

flints Planned breaks in a diamond or rectangular window, usually in the form of a curved triangle, to break up a strict geometric design.

fusing The art of adhering glass to other glass surfaces or melting one glass directly into another. The heat necessary for this is best applied in a kiln, though a torch may be used with very small pieces.

gemmaux A process whereby small pieces of colored glass are glued and then grouted to an underlying piece of clear window glass to form a pattern.

glass bending Sagging or draping glass over a mold, then heating the glass blank in a kiln until it either sags into or drapes over the mold.

glass globs Thick, rounded pieces of stained glass of varied colors and sizes used as glass "jewels" to enhance a design.

glass jewels These may be faceted, hollow-backed, reflective, or bulls-eyed. Unlike globs, which are allowed to assume their own shape, or chunks, which are hacked off a dalle at random, jewels are formulated in a mold of Swedish steel and then polished.

glass thickness Anywhere from ⅛″ in machine-made (cathedral) glass to nearly ½″ in certain heavy antique glass. Thickness in antique glass may not be uniform within the same sheet. This is liable to cause a rocking of the glass on the cutting surface, which must be compensated for by the worker.

granite-backed glass A form of textured glass with one side roughened (also called "pebble glass").

grisaille A process developed in the thirteenth century for windows having the bulk of the glass white or gray with extensive leading. The most famous example is the Five Sisters window at York Cathedral.

grozzing Wearing away the small pinpoints and chips of glass along a cut surface using a finetooth pliers especially made for the purpose.

hammered glass A type of textured cathedral glass with multiple small indentations.

hydrofluoric acid The only material that attacks silica (a basic constituent of glass). It is used for etching.

joint The area where one lead line meets another. Such joints usually butt one against another.

kiln An oven made of firebrick. Kilns can be electric, gas-heated, or wood-burning.

knapping The process of faceting slab glass by chipping away at the edges with the slab glass hammer.

lead came Extruded pure lead that is channeled to specific dimensions either on one or both sides. The channels then accept and hold the glass to shape.

leaded glass Glass held together by lead cames.

leading Assembling a work of stained glass where lead came is the holding material.

millefiore Beads of glass heated in a kiln and spread out into whorls of color. The use of this material goes back to ancient Egypt.

mold High-temperature firing shapes into which glass can be sagged or over which it can be bent or folded.

mold release A substance applied to the surface of a mold to prevent the glass from sticking to it at high temperature. Powdered mica, Kay Kinney Mold Release®, graphite may be employed.

mosaic glass An opaque glass where the colors have been heavily mixed (also called "puddle glass").

Murano An island off the coast of Venice; trational home of famous glassworks.

opalescent glass Nontransparent glass; the colors are seen by reflected light.

oxidation The tough, outer coat on lead came that must be wirebrushed before soldering.

pattern A paper (or thin sheet metal) template from which the glass pieces are cut.

ponce bag A piece of tied-up rag with whiting inside used as a stencil.

pontil The blowpipe used in gathering and blowing molten glass.

pot metal The medieval name for the molten glass "batch." It was heated in a large pot and metallic oxides were added for color.

reamies Sheets of antique glass containing faint and delicate streaks of color.

reinforcing rods Galvanized steel rods used to span a window to prevent it from bowing.

resist material Used to protect areas of the glass to be left unchanged, as in etching and silkscreening. Asphaltum and beeswax are resist materials.

rolled edges Usually found only on antique sheets where the cylinder of glass was cut. This has smoothed over from the oven and bulged somewhat from the surface. It must be cut away before the sheet can be worked.

sandblasting Another form of glass abrading.

score The line imposed by a glass cutter or diamond upon the surface of a piece of glass. The fracture line weakens the glass along its length.

semiantique glass Machine-made glass with little movement or texture but with brilliant tones.

silver stain Really an etch; it imparts a golden color to clear glass.

streakies Glass sheets with streaks of color running through them. Colors may be many and varied against a background of yet another color, either opalescent or antique.

tapping One of the techniques of breaking out a score. A ball-ended glass cutter is used, though the heavy end of a regular cutter is also effective. Glass must always be tapped from the bottom.

tinning Soldering completely over the surface of another metal either to stiffen it or to allow its color to be changed.

tints Lightly colored hues and tones of stained glass.

tracer A special brush used in painting on glass.

Bibliography

Amaya, Mario, *Tiffany Glass*. New York: Walker & Co., 1967.

Anderson, Harriet. *Kiln-Fired Glass*. Philadelphia: Chilton, 1970.

Armitage, E.L. *Stained Glass*. Newton Centre, Mass.: Branford, 1959.

Beyer, Victor. *Stained Glass Windows*. London: Oliver & Boyd, 1964.

Chagall, Marc. *The Jerusalem Windows*. New York: George Braziller, 1967.

Davidson, Marshall B., ed. *American Heritage History of Antiques from the Civil War to World War I*. New York: American Heritage, 1969.

Davis, Frank. *The Country Life Book of Glass*. Glasgow: University Press, 1968.

Dierick, Alfons. *The Stained Glass at Chartres*. Berne: Hallwag, n.d.

Drake, Maurice. *A History of English Glass Painting*. London: T. Wernew Laurie, 1912.

Gandy, Walter. *The Romance of Glass Making*. London: 1898.

Hancock, E. Campbell. *The Amateur Pottery and Glass Painter*. London: Chapman and Hall, n.d.

Harrison, F. *The Painted Glass of York,* New York: Macmillian, 1927.

Harvard University. *Glass Flowers from the Ware Collection in the Botanical Museum of Harvard University*. New York: Harcourt, Brace, 1940.

Kinney, Kay. *Glass Craft: Designing, Forming, Decorating,* Philadelphia: Chilton, 1962.

Koch, Robert. *Rebel in Glass: Louis C. Tiffany* New York: Crown, 1964.

Lee, Lawrence. *Stained Glass*. Oxford Paperback Handbooks for Artists. Oxford University Press, n.d.

Lethaby, W.R. *Leadwork: Old and Ornamental*. London and New York: Macmillan, 1893.

Marchini, G. *Italian Stained Glass Windows*. New York: Harry N. Abrams, Inc., 1956.

Mayer, Ralph. *The Artist's Handbook of Materials and Techniques*. New York: Viking Press, 1940.

Metropolitan Museum of Art. *Medieval Art from Private Collections*. New York, 1968.

Metropolitan Museum of Art. *The Year 1200*. Edited by Konrad Hoffman. 2 vols., 1970.

Osgood, Adelaide H. *How to Apply Royal Worcester, Matt, Bronze, La Croix and Dresden Colors to China* (also serves for glass). New York: Osgood Art School Pub., 1891.

Piper, John. *Stained Glass: Art or Anti-Art*. New York: Reinhold, 1968.

Plowman, George. *Etching and Other Graphic Arts*. New York: Dodd, Mead, 1929.

Reyntiens, Patrick R. *The Technique of Stained Glass*. New York: Watson-Guptil, 1967.

Rorimer, James J. *The Cloisters: The Building and the Collection of Medieval Art in Fort Tryon Park*. New York: Metropolitan Museum of Art, 1963.

Saint, L., and Arnold, H. *Stained Glass of the Middle Ages in England and France*. London: Black, 1913.

Sauzay. A. *Marvels of Glass Making in All Ages*. London: Sampson, Low, Son and Marston, 1870.

Schmutzler, Robert, *Art Nouveau*. New York: Harry N. Abrams, 1962.

Schuler, Frederick W., and Lilli Schuler. *Glass Forming: Glass Making for the Craftsmen*. Philadelphia: Chilton, 1970.

Sherrell, C.H. *Stained Glass Tours in France*. New York: John Lane, 1922.
Stained Glass Tours in England. New York: John Lane, 1910.
Stained Glass Tours in Germany, Austria &

the Rhinelands. New York: John Lane, 1927. *Stained Glass Tours in Spain & Flanders.* New York: Dodd, Mead, n.d.

Snell, Henry James. *Practical Instructions in Enamel Painting on Glass.* London: Brodie and Middleton, n.d.

Sturgis, Russell. *A Study of the Artist's Way of Working in the Various Handicrafts and Arts of Design.* 2 vols. New York: Dodd, Mead, 1905.

Twining, E.W. *Art and Craft of Stained Glass.* London: Sir Isaac Pitman & Sons, 1928.

Van Tassel, Valentine. *American Glass.* New York: Gramercy, n.d.

Werck, Alfred. *Stained Glass: A Handbook on The Art.* New York: Adelphi, 1926.

Whall, C.W. *Stained Glass Work.* London: John Hogg, 1905.

Winston, C. *Ancient Glass Paintings.* 2 vols. England: John Henry Parker, 1927.

Woodforde, Christopher. *The Norwich School of Glass-Painting in the 15th Century.* London: Oxford University Press, 1950.

Index

Page numbers followed by the letter "f" indicate information in illustrations.

Fitting the glass, for window making, 173–174, 173f, 175

Flaking, 119

Flammable substances. *See* Toxins and flammable substances

Flashed glass, characteristics, 19, 19f

Flat-jaw grozzers, 92

Flemish glass, 21–22, 28

Fletcher cutters, 115

Fletcher point driver, 237, 237f

Fletcher's Plate Glass Breaker, 125, 126f, 127f

Flux(es), 39, 51, 53, 58–59, 111, 178
 brands of, 59–60, 59f
 classes, 59
 correct use in soldering, 57–58
 forms of, 59, 70
 requirements, 53
 residues, 58, 155
 resinous, 56
 spreading of, 104, 104f
 use, 151, 157

Flux brushes, acid-resist, 57f, 58

Foil, use, 7. *See also* Copper Foil

Foiling machines, 152f, 153–154, 153f

Force, application of, for scoring, 118–119, 120

Fracture. *See* Fissure, Scoring

Fracture-backed glass, use, 28

Fracture glass, features, 22–23

Frame(s)
 for epoxy panel, 162–163, 164f
 silkscreen, 241, 242f

Framing, 234, 235, 236–238, 236f

Freehand cutting, 136

Freestanding objects, 225

Frosted glass, 28

Frosting, in sandblasting, 259

Fulcrum method, for breaking of score, 122–123

Furnace, thickness of, 16

Fusing, procedure, 227, 228

Gelatin, use as glue, 250

Generic type of glass, 25

Geometric figurations, 169

Geometric panels, interweaving leaded lines in, 308–312f

Gift shop, for selling stained glass items, 298–299
 mail orders, 299
 mass-produced items, 300
 packaging, 300

Glasflux, 59–60, 59f

Glass
 bonding of, for bent-panel lamps, 209, 210
 characteristics, 16, 28
 cleaning of, 155, 156
 cutting for multipaneled lamp, 197, 198f, 199–200, 199f
 cutting for window making, 172, 173
 defined, 15
 fitting to came, 36–37, 36f
 fitting for window making, 173f, 173–174, 175
 historical perspective, 1, 2

Glass, *cont'd.*
 poorly cut, 151–152
 pouring of, for epoxy panel, 163
 preparing for glue chipping, 252
 preparing for silkscreening, 247–248, 248f
 purchasing of, 25
 scoring of. *See* Scoring
 surfaces, for sandblasting, 259, 259f, 260
 tapping of, into came, 37
 use, safety in, 315
 workable, 25

Glass beads. *See* Beads

Glass bins, size of, 184, 184f

Glass breakers. *See* Breaking pliers

Glass chunks, use, 165, 234

Glass cutters, 71–72
 ball-ended, 74, 121, 121f, 122, 123
 bevel angle, 73
 carbide, 74
 choosing of, 115, 116f, 120
 circle cutters, 80, 80f, 81f
 classic, 72–73
 diamond, 80
 force and speed, 118–119, 120
 grozzing teeth, 74
 handles, 73–74
 holding of, 117–118, 120
 odd-shape, 80, 81f
 oil hand cutter, 78, 79
 Palm Rest and Scoremaster, 75–77, 78f
 Raven glass cutter, 79–80
 for scoring of slab-glass, 159
 sharpening of, 74, 75f
 strip-cutting devices, 80, 81–82, 83f, 84f
 testing for sharpness, 75
 types, 72
 Ultima 9000, 77, 78, 78f
 use, 112, 121
 wheel lubrication, 74
 wheel size, 73, 73f

Glass drills, 98
 types, 98, 98f, 100f
 use, 98, 99f, 99

Glass globs, 108, 110, 110f, 234
 uses, 110, 111

Glass grinder, 101f, 288
 heads, 99, 100f
 use, 99, 101f
 use in glass painting, 187f

Glass jewels, 106, 107f, 108f, 278
 making of, 107f
 use, 108f

Glass nippers, 85f
 use, 89, 90f

Glass paint, firing of, 186

Glass pliers, 82
 breaking pliers, 82, 83f, 86, 86f, 87f
 breaking of score with, 124, 125f
 came cutting pliers, 91f, 92
 categories, 82, 84f, 85f
 chain pliers, 92

Glass pliers, *cont'd.*
glass nippers, 89, 90f
grozzing pliers. *See* Grozzers, grozzing pliers
pull, 199
underslung jaw breakers, 90f, 91
use, 126, 128, 199
Glass rods, use, 112
Glass router. *See* Glass grinder
Glass stainers' paint, 186, 187f
vinegar trace, 186, 187, 188–189
Glasses, safety, for sandblasting, 261f, 263, 264
Glassnapper, 88–89
Glastar survey, on stained glass classes, 287–288
Glazing. *See* Double glazing
Globes, of lamp, 217
embedding of, 234
Globs, *See* Glass globs
Glossary, 318–320
Glue, use in lead channel, 220
Glue-chip glass, features, 23, 24
Glue chipping, 251
chipping procedure, 253–255, 256, 257f
designing chip area, 252–253
drying stages, 255–256, 275
preparing the glass, 252
supplies, 251, 252f
Gluing, 231f
of drinking glasses and candleholders, 227, 228f
of mosaic windows, 226–227, 227f
Goggles, use, 160, 161
Gold Tip glass cutters, 72
Grain, of glass, 18
Granite-backed glass, 20
Granite ripple glass, 20
Graph paper, use, 209
in mold method, 205
Green color, chemicals used for, 16
Greeting cards, crushed glass, 233
Grinders. *See* Glass grinders
Grinding, 24
of stain, 190
Grinding machine, 252
Grinding wheel, use, 279
Grip, for glass-cutting, 76f, 78f
Grooving, 71
Grozzers, grozzing pliers, 74, 85f
barrel-jaw, 90f
features, 86f, 87, 87f
flat-jaw, 92
heavy duty, 84f, 89, 90
round-barrel, 89, 90f
round-jaw, 91f, 92
use, 86f
Grozzing, 74, 74f, 174, 194
in lamp repair, 297
in window repair, 295
Grozzing heads, 100f
Grozzing slats, 74
Grozzing teeth, 74, 74f, 77
position of, 118
for tapping of glass, 122

Gum arabic, use, 190
in glass painting, 188

H came(s), 29, 30, 34, 49, 111
anatomy, 31f
for lamp repair, 296
for multipaneled lamp, 200, 201
as outside lead, 50
sizes and uses, 44, 45, 46–47, 49
H channel, 47
hacksaw blade, cutting bottles with, 112
Half-a-lead replacement method, for window repair, 295–296
Hammer
chipping, 159
slab glass, 103, 103f, 104, 159
Hammered glass, 21, 28
use, 28
Hand(s)
breaking of score by, 123, 124f
position of, in cutting, 115
Hand-blown glass. *See* Antique glass
Hand drill, 99
Hangers, 217
Hanging loops, applying of, 158
"Hard" foil, 146
Hatchet irons, 73
Heat, soldering and, 53, 58, 60–61
Heavyweight soldering iron, 60–61
Hexagon deflector, 63
Hexagonal buildup, cutting lead for, 311f–312f
"High heart" lead, 31, 34
Hobbyist, stained glass and, 10–12
Hole, cutting of, 99f, 99
Horseshoe nail, 97f, 98, 177
Humidity, 16, 39
Hydraulics, laws of, 16
Hydrochloric acid, 39, 111
Hydrofluoric acid, use in etching, 193–194

Iceberg chip, 253f, 254
Inner curves, cutting of, 128f, 129, 129f, 130f
Installation of window, 182–183
Instant solder, 60
Iridescence, applying, 7
Iridized glass, use, 23, 28
Iron, percentage in stained glass, 16

Jaw breakers. *See* Underslung jaw breakers
Jewel(s). *See* Glass jewels
Jewelry box, making of, 232f, 233, 233f, 234
Joints, 171
soldering of, 178
See also Solder joints

Kiln use
for firing oil-base paints, 191, 192
for firing silkscreens, 250–251
in glue chipping, 255
for sculpturing, 277
in torching, 227